REMINISCENCES OF MY CHILDHOOD AND YOUTH

BY

GEORGE BRANDES

NEW YORK

DUFFIELD & COMPANY

1906

CONTENTS

CONTENTS

FIRST LONG SOJOURN ABROAD

EARLY MANHOOD

SECOND LONGER STAY ABROAD

CONTENTS

FILOMENA

SECOND LONGER STAY ABROAD—*Continued*

REMINISCENCES OF
MY CHILDHOOD
AND YOUTH

DISCOVERING THE WORLD

I.

HE was little and looked at the world from below.
All that happened, went on over his head. Everyone looked down to him.

But the big people possessed the enviable power of lifting him to their own height or above it. It might so happen
that suddenly, without preamble, as he lay on the floor, rum-
maging and playing about and thinking of nothing at all, his
father or a visitor would exclaim: "Would you like to see
the fowls of Kjöge?" And with the same he would feel
two large hands placed over his ears and the arms belonging
to them would shoot straight up into the air. That was delightful. Still, there was some disappointment mingled with
it. "Can you see Kjöge now?" was a question he could
make nothing of. What could Kjöge be? But at the other
question: "Do you see the fowls?" he vainly tried to see
something or other. By degrees he understood that it was
only a phrase, and that there was nothing to look for.

It was his first experience of empty phrases, and it made
an impression.

It was just as great fun, though, when the big people
said to him: "Would you like to be a fat lamb? Let us
play at fat lamb." He would be flung over the man's
shoulder, like a slaughtered lamb, and hang there, or jump up
and ride with his legs round the man's hips, then climb val-
iantly several steps higher, get his legs round his shoulders,

and behold! be up on the giddy height! Then the man would take him round the waist, swing him over, and after a mighty somersault in the air, he would land unscathed on his feet upon the floor. It was a composite kind of treat, of three successive stages: first came the lofty and comfortable seat, then the more interesting moment, with a feeling, nevertheless, of being on the verge of a fall, and then finally the jump, during which everything was upside down to him.

But, too, he could take up attitudes down on the floor that added to his importance, as it were, and obliged the grown-up people to look at him. When they said: " Can you stand like the Emperor Napoleon? " he would draw himself up, bring one foot a little forward, and cross his arms like the little figure on the bureau.

He knew well enough just how he had to look, for when his stout, broad-shouldered Swedish uncle, with the big beard and large hands, having asked his parents about the little fellow's accomplishments, placed himself in position with his arms crossed and asked: " Who am I like? " he replied: " You are like Napoleon's lackey." To his surprise, but no small delight, this reply elicited a loud exclamation of pleasure from his mother, usually so superior and so strict, and was rewarded by her, who seldom caressed, with a kiss.

II.

The trying moment of the day was when he had to go to bed. His parents were extraordinarily prejudiced about bedtime, just when he was enjoying himself most. When visitors had arrived and conversation was well started— none the less interesting to him because he understood scarcely half of what was said—it was: " Now, to bed! "

But there were happy moments after he was in bed, too. When Mother came in and said prayers with him, and he lay there safely fenced in by the tall trellis-work, each bar of which, with its little outward bend in the middle, his fingers knew so well, it was impossible to fall out through them. It was very pleasant, the little bed with its railing, and he slept in it as he has never slept since.

It was nice, too, to lie on his back in bed and watch his parents getting ready to go to the theatre, Father in a shining white shirt and with his curly hair beautifully parted on one side, Mother with a crêpe shawl over her silk dress, and light gloves that smelled inviting as she came up to say goodnight and good-bye.

III.

I was always hearing that I was pale and thin and small. That was the impression I made on everyone. Nearly thirty years afterwards an observant person remarked to me: "The peculiarity about your face is its intense paleness." Consequently I looked darker than I was; my brown hair was called black.

Pale and thin, with thick brown hair, difficult hair. That was what the hairdresser said—Mr.[1] Alibert, who called Father Erré: "Good-morning, Erré," "Good-bye, Erré." And all his assistants, though as Danish as they could be, tried to say the same. Difficult hair! "There is a little round place on his crown where the hair will stand up, if he does not wear it rather long," said Mr. Alibert.

I was forever hearing that I was pale and small, pale in particular. Strangers would look at me and say: "He is rather pale." Others remarked in joke: "He looks rather green in the face." And so soon as they began talking about me the word "thin" would be uttered.

I liked my name. My mother and my aunts said it in such a kindly way. And the name was noteworthy because it was so difficult to pronounce. No boy or girl smaller than I could pronounce it properly; they all said *Gayrok*.

I came into the world two months too soon, I was in such a hurry. My mother was alone and had no help. When the midwife came I had arrived already. I was so feeble that the first few years great care had to be taken of me to keep me alive. I was well made enough, but not strong, and this was the source of many vexations to me during those years when a boy's one desire and one ambition is to be strong.

[1] Danish *Herre*.

I was not clumsy, very agile if anything; I learnt to be a good high jumper, to climb and run well, was no contemptible wrestler, and by degrees became an expert fighter. But I was not muscularly strong, and never could be compared with those who were so.

IV.

The world, meanwhile, was so new, and still such an unknown country. About that time I was making the discovery of fresh elements.

I was not afraid of what I did not like. To overcome dislike of a thing often satisfied one's feeling of honour.

" Are you afraid of the water? " asked my brisk uncle from Fünen one day. I did not know exactly what there was to be afraid of, but answered unhesitatingly: " No." I was five years old; it was Summer, consequently rainy and windy.

I undressed in the bathing establishment; the old sailor fastened a cork belt round my waist. It was odiously wet, as another boy had just taken it off, and it made me shiver. Uncle took hold of me round the waist, tossed me out into the water, and taught me to take care of myself. Afterwards I learnt to swim properly with the help of a long pole fastened to the cork belt and held by the bathing-man, but my familiarity with the salt element dated from the day I was flung out into it like a little parcel. Without by any means distinguishing myself in swimming, any more than in any other athletic exercise, I became a very fair swimmer, and developed a fondness for the water and for bathing which has made me very loth, all my life, to miss my bath a single day.

There was another element that I became acquainted with about the same time, and which was far more terrifying than the water. I had never seen it uncontrolled: fire.

One evening, when I was asleep in the nursery, I was awaked by my mother and her brother, my French uncle. The latter said loudly: " We must take the children out of bed."

I had never been awaked in the night before. I opened

my eyes and was thrilled by a terror, the memory of which has never been effaced. The room was brightly illuminated without any candle having been lighted, and when I turned my head I saw a huge blaze shoot up outside the window. Flames crackled and sparks flew. It was a world of fire. It was a neighbouring school that was burning. Uncle Jacob put his hand under my " night gown," a long article of clothing with a narrow cotton belt round the waist, and said laughing: " Do you have palpitations of the heart when you are afraid? " I had never heard of palpitations of the heart before. I felt about with my hand and for the first time found my heart, which really was beating furiously. Small though I was, I asked the date and was told that it was the 25th of November; the fright I had had was so great that I never forgot this date, which became for me the object of a superstitious dread, and when it drew near the following year, I was convinced that it would bring me fresh misfortune. This was in so far the case that next year, at exactly the same time, I fell ill and was obliged to spend some months in bed.

v.

I was too delicate to be sent to school at five years old, like other boys. My doctor uncle said it was not to be thought of. Since, however, I could not grow up altogether in ignorance, it was decided that I should have a tutor of my own.

So a tutor was engaged who quickly won my unreserved affection and made me very happy. The tutor came every morning and taught me all I had to learn. He was a tutor whom one could ask about anything under the sun and he would always know. First, there was the A B C. That was mastered in a few lessons. I could read before I knew how to spell. Then came writing and arithmetic and still more things. I was soon so far advanced that the tutor could read *Frithiof's Saga* aloud to me in Swedish and be tolerably well understood; and, indeed, he could even take a short German extract, and explain that I must say *ich* and not *ish*, as seemed so natural.

Mr. Voltelen was a poor student, and I quite under-stood from the conversation of my elders what a pleasure and advantage it was to him to get a cup of coffee extra and fine white bread and fresh butter with it every day. On the stroke of half-past ten the maid brought it in on a tray. Lessons were stopped, and the tutor ate and drank with a relish that I had never seen anyone show over eating and drinking before. The very way in which he took his sugar—more sugar than Father or Mother took—and dissolved it in the coffee before he poured in the cream, showed what a treat the cup of coffee was to him.

Mr. Voltelen had a delicate chest, and sometimes the grown-up people said they were afraid he could not live. There was a report that a rich benefactor, named Nobel, had offered to send him to Italy, that he might recover in the warmer climate of the South. It was generous of Mr. Nobel, and Mr. Voltelen was thinking of starting. Then he caught another complaint. He had beautiful, brown, curly hair. One day he stayed away; he had a bad head, he had con-tracted a disease in his hair from a dirty comb at a bathing establishment. And when he came again I hardly recog-nised him. He wore a little dark wig. He had lost every hair on his head, even his eyebrows had disappeared. His face was of a chalky pallor, and he coughed badly too.

Why did not God protect him from consumption? And how could God find it in His heart to give him the hair dis-ease when he was so ill already? God was strange. He was Almighty, but He did not use His might to take care of Mr. Voltelen, who was so good and so clever, and so poor that he needed help more than anyone else. Mr. Nobel was kinder to Mr. Voltelen than God was. God was strange, too, in other ways; He was present everywhere, and yet Mother was cross and angry if you asked whether He was in the new moderator lamp, which burnt in the drawing-room with a much brighter light than the two wax candles used to give. God knew everything, which was very uncomfortable, since it was impossible to hide the least thing from Him. Strangest of all was it when one reflected that, if one knew what God thought one was going to say, one could say something else and His omniscience would be foiled. But of course one did not know what He thought would come next. The worst of all, though, was that He left Mr. Voltelen in the lurch so.

VI.

Some flashes of terrestrial majesty and magnificence shone on my modest existence. Next after God came the King. As I was walking along the street one day with my father, he exclaimed: "There is the King!" I looked at the open carriage, but saw nothing noticeable there, so fixed my attention upon the coachman, dressed in red, and the footman's plumed hat. "The King wasn't there!" "Yes, indeed he was—he was in the carriage." "Was that the King? He didn't look at all remarkable—he had no crown on." "The King is a handsome man," said Father. "But he only puts on his state clothes when he drives to the Supreme Court."

So we went one day to see the King drive to the Supreme Court. A crowd of people were standing waiting at the Naval Church. Then came the procession. How splendid it was! There were runners in front of the horses, with white silk stockings and regular flower-pots on their heads; I had never seen anything like it; and there were postillions riding on the horses in front of the carriage. I quite forgot to look inside the carriage and barely caught a glimpse of the King. And that glimpse made no impression upon me. That he was Christian VIII. I did not know; he was only "the King."

Then one day we heard that the King was dead, and that he was to lie in state twice. These lyings in state were called by forced, unnatural names, *Lit de Parade* and *Castrum doloris;* I heard them so often that I learnt them and did not forget them. On the *Lit de Parade* the body of the King himself lay outstretched; that was too sad for a little boy. But *Castrum doloris* was sheer delight, and it really was splendid. First you picked your way for a long time along narrow corridors, then high up in the black-draped hall appeared the coffin covered with black velvet, strewn with

shining, twinkling stars.　And a crowd of candles all round.
It was the most magnificent sight I had ever beheld.

VII.

I was a town child, it is true, but that did not prevent
me enjoying open-air life, with plants and animals.　The
country was not so far from town then as it is now.　My paternal grandfather had a country-house a little way beyond
the North gate, with fine trees and an orchard; it was the
property of an old man who went about in high Wellington
boots and had a regular collection of wax apples and pears—
such a marvellous imitation that the first time you saw them
you couldn't help taking a bite out of one.　Driving out to the
country-house in the Summer, the carriage would begin to
lumber and rumble as soon as you passed through the North
gate, and when you came back you had to be careful to come
in before the gate was closed.

We lived in the country ourselves, for that matter, out in
the western suburb, near the Black Horse (as later during the
cholera Summer), or along the old King's Road, where there
were beautiful large gardens.　In one such a huge garden I
stood one Summer day by my mother's side in front of a large
oblong bed with many kinds of flowers.　" This bed shall be
yours," said Mother, and happy was I.　I was to rake the
paths round it myself and tend and water the plants in it.
I was particularly interested to notice that a fresh set of flowers came out for every season of the year.　When the asters
and dahlias sprang into bloom the Summer was over.　Still
the garden was not the real country.　The real country was
at Inger's, my dear old nurse's.　She was called my nurse because she had looked after me when I was small.　But she
had not fed me, my mother had done that.

Inger lived in a house with fields round it near High
Taastrup.　There was no railway there then, and you drove
out with a pair of horses.　It was only later that the
wonderful railway was laid as far as Roskilde.　So it was an
unparalleled event for the children, to go by train to Valby
and back.　Their father took them.　Many people thought

that it was too dangerous. But the children cared little for the danger. And it went off all right and they returned alive.

Inger had a husband whose name was Peer. He was nice, but had not much to say. Inger talked far more and looked after everything. They had a baby boy named Niels, but he was in the cradle and did not count. Everything at Inger and Peer's house was different from the town. There was a curious smell in the rooms, with their chests of drawers and benches, not exactly disagreeable, but unforgettable. They had much larger dishes of curds and porridge than you saw in Copenhagen. They did not put the porridge or the curds on plates. Inger and Peer and their little visitor sat round the milk bowl or the porridge dish and put their spoons straight into it. But the guest had a spoon to himself. They did not drink out of separate glasses, but he had a glass to himself.

It was jolly in the country. A cow and little pigs to play with and milk warm from the cow. Inger used to churn, and there was buttermilk to drink. It was great fun for a little Copenhagen boy to roll about in the hay and lie on the hay-waggons when they were driven home. And every time I came home from a visit to Inger Mother would laugh at me the moment I opened my mouth, for, quite unconsciously, I talked just like Inger and the other peasants.

VIII.

In the wood attic, a little room divided from the main garret by wooden bars, in which a quantity of split firewood and more finely chopped fir sticks, smelling fresh and dry, are piled up in obliquely arranged heaps, a little urchin with tightly closed mouth and obstinate expression has, for more than two hours, been bearing his punishment of being incarcerated there.

Several times already his anxious mother has sent the housemaid to ask whether he will beg pardon yet, and he has only shaken his head. He is hungry; for he was brought up here immediately after school. But he will not give in, for he is in the right. It is not his fault that the grown-up people cannot understand him.　They do not know that what he is suffering now is nothing to what he has had to suffer. It is true that he would not go with the nurse and his little brother into the King's Gardens.　But what do Father and Mother know of the ignominy of hearing all day from the other schoolboys:　"Oh! so you are fetched by the nurse!" or "Here comes your nurse to fetch you!"　He is overwhelmed with shame at the thought of the other boys' scorn. She is not *his* nurse, she is his brother's.　He could find his way home well enough, but how can he explain to the other boys that his parents will not trust him with the little one yet, and so send for them both at the same time!　Now there shall be an end to it; he will not go to the King's Gardens with the nurse again.

It is the housemaid, once more, come to ask if he will not beg pardon now.　In vain.　Everything has been tried with him, scolding, and even a box on the ear; but he has not been humbled.　Now he stands here; he will not give in.

But this time his kind mother has not let the girl come empty-handed.　His meal is passed through the bars and he eats it.　It is so much the easier to hold out.　And some hours later he is brought down and put to bed without having apologised.

Before I had so painfully become aware of the ignominy of going with the maid to the King's Gardens, I had been exceedingly fond of the place.　What gardens they were for hide and seek, and puss in the corner!　What splendid alleys for playing Paradise, with Heaven and Hell!　To say nothing of playing at horses!　A long piece of tape was passed over and under the shoulders of two playfellows, and you drove them with a tight rein and a whip in your hand.　And if it were fun in the old days when I only had tape for reins, it was ever so much greater fun now that I had had a present from my father of splendid broad reins of striped wool, with bells, that you could hear from far enough when the pair came tearing down the wide avenues.

I was fond of the gardens, which were large and at that time much larger than they are now; and of the trees, which were many, at that time many more than now.　And every part of the park had its own attraction. The Hercules pavilion was mysterious; Hercules with the lion, instructive and powerful. A pity that it had become such a disgrace to go there!

I had not known it before. One day, not so long ago, I had felt particularly happy there. I had been able for a long time to read correctly in my reading-book and write on my slate. But one day Mr. Voltelen had said to me: " You ought to learn to read writing." And from that moment forth my ambition was set upon reading *writing,* an idea which had never occurred to me before. When my tutor first showed me *writing,* it had looked to me much as cuneiform inscriptions and hieroglyphics would do to ordinary grown-up people, but by degrees I managed to recognize the letters I was accustomed to in this their freer, more frivolous disguise, running into one another and with their regularity broken up. In the first main avenue of the King's Gardens I had paced up and down, in my hand the thin exercise-book, folded over in the middle,—the first book of writing I had ever seen,—and had already spelt out the title, " Little Red Riding-Hood." The story was certainly not very long; still, it filled several of the narrow pages, and it was exciting to spell out the subject, for it was new to me. In triumphant delight at having conquered some difficulties and being on the verge of conquering others, I kept stopping in front of a strange nurse-girl, showed her the book, and asked: " Can you read writing? "

Twenty-three years later I paced up and down the same avenue as a young man, once more with a book of manuscript, that I was reading, in my hand. I was fixing my first lecture in my mind, and I repeated it over and over again to myself until I knew it almost by heart, only to discover, to my disquiet, a few minutes later, that I had forgotten the whole, and that was bad enough; for what I wished to say in my lecture were things that I had very much at heart.

The King's Garden continued to occupy its place in my life. Later on, for so many years, when Spring and Summer passed by and I was tied to the town, and pined for trees and the scent of flowers, I used to go to the park, cross it obliquely to the beds near the beautiful copper beeches, by the entrance from the ramparts, where there were always flowers, well cared for and sweet scented. I caressed them with my eyes, and inhaled their perfume leaning forward over the railings.

But just now I preferred to be shut up in the wood-loft to being fetched by the nurse from school to the Gardens. It was horrid, too, to be obliged to walk so slowly with the girl, even though no longer obliged to take hold of her skirt. How I envied the boys contemptuously called street boys! They could run in and out of the courtyard, shout and make as much noise as they liked, quarrel and fight out in the street, and move about freely. I knew plenty of streets. If sent into the town on an errand I should be able to find my way quite easily.

And at last I obtained permission. Happy, happy day! I flew off like an arrow. I could not possibly have walked. And I ran home again at full galop. From that day forth I always ran when I had to go out alone. Yes, and I could not understand how grown-up people and other boys could walk. I tried a few steps to see, but impatience got the better of me and off I flew. It was fine fun to run till you positively felt the hurry you were in, because you hit your back with your heels at every step.

My father, though, could run very much faster. It was impossible to compete with him on the grass. But it was astonishing how slow old people were. Some of them could not run up a hill and called it trying to climb stairs.

IX.

On the whole, the world was friendly. It chiefly depended on whether one were good or not. If not, Karoline was especially prone to complain and Father and Mother were transformed into angry powers. Father was, of course, a much more serious power than Mother, a more distant, more hard-handed power. Neither of them, in an ordinary way, inspired any terror. They were in the main protecting powers.

The terrifying power at this first stage was supplied by the bogey-man. He came rushing suddenly out of a corner with a towel in front of his face and said: "Bo!" and you jumped. If the towel were taken away there soon emerged a laughing face from behind it. That at once made the bogey-man less terrible. And perhaps that was the reason Maren's threat: "Now, if you are not good, the bogey-man will come and take you," quickly lost its effect. And yet it was out of this same bogey-man, so cold-bloodedly shaken off, that at a later stage a personality with whom there was no jesting developed, one who was not to be thrust aside in the same way, a personality for whom you felt both fear and trembling—the Devil himself.

But it was only later that he revealed himself to my ken. It was not he who succeeded first to the bogey-man. It was—the police. The police was the strange and dreadful power from which there was no refuge for a little boy. The police came and took him away from his parents, away from the nursery and the drawing-room, and put him in prison.

In the street the police wore a blue coat and had a large cane in his hand. Woe to the one who made the acquaintance of that cane!

My maternal grandfather was having his warehouse done up, a large warehouse, three stories high. Through doors at the top, just under the gable in the middle, there issued a crane, and from it hung down a tremendously thick rope at the end of which was a strong iron hook. By means of it the large barrels of sky-blue indigo, which were brought on waggons, were hoisted. Inside the warehouse the ropes passed through every storey, through holes in the floors. If you pulled from the inside at the one or the other of the ropes, the rope outside with the iron crook went up or down.

In the warehouse you found Jens; he was a big, strong, taciturn, majestic man with a red nose and a little pipe in his mouth, and his fingers were always blue from the indigo. If you had made sure of Jens' good-will, you could play in the warehouse for hours at a time, roll the empty barrels about, and—which was the greatest treat of all—pull the ropes. This last was a delight that kept all one's faculties at extreme tension. The marvellous thing about it was that you yourself stood inside the house and pulled, and yet at the same time you could watch through the open doors in the wall how the rope outside went up or down. How it came about was an enigma. But you had the refreshing consciousness of having accomplished something—saw the results of your efforts before your eyes.

Nor could I resist the temptation of pulling the ropes when Jens was out and the warehouse empty. My little brother had whooping cough, so I could not live at home, but had to be at my grandfather's. One day Jens surprised me and pretty angry he was. "A nice little boy you are! If you pull the rope at a wrong time you will cut the expensive rope through, and it cost 90 Rigsdaler! What do you think your grandfather will say?"[1]

It was, of course, very alarming to think that I might destroy such a valuable thing. Not that I had any definite ideas of money and numbers. I was well up in the multiplication table and was constantly wrestling with large numbers, but they did not correspond to any actual conception in my mind. When I reckoned up what one number of several digits came to multiplied by another of much about the same value, I had not the least idea whether Father or Grandfather had so many Rigsdaler, or less, or more. There was only one of the uncles who took an interest in my gift for multiplication, and that was my stout, rich uncle with the crooked mouth, of whom it was said that he owned a million, and who was always thinking of figures. He was hardly at the door of Mother's drawing-room before he called out: "If you are a sharp boy and can tell me what 27,374 times 580,208 are, you shall have four skilling;" and quickly slate and pencil appeared and the sum was finished in a moment and the four skilling pocketed.[2]

I was at home then in the world of figures, but not in

---

[1] A Rigsdaler was worth about two shillings and threepence, English money. It is a coin that has been out of use about 40 years.

[2] Four skilling would be a sum about equal to 1½d. English money.

that of values. All the same, it would be a terrible thing to destroy such a value as 90 Rigsdaler seemed to be. But might it not be that Jens only said so? He surely could not see from the rope whether it had been pulled or not.

So I did it again, and one day when Jens began questioning me sternly could not deny my guilt. " I saw it," said Jens; " the rope is nearly cut in two, and now you will catch it, now the policeman will come and fetch you."

For weeks after that I did not have one easy hour. Wherever I went, or whatever I did, the fear of the police followed me. I dared not speak to anyone of what I had done and of what was awaiting me. I was too much ashamed, and I noticed, too, that my parents knew nothing. But if a door opened suddenly I would look anxiously at the incomer. When I was walking with the nurse and my little brother I looked all round on every side, and frequently peeped behind me, to see whether the police were after me. Even when I lay in my bed, shut in on all four sides by its trellis-work, the dread of the police was upon me still.

There was only one person to whom I dared mention it, and that was Jens. When a few weeks had gone by I tried to get an answer out of him. Then I perceived that Jens did not even know what I was talking about. Jens had evidently forgotten all about it. Jens had been making fun of me. If my relief was immense, my indignation was no less. So much torture for nothing at all! Older people, who had noticed how the word " police " was to me an epitome of all that was terrible, sometimes made use of it as an explanation of things that they thought were above my comprehension.

When I was six years old I heard the word " war " for the first time. I did not know what it was, and asked. " It means," said one of my aunts, " that the Germans have put police in Schleswig and forbidden the Danes to go there, and that they will beat them if they stay there." That I could understand, but afterwards I heard them talking about soldiers. " Are there soldiers as well? " I asked. " Police and soldiers," was the answer. But that confused me altogether, for the two things belonged in my mind to wholly different categories. Soldiers were beautiful, gay-coloured men with shakos, who kept guard and marched in step to the sound of drums and fifes and music, till you longed to go with them. That was why soldiers were copied in tin and you got them on your birthday in boxes. But police went by themselves, without music, without beautiful colours on their uniforms, looked stern and threatening, and had a stick in their hands. Nobody dreamt of copying them in tin. I was very much annoyed to find out, as I soon did, that I had been misled by the explanation and that it was a question of soldiers only.

Not a month had passed before I began to follow eagerly, when the grown-up people read aloud from the far-thing newspaper sheets about the battles at Bov, Nybböl, etc. The Danes always won. At bottom, war was a cheerful thing.

Then one day an unexpected and overwhelming thing happened. Mother was sitting with her work on the little raised platform in the drawing-room, in front of the sewing-table with its many little compartments, in which, under the loose mahogany lid, there lay so many beautiful and wonder-ful things—rings and lovely earrings, with pearls in them— when the door to the kitchen opened and the maid came in. " Has Madame heard? The *Christian VIII.* has been blown up at Eckernförde and the *Gefion* is taken."

" Can it be possible? " said Mother. And she leaned over the sewing-table and burst into tears, positively sobbed. It impressed me as nothing had ever done before. I had never seen Mother cry. Grown-up people did not cry. I did not even know that they could. And now Mother was cry-ing till the tears streamed down her face. I did not know what either the *Christian VIII.* or the *Gefion* were, and it was only now that the maid explained to me that they were ships. But I understood that a great misfortune had happened, and soon, too, how people were blown up with gunpowder, and what a good thing it was that one of our acquaintances, an active young man who was liked by everyone and always got on well, had escaped with a whole skin, and had reached Copenhagen in civilian's dress.

X.

About this time it dawned upon me in a measure what birth and death were. Birth was something that came quite unexpectedly, and afterwards there was one child more in the house. One day, when I was sitting on the sofa between Grandmamma and Grandpapa at their dining-table in Klareboderne, having dinner with a fairly large company, the door at the back of the room just opposite to me opened. My father stood in the doorway, and, without a good-morning, said: " You have got a little brother "—and there really was a little one in a cradle when I went home.

Death I had hitherto been chiefly acquainted with from a large, handsome painting on Grandfather's wall, the death of the King not having affected me. The picture represented a garden in which Aunt Rosette sat on a white-painted bench, while in front of her stood Uncle Edward with curly hair and a blouse on, holding out a flower to her. But Uncle Edward was dead, had died when he was a little boy, and as he had been such a very good boy, everyone was very sorry that they were not going to see him again. And now they were always talking about death. So and so many dead, so and so many wounded! And all the trouble was caused by the Enemy.

XI.

There were other inimical forces, too, besides the police and the Enemy, more uncanny and less palpable forces. When I dragged behind the nursemaid who held my younger brother by the hand, sometimes I heard a shout behind me, and if I turned round would see a grinning boy, making faces and shaking his fist at me. For a long time I took no particular notice, but as time went on I heard the shout oftener and asked the maid what it meant. " Oh, nothing! " she replied. But on my repeatedly asking she simply said: " It is a bad word."

But one day, when I had heard the shout again, I made up my mind that I would know, and when I came home asked my mother: ' What does it mean? " " Jew! " said Mother.

" Jews are people." " Nasty people ? " " Yes," said Mother, smiling, " sometimes very ugly people, but not always." " Could I see a Jew ? " " Yes, very easily," said Mother, lifting me up quickly in front of the large oval mirror above the sofa.

I uttered a shriek, so that Mother hurriedly put me down again, and my horror was such that she regretted not having prepared me.   Later on she occasionally spoke about it.

XII.

Other inimical forces in the world cropped up by degrees.   When you had been put to bed early the maids often sat down at the nursery table, and talked in an undertone until far on into the evening.   And then they would tell stories that were enough to make your hair stand on end.   They talked of ghosts that went about dressed in white, quite noiselessly, or rattling their chains through the rooms of houses appeared to people lying in bed, frightened guilty persons of figures that stepped out of their picture-frames and moved across the floor; of the horror of spending a night in the dark in a church—no one dared do that; of what dreadful places churchyards were, how the dead in long grave-clothes rose up from their graves at night and frightened the life out of people, while the Devil himself ran about the churchyard in the shape of a black cat.   In fact, you could never be sure when you saw a black cat towards evening, that the Devil was not inside it.   And as easily as winking the Devil could transform himself into a man and come up behind the person he had a grudge against.

It was a terrifying excitement to lie awake and listen to all this.   And there was no doubt about it.   Both Maren and Karoline had seen things of the sort themselves and could produce witnesses by the score.   It caused a revolution in my consciousness.   I learnt to know the realm of Darkness and the Prince of Darkness.   For a time I hardly ventured to pass through a dark room.   I dared not sit at my book with an open door behind me.   Who might not step noiselessly in !   And if there were a mirror on the wall in front of me would tremble with fear lest I might see the Devil, standing with gleaming eyes at the back of my chair.

When at length the impression made upon me by all these ghost and devil stories passed away, I retained a strong repugnance to all darkness terror, and to all who take advantage of the defenceless fear of the ignorant for the powers of darkness.

XIII.

The world was widening out. It was not only home and the houses of my different grandparents, and the clan of my uncles, aunts, and cousins; it grew larger.

I realized this at the homecoming of the troops. They came home twice. The impression they produced the first time was certainly a great, though not a deep one. It was purely external, and indistinctly merged together: garlands on the houses and across the streets, the dense throng of people, the flower-decked soldiers, marching in step to the music under a constant shower of flowers from every window, and looking up smiling. The second time, long afterwards, I took things in in much greater detail. The wounded, who went in front and were greeted with a sort of tenderness; the officers on horseback, saluting with their swords, on which were piled wreath over wreath; the bearded soldiers, with tiny wreaths round their bayonets, while big boys carried their rifles for them. And all the time the music of *Den tapre Landsoldat,* when not the turn of *Danmark dejligst* or *Vift stolt!*[1]

But the second time I was not wholly absorbed by the sight, for I was tormented by remorse. My aunt had presented me the day before with three little wreaths to throw at the soldiers; the one I was to keep myself, and I was to give each of my two small brothers one of the others; I had promised faithfully to do so. And I had kept them all three, intending to throw them all myself. I knew it was wrong and deceitful; I was suffering for it, but the delight of throwing all the wreaths myself was too great. I flung them

[1] Three favourite Danish tunes: "The Brave Soldier," "Fairest Denmark," and "Proudly Wave."

down. A soldier caught one on his bayonet; the others fell to the ground. I was thoroughly ashamed of myself, and have never forgotten my shame.

XIV.

I knew that the theatre (where I had never been) was the place where Mother and Father enjoyed themselves most. They often talked of it, and were most delighted if the actors had " acted well," words which conveyed no meaning to me.

Children were not at that time debarred from the Royal Theatre, and I had no more ardent wish than to get inside. I was still a very small child when one day they took me with them in the carriage in which Father and Mother and Aunt were driving to the theatre. I had my seat with the others in the pit, and sat speechless with admiration when the curtain went up. The play was called *Adventures on a Walking Tour*. I could not understand anything. Men came on the stage and talked together. One crept forward under a bush and sang. I could not grasp the meaning of it, and when I asked I was only told to be quiet. But my emotion was so great that I began to feel ill, and had to be carried out. Out in the square I was sick and had to be taken home. Unfortunately for me, that was precisely what happened the second time, when, in response to my importunity, another try was made. My excitement, my delight, my attention to the unintelligible were too overwhelming. I nearly fainted, and at the close of the first act had to leave the theatre. After that, it was a very long time before I was regarded as old enough to stand the excitement.

Once, though, I was allowed to go to see a comedy. Mr. Voltelen gave me a ticket for some students' theatricals at the Court Theatre, in which he himself was going to appear. The piece was called *A Spendthrift*, and I saw it without suffering for it. There was a young, flighty man in it who used to throw gold coins out of the window, and there was an ugly old hag, and a young, beautiful girl as well. I sat and kept a sharp lookout for when my master should

come on, but I was disappointed; there was no Mr. Voltelen
to be seen.

Next day, when I thanked him for the entertainment, I
added: "But you made game of me. You were not in it
at all." "What? I was not in it? Did you not see the
old hag? That was I. Didn't you see the girl? That was
I." It was incomprehensible to me that anyone could disguise himself so. Mr. Voltelen must most certainly have
"acted well." But years afterwards, I could still not understand how one judged of this. Since plays affected me exactly like real life, I was, of course, not in a position to single
out the share the actors took.

XV.

The war imbued my tin soldiers with quite a new interest. It was impossible to have boxes enough of them. You
could set them out in companies and battalions; they opened
their ranks to attack, stormed, were wounded, and fell.
Sometimes they lay down fatigued and slept on the field of
battle. But a new box that came one day made the old ones
lose all value for me. For the soldiers in the new box were
proper soldiers, with chests and backs, round to the touch,
heavy to hold. In comparison with them, the older ones, profile soldiers, so small that you could only look at them side-
ways, sank into utter insignificance. A step had been taken
from the abstract to the concrete. It was no longer any pleasure to me to play with the smaller soldiers. I said: "They
amused me last year, when I was little." There was a similar change, a similar picture of historic progress, when the
hobby-horse on which I had spent so many happy hours, and
on which I had ridden through rooms and passages, was put
in the corner in favour of the new rocking-horse which, long
coveted and desired, was carried in through the door, and
stood in the room, rocking slightly, as though ready for the
boldest ride, the moment its rider flung himself into the
saddle.

I mounted it and oh, happiness! I began to ride, and
rode on with passionate delight till I nearly went over the

horse's head. "When I was a little boy the hobby-horse amused me, but it does not now." Every time I climbed a fresh rung of the ladder, no matter how low an one, the same feeling possessed me, and the same train of thought. Mother often joked about it, up to the time when I was a full grown man. If I quickly outgrew my fancies, if I had quite done with anything or anybody that had absorbed me a little while before, she would say, with a smile: "Last year, when I was a little boy, the hobby-horse amused me."

Still, progress was not always smooth. When I was small I had pretty blouses, one especially, grey, with brown worsted lace upon it, that I was fond of wearing; now I had plain, flat blouses with a leather belt round the waist. Later on, I was ambitious to have a jacket, like big boys, and when this wish had been gratified there awoke in me, as happens in life, a more lofty ambition still, that to wear a frock coat. In the fulness of time an old frock coat of my father's was altered to fit me. I looked thin and lank in it, but the dress was honourable. Then it occurred to me that everybody would see I was wearing a frock coat for the first time. I did not dare to go out into the streets with it on, but went out of my way round the ramparts for fear of meeting anyone.

When I was a little boy I did not, of course, trouble much about my appearance. I did not remember that my portrait had been drawn several times. But when I was nine years old, Aunt Sarah—at that time everybody was either uncle or aunt—determined that we brothers should have our portraits taken in daguerreotype for Father's birthday. The event made a profound impression, because I had to stand perfectly still while the picture was being taken, and because the daguerreotypist, a German, whose name was Schätzig, rolled his *r*s and hissed his *s*s. The whole affair was a great secret, which was not to be betrayed. The present was to be a surprise, and I was compelled to promise perfect silence. I kept my promise for one day. But next day, at the dinner-table, I accidentally burst out: "Now! quite shtill! *as the man said.*" "What man?" "Ah! that was the secret!"

The visit to Schätzig in itself I had reason to remember a long time.   Some one or another had said that I
had a slender neck, and that it was pretty.   Just as we were
going in, my aunt said: " You will catch cold inside," and
in spite of my protests tied a little silk handkerchief round my
neck.   That handkerchief spoilt all my pleasure in being im-
mortalised.   And it is round my neck on the old picture to
this day.

XVI.

The tin soldiers had called all my warlike instincts into
being.   After the rocking-horse, more and more military ap-
purtenances followed.   A shining helmet to buckle firmly under the chin, in which one looked quite imposing; a cuirass of
real metal like the Horseguards', and a short rapier in a
leather scabbard, which went by the foreign name of Hirschfänger, and was a very awe-inspiring weapon in the eyes of
one's small brothers, when they were mercilessly massacred
with it.   Sitting on the rocking-horse, arrayed in all this
splendour, wild dreams of military greatness filled the soul,
dreams which grew wilder and more ambitious from year to
year until between the age of 8 and 9 they received a fresh
and unwholesome stimulus from Ingemann's novels.[1]

On horseback, at the head of a chosen band, fighting like
the lost against unnumbered odds!   Rock goes the rocking-
horse, violently up and down.   The enemy wavers, he begins
to give way.   The rocking-horse is pulled up.   A sign with
the Hirschfänger to the herd of common troops.   The enemy
is beaten and flies, the next thing is to pursue him.   The
rocking-horse is set once more in furious motion.   Complete
victory.   Procession into the capital; shouts of jubilation and
wreaths of flowers, for the victor and his men.

XVII.

Just about this time, when in imagination I was so great
a warrior, I had good use in real life for more strength, as

---

[1] B. S. Ingemann (1789-1862), a Danish writer celebrated chiefly as
the author of many historical novels, now only read by very young children.

I was no longer taken to school by the nurse, but instead had myself to protect my brother, two years my junior. The start from home was pleasant enough. Lunch boxes of tin with the Danish greeting after meals in gold letters upon them, stood open on the table. Mother, at one end of the table, spread each child six pieces of bread and butter, which were then placed together, two and two, white bread on brown bread, a mixture which was uncommonly nice. The box would take exactly so many. Then it was put in the school-bag with the books. And with bag on back you went to school, always the same way. But those were days when the journey was much impeded. Every minute you met boys who called you names and tried to hit the little one, and you had to fight at every street corner you turned. And those were days when, even in the school itself, despite the humanity of the age (not since attained to), terms of abuse, buffets and choice insults were one's daily bread, and I can see myself now, as I sprang up one day in a fight with a much bigger boy and bit him in the neck, till a master was obliged to get me away from him, and the other had to have his neck bathed under the pump.

I admired in others the strength that I lacked myself. There was in the class one big, stout, squarely built, inexpressibly good-natured boy, for whom no one was a match in fighting. He was from Lolland, and his name was Ludvig; he was not particularly bright, but robust and as strong as a giant. Then one day there arrived at the school a West Indian of the name of Muddie, dark of hue, with curly hair, as strong and slim as a savage, and with all the finesse and feints which he had at his command, irresistible, whether wrestling or when fighting with his fists. He beat all the strongest boys in the school. Only Ludvig and he had not challenged each other. But the boys were very anxious to see a bout between the two, and a wrestling match between them was arranged for a free quarter of an hour. For the boys, who were all judges, it was a fine sight to see two such fighters wrestle, especially when the Lollander flung himself down on the other and the West Indian struggled vainly, writhing like a very snake to twist himself out of his grasp.

One day two new boys came to school, two brothers; the elder, Adam, was small and sallow, extraordinarily withered, looking like a cripple, without, however, being one; the somewhat younger brother, Sofus, was splendidly made and amazed us in the very first lesson in which the new arrivals took part—a gymnastic class—by his unusual agility in swarming and walking up the sloping bar. He seemed to be as strong as he was dexterous, and in a little boy with a reverence for those who were strong, he naturally aroused positive enthusiasm. This was even augmented next day, when a big, malicious boy, who had scoffed at Adam for being puny, was, in a trice, so well thrashed by Sofus that he lost both his breath and his courage.

Sofus, the new arrival, and I, who had achieved fighting exploits from the rocking-horse only, were henceforth, for some time, inseparable friends. It was one of the usual friendships between little boys, in which the one admires and the other allows himself to be worshipped. The admirer in this case could only feed his feelings by presenting the other with the most cherished thing he possessed. This most cherished thing happened to be some figures cut out in gold paper, from France, representing every possible object and personage, from ships with masts and sails, to knights and ladies. I had collected them for a long time and preserved them, piece by piece, by gumming them into a book which was the pride of my existence. I gave the book, without the slightest hesitation, to Sofus, who accepted it without caring for it in the least.

And then by reason of the exaggerated admiration of which he was the object, Sofus, who hitherto had been so straightforward, began to grow capricious. It was a settled rule that he and I went home from school together. But one day a difficulty cropped up; Sofus had promised Valdemar, a horrid boy, who cheated at lessons, to go home with him. And next day something else prevented him. But when, suddenly having learnt to know all the pangs of neglect and despised affection, I met him the third day, after having waited vainly for him, crossing Our Lady's Square with Valdemar, in my anger I seized my quondam friend roughly by

the arm, my face distorted with rage, and burst out: "You
are a rascal!" then rushed off, and never addressed him
again.   It was a very ill-advised thing to do, in fact, the
very most foolish thing I could have done.   But I was too
passionate to behave sensibly.   Valdemar spread the account
of my conduct all through the class, and next day, in our
quarter of an hour's playtime, I heard on every side from the
laughing boys: "You are a rascal!   You are a rascal!"

XVIII.

The world was widening out.   The instruction I received grew more varied.   There were a great many lessons
out of school.   From my drawing mistress, a pleasant girl,
who could draw Fingal in a helmet in charcoal, I learnt to see
how things looked in comparison with one another, how they
hid one another and revealed themselves, in perspective; from
my music mistress, my kind aunt, to recognise the notes and
keys, and to play, first short pieces, then sonatas, alone,
then as duets.   But alas!   Neither in the arts of sight nor
hearing did I ever prove myself more than mediocre.   I
never attained, either in drawing or piano-playing, to more
than a soulless accuracy.   And I hardly showed much greater
aptitude when, on bright Sunday mornings, which invited not
at all to the delights of dancing, with many another tiny lad
and lass I was marshalled up to dance in the dancing saloon
of Mr. Hoppe, the royal dancer, and learnt to take up the
first to the fifth positions and swing the girls round in the
polka mazurka.   I became an ardent, but never a specially
good, dancer.

XIX.

The world was widening out.   Father brought from
Paris a marvellous game, called Fortuna, with bells over
pockets in the wood, and balls which were pushed with cues.
Father had travelled from Paris with it five days and six
nights.   It was inexpressibly fascinating; no one else in Copenhagen had a game like it.   And next year, when Father
came home from Paris again, he brought a large, flat, pol-

ished box, in which there were a dozen different games, French games with balls, and battledores and shuttlecocks, games which grown-up people liked playing, too; and there were carriages which went round and round by clockwork, and a tumbler who turned somersaults backwards down a flight of steps as soon as he was placed on the top step. Those were things that the people in France could do.

The world was widening out more and more. Relations often came over from Göteborg. They spoke Swedish, but if you paid great attention you could understand quite well what they said. They spoke the language of *Frithiof's Saga,* but pronounced it differently from Mr. Voltelen. And there came a young French count whose relations my father's brother had known; he had come as a sailor on a French man-o'-war, and he came and stayed to dinner and sang the Marseillaise. It was from him that I heard the song for the first time. He was only fifteen, and very good-looking, and dressed like an ordinary sailor, although he was a count.

And then there were my two uncles, Uncle Jacob and Uncle Julius—my mother's brother Jacob and my father's brother Julius, who had both become Frenchmen long ago and lived in Paris. Uncle Jacob often came for a few weeks or more at a time. He was small and broad-shouldered and good-looking. Everybody was fond of Uncle Jacob; all the ladies wanted to be asked to the house when Uncle Jacob came. He had a wife and four children in Paris. But I had pieced together from the conversation of the grown-up people that Aunt Victorine was his wife and yet not his wife. Grandmother would have nothing to do with her. And Uncle Jacob had gone all the way to the Pope in Rome and asked for her to remain his wife. But the Pope had said No. Why? Because Aunt Victorine had had another husband before, who had been cruel to her and beaten her, and the man came sometimes, when Uncle was away, and took her furniture away from her. It was incomprehensible that he should be allowed to, and that the Pope would do nothing to prevent it, for after all she was a Catholic.

Uncle Jacob had a peculiar expression about his mouth when he smiled. There was a certain charm about everything he said and did, but his smile was sad. He had acted thoughtlessly, they said, and was not happy. One morning, while he was visiting Father and Mother and was lying asleep in the big room, there was a great commotion in the house; a messenger was sent for the doctor and the word *morphia* was spoken. He was ill, but was very soon well again. When he asked his sister next day: " What has become of my case of pistols? " she replied with a grave face: " I have taken it and I shall keep it."

I had not thought as a boy that I should ever see Uncle Jacob's wife and children. And yet it so happened that I did. Many years afterwards, when I was a young man and went to Paris, after my uncle's death, I sought out Victorine and her children. I wished to bring her personally the monthly allowance that her relatives used to send her from Denmark. I found her prematurely old, humbled by poverty, worn out by privation. How was it possible that she should be so badly off? Did she not receive the help that was sent from Copenhagen every month to uncle's best friend, M. Fontane, in the Rue Vivienne? Alas, no! M. Fontane gave her a little assistance once in a while, and at other times sent her and her children away with hard words.

It turned out that M. Fontane had swindled her, and had himself kept the money that had been sent for years to the widow of his best friend. He was a tall, handsome man, with a large business. No one would have believed that a scoundrel could have looked as he did. He was eventually compelled to make the money good. And when the cousin from Denmark rang after that at his French relatives' door, he was immediately hung round, like a Christmas tree, with little boys and one small girl, who jumped up and wound their arms round his neck, and would not let him go.

BOYHOOD'S YEARS

I.

THE house belonged to my father's father, and had been in his possession some twenty years. My parents lived on the second floor. It was situated in the busy part of the town, right in the heart of Copenhagen. On the first floor lived a West Indian gentleman who spoke Danish with a foreign accent; sometimes there came to see him a Danish man of French descent, Mr. Lafontaine, who, it was said, was so strong that he could take two rifles and bayonets and hold them out horizontally without bending his arm. I never saw Mr. Lafontaine, much less his marvellous feat of strength, but when I went down the stairs I used to stare hard at the door behind which these wonderful doings went on.

In the basement lived Niels, manservant to the family, who, besides his domestic occupations, found time to develop a talent for business. In all secrecy he carried on a commerce, very considerable under the circumstances, in common watches and in mead, two kinds of wares that in sooth had no connection with each other. The watches had no particular attraction for a little boy, but the mead, which was kept in jars, on a shelf, appealed to me doubly. It was the beverage the old Northmen had loved so much that the dead drank it in Valhalla. It was astonishing that it could still be had. How nice it must be! I was allowed to taste it and

29

it surpassed all my expectations. Sweeter than sugar! More
delicious than anything else on earth that I had tasted! But
if you drank more than a very small glass of it, you felt sick.

And I profoundly admired the dead warriors for having
been able to toss off mead from large drinking-horns and eat
fat pork with it. What a choice! And they never had
stomach-ache!

II.

On the ground floor was the shop, which occupied the
entire breadth and nearly the entire depth of the house, a
silk and cloth business, large, according to the ideas of the
time, which was managed by my father and grandfather together until my eleventh year, when Father began to deal
wholesale on his own account. It was nice in the shop, because when you went down the assistants would take you
round the waist and lift you over to the other side of the
semi-circular counter which divided them from the customers.
The assistants were pleasant, dignified gentlemen, of fine appearance and behaviour, friendly without wounding condescension.

Between my fifth and sixth years some alterations were
done at the shop, which was consequently closed to me for a
long time. When it was once more accessible I stood amazed
at the change. A long, glass-covered gallery had been
added, in which the wares lay stored on new shelves. The
extension of the premises was by no means inconsiderable, and
simultaneously an extension had been made in the staff.
Among the new arrivals was an apprentice named Gerhard,
who was as tall as a grown man, but must have been very
young, for he talked to me, a six-year-old child, like a companion. He was very nice-looking, and knew it. "You
don't want harness when you have good hips," he would say,
pointing to his mightily projecting loins. This remark made
a great impression upon me, because it was the first time I had
heard anyone praise his own appearance. I knew that one
ought not to praise one's self and that self-praise was no recommendation. So I was astonished to find that self-praise
in Gerhard's mouth was not objectionable; in fact, it actually

suited him.   Gerhard often talked of what a pleasure it was
to go out in the evenings and enjoy one's self—what the devil
did it matter what old people said?—and listen to women
singing—amusements which his hearer could not manage to
picture very clearly to himself.

It soon began to be said that Gerhard was not turning
out well.   The manner in which he procured the money
for his pleasures resulted, as I learnt long afterwards, in his
sudden dismissal.   But he had made some slight impression
on my boyish fancy—given me a vague idea of a heedless life
of enjoyment, and of youthful defiance.

III.

On the landing which led from the shop to the stock-
room behind, my grandfather took up his position.   He
looked very handsome up there, with his curly white hair.
Thence, like a general, he looked down on everything—on the
customers, the assistants, the apprentices, both before and behind him.   If some specially esteemed lady customer came
into the shop, he hurriedly left his exalted position to give
advice.   If the shopman's explanations failed to satisfy her,
he put things right.   He was at the zenith of his strength,
vigour, and apparently of his glory.

The glory vanished, because from the start he had
worked his way up without capital.   The Hamburg firm that
financed the business lent money at too high a rate of interest
and on too hard conditions for it to continue to support two
families.

But when later on my grandfather had his time at his
own disposal, he took up the intellectual interests which in his
working years he had had to repress.   In his old age, for instance, he taught himself Italian, and his visitors would find
him, with Tasso's *Gerusalemme liberata* in front of him, looking out in a dictionary every word that presented any difficulty to him, and of such there were many.

The old man was an ardent Buonapartist, and, strangely
enough, an even more ardent admirer of the Third Napoleon
than of the First, because he regarded him as shrewder, and

was convinced that he would bequeath the Empire to his son.
But he and I came into collision on this point from the time I
was fourteen years of age. For I was of course a Republican,
and detested Napoleon III. for his breach of the Constitution, and used to write secretly in impossible French, and in a
still more impossible metre (which was intended to represent
hexameters and pentameters) verses against the tyrant. An
ode to the French language began:

> "Ah! quelle langue magnifique, si belle, si riche, si sonore,
> Langue qu'un despote cruel met aux liens et aux fers!"

On the subject of Napoleon III. grandfather and grandson
could not possibly agree. But this was the only subject on
which we ever had any dispute.

IV.

My maternal grandfather was quite different, entirely
devoid of impetuosity, even-tempered, amiable, very handsome. He too had worked his way up from straightened circumstances; in fact, it was only when he was getting on for
twenty that he had taught himself to read and write, well-
informed though he was at the time I write of. He had
once been apprentice to the widow of Möller the dyer, when
Oehlenschläger and the Œrsteds used to dine at the house.
After the patriarchal fashion of the day, he had sat daily at
the same table as these great, much-admired men, and he
often told how he had clapped his hands till they almost bled
at Oehlenschläger's plays, in the years when, by reason of
Baggesen's attack, opinions about them at the theatre were
divided.

My great-grandfather, the father of my mother's step-
mother, who wore high boots with a little tassel in front, belonged to an even older generation. He used to say: "If
I could only live to see a Danish man-o'-war close with an
English ship and sink it, I should be happy; the English are
the most disgraceful pack of robbers in the world." He was
so old that he had still a vivid recollection of the battle in the
roadstead and of the bombardment of Copenhagen.

V.

School and Home were two different worlds, and it often struck me that I led a double life.   Six hours a day I lived under school discipline in active intercourse with people none of whom were known to those at home, and the other hours of the twenty-four I spent at home, or with relatives of the people at home, none of whom were known to anybody at school.

On Oct. 1st, 1849, I was taken to school, led in through the sober-looking doorway, and up into a classroom, where I was received by a kindly man, the arithmetic master, who made me feel at my ease.   I noticed at once that when the master asked a boy anything which another knew, this other had a right to publish his knowledge by holding up a finger— a right of which I myself made an excessive use in the first lessons, until I perceived the sense of not trying, in season and out of season, to attract attention to my knowledge or superiority, and kept my hands on the table in front of me.

VI.

Suddenly, with surprising vividness, a little incident of my childhood rises up before me.   I was ten years old.   I had been ill in the Winter and my parents had boarded me out in the country for the Summer holidays; all the love of adventure in me surged up.   At the Straw Market a fat, greasy, grinning peasant promised to take me in his cart as far as the little town of Farum, where I was to stay with the schoolmaster.   He charged two dalers, and got them.   Any sum, of course, was the same to me.   I was allowed to drive the brown horses, that is to say, to hold the reins, and I was in high glee.   Where Farum was, I did not know and did not care, but it was a new world.   Until now I, who was a town child, had seen nothing of the country except my nurse's house and land at Glostrup,—but what lay in front of me was a village, a schoolhouse, a large farm, in short an adventure in grand style.

I had my shirts and blouses and stockings in a portmanteau, and amongst them a magnificent garment, never yet worn, a blue cloth jacket, and a white waistcoat belonging to it, with gold buttons, which my mother had given me permission to wear on Sundays. For days, I always wore blouses, so the jacket implied a great step forward. I was eager to wear it, and regretted profoundly that it was still only Monday.

Half-way there, the peasant pulled up. He explained to me that he could not very well drive me any farther, so must put me down; he was not going to Farum himself at all. But a peat cart was coming along the road yonder, the driver of which was going to Farum, and he transferred me, poor defenceless child as I was, to the other conveyance. He had had my money; I had nothing to give the second man, and sadly I exchanged the quick trot of the brown horses for the walking pace of the jades in the peat-cart.

My first experience of man's perfidy.

At last I was there. On a high, wide hill—high and wide as it seemed to me then—towered the huge schoolhouse, a miniature Christiansborg Castle, with the schoolmaster's apartments on the right and the schoolroom on the left. And the schoolmaster came out smiling, holding a pipe which was a good deal taller than I, held out his hand, and asked me to come in, gave me coffee at once, and expressed the profoundest contempt for the peasant who had charged two rigsdaler for such a trifle, and then left me in the road.

I asked at once for pen and paper, and wrote in cipher to a comrade, with whom I had concocted this mysterious means of communication, asking him to tell my parents that I had been most kindly received. I felt a kind of shyness at the schoolmaster seeing what I wrote home from his house. I gave him the sheet, and begged him to fold it up, as I could not do it myself. There were no envelopes in those days. But what was my surprise to hear him, without further ado, read aloud with a smile, from my manufactured cipher: " I have been most kindly received," etc. I had never thought such keen-wittedness possible. And my respect for him and his long pipe rose.

Just then there was a light knock at the door. In walked two girls, one tall and one short, the former of whom positively bewildered me. She was fair, her sister as dark as a negro. They were ten and eight years old respectively, were named Henrietta and Nina K., came from Brazil, where their home was, and were to spend a few years in Denmark; came as a rule every day, but had now arrived specially to inspect the strange boy. After gazing for two minutes at the lovely Henrietta's fair hair and wonderful grey eyes, I disappeared from the room, and five minutes afterwards reappeared again, clothed in the dark-blue jacket and the white waistcoat with gold buttons, which I had been strictly forbidden to wear except on Sundays. And from that time forth, sinner that I was, I wore my Sunday clothes every blessed day,—but with what qualms of conscience!

I can still see lovely fields, rich in corn, along the sides of which we played; we chased beautiful, gaudy butterflies, which we caught in our hats and cruelly stuck on pins, and the little girls threw oats at my new clothes, and if the oats stuck fast it meant something, sweethearts, I believe. Sweethearts—and I!

Then we were invited to the manor, a big, stately house, a veritable castle. There lived an old, and exceedingly handsome, white-haired Chamberlain, called the General, who frequently dined with Frederik VII., and invariably brought us children goodies from dessert, lovely large pieces of barley sugar in papers with gay pictures on the outside of shepherd lovers, and crackers with long paper fringes. His youngest son, who owned a collection of insects and many other fine things, became my sworn friend, which means that I was his, for he did not care in the least about me; but I did not notice that, and I was happy and proud of his friendship and sailed with him and lots of other boys and girls on the pretty Farum lake, and every day was more convinced that I was quite a man. It was a century since I had worn blouses.

Every morning I took all the newspapers to Dr. Dörr, the German tutor at the castle, and every morning I accidentally met Henrietta, and after that we were hardly separated all day. I had no name for the admiration that attached me to her. I knew she was lovely, that was all. We were anxious to read something together, and so read the whole of a translation of *Don Quixote,* sitting cheek against cheek in the summer-house. Of course, we did not understand one-half of it, and I remember that we tried in vain to get an explanation of the frequently recurring word " doxy "; but we laughed till we cried at what we did understand. And after all, it is this first reading of *Don Quixote* which has dominated all my subsequent attempts to understand the book.

But Henrietta had ways that I did not understand in the least; she used to amuse herself by little machinations, was inventive and intriguing. One day she demanded that I should play the school children, small, white-haired boys and girls, all of whom we had long learnt to know, a downright trick. I was to write a real love-letter to a nine-year-old little girl named Ingeborg, from an eleven or twelve-year-old boy called Per, and then Henrietta would sew a fragrant little wreath of flowers round it. The letter was completed and delivered. But the only result of it was that next day, as I was walking along the high road with Henrietta, Per separated himself from his companions, called me a dandy from Copenhagen, and asked me if I would fight. There was, of course, no question of drawing back, but I remember very plainly that I was a little aghast, for he was much taller and broader than I, and I had, into the bargain, a very bad cause to defend. But we had hardly exchanged the first tentative blows before I felt overwhelmingly superior. The poor cub! He had not the slightest notion how to fight. From my everyday school life in Copenhagen, I knew hundreds of tricks and feints that he had never learnt, and as soon as I perceived this I flung him into the ditch like a glove. He sprang up again, but, with lofty indifference, I threw him a second time, till his head buzzed. That satisfied me that I had not been shamed before Henrietta, who, for that matter, took my exploit very coolly and did not fling me so much as a word for it. However, she asked me if I would meet her the same evening under the old May-tree. When we met, she had two long straps with her, and at once asked me, somewhat mockingly and dryly, whether I had the courage to let myself be bound. Of course I said I had, whereupon, very carefully and thoroughly, she fastened my hands together with the one strap. Could I move my arms? No. Then, with eager haste, she swung the other strap and let it fall on my back. Again and again.

My first smart jacket was a well-thrashed one. She thoroughly enjoyed exerting her strength. Naturally, my boyish ideas of honour would not permit me to scream or complain; I merely stared at her with the profoundest astonishment. She gave me no explanation, released my hands, we each went our own way, and I avoided her the rest of my stay.

This was my first experience of woman's perfidy.

Still, I did not bear a grudge long, and the evening before I left we met once again, at her request, and then she gave me the first and only kiss, neither of us saying anything but the one word, " Good-bye."

I have never seen her since. I heard that she died twenty years ago in Brazil. But two years after this, when I was feeling my first schoolboy affection for an eleven-year-old girl, she silenced me at a children's ball with the scoffing remark: " Ah! it was you who let Henrietta K. thrash you under the May-tree at Farum." Yes, it was I. So cruel had my fair lady been that she had not even denied herself the pleasure of telling her friends of the ignominious treatment to which she had subjected a comrade who, from pure feeling of honour, had not struck back.

This was my first real experience of feminine nature.

VII.

For nearly ten years I went to one and the same school. I came to know the way there and back, to and from the three different places, all near together, where my parents lived during the time, as I knew no other. In that part of the town, all about the Round Tower, I knew, not only every house, but every archway, every door, every window, every paving-stone. It all gradually imprinted itself so deeply upon

me that in after years, when gazing on foreign sights and
foreign towns, even after I had been living for a long time
in the same place, I had a curious feeling that, however beautiful and fascinating it all might be, or perhaps for that very
reason, it was dreamland, unreality, which would one day
elude me and vanish; reality was the Round Tower in Copenhagen and all that lay about it. It was ugly, and altogether
unattractive, but it was reality. That you always found
again.

Similarly, though in a somewhat different sense, the wooded landscape in the neighbourhood of Copenhagen, to be
exact, the view over the Hermitage Meadows down to the
Sound, as it appears from the bench opposite the Slesvig
Stone, the first and dearest type of landscape beauty with
which I became acquainted, was endowed to me with an im-
print of actuality which no other landscape since, be it never
so lovely or never so imposing, has ever been able to acquire.

VIII.

The instruction at school was out of date, inasmuch as,
in every branch, it lacked intelligibility. The masters were
also necessarily, in some instances, anything but perfect, even
when not lacking in knowledge of their subject. Nevertheless, the instruction as a whole, especially when one bears in
mind how cheap it was, must be termed good, careful and
comprehensive; as a rule it was given conscientiously. When
as a grown up man I have cast my thoughts back, what has
surprised me most is the variety of subjects that were in-
stilled into a boy in ten years. There certainly were teachers
so lacking in understanding of the proper way to communi-
cate knowledge that the instruction they gave was altogether
wasted. For instance, I learnt geometry for four or five
years without grasping the simplest elements of the science.
The principles of it remained so foreign to me that I did not
even recognise a right-angled triangle, if the right angle were
uppermost. It so happened that the year before I had to
sit for my examinations, a young University student in his
first year, who had been only one class in front of the rest of

us, offered us afternoon instruction in trigonometry and spher-
ical geometry gratis, and all who appreciated the help that
was being offered to them streamed to his lessons. This young
student, later Pastor Jörgen Lund, had a remarkable gift for
mathematics, and gave his instruction with a lucidity, a fire,
and a swing that carried his hearers with him.   I, who had
never before been able to understand a word of the subject,
became keenly interested in it, and before many lessons were
over was very well up in it.   As Jörgen Lund taught mathematics, so all the other subjects ought to have been taught.
We were obliged to be content with less.

Lessons might have been a pleasure.   They never were,
or rather, only the Danish ones.   But in childhood's years,
and during the first years of boyhood they were fertilising.
As a boy they hung over me like a dread compulsion; yet
the compulsion was beneficial.   It was only when I was
almost fourteen that I began inwardly to rebel against
the time which was wasted, that the stupidest and laziest of
the boys might be enabled to keep up with the industrious and
intelligent.   There was too much consideration shown towards
those who would not work or could not understand.   And
from the time I was sixteen, school was my despair.   I had
done with it all, was beyond it all, was too matured to submit
to the routine of lessons; my intellectual pulses no longer beat
within the limits of school.   What absorbed my interest
was the endeavour to become master of the Danish language
in prose and verse, and musings over the mystery of existence.   In school I most often threw up the sponge entirely,
and laid my head on my arms that I might neither see nor
hear what was going on around me.

There was another reason, besides my weariness of it all,
which at this latter period made my school-going a torture
to me.   I was by now sufficiently schooled for my sensible
mother to think it would be good for me to make, if it were
but a small beginning, towards earning my own living.   Or
rather, she wanted me to earn enough to pay for my amusements myself.   So I tried, with success, to find pupils, and
gave them lessons chiefly on Sunday mornings; but in order
to secure them I had called myself *Studiosus*.   Now it was

an ever present terror with me lest I should meet any of my
pupils as I went to school in the morning, or back at midday,
with my books in a strap under my arm. Not to betray myself, I used to stuff these books in the most extraordinary
places, inside the breast of my coat till it bulged, and in all my
pockets till they burst.

IX.

School is a foretaste of life. A boy in a large Copenhagen school would become acquainted, as it were in miniature, with Society in its entirety and with every description
of human character. I encountered among my comrades the
most varied human traits, from frankness to reserve, from
goodness, uprightness and kindness, to brutality and baseness.

In our quarter of an hour's playtime it was easy to see
how cowardice and meanness met with their reward in the
boy commonwealth. There was a Jewish boy of repulsive
appearance, very easy to cow, with a positively slavish disposition. Every single playtime his schoolfellows would
make him stand up against a wall and jump about with his
feet close together till playtime was over, while the others
stood in front of him and laughed at him. He became later
a highly respected Conservative journalist.

In lesson time it was easy to see that the equality under
one discipline, under the hierarchy of merit, which was expressed in the boys' places on the forms, from highest to lowest, was not maintained when opposed to the very different
hierarchy of Society. On the lowest form sat a boy whose
gifts were exceedingly mediocre, and who was ignorant,
moreover, from sheer laziness; to him were permitted things
forbidden to all the others: he was the heir of a large feudal
barony. He always came late to school, and even at that
rode in followed by a groom on a second horse. He wore
a silk hat and, when he came into the schoolroom, did not
hang it up on the peg that belonged to him, where he was
afraid it might be interfered with, but in the school cupboard,
in which only the master was supposed to keep his things; and
the tall hat crowning so noble a head impressed the masters

to such an extent that not one of them asked for it to be removed. And they acquiesced like lambs in the young lord's departure half-way through the last lesson, if the groom happened to be there with his horse to fetch him.

It seemed impossible to drive knowledge of any sort into the head of this young peer, and he was taken from school early. To what an extent he must have worked later to make up for lost time was proved by results. For he became nothing less than a Minister.

x.

The reverence with which the boys, as youngsters, had looked up to the masters, disappeared with striking rapidity. The few teachers in whose lessons you could do what you liked were despised. The masters who knew how to make themselves respected, only in exceptional cases inspired affection. The love of mockery soon broke out. Children had not been at school long before the only opinion they allowed scope to was that the masters were the natural enemies of the boys. There was war between them, and every stratagem was permissible. They were fooled, misled, and plagued in every conceivable manner. Or they were feared and we flattered them.

A little boy with a natural inclination to reverence and respect and who brought both industry and good-will to his work, felt confused by all the derogatory things he was constantly hearing about the masters, and, long before he was half grown up, formed as one result of it the fixed determination that, whatever he might be when he grew up, there was one thing he would never, under any circumstances be, and that was—master in a school.

From twelve years of age upwards, contempt for the masters was the keynote of all conversation about them. The Latin master, a little, insignificant-looking man, but a very good teacher, was said to be so disgracefully enfeebled by debauchery that an active boy could throw him without the least difficulty. The Natural History master, a clever, outspoken young man, who would call out gaily: " Silence there, or you'll get a dusting on the teapot that will make the spout fly off!" sank deeply in our estimation when one of the boys told us that he spent his evenings at music-halls. One morning there spread like wildfire through the class the report that the reason the Natural History master had not come that day was because he had got mixed up the night before in a fight outside a music-pavilion. The contempt and the ridicule that were heaped upon him in the conversation of the boys were immeasurable. When he came next morning with a black, extravasated eye, which he bathed at intervals with a rag, he was regarded by most of us as absolute scum. The German master, a tall, good-looking man, was treated as utterly incompetent because, when he asked a question in grammar or syntax, he walked up and down with the book in front of him, and quite plainly compared the answer with the book. We boys thought that anyone could be a master, with a book in his hand. History and Geography were taught by an old man, overflowing with good-humour, loquacious, but self-confident, liked for his amiability, but despised for what was deemed unmanliness in him. The boys pulled faces at him, and imitated his expressions and mannerisms.

The Danish master, Professor H. P. Holst, was not liked. He evidently took no interest in his scholastic labours, and did not like the boys. His coolness was returned. And yet, that which was the sole aim and object of his instruction he understood to perfection, and drilled into us well. The unfortunate part of it was that there was hardly more than one boy in the class who enjoyed learning anything about just that particular thing. Instruction in Danish was, for Holst, instruction in the metrical art. He explained every metre and taught the boys to pick out the feet of which the verses were composed. When we made fun of him in our playtime, it was for remarks which we had invented and placed in his mouth ourselves; for instance: "Scan my immortal poem, *The Dying Gladiator*." The reason of this was simply that, in elucidation of the composition of the antique distich, he made use of his own poem of the above name, which he had included in a Danish reading-book edited by himself. As soon as he took up his position in the desk, he began:

" Hark ye the—storm of ap—plause from the— thea-tre's—echoing circle! Go on, Möller!"

How could he find it in his heart, his own poem!

XI.

The French master knew how to command respect; there was never a sound during his lessons. He was alto-gether absorbed in his subject, was absolutely and wholly a Frenchman; he did not even talk Danish with the same ac-centuation as others, and he had the impetuous French dispo-sition of which the boys had heard. If a boy made a mess of his pronunciation, he would bawl, from the depths of his full brown beard, which he was fond of stroking: " You speak French *comme un paysan d'Amac.*" When he swore, he swore like a true Frenchman: " *Sacrebleu-Mops-Carot-ten-Rapée!*"[1] If he got angry, and he very often did, he would unhesitatingly pick up the full glass of water that al-ways stood in front of him on the desk, and in Gallic exasper-ation fling it on the floor, when the glass would be smashed to atoms and the water run about, whereupon he would quietly, with his *Grand seigneur* air, take his purse out of his pocket and lay the money for the glass on the desk.

For a time I based my ideas of the French mind and manner upon this master, although my uncle Jacob, who had lived almost all his life in Paris, was a very different sort of Frenchman. It was only later that I became acquainted with a word and an idea which it was well I did not know, as far as the master's capacity for making an impression was con-cerned—the word *affected.*

At last, one fine day, a little event occurred which was not without its effect on the master's prestige, and yet aroused my compassion almost as much as my surprise. The parents of one of my best friends were expecting a French business friend for the evening. As they knew themselves to be very weak in the language, they gave their son a polite note to the

---

[1] Needless to say, this is impossible French, composed chiefly of distorted Danish words.   (Trans.)

French master, asking him to do them the honour of spending the next evening at their house, on the occasion of this visit, which rendered conversational support desirable. The master took the note, which we two boys had handed to him, grew —superior though he usually was—rather red and embarrassed, and promised a written reply. To our astonishment we learnt that this reply was to the effect that he must unfortunately decline the honour, as he had never been in France, had never heard anyone speak French, and was not proficient in the language. Thus this tiger of a savage Frenchman suddenly cast his tiger's skin and revealed himself in his native wool.

Unfortunately, the instruction of this master left long and deep traces upon me. When I was fifteen and my French uncle began to carry on his conversations with me in French, the Parisian was appalled at my abominable errors of pronunciation. The worst of them were weeded out in those lessons. But there were enough left to bring a smile many a time and oft to the lips of the refined young lady whom my friends procured me as a teacher on my first visit to Paris.

XII.

Among the delights of Summer were picnics to the woods. There would be several during the course of the season. When the weather seemed to inspire confidence, a few phaetons would be engaged for the family and their relations and friends, and some Sunday morning the seat of each carriage would be packed full of good things. We took tablecloth and serviettes with us, bread, butter, eggs and salmon, sausages, cold meat and coffee, as well as a few bottles of wine. Then we drove to some keeper's house, where for money and fair words they scalded the tea for us, and the day's meal was seasoned with the good appetite which the outdoor air gave us.

As a child I preserved an uncomfortable and instructive recollection of one of these expeditions. The next day my mother said to me: " You behaved very ridiculously yesterday, and made a laughing stock of yourself." " How ? "

" You went on in front of the grown-up people all the time, and sang at the top of your voice.   In the first place, you ought not to go in front, and in the next place, you should not disturb other people by singing."   These words made an indelible impression upon me, for I was conscious that I had not in the least intended to push myself forward or put on airs.   I could only dimly recollect that I had been singing, and I had done it for my own pleasure, not to draw attention to myself.

I learnt from this experience that it was possible, without being naughty or conceited, to behave in an unpleasing manner, understood that the others, whom I had not been thinking about, had looked on me with disfavour, had thought me a nuisance and ridiculous, my mother in particular; and I was deeply humiliated at the thought.

It gradually dawned upon me that there was no one more difficult to please than my mother.   No one was more chary of praise than she, and she had a horror of all sentimentality.   She met me with superior intelligence, corrected me, and brought me up by means of satire.   It was possible to impress my aunts, but not her.   The profound dread she had of betraying her feelings or talking about them, the shrewdness that dwelt behind that forehead of hers, her consistently critical and clear-sighted nature, the mocking spirit that was so conspicuous in her, especially in her younger days, gave me, with regard to her, a conviction that had a stimulating effect on my character—namely, that not only had she a mother's affection for me, but that the two shrewd and scrutinising eyes of a very clever head were looking down upon me.   Rational as she was through and through, she met my visionary inclinations, both religious and philosophical, with unshaken common sense, and if I were sometimes tempted, by lesser people's over-estimating of my abilities, to over-estimate them myself, it was she who, with inflexible firmness, urged her conviction of the limitations of my nature.   None of my weaknesses throve in my mother's neighbourhood.

This was the reason why, during the transitional years between boyhood and adolescence, the years in which a boy

feels a greater need of sympathy than of criticism and of indulgence than of superiority, I looked for and found comprehension as much from a somewhat younger sister of my
mother's as from the latter herself.   This aunt was all heart.
She had an ardent, enthusiastic brain, was full of tenderness
and goodness and the keenest feeling for everything deserving of sympathy, not least for me, while she had not my mother's critical understanding.   Her judgment might be obscured by passion; she sometimes allowed herself to be carried to imprudent extremes; she had neither Mother's equilibrium nor her satirical qualities.   She was thus admirably
adapted to be the confidant of a big boy whom she gave to
understand that she regarded as extraordinarily gifted.   When
these transitional years were over, Mother resumed undis-
puted sway, and the relations between us remained in all essentials the same, even after I had become much her superior in
knowledge and she in some things my pupil.   So that it affected me very much when, many years after, my younger
brother said to me somewhat sadly: "Has it struck you,
too, that Mother is getting old?" "No, not at all," I replied.   "What do you think a sign of it?"   "I think, God
help me, that she is beginning to admire us."

XIII.

My mind, like that of all other children, had been exercised by the great problem of the mystery of our coming
into the world.   I was no longer satisfied with the explanation that children were brought by the stork, or with that
other, advanced with greater seriousness, that they drifted up
in boxes, which were taken up out of Peblinge Lake.   As a
child I tormented my mother with questions as to how you
could tell whom every box was for.   That the boxes were
numbered, did not make things much clearer.   That they
were provided with addresses, sounded very strange.   Who
had written the addresses?   I then had to be content with
the assurance that it was a thing that I was too small to understand; it should be explained to me when I was older.
My thoughts were not directed towards the other sex.

I had no little girl playfellows, and as I had no sister, knew very few. When I was eight or nine years old, it is true, there was one rough and altogether depraved boy whose talk touched upon the sexual question in expressions that were coarse and in a spirit coarser still. I was scoffed at for not knowing how animals propagated themselves, and that human beings propagated themselves like animals.

I replied: " My parents, at any rate, never behaved in any such manner." Then, with the effrontery of childhood, my schoolfellows went on to the most shameless revelations, not only about a morbid development of natural instincts, but actual crimes against nature and against the elementary laws of society. In other words, I was shown the most repulsive, most agitating picture of everything touching the relations of the sexes and the propagation of the species.

It is probable that most boys in a big school have the great mystery of Nature sullied for them in their tender years by coarseness and depravity. Whereas, in ancient Greek times, the mystery was holy, and with a pious mind men worshipped the Force of Nature without exaggerated prudery and without shamelessness, such conditions are impossible in a society where for a thousand years Nature herself has been depreciated by Religion, associated with sin and the Devil, stamped as unmentionable and in preference denied, in which, for that very reason, brutality takes so much more terrible a satisfaction and revenge. As grown-up people never spoke of the forces of Nature in a pure and simple manner, it became to the children a concealed thing. Individual children, in whom the sexual impulse had awakened early, were taught its nature by bestial dispositions, and the knowledge was interpreted by them with childish shamelessness. These children then filled the ears of their comrades with filth.

In my case, the nastiness hit, and rebounded, without making any impression. I was only infected by the tone of the other scholars in so far as I learnt from them that it was manly to use certain ugly words. When I was twelve years old, my mother surprised me one day, when I was standing alone on the stairs, shouting these words out. I was reproved for it, and did not do it again.

XIV.

I hardly ever met little girls except at children's balls, and in my early childhood I did not think further of any of them. But when I was twelve years old I caught my first strong glimpse of one of the fundamental forces of existence, whose votary I was destined to be for life—namely, Beauty.

It was revealed to me for the first time in the person of a slender, light-footed little girl, whose name and personality secretly haunted my brain for many a year.

One of my uncles was living that Summer in America Road, which at that time was quite in the country, and there was a beautiful walk thence across the fields to a spot called *The Signal,* where you could watch the trains go by from Copenhagen's oldest railway station, which was not situated on the western side of the town, where the present stations are. Near here lived a family whose youngest daughter used to run over almost every day to my uncle's country home, to play with the children.

She was ten years old, as brown as a gipsy, as agile as a roe, and from her childish face, from all the brown of her hair, eyes, and skin, from her smile and her speech, glowed, rang, and as it were, struck me, that overwhelming and hitherto unknown force, Beauty. I was twelve, she was ten. Our acquaintance consisted of playing touch, not even alone together, but with other children; I can see her now rushing away from me, her long plaits striking against her waist. But although this was all that passed between us, we both had a feeling as of a mysterious link connecting us. It was delightful to meet. She gave me a pink. She cut a Queen of Hearts out of a pack of cards, and gave it to me; I treasured it for the next five years like a sacred thing.

That was all that passed between us and more there never was, even when at twelve years of age, at a children's ball, she confessed to me that she had kept everything I had given her—gifts of the same order as her own. But the impression of her beauty filled my being.

Some one had made me a present of some stuffed humming-birds, perched on varnished twigs under a glass case. I always looked at them while I was reading in the nursery; they stood on the bookshelves which were my special property. These birds with their lovely, shining, gay-coloured plumage, conveyed to me my first impression of foreign or tropical vividness of colouring. All that I was destined to love for a long time had something of that about it, something foreign and afar off.

The girl was Danish as far as her speech was concerned, but not really Danish by descent, either on her father or her mother's side; her name, too, was un-Danish. She spoke English at home and was called Mary at my uncle's, though her parents called her by another name. All this combined to render her more distinctive.

Once a year I met her at a children's ball; then she had a white dress on, and was, in my eyes, essentially different from all the other little girls. One morning, after one of these balls, when I was fourteen, I felt in a most singular frame of mind, and with wonder and reverence at what I was about to do, regarding myself as dominated by a higher, incomprehensible force, I wrote the first poetry I ever composed.

There were several strophes of this heavenly poetry. Just because I so seldom met her, it was like a gentle earthquake in my life, when I did. I had accustomed myself to such a worship of her name that, for me, she hardly belonged to the world of reality at all. But when I was sixteen and I met her again, once more at a young people's ball, the glamour suddenly departed. Her appearance had altered and corresponded no longer to my imaginary picture of her. When we met in the dance she pressed my hand, which made me indignant, as though it were an immodest thing. She was no longer a fairy. She had broad shoulders, a budding bust, warm hands; there was youthful coquetry about her— something that, to me, seemed like erotic experience. I soon lost sight of her. But I retained a sentiment of gratitude towards her for what, as a ten-year-old child, she had afforded me, this naturally supernatural impression, my first revelation of Beauty.

XV.

The person upon whom the schoolboys' attention centred was, of course, the Headmaster. To the very young ones, the Headmaster was merely powerful and paternal, up above everything. As soon as the critical instinct awoke, its utterances were specially directed, by the evil-disposed, at him, petty and malicious as they were, and were echoed slavishly by the rest.

As the Head was a powerful, stout, handsome, distinguished-looking man with a certain stamp of joviality and innocent good-living about him, these malicious tongues, who led the rest, declared that he only lived for his stomach. In the next place, the old-fashioned punishment of caning, administered by the Head himself in his private room, gave some cause of offence. It was certainly only very lazy and obdurate boys who were thus punished; for others such methods were never even dreamt of. But when they were ordered to appear in his room after school-time, and the Head took them between his knees, thrashed them well and then afterwards caressed them, as though to console them, he created ill-feeling, and his dignity suffered. If there were some little sense in the disgust occasioned by this, there was certainly none at all in certain other grievances urged against him.

It was the ungraceful custom for the boys, on the first of the month, to bring their own school fees. In the middle of one of the lessons the Head would come into the schoolroom, take his seat at the desk, and jauntily and quickly sweep five-daler bills[1] into his large, soft hat and thence into his pockets. One objection to this arrangement was that the few poor boys who went to school free were thus singled out to their schoolfellows, bringing no money, which they felt as a humiliation. In the next place, the sight of the supposed wealth that the Head thus became possessed of roused ill-feeling and derision. It became the fashion to call him boy-dealer, because the school, which in its palmy days had 550 scholars, was so well attended. This extraordinary influx, which in all common sense ought to have been regarded as a

---

[1] Five daler, a little over 11/— English money.

proof of the high reputation of the school, was considered a proof of the Head's avarice.

It must be added that there was in his bearing, which was evidently and with good reason, calculated to impress, something that might justly appear unnatural to keen-sighted boys. He always arrived with blustering suddenness; he always shouted in a stentorian voice, and, when he gave the elder boys a Latin lesson, he always appeared, probably from indolence, a good deal behind time, but to make up, and as though there were not a second to waste, began to hurl his questions at them the moment he arrived on the threshold. He liked the pathetic, and was certainly a man with a naturally warm heart. On a closer acquaintance, he would have won much affection, for he was a clever man and a gay, optimistic figure. As the number of his scholars was so great, he produced more effect at a distance.

XVI.

Neither he nor any of the other masters reproduced the atmosphere of the classical antiquity round which all the instruction of the Latin side centred. The master who taught Greek the last few years did so, not only with sternness, but with a distaste, in fact, a positive hatred for his class, which was simply disgusting.

The Head, who had the gift of oratory, communicated to us some idea of the beauty of Latin poetry, but the rest of the instruction in the dead languages was purely grammatical, competent and conscientious though the men who gave it might have been. Madvig's[1] spirit brooded over the school. Still, there was no doubt in the Head's mind as to the greatness of Virgil or Horace, so that a boy with perception of stylistic emphasis and metre could not fail to be keenly interested in the poetry of these two men. Being the boy in the class of whom the Head entertained the greatest hopes, I began at once secretly to translate them. I made a Danish

---

[1] Johan Nicolai Madvig (1804-1886), a very celebrated Danish philologist, for fifty years professor at the University of Copenhagen. He is especially noted for his editions of the ancient classics, with critical notes on the text, and for his Latin Grammar.—[Translator's note.]

version of the second and fourth books of the Æneid, and
Danicised a good part of the Songs and Epistles of Horace in
imperfect verse.

XVII.

Nothing was ever said at home about any religious creed.
Neither of my parents was in any way associated with the
Jewish religion, and neither of them ever went to the Syna-
gogue. As in my maternal grandmother's house all the Jewish laws about eating and drinking were observed, and they
had different plates and dishes for meat and butter and a
special service for Easter, orthodox Judaism, to me, seemed
to be a collection of old, whimsical, superstitious prejudices,
which specially applied to food. The poetry of it was a
sealed book to me. At school, where I was present at the
religious instruction classes as an auditor only, I always heard
Judaism alluded to as merely a preliminary stage of Christianity, and the Jews as the remnant of a people who, as a
punishment for slaying the Saviour of the world, had been
scattered all over the earth. The present-day Israelites were
represented as people who, urged by a stiff-necked wilfulness
and obstinacy and almost incomprehensible callousness, clung
to the obsolete religious ideal of the stern God in opposition
to the God of Love.

When I attempted to think the matter out for myself,
it annoyed me that the Jews had not sided with Jesus, who
yet so clearly betokened progress within the religion that He
widened and unintentionally overthrew. The supernatural
personality of Jesus did not seem credible to me. The demand made by faith, namely, that reason should be fettered,
awakened a latent rebellious opposition, and this opposition
was fostered by my mother's steady rationalism, her unconditional rejection of every miracle. When the time came for
me to be confirmed, in accordance with the law, I had advanced so far that I looked down on what lay before me as a
mere burdensome ceremony. The person of the Rabbi only
inspired me with distaste; his German pronunciation of Danish was repulsive and ridiculous to me. The abominable
Danish in which the lesson-book was couched offended me, as

I had naturally a fine ear for Danish. Information about ancient Jewish customs and festivals was of no interest to me, with my modern upbringing. The confirmation, according to my mocking summary of the impression produced by it, consisted mainly in the hiring of a tall silk hat from the hatmaker, and the sending of it back next day, sanctified. The silly custom was at that time prevalent for boys to wear silk hats for the occasion, idiotic though they made them look. With these on their heads, they went, after examination, up the steps to a balustrade where a priest awaited, whispered a few affecting words in their ear about their parents or grandparents, and laid his hand in blessing upon the tall hat. When called upon to make my confession of faith with the others, I certainly joined my first " yes," this touching a belief in a God, to theirs, but remained silent at the question as to whether I believed that God had revealed Himself to Moses and spoken by His prophets. I did not believe it.

I was, for that matter, in a wavering frame of mind unable to arrive at any clear understanding. What confused me was the unveracious manner in which historical instruction, which was wholly theological, was given. The History masters, for instance, told us that when Julian the Apostate wanted to rebuild the Temple at Jerusalem, flames had shot out of the earth, but they interpreted this as a miracle, expressing the Divine will. If this were true—and I was unable to refute it then—God had expressly taken part against Judaism and the Jews as a nation. The nation, in that case, seemed to be really cursed by Him. Still, Christianity fundamentally repelled me by its legends, its dogmatism, and its church rites. The Virgin birth, the three persons in the Trinity, and the Sacrament of the Lord's Supper in particular, seemed to me to be remnants of the basest barbarism of antiquity.

Under these circumstances, my young soul, feeling the need of something it could worship, fled from Asia's to Europe's divinities, from Palestine to Hellas, and clung with vivid enthusiasm to the Greek world of beauty and the legends of its Gods. From all the learned education I had had, I only extracted this one thing: an enthusiasm for an-

cient Hellas and her Gods; they were my Gods, as they had
been those of Julian.   Apollo and Artemis, Athene and Eros
and Aphrodite grew to be powers that I believed in and rejoiced over in a very different sense from any God revealed
on Sinai or in Emmaus.   They were near to me.

And under these circumstances the Antiquities Room at
Charlottenburg, where as a boy I had heard Höyen's lectures,
grew to be a place that I entered with reverence, and Thorwaldsen's Museum my Temple, imperfectly though it reproduced the religious and heroic life and spirit of the Greeks.
But at that time I knew no other, better door to the world
of the Gods than the Museum offered, and Thorwaldsen and
the Greeks, from fourteen to fifteen, were in my mind merged
in one.   Thorwaldsen's Museum was to me a brilliant illustration of Homer.   There I found my Church, my Gods, my
soul's true native land.

XVIII.

I had for several years been top of my class, when a
boy was put in who was quite three years older than I, and
with whom it was impossible for me to compete, so much
greater were the newcomer's knowledge and maturity.   It
very soon became a settled thing for the new boy always to be
top, and I invariably No. 2.   However, this was not in the
least vexatious to me; I was too much wrapped up in Sebastian for that.   The admiration which as a child I had
felt for boys who distinguished themselves by muscular
strength was manifested now for superiority in knowledge or
intelligence.   Sebastian was tall, thin, somewhat disjointed in
build, with large blue eyes, expressive of kindness, and intelligence; he was thoroughly well up in all the school subjects,
and with the ripeness of the older boy, could infer the right
thing even when he did not positively know it.   The reason
why he was placed at lessons so late was doubtless to be found
in the narrow circumstances of his parents.   They considered
that they had not the means to allow him to follow the path
towards which his talents pointed.   But the Head, as could
be seen on pay days, was now permitting him to come to

school free.   He went about among his jacketed schoolfellows in a long frock coat, the skirts of which flapped round
his legs.

No. 2 could not help admiring No. 1 for the confidence
with which he disported himself among the Greek aorists, in
the labyrinths of which I myself often went astray, and for
the knack he had of solving mathematical problems.   He
was, moreover, very widely read in belles lettres, and had
almost a grown-up man's taste with regard to books at a time
when I still continued to admire P. P.'s[1] novels, and was incapable of detecting the inartistic quality and unreality of
his popular descriptions of the exploits of sailor heroes.   As
soon as my eyes were opened to the other's advanced acquirements, I opened my heart to him, gave him my entire confidence, and found in my friend a well of knowledge and superior development from which I felt a daily need to draw.

When at the end of the year the large number of newcomers made it desirable for the class to be divided, it was a
positive blow to me that in the division, which was effected
by separating the scholars according to their numbers, odd or
even, Sebastian and I found ourselves in different classes.   I
even took the unusual step of appealing to the Head to be
put in the same class as Sebastian, but was refused.

However, childhood so easily adapts itself to a fresh situation that during the ensuing year, in which I myself advanced right gaily, not only did I feel no lack, but I forgot my elder comrade.   And at the commencement of the
next school year, when the two parallel classes, through several boys leaving, were once more united, and I again found
myself No. 2 by the side of my one-time friend, the relations
between us were altogether altered, so thoroughly so, in fact,
that our rôles were reversed.   If formerly the younger had
hung upon the elder's words, now it was the other way
about.   If formerly Sebastian had shown the interest in me
that the half-grown man feels for a child, now I was too
absorbed by my own interests to wish for anything but a lis-

---

[1] *P. P.* was a writer whose real name was Rumohr.   He wrote a number
of historical novels of a patriotic type, but which are only read by children
up to 14.

tener in him when I unfolded the supposed wealth of my ideas and my soaring plans for the future, which betrayed a boundless ambition. I needed a friend at this stage only in the same sense as the hero in French tragedies requires a confidant, and if I attached myself as before, wholly and completely to him, it was for this reason. It is true that the other was still a good deal in front of me in actual knowledge, so that there was much I had to consult him about; otherwise our friendship would hardly have lasted; but the importance of this superiority was slight, inasmuch as Sebastian henceforward voluntarily subordinated himself to me altogether; indeed, by his ready recognition of my powers, contributed more than anyone else to make me conscious of these powers and to foster a self-esteem which gradually assumed extraordinary forms.

XIX.

This self-esteem, in its immaturity, was of a twofold character. It was not primarily a belief that I was endowed with unusual abilities, but a childish belief that I was one set apart, with whom, for mysterious reasons, everything must succeed. The belief in a personal God had gradually faded away from me, and there were times when, with the conviction of boyhood, I termed myself an atheist to my friend; my attitude towards the Greek gods had never been anything more than a personification of the ideal forces upon which I heaped my enthusiasm. But I believed in my star. And I hypnotised my friend into the same belief, infected him so that he talked as if he were consecrating his life to my service, and really, as far as was possible for a schoolboy, lived and breathed exclusively for me, I, for my part, being gratified at having, as my unreserved admirer and believer, the one whom, of all people I knew, I placed highest, the one whose horizon seemed to me the widest, and whose store of knowledge was the greatest; for in many subjects it surpassed even that of the masters in no mean degree.

Under such conditions, when I was fifteen or sixteen, I was deeply impressed by a book that one might think was infinitely beyond the understanding of my years, Lermontof's

A Hero of Our Time, in Xavier Marmier's French translation. The subject of it would seem utterly unsuited to a schoolboy who had never experienced anything in the remotest degree resembling the experiences of a man of the world, at any rate those which produced the sentiments pervading this novel. Nevertheless, this book brought about a revolution in my ideas. For the first time I encountered in a book a chief character who was not a universal hero, a military or naval hero whom one had to admire and if possible imitate, but one in whom, with extreme emotion, I fancied that I recognised myself!

I had certainly never acted as Petsjórin did, and never been placed in such situations as Petsjórin. No woman had ever loved me, still less had I ever let a woman pay with suffering the penalty of her affection for me. Never had any old friend of mine come up to me, delighted to see me again, and been painfully reminded, by my coolness and indifference, how little he counted for in my life. Petsjórin had done with life; I had not even begun to live. Petsjórin had drained the cup of enjoyment; I had never tasted so much as a drop of it. Petsjórin was as blasé as a splendid Russian Officer of the Guards could be; I, as full of expectation as an insignificant Copenhagen schoolboy could be. Nevertheless, I had the perplexing feeling of having, for the first time in my life, seen my inmost nature, hitherto unknown even to myself, understood, interpreted, reproduced, magnified, in this unharmonious work of the Russian poet who was snatched away so young.

XX.

The first element whence the imaginary figure which I fancied I recognized again in Lermontof had its rise was doubtless to be found in the relations between my older friend and myself (in the reversal of our rôles, and my consequent new feeling of superiority over him). The essential point, however, was not the comparatively accidental shape in which I fancied I recognised myself, but that what was at that time termed *reflection* had awaked in me, introspection, self-consciousness, which after all had to awake some day, as all other impulses awake when their time comes. This introspection was not, however, by any means a natural or permanent quality in me, but on the contrary one which made me feel ill at ease and which I soon came to detest. During these transitional years, as my pondering over myself grew, I felt more and more unhappy and less and less sure of myself. The pondering reached its height, as was inevitable, when there arose the question of choosing a profession and of planning the future rather than of following a vocation. But as long as this introspection lasted, I had a torturing feeling that my own eye was watching me, as though I were a stranger, a feeling of being the spectator of my own actions, the auditor of my own words, a double personality who must nevertheless one day become one, should I live long enough. After having, with a friend, paid a visit to Kaalund, who was prison instructor at Vridslöselille at the time and showed us young fellows the prison and the cells, I used to picture my condition to myself as that of a prisoner enduring the torture of seeing a watchful eye behind the peep-hole in the door. I had noticed before, in the Malmö prison, how the prisoners tried to besmear this glass, or scratch on it, with a sort of fury, so that it was often impossible to see through it. My natural inclination was to act naïvely, without premeditation, and to put myself wholly into what I was doing. The cleavage that introspection implies, therefore, was a horror to me; all bisection, all dualism, was fundamentally repellent to me; and it was consequently no mere chance that my first appearance as a writer was made in an attack on a division and duality in life's philosophy, and that the very title of my first book was a branding and rejection of a *Dualism*. So that it was only when my self-contemplation, and with it the inward cleavage, had at length ceased, that I attained to quietude of mind.

XXI.

Thus violently absorbing though the mental condition here suggested was, it was not permanent. It was childish and child-like by virtue of my years; the riper expressions which I here make use of to describe it always seem on the verge of distorting its character. My faith in my lucky star barely persisted a few years unassailed. My childish idea had been very much strengthened when, at fifteen years of age, in the first part of my finishing examination, I received *Distinction* in all my subjects, and received a mighty blow when, at seventeen, I only had *Very Good* in five subjects, thus barely securing Distinction for the whole.

I ceased to preoccupy myself about my likeness to Petsjórin, after having recovered from a half, or quarter, falling in love, an unharmonious affair, barren of results, which I had hashed up for myself through fanciful and affected reverie, and which made me realise the fundamental simplicity of my own nature,—and I then shook off the unnatural physiognomy like a mask. Belief in my own unbounded superiority and the absolutely unmeasured ambition in which this belief had vented itself, collapsed suddenly when at the age of eighteen, feeling my way independently for the first time, and mentally testing people, I learnt to recognise the real mental superiority great writers possess. It was chiefly my first reading of the principal works of Kierkegaard that marked this epoch in my life. I felt, face to face with the first great mind that, as it were, had personally confronted me, all my real insignificance, understood all at once that I had as yet neither lived nor suffered, felt nor thought, and that nothing was more uncertain than whether I might one day evince talent. The one certain thing was that my present status seemed to amount to nothing at all.

XXII.

In those boyhood's years, however, I revelled in ideas of greatness to come which had not so far received a shock. And I was in no doubt as to the domain in which when grown up I should distinguish myself. All my instincts drew me towards Literature. The Danish compositions which were set at school absorbed all my thoughts from week to week; I took the greatest pains with them, weighed the questions from as many sides as I could and endeavoured to give good

form and style to my compositions.   Unconsciously I tried
to find expressions containing striking contrasts; I sought
after descriptive words and euphonious constructions.   Although not acquainted with the word *style* in any other sense
than that it bears in the expression " style-book," the Danish
equivalent for what in English is termed an " exercise-book,"
I tried to acquire a certain style, and was very near falling
into mannerism, from sheer inexperience, when a sarcastic
master, to my distress, reminded me one day of Heiberg's
words :   " The unguent of expression, smeared thickly over
the thinness of thoughts."

XXIII.

Together with a practical training in the use of the language, the Danish lessons afforded a presentment of the history of our national literature, given intelligently and in a
very instructive manner by a master named Driebein, who,
though undoubtedly one of the many Heibergians of the time,
did not in any way deviate from what might be termed the
orthodoxy of literary history.   Protestantism carried it against
Roman Catholicism, the young Oehlenschläger against Baggesen, Romanticism against Rationalism; Oehlenschläger as
the Northern poet of human nature against a certain Björnson, who, it was said, claimed to be more truly Norse than
he.   In Mr. Driebein's presentment, no recognised great
name was ever attacked.   And in his course, as in Thortsen's
History of Literature, literature which might be regarded
as historic stopped with the year 1814.

The order in which in my private reading I became acquainted with Danish authors was as follows: Ingemann,
Oehlenschläger, Grundtvig, Poul Möller, many books by
these authors having been given me at Christmas and on
birthdays.   At my grandfather's, I eagerly devoured Heiberg's vaudevilles as well.   As a child, of course, I read un-
critically, merely accepting and enjoying.   But when I heard
at school of Baggesen's treatment of Oehlenschläger, thus
realising that there had been various tendencies in literature
at that time, and various opinions as to which was preferable,

I read with enthusiasm a volume of selected poems by Baggesen, which I had had one Christmas, and the treatment of
language in it fascinated me exceedingly, with its gracefulness
and light, conversational tone.   Then, when Hertz's[1] *Ghost
Letters* fell into my hands one day, and the diction of them
appealed to me almost more, I felt myself, first secretly,
afterwards more consciously, drawn towards the school
of form in Danish literature, and rather enjoyed being
a heretic on this point.   For to entertain kindly sentiments for the man who had dared to profane Oehlenschläger was like siding with Loki against Thor.   Poul
Möller's Collected Works I had received at my confirmation,
and read again and again with such enthusiasm that I almost
wore the pages out, and did not skip a line, even of the philosophical parts, which I did not understand at all.   But
Hertz's Lyrical Poems, which I read in a borrowed copy,
gave me as much pleasure as Poul Möller's Verses had done.
And for a few years, grace and charm, and the perfect control of language and poetic form, were in my estimation the
supreme thing until, on entering upon my eighteenth year,
a violent reaction took place, and resonance, power and
grandeur alone seemed to have value.   From Hertz my sympathies went over to Christian Winther, from Baggesen to
Homer, Æschylus, the Bible, Shakespeare, Goethe.   One of
the first things I did as a student was to read the Bible through
in Danish and the Odyssey in Greek.

XXIV.

The years of approaching maturity were still distant,
however, and my inner life was personal, not real, so
that an element of fermentation was cast into my mind
when a copy of Heine's *Buch der Lieder* was one day
lent to me.   What took my fancy in it was, firstly, the
combination of enthusiasm and wit, then its terse, pithy

[1] Henrik Hertz, a Danish poet (1797-1870), published "Ghost Letters"
anonymously, and called them thus because in language and spirit they
were a kind of continuation of the long-deceased Baggesen's rhymed contribution to a literary dispute of his day.   Hertz, like the much greater Baggesen,
laid great stress upon precise and elegant form.—[Translator's note.]

form, and after that the parts describing how the poet
and his lady love, unable to overcome the shyness which
binds their tongues, involuntarily play hide and seek with
one another and lose each other; for I felt that I should
be equally unable to find natural and simple expression for my
feelings, should things ever come to such a pass with me.   Of
Heine's personality, of the poet's historic position, political
tendencies or importance, I knew nothing; in these love-poems
I looked more especially for those verses in which violent
self-esteem and blasé superiority to every situation find expression, because this fell in with the Petsjórin note, which,
since reading Lermontof's novel, was the dominant one in my
mind.   As was my habit in those years, when it was still out
of the question for me to buy books that pleased me, I copied
out of the *Buch der Lieder* all that I liked best, that I might
read it again.

XXV.

Of all this life of artistic desire and seeking, of external
impressions, welcomed with all the freshness and impulsive-
ness of a boy's mind, but most of self-study and self-dis-
covery, the elder of the two comrades was a most attentive
spectator, more than a spectator.   He made use of expressions and said things which rose to my head and made me
conceited.   Sebastian would make such a remark as: "It is
not for your abilities that I appreciate you, it is for your enthusiasm.   All other people I know are machines without
souls, at their best full of affected, set phrases, such as one
who has peeped behind the scenes laughs at; but in you there
is a fulness of ideality too great for you ever to be happy."
" Fulness of ideality " was the expression of the time for the
supremest quality of intellectual equipment.   No wonder,
then, that I felt flattered.

And my older comrade united a perception of my mental condition, which unerringly perceived its immaturity, with
a steadfast faith in a future for me which in spite of my arrogance, I thirsted to find in the one of all others who knew me
best and was most plainly my superior in knowledge.   One
day, when I had informed him that I felt " more mature and

clearer about myself," he replied, without a trace of indecision, that this was undoubtedly a very good thing, if it were true, but that he suspected I was laboring under a delusion. " I am none the less convinced," he added, " that you will soon reach a crisis, will overcome all obstacles and attain the nowadays almost giant's goal that you have set before you." This goal, for that matter, was very indefinite, and was to the general effect that I intended to make myself strongly felt, and bring about great changes in the intellectual world; of what kind, was uncertain.

Meanwhile, as the time drew near for us to enter the University, and I approached the years of manhood which the other, in spite of his modest position as schoolboy, had already long attained, Sebastian grew utterly miserable. He had, as he expressed it, made up his mind to be my *Melanchthon*. But through an inward collapse which I could not understand he now felt that the time in which he could be anything to me had gone by; it seemed to him that he had neglected to acquire the knowledge and the education necessary, and he reproached himself bitterly. " I have not been in the least what I might have been to you," he exclaimed one day, and without betraying it he endured torments of jealousy, and thought with vexation and anxiety of the time when a larger circle would be opened to me in the University, and he himself would become superfluous.

His fear was thus far unfounded, that, naïve in my selfishness, as in my reliance on him, I still continued to tell him everything, and in return constantly sought his help when philological or mathematical difficulties which I could not solve alone presented themselves to me.

But I had scarcely returned to Copenhagen, after my first journey abroad (a very enjoyable four weeks' visit to Göteborg), I had scarcely been a month a freshman, attending philosophical lectures and taking part in student life than the dreaded separation between us two so differently constituted friends came to pass. The provocation was trifling, in fact paltry. One day I was standing in the lecture-room with a few fellow-students before a lecture began, when a freshman hurried up to us and asked: " Is it true, what

Sebastian says, that he is the person you think most of in the world?" My reply was: "Did he say that himself?" "Yes." And, disgusted that the other should have made such a remark in order to impress perfect strangers, though it might certainly very easily have escaped him in confidence, I said hastily: "Oh! he's mad!" which outburst, bearing in mind young people's use of the word "mad," was decidedly not to be taken literally, but was, it is quite true, ill-naturedly meant.

The same evening I received a short note from Sebastian in which, though in polite terms, he repudiated his allegiance and fidelity; the letter, in which the polite form *you* was used instead of the accustomed *thou,* was signed: "Your 'mad' and 'foolish,' but respectful Sebastian."

The impression this produced upon me was exceedingly painful, but an early developed mental habit of always accepting a decision, and a vehement repugnance to renew any connection deliberately severed by another party, resulted in my never even for a moment thinking of shaking his resolution, and in my leaving the note unanswered. However, the matter was not done with, and the next few months brought me many insufferable moments, indeed hours, for Sebastian, whose existence had for so long centred round mine that he was evidently incapable of doing without me altogether, continually crossed my path, planted himself near me on every possible occasion, and one evening, at a students' gathering, even got a chair outside the row round the table, sat himself down just opposite to me, and spent a great part of the evening in staring fixedly into my face. As may be supposed, I felt exceedingly irritated.

Three months passed, when one day I received a letter from Sebastian, and at intervals of weeks or months several others followed. They were impressive letters, splendidly written, with a sort of grim humour about them, expressing his passionate affection and venting his despair. This was the first time that I had come in contact with passion, but it was a passion that without having any unnatural or sensual element in it, nevertheless, from a person of the same sex, excited a feeling of displeasure, and even disgust, in me.

Sebastian wrote: " I felt that it was cheating you to take so much without being able to give you anything in return; I thought it mean to associate with you; consequently, I believe that I did perfectly right to break with you. Still, it is true that I hardly needed to do it. Time and circumstances would have effected the breach." And feeling that our ways were now divided, he continued:

> Hic locus est, partes ubi se via findit in ambas.
> Dextera, quæ Ditis magni sub moenia tendit,
> Hac iter Elysium nobis; at læva malorum
> Exercet poenas et ad impia Tartara mittit.

" I cannot kill myself at present, but as soon as I feel able I shall do so."

Or he wrote: " Towards the end of the time when we were friends, I was not quite myself when talking to you; I was unbalanced; for I was convinced that you wasted your valuable time talking to me, and at the same time was oppressed with grief at the thought that we must part. Then I tried to make you angry by pretending to question your abilities, by affecting indifference and scorn; but it was the dog baying at the moon. I had to bring about the severance that I did. That I should be so childish as to be vexed about a slight from you, you cannot yourself believe. I cannot really regret it, for I could no longer be of use to you; you doubtless think the same yourself; but I cannot do without you; my affection for you is the only vital thing in me; your life throbbed in mine."

Sometimes the letters ended with an outburst of a sort of despairing humour, such as: " Vale! (Fanfare! somersaults by Pagliaccio.)" But whether Sebastian assumed a serious or a desperate tone, the renewal of our old companionship was equally impossible to me. I could not ignore what had happened, and I could not have a friend who was jealous if I talked to others. Since my intellectual entity had awakened, all jealousy had been an abomination to me, but jealousy in one man of another man positively revolted me. I recognised Sebastian's great merits, respected his character, and admired his wide range of knowledge, but I could not associate with him again, could not even so much as walk down the street by his side. All his affectionate and beautiful letters glanced off ineffectual from this repugnance. Something in me had suddenly turned stony, like a plant plunged in petrifying water.

Six years passed before we saw each other again. We met then with simple and sincere affection. Sebastian's old passion had evaporated without leaving a trace; he himself could no longer understand it. And, though far apart, and with nothing to connect us closely, we continued to think kindly of one another and to exchange reflections, until, after a few years, Death carried him away, ere he had reached the years of real manhood, or fulfilled any of the promises of his gifted and industrious youth.

TRANSITIONAL YEARS

I.

MY second schoolboy fancy dated from my last few
months at school.   It was a natural enough outcome of the attraction towards the other sex which,
never yet encouraged, was lurking in my mind; but it was not
otherwise remarkable for its naturalness.   It had its origin
partly in my love of adventure, partly in my propensity
for trying my powers, but, as love, was without root,
inasmuch as it was rooted neither in my heart nor in my
senses.

The object of it was again a girl from another country.
Her name and person had been well known to me since I was
twelve years old.   We had even exchanged compliments, been
curious about one another, gone so far as to wish for a lock
of each other's hair.   There was consequently a romantic
background to our first meeting.   When I heard that she was
coming to Denmark I was, as by chance, on the quay, and
saw her arrive.

She was exactly the same age as I, and, without real
beauty, was very good-looking and had unusually lovely
eyes.   I endeavoured to make her acquaintance through
relatives of hers whom I knew, and had no difficulty in getting into touch with her.   An offer to show her the museums
and picture galleries in Copenhagen was accepted.   Although
I had very little time, just before my matriculation examination, my new acquaintance filled my thoughts to such an extent

that I did not care how much of this valuable time I sacrificed to her. In the Summer, when the girl went out near Charlottenlund, whereas my parents were staying much nearer to the town, I went backwards and forwards to the woods nearly every day, in the uncertain but seldom disappointed hope of seeing her. Sometimes I rowed her about in the Sound.

Simple and straightforward though the attraction I felt might seem, the immature romance I built up on it was anything but simple.

It was, as stated, not my senses that drew me on. Split and divided up as I was just then, a merely intellectual love seemed to me quite natural; one might feel an attraction of the senses for an altogether different woman. I did not wish for a kiss, much less an embrace; in fact, was too much a child to think of anything of the sort.

But neither was it my heart that drew me on; I felt no tenderness, hardly any real affection, for this young girl whom I was so anxious to win. She only busied my brain.

In the condition of boyish self-inquisition in which I then found myself, this acquaintance was a fresh element of fermentation, and the strongest to which my self-examination had hitherto been subjected. I instinctively desired to engage her fancy; but my attitude was from myself through her to myself. I wanted less to please than to dominate her, and as it was only my head that was filled with her image, I wholly lacked the voluntary and cheerful self-humiliation which is an element of real love. I certainly wished with all my heart to fascinate her; but what I more particularly wanted was to hold my own, to avoid submission, and retain my independence. My boyish pride demanded it.

The young foreigner, whose knowledge of the world was hardly greater than my own, had certainly never, during her short life, come in contact with so extraordinary a phenomenon; it afforded matter for reflection. She certainly felt attracted, but, woman-like, was on her guard. She was of a quiet, amiable disposition, innocently coquettish, naturally adapted for the advances of sound common sense and affectionate good-will, not for the volts of passion; she was, moreover, femininely practical.

She saw at a glance that this grown-up schoolboy, who almost staggered her with his eloquence, his knowledge, his wild plans for the future, was no wooer, and that his advances were not to be taken too seriously. Next, with a woman's unfailing intuition, she discovered his empty love of power. And first involuntarily, and then consciously, she placed herself in an attitude of defence. She did not lack intelligence. She showed a keen interest in me, but met me with the self-control of a little woman of the world, now and then with coolness, on one occasion with well-aimed shafts of mockery.

Our mutual attitude might have developed into a regular war between the sexes, had we not both been half-children. Just as I, in the midst of a carefully planned assault on her emotions, occasionally forgot myself altogether and betrayed the craving to be near her which drove me almost every day to her door, she also would at times lose the equilibrium she had struggled for, and feverishly reveal her agitated state of mind. But immediately afterwards I was again at the assault, she once more on the alert, and after the lapse of four months our ways eparated, without a kiss, or one simple, affectionate word, ever having passed between us.

In my morbid self-duplication, I had been busy all this time fixing in my memory and writing down in a book all that I had said to her or she to me, weighing and probing the scope and effect of the words that had been uttered, laying plans for future methods of advance, noting actual victories and defeats, pondering over this inanity, bending over all this abnormality, like a strategist who, bending over the map, marks with his nail the movements of troops, the carrying or surrender of a fortified position.

This early, unsatisfactory and not strictly speaking erotic experience had the remarkable effect of rendering me for the next seven years impervious to the tender passion, so that, undisturbed by women or erotic emotions, I was able to absorb myself in the world of varied research that was now opening up to me.

II.

A school-friend who was keenly interested in astronomy and had directed my nightly contemplations of the heavens, drew me, just about this time, a very good map of the stars, by the help of which I found those stars I knew and extended my knowledge further.

The same school-friend sometimes took me to the Observatory, to see old Professor d'Arrest—a refined and sapient man—and there, for the first time, I saw the stellar heavens through a telescope. I had learnt astronomy at school, but had lacked talent to attain any real insight into the subject. Now the constellations and certain of the stars began to creep into my affections; they became the nightly witnesses of my joys and sorrows, all through my life; the sight of them sometimes comforted me when I felt lonely and forsaken in a foreign land. The Lyre, the Swan, the Eagle, the Crown and Boötes, Auriga, the Hyades and the Pleiades, and among the Winter constellations, Orion; all these twinkling groups, that human eyes have sought for thousands of years, became distant friends of mine, too. And the thoughts which the sight of the countless globes involuntarily and inevitably evokes, were born in me, too,—thoughts of the littleness of the earth in our Solar System, and of our Solar System in the Universe, of immeasurable distances—so great that the stars whose rays, with the rapidity of light's travelling, are striking against our eyes now, may have gone out in our childhood; of immeasurable periods of time, in which a human life, or even the lifetime of a whole people, disappears like a drop in the ocean. And whereas at school I had only studied astronomy as a subject, from its mathematical aspect, I now learnt the results of spectroscopic analysis, which showed me how the human genius of Bunsen and Kirchhoff had annihilated the distance between the Earth and the Sun; and at the same time I perceived the inherent improbability of the culture of our Earth ever being transmitted to other worlds, even as the Earth had never yet received communications from the civilisation of any of the stars.

This circumstance, combined with the certainty of the

gradual cooling and eventual death of the Earth, gave me a conclusive impression of the finality of all earthly existence and of the merely temporary character of all progress.

Feeling that all religions built up on a belief in a God were collapsing, Europe had long inclined towards the religion of Progress as the last tenable. Now I perceived as I raised my eyes to the starry expanse and rejoiced in my favourite stars, Sirius in the Great Dog, and Vega in the Lyre or Altair in the Eagle, that it, too, was tottering, this last religion of all.

III.

At school, I had known a score of boys of my own age, and naturally found few amongst them who could be anything to me. Among the advantages that the freedom of student life afforded was that of coming in contact all at once with hundreds of similarly educated young men of one's own age. Young men made each other's acquaintance at lectures and banquets, were drawn to one another, or felt themselves repulsed, and elective affinity or accident associated them in pairs or groups for a longer or shorter period.

A young fellow whose main passion was a desire for intellectual enrichment was necessarily obliged to associate with many of the other young men of his own age, in order to learn to know them, in order, externally and internally, to gain as much experience as possible and thereby develop himself.

In the case of many of them, a few conversations were enough to prove that any fruitful intimacy was out of the question. I came into fleeting contact with a number of suave, or cold, or too ordinary young students, without their natures affecting mine or mine theirs. But there were others who, for some months, engaged my attention to a considerable extent.

The first of these was a type of the student of the time. Vilsing was from Jutland, tall, dark, neither handsome nor plain, remarkable for his unparalleled facility in speaking. He owed his universal popularity to the fact that at students' parties he could at any time stand up and rattle off at a furi-

ous rate an apparently unprepared speech, a sort of stump
speech in which humorous perversions, distortions, lyric remarks, clever back-handed blows to right and left, astonishing incursions and rapid sorties, were woven into a whole
so good that it was an entertaining challenge to common
sense.

The starting point, for instance, might be some travesty
of Sibbern's whimsical definition of life, which at that time
we all had to learn by heart for the examination.   It ran:

> "Life altogether is an activity and active process, proceding from an
> inner source and working itself out according to an inner impulse, pro-
> ducing and by an eternal change of matter, reproducing, organising and
> individualising, and, since it by a certain material or substratum constitutes
> itself a certain exterior, within which it reveals itself, it simultaneously
> constitutes itself as the subsisting activity and endeavour in this, its exterior,
> of which it may further be inquired how far a soul can be said to live and
> subsist in it, as a living entity appearing in such a life."

It is not difficult to conceive what delightful nonsense
this barbaric elucidation might suggest, if a carouse, or love,
woman or drunkenness were defined in this vein; and he
would weave in amusing attacks on earlier, less intrepid
speakers, who, as Vilsing put it, reminded one of the bash-
ful forget-me-not, inasmuch as you could read in the
play of their features: "Forget me not!   I, too, was an
orator."

Vilsing, who had been studying for some years already,
paid a freshman a compliment by desiring his acquaintance
and seeking his society. He frequented the Students' Union,
was on terms of friendship with those who led the fashion,
and was a favourite speaker. It was a species of condescension on his part to seek out a young fellow just escaped from
school, a fellow who would have sunk into the earth if he had
had to make a speech, and who had no connection with the
circle of older students.

Vilsing was a young man of moods, who, like many at
that time, like Albrecht, the chief character in Schandorph's[1]
Without a Centre, would exhibit all the colours of the

[1] Sophus Schandorph, b. 1820, d. 1901; a prominent Danish novelist, who
commenced his literary activity in the sixties.—[Translator's note.]

ainbow in one morning. He would give himself, and take
imself back, show himself affectionate, cordial, intimate,
onfidential, full of affectionate anxiety for me his young
riend, and at the next meeting be as cursory and cool as
f he scarcely remembered having seen me before; for he
would in the meantime have been attacked by vexation at his
oo great friendliness, and wish to assert himself, as know-
ng his own value.

He impressed me, his junior, by revealing himself, not
precisely as a man of the world, but as a much sought after
ociety man. He told me how much he was asked out, and
how he went from one party and one ball to another, which,
o me, with my hankering after experiences, seemed to be an
nviable thing. But I was more struck by what Vilsing told
me of the favour he enjoyed with the other sex. One girl—
a charming girl!—he was engaged to, another loved him and
he her; but those were the least of his erotic triumphs; wherever he showed himself, he conquered. And proofs were to
hand. For one day, when he had dragged me up to his
room with him, he bewildered me by shaking out before my
eyes a profusion of embroidered sofa-cushions, fancy pillows,
cigar-cases, match-holders, crocheted purses, worked waist-
coats, etc.; presents from every description of person of the
feminine gender. In every drawer he pulled out there
were presents of the sort; they hung over chairs and
on pegs.

I was young enough to feel a certain respect for a man
so sought after by the fair sex, although I thought his frankness too great. What first began to undermine this feeling
was not doubt of the truth of his tales, or the genuineness
of the gifts, but the fact that one after another of my comrades, when the first cool stages of acquaintance were passed,
invariably found a favourable opportunity of confidentially
informing me—he could not explain why it was himself, but
it was a fact—that wherever he showed himself women were
singularly fascinated by the sight of him; there must be something about him which vanquished them in spite of him.
When at last one evening the most round-backed of all of
them, a swain whose blond mustache, of irregular growth,

resembled an old, worn-out toothbrush more than anything else, also confided in me that he did not know how it was or what could really be the cause of it, but there must be something about him, etc.,—then my belief in Vilsing's singularity and my admiration for him broke down.

It must not be supposed that Vilsing regarded himself as a sensual fiend. He did not pose as cold and impudent but as heartfelt and instinct with feeling. He was studying theology, and cherished no dearer wish than eventually to become a priest. He constantly alternated between contrition and self-satisfaction, arrogance and repentance, enjoyed the consciousness of being exceptionally clever, an irresistible charmer, and a true Christian. It seemed to him that in the freshman whom he had singled out from the crowd and given a place at his side, he had found an intellectual equal, or even superior, and this attracted him; he met with in me an inexperience and unworldliness so great that the inferiority in ability which he declared he perceived was more than counterbalanced by the superiority he himself had the advantage of, both in social accomplishments and in dealing with women.

It thus seemed as though many of the essential conditions of a tolerably permanent union between us were present. But during the first conversation in which he deigned to be interested in my views, there occurred in our friendship a little rift which widened to a chasm. Vilsing sprang back horrified when he heard how I, greenhorn though I was, regarded life and men and what I considered right. " You are in the clutches of Evil, and your desire is towards the Evil. I have not time or inclination to unfold an entire Christology now, but what you reject is the Ideal, and what you appraise is the Devil himself. God! God! How distressed I am for you! I would give my life to save you. But enough about it for the present; I have not time just now; I have to go out to dinner."

This was our last serious conversation. I was not saved. He did not give his life. He went for a vacation tour the following Summer holidays, avoided me on his return, and soon we saw no more of each other.

IV.

The theory, the intimation of which roused Vilsing to such a degree, bore in its form witness to such immaturity that it could only have made an impression on a youth whose immaturity, in spite of his age, was greater still. To present it with any degree of clearness is scarcely possible; it was not sufficiently clear in itself for that. But this was about what it amounted to:

The introspection and energetic self-absorption to which I had given myself up during my last few years at school became even more persistent on my release from the restraint of school and my free admission to the society of grown-up people.

I took advantage of my spare time in Copenhagen, and on the restricted travels that I was allowed to take, to slake my passionate thirst for life; firstly, by pondering ever and anon over past sensations, and secondly, by plunging into eager and careful reading of the light literature of all different countries and periods that I had heard about, but did not yet myself know at first hand.

Through all that I experienced and read, observed and made my own, my attitude towards myself was, that before all, I sought to become clear as to what manner of man I really, in my inmost being, was. I asked myself who I was. I endeavoured to discover the mysterious word that would break the charm of the mists in which I found myself and would answer my fundamental question, *What* was I? And then at last, my ponderings and my readings resulted in my finding the word that seemed to fit, although nowadays one can hardly hear it without a smile, the word *Dæmonic.*

I was *dæmonic;* and in giving myself this reply it seemed to me that I had solved the riddle of my nature. I meant thereby, as I then explained it to myself, that the choice between good and evil did not present itself to me, as to others, since evil did not interest me. For me, it was not a question of a choice, but of an unfolding of my *ego,* which had its justification in itself.

That which I called the *dæmonic* I had encountered f(
the first time outside my own mind in Lermontof's her(
Petsjórin was compelled to act in pursuance of his natur:
bent, as though possessed by his own being.   I felt myself i
a similar manner possessed.   I had met with the word *Dæ*
mon and *Daimones* in Plato; Socrates urges that by *dæmor*
the Gods, or the children of the Gods, were meant.   I fe
as though I, too, were one of the children of the Gods.   I
all the great legendary figures of the middle ages I detecte
the feature of divine possession, especially in the two wh
had completely fascinated the poets of the nineteenth centur
Don Juan and Faust.   The first was the symbol of mag
power over women, the second of the thirst for knowledg
giving dominion over humanity and Nature.   Among m
comrades, in Vilsing, even in the hunch-backed fellow wit
the unsuccessful moustache, I had seen how the Don Jua
type which had turned their heads still held sway over th
minds of young people; I myself could quite well understan
the magic which this beautiful ideal of elementary irresistibi
ity must have; but the Faust type appealed to me, with m
thirst for knowledge, very much more.   Still, the main thin
for me was that in the first great and wholly modern poe
that I made acquaintance with, Byron and his intellectual su
cessors, Lormontof and Heine, I recognised again the ver
fundamental trait that I termed *dæmonic*, the worship c
one's own originality, under the guise of an uncompromisin
love of liberty.

I was always brooding over this idea of the *dæmon*
with which my mind was filled.   I recorded my thoughts o
the subject in my first long essay (lost, for that matter), *O*
the Dæmonic, as it Reveals Itself in the Human Cha
acter.

When a shrewdly intelligent young fellow of my ow
age criticised my work from the assumption that the *dæmon*
did not exist, I thought him ridiculous.   I little dreamt tha
twenty-five years later Relling, in *The Wild Duck*, woul
show himself to be on my friend's side in the emphati
words: " What the Devil does it mean to be dæmonic!   It
sheer nonsense."

v.

The " dæmonic " was also responsible for the mingled attraction that was exerted over me at this point by a young foreign student, and for the intercourse which ensued between us. Kappers was born somewhere in the West Indies, was the son of a well-to-do German manufacturer, and had been brought up in a North German town. His father, for what reason I do not know, wished him to study at Copenhagen University, and there take his law examination. There was coloured blood in his veins, though much diluted, maybe an eighth or so. He was tall and slender, somewhat loose in his walk and bearing, pale-complexioned, with dark eyes and negro hair. His face, though not handsome, looked exceedingly clever, and its expression was not deceptive, for the young man had an astonishing intellect.

He was placed in the house of a highly respected family in Copenhagen, that of a prominent scientist, a good-natured, unpractical savant, very unsuited to be the mentor of such an unconventional young man. He was conspicuous among the native Danish freshmen for his elegant dress and cosmopolitan education, and was so quick at learning that before very many weeks he spoke Danish almost without a mistake, though with a marked foreign accent, which, however, lent a certain charm to what he said. His extraordinary intelligence was not remarkable either for its comprehensiveness or its depth, but it was a quicker intelligence than any his Copenhagen fellow-student had ever known, and so keen that he seemed born to be a lawyer.

Kappers spent almost all his day idling about the streets, talking to his companions; he was always ready for a walk; you never saw him work or heard him talk about his work. Nevertheless, he, a foreigner, who had barely mastered the language, presented himself after six months—before he had attended all the lectures, that is,—for the examination in philosophy and passed it with *Distinction* in all three subjects; indeed, Rasmus Nielsen, who examined him in Propædeutics, was so delighted at the foreigner's shrewd and ready answers that he gave him *Specially excellent,* a mark which did not exist.

His gifts in the juridical line appeared to be equally remarkable. When he turned up in a morning with his Danish fellow-students at the coach's house it might occasionally happen that he was somewhat tired and slack, but more often he showed a natural grasp of the handling of legal questions, and a consummate skill in bringing out every possible aspect of each question, that were astonishing in a beginner.

His gifts were of unusual power, but for the externalities of things only, and he possessed just the gifts with which the sophists of old time distinguished themselves. He himself was a young sophist, and at the same time a true comedian, adapting his behaviour to whomsoever he might happen to be addressing, winning over the person in question by striking his particular note and showing that side of his character with which he could best please him. Endowed with the capacity of mystifying and dazzling those around him, exceedingly keen-sighted, adaptable but in reality empty, he knew how to set people thinking and to fascinate others by his lively, unprejudiced and often paradoxical, but entertaining conversation. He was now colder, now more confidential; he knew how to assume cordiality, and to flatter by appearing to admire.

With a young student like myself who had just left school, was quite inexperienced in all worldly matters, and particularly in the chapter of women, but in whom he detected good abilities and a very strained idealism, he affected ascetic habits. With other companions he showed himself the intensely reckless and dissipated rich man's son he was; indeed, he amused himself by introducing some of the most inoffensive and foolish of them into the wretched dens of vice and letting them indulge themselves at his expense.

Intellectually interested as he was, he proposed, soon after our first meeting, that we should start a " literary and scientific " society, consisting of a very few freshmen, who, at the weekly meetings, should read a paper one of them had composed, whereupon two members who had previously read the paper should each submit it to a prepared criticism and after that, general discussion of the question. All that concerned the proposed society was carried out with a genuine Kappers-like mystery, as if it were a conspiracy, and with forms and ceremonies worthy of a diplomat's action.

Laws were drafted for the society, although it eventually consisted only of five members, and elaborate minutes were kept of the meetings. Among the members was V. Topsöe, afterwards well known as an editor and author, at that time a cautious and impudent freshman, whose motto was: "It is protection that we people must live by." He read the society a paper *On the Appearance,* dealing with how one ought to dress, behave, speak, do one's hair, which revealed powers of observation and a sarcastic tendency. Amongst those who eagerly sought for admission but never secured it was a young student, handsome, and with no small love of study, but stupid and pushing, for whom I, who continued to see myself in Lermontof's Petsjórin, cherished a hearty contempt, for the curious reason that he in every way reminded me of Petsjórin's fatuous and conceited adversary, Gruchnitski. Vilsing was asked to take part in the society's endeavours, but refused. "What I have against all these societies," he said, "is the self-satisfaction they give rise to; the only theme I should be inclined to treat is that of how the modern Don Juan must be conceived; but that I cannot do, since I should be obliged to touch on so many incidents of my own life."

This was the society before which I read the treatise on *The Dæmonic,* and it was Kappers who, with his well-developed intelligence, would not admit the existence of anything of the sort.

The regular meetings went on for six months only, the machinery being too large and heavy in comparison with the results attained. Kappers and his intimate friends, however, saw none the less of each other. The brilliant West Indian continued to pursue his legal studies and to carry on his merry life in Copenhagen for some eighteen months. But his studies gradually came to a standstill, while his gay life took up more and more of his time. He was now living alone in a flat which, to begin with, had been very elegantly furnished, but grew emptier and emptier by degrees, as his furniture was sold, or went to the pawnbroker's. His furniture was followed by his books, and when Schou's " *Orders in Council* " had also been turned into money, his legal studies ceased of themselves. When the bookshelves were empty it was the turn of the wardrobe and the linen drawers, till one Autumn day in 1861, an emissary of his father, who had been sent to Copenhagen to ascertain what the son was really about, found him in his shirt, without coat or trousers, wrapped up in his fur overcoat, sitting on the floor in his drawing-room, where there was not so much as a chair left. Asked how it was that things had come to such a pass with him, he replied: " It is the curse that follows the coloured race."

A suit of clothes was redeemed for Kappers junior, and he was hurried away as quickly as possible to the German town where his father lived, and where the son explained to everyone who would listen that he had been obliged to leave Copenhagen suddenly " on account of a duel with a gentleman in a very exalted position."

VI.

My first experiences of academic friendship made me smile in after years when I looked back on them. But my circle of acquaintances had gradually grown so large that it was only natural new friendships should grow out of it.

One of the members of Kappers' " literary and scientific " society, and the one whom the West Indian had genuinely cared most for, was a young fellow whose father was very much respected, and to whom attention was called for that reason; he was short, a little heavy on his feet, and a trifle indolent, had beautiful eyes, was warm-hearted and well educated, had good abilities without being specially original, and was somewhat careless in his dress, as in other things.

His father was C. N. David, well known in his younger days as a University professor and a liberal politician, who later became the Head of the Statistical Department and a Member of the Senate. He had been in his youth a friend of

Johan Ludvig Heiberg,[1] and had been dramatic contributor to the latter's paper.

He was a very distinguished satirist and critic and his influence upon the taste and critical opinion of his day can only be compared with that of Holberg in the 18th century.

Now, in concert with Bluhme and a few other of the elder politicians, he had formed a Conservative Fronde, opposed to the policy of the National Liberals. One day as we two young men were sitting in his son's room, drafting the rules for the freshmen's society of five members, the old gentleman came through and asked us what we were writing. " Rules for a society; we want to get them done as quickly as we can." "That is right. That kind of constitution may very well be written out expeditiously. There has not been very much more trouble or forethought spent on the one we have in this country."

It was not, however, so much the internal policy of the National Liberals that he objected to—it was only the Election Law that he was dissatisfied with—as their attitude towards Germany. Whenever a step was taken in the direction of the incorporation of Slesvig, he would exclaim: " We are doing what we solemnly promised not to do. How can anyone be so childish as to believe that it will turn out well! "

The son, whose home impressions in politics had been Conservative, was a happy young man with a somewhat embarrassed manner, who sometimes hid his uncertainty under the cloak of a carelessness that was not altogether assumed. Behind him stood his family, to whom he hospitably introduced those of his companions whom he liked, and though the family were not gentle of origin, they belonged, nevertheless, to the highest circles in the country and exercised their attraction through the son.

I, whom Ludvig David was now eagerly cultivating,

---

[1] J. L. Heiberg, to whom such frequent allusion is made, was a well-known Danish author of the last century (1791-1860). Among many other things, he wrote a series of vaudevilles for the Royal Theatre at Copenhagen, which he was manager. In every piece he wrote there was a special part for his wife, Johanne Luise Heiberg, who was the greatest Danish actress of the 19th century.

had known him for many years, as we had been school-fellows and even classmates, although David was considera-bly older. I had never felt drawn to him as a boy, in fact, had not liked him. Neither had David, in our school-days, ever made any advances to me, having had other more in-timate friends. Now, however, he was very cordial to me, and expressed in strong terms his appreciation of my industry and abilities; he himself was often teased at home for his lack of application.

C. N. David was the first public personality with whom, as a student, I became acquainted and into whose house I was introduced. For many years I enjoyed unusual kind-ness and hospitality at the hands of the old politician, after-wards Minister of Finance.

VII.

I had hitherto been only mildly interested in politics I had, of course, as a boy, attentively followed the course of the Crimean war, which my French uncle, on one of his visits had called the fight for civilisation against barbarism, al though it was a fight for Turkey! now, as a student I followed with keen interest the Italian campaign and the revolt against the Austrian Dukes and the Neapolitan Bour bons. But the internal policy of Denmark had little attrac tion for me. As soon as I entered the University I felt my self influenced by the spirit of such men as Poul Möller, J. L Heiberg, Sören Kierkegaard, and distinctly removed from the belief in the power of the people which was being preached everywhere at that time. This, however, wa hardly more than a frame of mind, which did not preclude m feeling myself in sympathy with what at that time was calle broad thought (i.e., Liberalism). Although I was often in dignant at the National Liberal and Scandinavian terrorisn which obtained a hearing at both convivial and serious mee ings in the Students' Union, my feelings in the matter o Denmark's foreign policy with regard to Sweden and Nor way, as well as to Germany, were the same as those held b all the other students. I felt no intellectual debt to eithe

Sweden or Norway, but I was drawn by affection towards the Swedes and the Norsemen, and in Christian Richardt's lovely song at the Northern Celebration in 1860, *For Sweden and Norway,* I found the expression of the fraternal feelings that I cherished in my breast for our two Northern neighbours. On the other hand, small as my store of knowledge still was, I had already acquired some considerable impression of German culture. Nevertheless, the increasingly inimical attitude of the German people towards Denmark, and the threatenings of war with Germany, together with my childish recollections of the War of 1848-50, had for their effect that in the Germany of that day I only saw an enemy's country. A violent affection that I felt at sixteen for a charming little German girl made no difference to this view.

VIII.

The old men, who advocated the greatest caution in dealing with the impossible demands of the German Federation, and were profoundly distrustful as to the help that might be expected from Europe, were vituperated in the press. As *Whole-State Men,* they were regarded as unpatriotic, and as so-called *Reactionaries,* accused of being enemies to freedom. When I was introduced into the house of one of these politically ill-famed leaders, in spite of my ignorance, I knew enough of politics, as of other subjects, to draw a sharp distinction between that which I could in a measure grasp, and that which I did not understand; I was sufficiently educated to place Danish constitutional questions in the latter category, and consequently I crossed, devoid of prejudice, the threshold of a house whence proceeded, according to the opinion of the politically orthodox, a pernicious, though fortunately powerless, political heterodoxy.

It must not be supposed that I came into close touch with anything of the sort. The old Minister never opened his mouth on political matters in the bosom of his family. But the impression of superior intelligence and knowledge of men that he conveyed was enough to place him in a different light from that in which he was depicted in *The*

Fatherland, the paper whose opinions were swallowed blindly
by the student body.   And my faith in the infallibility of the
paper was shaken even more one day, when I saw the Leader
of the Reactionary Party himself, Privy Councillor Bluhme
at the house, and sat unnoticed in a corner, listening to his
conversation.   He talked a great deal, although, like the mas
ter of the house, he did not allude to his public work.   Like a
statesman of the old school, he expressed himself with exquis
ite politeness and a certain ceremony.   But of the affectation
of which *The Fatherland* accused him, there was not a trace.
What profoundly impressed me was the Danish the old gen
tleman spoke, the most perfect Danish.   He told of his
travels in India—once upon a time he had been Governor
of Trankebar—and you saw before you the banks of the
Ganges and the white troops of women, streaming down to
bathe in the river, as their religion prescribed.

I never forgot the words with which Bluhme rose to
go: " May I borrow the English blue-books for a few days ?
There might be something or other that the newspapers have
not thought fit to tell us."   I started at the words.   It
dawned upon me for the first time, though.merely as a re
mote possibility, that the Press might purposely and with in
tent to mislead keep silence about facts that had a claim upon
the attention of the public.

IX.

Young David had once asked me to read Ovid's Ele
giacs with him, and this was the beginning of our closer
acquaintance.   In town, in the Winter, we two younger ones
were only rarely with the rest of the family, but in Summer it
was different.   The Minister had built a house at Rung
sted, on a piece of land belonging to his brother, who was a
farmer and the owner of Rungstedgaard, Rungstedlund and
Folehavegaard, a shrewd and practical man.   To this villa
which was in a beautiful situation, overlooking the sea, I was
often invited by my friend to spend a few days in the Summer,
sometimes even a month at a time.   At first, of course, I was
nothing to the rest of the family; they received me for the

son's sake; but by degrees I won a footing with them, too. The handsome, clever and sprightly mistress of the house took a motherly interest in me, and the young daughters showed me kindness for which I was very grateful.

The master of the house sometimes related an anecdote, as, for instance, about Heiberg's mad pranks as a young man. When he went off into the woods and got hungry, he used to take provisions from the stores in the lockers of the phaetons that put up at Klampenborg, while the people were walking about in the park, and the coachmen inside the public-house. One day, with Möhl and David, he got hold of a huge layer-cake. The young fellows had devoured a good half of it and replaced it under the seat of the carriage, when the family came back, caught sight of Heiberg, whom they knew, and invited the young men to have a piece of cake and a glass of wine. When they made the horrifying discovery of the havoc that had been wrought, they themselves would not touch it, and the robbers, who were stuffed already, were obliged to consume the remainder of the cake between them.

There was often music at the Villa; sometimes I was asked to read aloud, and then I did my best, choosing good pieces not well known, and reading carefully. The pleasant outdoor life gave me a few glimpses of that rare and ardently desired thing, still contentment. It was more particularly alone with Nature that I felt myself at home.

A loose page from my diary of those days will serve to indicate the untried forces that I felt stirring within me:

On the way down, the sky was dappled with large and many-coloured clouds. I wandered about in the woods to-day, among the oaks and beeches, and saw the sun gilding the leaves and the tree-trunks, lay down under a tree with my Greek Homer and read the first and second books of the Odyssey. Went backwards and forwards in the clover field, revelled in the clover, smelt it, and sucked the juice of the flowers. I have the same splendid view as of old from my window. The sea, in all its flat expanse, moved in towards me to greet me, when I arrived. It was roaring and foaming mildly. Hveen could be seen quite clearly. Now the wind is busy outside my window, the sea is stormy, the dark heavens show streaks of moonlight. . . .

East wind and rain. Went as far as Valloröd in a furious wind. The sky kept clear; a dark red patch of colour showed the position of the Sun on the horizon. The Moon has got up hurriedly, has turned from red to yellow, and looks lovely. I am drunk with the beauties of Nature. Go to Folehave and feel, like the gods in Homer, without a care. . . .

I can never get sleepy out in the open country on a windy night. Rested a little, got up at four o'clock, went at full speed along soaked roads to Humlebæk, to Gurre Ruins and lake, through the woods to Fredensborg park, back to Humlebæk, and came home to Rungsted by steamer. Then went up on the hill. Quiet beauty of the landscape. Feeling that Nature raises even the fallen into purer, loftier regions. Took the Odyssey and went along the field-path to the stone table; cool, fresh air, harmony and splendour over Nature. "Wildly soars the hawk." Went up into the sunlit wood at Hörsholm, gazed at the melancholy expression in the faces of the horses and sheep. . . .

I made ducks and drakes and asked the others riddles. A woman came and begged for help to bury her husband; he had had such an easy death. (She is said to have killed him with a blow from a wooden shoe.) Sat under a giant beech in Rungsted Wood; then had a splendid drive after the heavy rain up to Folehave and thence to Hörsholm. Everything was as fresh and lovely as in an enchanted land. What a freshness! The church and the trees mirrored themselves in the lake. The device on my shield shall be three lucky peas.[1]

To Vedbæk and back. We were going for a row. My hostess agreed, but as we had a large, heavy and clumsy boat, they were all nervous. Then Ludvig's rowlock snapped and he caught a crab. It was no wonder, as he was rowing too deep. So I took both sculls myself. It was tiring to pull the heavy boat with so many, but the sea was inexpressibly lovely, the evening dead calm. Silver sheen on the water, visible to the observant and initiated Nature-lover. Ripple from the west wind ($\Phi\rho\grave{\iota}\xi$).

Grubbed in the shingle, and went to Folehave. Gathered flowers and strawberries. My fingers still smell of strawberries.

Went out at night. Pictures of my fancy rose around me. A Summer's night, but as cold as Winter, the clouds banked up on the horizon. Suppose in the wind and cold and dark I were to meet one I know! Over the corn the wind whispered or whistled a name. The waves dashed in a short little beat against the shore. It is only the sea that is as Nature made it; the land in a thousand ways is robbed of its virginity by human hands, but the sea now is as it was thousands of years ago. A thick fog rose up. The birches bent their heads and went to sleep. But I can hear the grass grow and the stars sing.

Gradually my association with Ludvig David grew more and more intimate, and the latter proved himself a constant friend. A few years after our friendship had begun, when things were looking rather black for me, my father having suffered great business losses, and no longer being able to give me the same help as before, Ludvig David invited me to go and live altogether at his father's house, and be like a son there—an offer which I of course refused, but which affected me deeply, especially when I learnt that it had only been made after the whole family had been consulted.

[1] There seems to be some such legendary virtue attached in Denmark to a pea-pod containing *three* or *nine* peas, as with us to a four-leaved clover.— [Translator's note.]

x.

In November, 1859, at exactly the same time as Kappers' "literary and scientific" society was started, a fellow-student named Grönbeck, from Falster, who knew the family of Caspar Paludan-Müller, the historian, proposed my joining another little society of young students, of whom Grönbeck thought very highly on account of their altogether unusual knowledge of books and men.

In the old Students' Union in Boldhusgade, the only meeting-place at that time for students, which was always regarded in a poetic light, I had not found what I wanted. There was no life in it, and at the convivial meetings on Saturday night the punch was bad, the speeches were generally bad, and the songs were good only once in a way.

I had just joined one new society, but I never rejected any prospect of acquaintances from whom I could learn anything, and nothing was too much for me. So I willingly agreed, and one evening late in November I was introduced to the society so extolled by Grönbeck, which called itself neither "literary" nor "scientific," had no other object than sociability, and met at Ehlers' College, in the rooms of a young philological student, Frederik Nutzhorn.

Expecting as I did something out of the ordinary, I was very much disappointed. The society proved to be quite vague and indefinite. Those present, the host, a certain Jens Paludan-Müller, son of the historian, a certain Julius Lange, son of the Professor of Pedagogy, and a few others, received me as though they had been waiting for me to put the society on its legs; they talked as if I were going to do everything to entertain them, and as if they themselves cared to do nothing; they seemed to be indolent, almost sluggish. First we read aloud in turns from Björnson's *Arne,* which was then new; a lagging conversation followed. Nutzhorn talked nonsense, Paludan-Müller snuffled, Julius Lange alone occasionally let fall a humorous remark. The contrast between Nutzhorn's band, who took sociability calmly and quietly, and Kappers' circle, which met to work and discuss things to its utmost

capacity, was striking. The band seemed exceedingly phleg-
matic in comparison.

This first impression was modified at subsequent meetings. As I talked to these young men I discovered, first and
foremost, how ignorant I was of political history and the history of art; in the next place, I seemed, in comparison with
them, to be old in my opinions and my habits. They called
themselves Republicans, for instance, whereas Republicanism
in Denmark had in my eyes hitherto been mere youthful folly.
Then again, they were very unconventional in their habits.
After a party near Christmas time, which was distinguished by
a pretty song by Julius Lange, they proposed—at twelve
o'clock at night!—that we should go to Frederiksborg. And
extravagances of this kind were not infrequent.

Still it was only towards midsummer 1860 that I became properly merged into the new circle and felt myself at
home in it. It had been increased by two or three first-rate
fellows, Harald Paulsen, at the present time Lord Chief Justice, a courageous young fellow, who was not afraid of tack-
ling any ruffian who interfered with him in a defile; Troels
Lund, then studying theology, later on the esteemed historian,
who was always refined, self-controlled, thoughtful, and on
occasion caustic, great at feints in the fencing class; and Emil
Petersen, then studying law (died in 1890, as Departmental
Head of Railways), gentle, dreamy, exceedingly conscientious, with a marked lyric tendency.

ʻ   One evening, shortly before Midsummer's eve, when
we had gone out to Vedbæk, fetched Emil Petersen from
Tryggeröd and thoroughly enjoyed the beautiful scenery, we
had a wrestling match out in the water off Skodsborg and a
supper party afterwards at which, under the influence of the
company, the gaiety rose to a wild pitch and eventually passed
all bounds. We made speeches, sang, shouted our witticisms
at each other all at once, seized each other round the waist
and danced, till we had to stop for sheer tiredness. Then
we all drank pledges of eternal friendship, and trooped into
the town together, and hammered at the doors of the
coffee-houses after midnight to try to get in somewhere where
we could have coffee. We had learnt all at once to know

and appreciate each other to the full; we were united by a feeling of brotherhood and remained friends for life. The life allotted to several of the little band was, it is true, but short; Jens Paludan-Müller fell at Sankelmark three and a half years later; Nutzhorn had only five years and a half to l've. Of the others, Emil Petersen and Julius Lange are dead. But, whether our lives were long or short, our meetings frequent or rare, we continued to be cordially attached to one another, and no misunderstanding or ill-feeling ever cropped up between us.

XI.

Among my Danish excursions was one to Slesvig in July, 1860. The Copenhagen students had been asked to attend a festival to be held at Angel at the end of July for the strengthening of the sparse Danish element in that German-minded region. There were not many who wished to go, but several of those who did had beautiful voices, and sang feelingly the national songs with which it was hoped the hearts of the Angel people, and especially of the ladies, might be touched. Several gentlemen still living, at that time among the recognised leaders of the students, went with us.

We sailed from Korsör to Flensborg one exquisite Summer night; we gave up the berths we had secured and stayed all night on deck with a bowl of punch. It was a starlight night, the ship cut rapidly through the calm waters, beautiful songs were sung and high-flown speeches made. One speech was held in a whisper, the one in honour of General de Meza, who was still a universal favourite, and who was sitting in his stateroom, waked up out of his sleep, with his white gloves and gaufred lace cuffs on and a red and white night-cap on his head. We young ones only thought of him as the man who, during the battle of Fredericia, had never moved a muscle of his face, and when it was over had said quietly: "The result is very satisfactory."

Unfriendly and sneering looks from the windows at Flensborg very soon showed the travellers that Danish students' caps were not a welcome sight there. The Angel peasants, however, were very pleasant. The festival, which lasted all day and concluded with dancing and fireworks, was a great success, and a young man who had been carousing all night, travelling all day, and had danced all the evening with pretty girls till his senses were in a whirl, could not help regarding the scene of the festival in a romantic light, as he stood there alone, late at night, surrounded by flaring torches, the fireworks sputtering and glittering about him. Some few of the students sat in the fields round flaming rings of pitch, an old Angel peasant keeping the fires alight and singing Danish songs. Absolutely enraptured, and with tears in his eyes, he went about shaking hands with the young men and thanking them for coming. It was peculiarly solemn and beautiful.

Next day, when I got out at Egebæk station on my way from Flensborg, intending to go to Idsted, it seemed that three other young men had had the same idea, so we all four walked together. They were young men of a type I had not met with before. The way they felt and spoke was new to me. They all talked in a very affectionate manner, betrayed at once that they worshipped one another, and seemed to have strong, open natures, much resembling each other. They were Ernst Trier, Nörregaard, and Baagöe, later the three well-known High School men.

The little band arrived at a quick pace on Idsted's beautiful heath, all tufts of ling, the red blossoms of which looked lovely in the light of the setting sun. We sat ourselves down on the hill where Baudissin and his staff had stood. Then Baagöe read aloud Hammerich's description of the battle of Idsted, while each of us in his mind's eye saw the seething masses of troops advance and fall upon one another, as they had done just ten years before.

Our time was short, if we wanted to get under a roof that night. At 9 o'clock we were still eight miles from Slesvig. We did the first four at a pace that was novel to me. Three-parts of the way we covered in forty-five minutes, the last two miles took us twenty. When we arrived at the hotel, there stood Madam Esselbach, of war renown, in the doorway, with her hands on her hips, as in her portrait; she

summed up the arrivals with shrewd, sharp eyes, and exclaimed: " *Das ist ja das junge Dänemark.*" Inside, officers were sitting, playing cards. Major Sommer promised
us young men to show us Gottorp at 6 o'clock next morning;
we should then get a view of the whole of the town from
Hersterberg beforehand.

The Major, who was attacked in the newspapers after
the war, and whose expression " my maiden sword," was
made great fun of, showed us younger ones the magnificent
church, and afterwards the castle, which, as a barracks, was
quite spoilt. He acted as the father of the regiment, and,
like Poul Möller's artist, encouraged the efficient, and said
hard words to the slighty, praising or blaming unceasingly,
chatted Danish to the soldiers, Low German to the cook,
High German to the little housekeeper at the castle, and
called the attention of his guests to the perfect order and
cleanliness of the stables. He complained bitterly that a certain senior lieutenant he pointed out to us, who in 1848 had
flung his cockade in the gutter and gone over to the Germans,
had been reinstated in the regiment, and placed over the heads
of brave second-lieutenants who had won their crosses in
the war.

Here I parted with my Grundtvigian friends. When
I spoke of them to Julius Lange on my return, he remarked:
" They are a good sort, who wear their hearts in their button-
holes as decorations."

The society I fell in with for the rest of my journey was
very droll. This consisted of Borup, later Mayor of Finance,
and a journalist named Falkman (really Petersen), even at
that time on the staff of *The Daily Paper*. I little guessed
then that my somewhat vulgar travelling companion would
develop into the Cato who wished Ibsen's *Ghosts* " might be
thrust into the slime-pit, where such things belong," and
would write articles by the hundred against me. Neither had
I any suspicion, during my acquaintance with Topsöe, that the
latter would one day be one of my most determined persecu-
tors. Without exactly being strikingly youthful, the large,
broad-shouldered Borup was still a young man. Falkman
wrote good-humouredly long reports to Bille about Slesvig,

.which I corrected for him.   Borup and Falkman generally
exclaimed the moment I opened my mouth: " Not seraphic,
now ! "

We travelled together to Glücksborg, saw the camp
there, and, as we had had nothing since our morning coffee at
5 o'clock, ate between the three of us a piece of roast meat six
pounds weight.   We spent the night at Flensborg and drove
next day to Graasten along a lovely road with wooded banks
on either side.   It was pouring with rain, and we sat in dead
silence, trying to roll ourselves up in horse-cloths.   When
in an hour's time the rain stopped, and we put up at an inn,
our enforced silence gave place to the wildest merriment.   We
three young fellows—the future Finance Minister as well—
danced into the parlour, hopped about like wild men, spilt
milk over ourselves, the sofa, and the waitress; then sprang,
waltzing and laughing, out through the door again and up
into the carriage, after having heaped the girl with small copper coins.

From Graasten we proceeded to Sönderborg.   The
older men lay down and slept after the meal.   I went up to
Dybbölmölle.   On the way back, I found on a hill looking
out over Als a bench from which there was a beautiful view
across to Slesvig. I lay down on the seat and gazed up at the
sky and across the perfect country. The light fields, with their
tall, dark hedges, which give the Slesvig scenery its peculiar
stamp, from this high-lying position looked absolutely
lovely.

XII.

I was not given to looking at life in a rosy light.   My
nature, one uninterrupted endeavour, was too tense for that.
Although I occasionally felt the spontaneous enjoyments of
breathing the fresh air, seeing the sun shine, and listening to
the whistling of the wind, and always delighted in the fact
that I was in the heyday of my youth, there was yet a considerable element of melancholy in my temperament, and I
was so loth to abandon myself to any illusion that when I
looked into my own heart and summed up my own life it
seemed to me that I had never been happy for a day.   I did

not know what it was to be happy for a whole day at a time, scarcely for an hour.   I had only known a moment's rapture in the companionship of my comrades at a merry-making, in intercourse with a friend, under the influence of the beauties of Nature, or the charm of women, or in delight at gaining intellectual riches—during the reading of a poem, the sight of a play, or when absorbed in a work of art.

Any feeling that I was enriching my mind from those surrounding me was unfortunately rare with me.   Almost always, when talking to strangers, I felt the exact opposite, which annoyed me exceedingly, namely, that I was being intellectually sucked, squeezed like a lemon, and whereas I was never bored when alone, in the society of other people I suffered overwhelmingly from boredom.   In fact, I was so bored by the visits heaped upon me by my comrades and acquaintances, who inconsiderately wasted my time, in order to kill a few hours, that I was almost driven to despair; I was too young obstinately to refuse to see them.

By degrees, the thought of the boredom that I suffered at almost all social functions dominated my mind to such an extent that I wrote a little fairy tale about boredom, by no means bad (but unfortunately lost), round an idea which I saw several years later treated in another way in Sibbern's well-known book of the year 2135.   This fairy tale was read aloud to Nutzhorn's band and met with its approval.

But although I could thus by no means be called of a happy disposition, I was, by reason of my overflowing youth, in a constant state of elation, which, as soon as the company of others brought me out of my usual balance, acted like exuberant mirth and made me burst out laughing.

I was noted, among my comrades, and not always to my advantage, for my absolutely ungovernable risibility.   I had an exceedingly keen eye for the ridiculous, and easily influenced as I still was, I could not content myself with a smile. Not infrequently, when walking about the town, I used to laugh the whole length of a street.   There were times when I was quite incapable of controlling my laughter; I laughed like a child, and it was incomprehensible to me that people could go so soberly and solemnly about. If a person stared straight at me, it made me laugh. If a girl flirted a little with me, I laughed in her face. One day I went out and saw two drunken labourers, in a cab, each with a wreath on his knee; I was obliged to laugh; I met an old dandy whom I knew, with two coats on, one of which hung down below the other; I had to laugh at that, too. Sometimes, walking or standing, absorbed in thoughts, I was outwardly abstracted, and answered mechanically, or spoke in a manner unsuited to my words; if I noticed this myself, I could not refrain from laughing aloud at my own absent-mindedness. It occasionally happened that at an evening party, where I had been introduced by the son of the house to a stiff family to whom I was a stranger, and where the conversation at table was being carried on in laboured monosyllables, I would begin to laugh so unrestrainedly that every one stared at me in anger or amazement. And it occasionally happened that when some sad event, concerning people present, was being discussed, the recollection of something comical I had seen or heard the same day would crop up in my mind to the exclusion of all else, and I would be overtaken by fits of laughter that were both incomprehensible and wounding to those round me, but which it was impossible to me to repress. At funeral ceremonies, I was in such dread of bursting out laughing that my attention would involuntarily fix itself on everything it ought to avoid. This habit of mine was particularly trying when my laughter had a ruffling effect on others in a thing that I myself was anxious to carry through. Thus I spoilt the first rehearsals of Sophocles' Greek play *Philoctetes,* which a little group of students were preparing to act at the request of Julius Lange. Some of them pronounced the Greek in an unusual manner, others had forgotten their parts or acted badly —and that was quite enough to set me off in a fit of laughter which I had difficulty in stopping. Thus I often laughed, when I was tormented at being compelled to laugh, in reality feeling melancholy, and mentally worried; I used to think of Oechlenschläger's Œrvarodd, who does not laugh when he is happy, but breaks into a guffaw when he is deeply affected.

These fits of laughter were in reality the outcome of sheer youthfulness; with all my musings and reflection, I was still in many ways a child; I laughed as boys and girls laugh, without being able to stop, and especially when they ought not. But this painful trait in myself directed my thoughts to the nature proper of laughter; I tried to sum up to myself why I laughed, and why people in general laughed, pondered, as well as I was capable of doing the question of what the comical consisted of, and then recorded the fruits of my reflections in my second long treatise, *On Laughter,* which has been lost.

As I approached my twentieth year, these fits of laughter stopped. " I have," wrote I at the time, " seen into that Realm of Sighs, on the threshold of which I—like Parmeniscus after consulting the Oracle of Trophonius—have suddenly forgotten how to laugh."

XIII.

Meanwhile I had completed my eighteenth year and had to make my choice of a profession. But what was I fitted for? My parents, and those other of my relations whose opinions I valued, wished me to take up the law; they thought that I might make a good barrister; but I myself held back, and during my first year of study did not attend a single law lecture. In July, 1860, after I had passed my philosophical examination (with *Distinction* in every subject), the question became urgent. Whether I was likely to exhibit any considerable talent as a writer, it was impossible for me to determine. There was only one thing that I felt clear about, and that was that I should never be contented with a subordinate position in the literary world; better a hundred times be a judge in a provincial town. I felt an inward conviction that I should make my way as a writer. It seemed to me that a deathlike stillness reigned for the time being over European literature, but that there were mighty forces working in the silence. I believed that a revival was imminent. In August, 1860, I wrote in my private papers: " We Danes, with our national culture and our knowledge of the literatures of other countries, will stand well equipped when the literary horn of the Gods resounds again through the world, calling fiery youth to battle. I am firmly convinced that that time will come and that I shall be, if not the one who evokes it in the North, at any rate one who will contribute greatly towards it."

One of the first books I had read as a student was Goethe's *Dichtung und Wahrheit,* and this career had extraordinarily impressed me. In my childlike enthusiasm I determined to read all the books that Goethe says that he read as a boy, and thus commenced and finished Winckelmann's collected works, Lessing's *Laocoon* and other books of artistic and archæological research; in other words, studied the history and philosophy of Art in the first instance under aspects which, from the point of view of subsequent research, were altogether antiquated, though in themselves, and in their day, valuable enough.

Goethe's life fascinated me for a time to such an extent that I found duplicates of the characters in the book everywhere. An old language master, to whom I went early in the morning, in order to acquire from him the knowledge of English which had not been taught me at school, reminded me vividly, for instance, of the old dancing master in Goethe, and my impression was borne out when I discovered that he, too, had two pretty daughters. A more important point was that the book awoke in me a restless thirst for knowledge, at the same time that I conceived a mental picture of Goethe's monumental personality and began to be influenced by the universality of his genius.

Meanwhile, circumstances at home forced me, without further vacillation, to take up some special branch of study. The prospects literature presented were too remote. For Physics I had no talent; the logical bent of my abilities seemed to point in the direction of the Law; so Jurisprudentia was selected and my studies commenced.

The University lectures, as given by Professors Aagesen and Gram, were appalling; they consisted of a slow, sleepy dictation. A death-like dreariness brooded always over the lecture halls. Aagesen was especially unendurable;

there was no trace of anything human or living about his dictation. Gram had a kind, well-intentioned personality, but had barely reached his desk than it seemed as though he, too, were saying: " I am a human being, everything human is alien to me."

We consequently had to pursue our studies with the help of a coach, and the one whom I, together with Kappers, Ludvig David and a few others, had chosen, Otto Algreen-Ussing, was both a capable and a pleasant guide. Five years were yet to elapse before this man and his even more gifted brother, Frederik, on the formation of the Loyal and Conservative Society of August, were persecuted and ridiculed as reactionaries, by the editors of the ascendant Press, who, only a few years later, proved themselves to be ten times more reactionary themselves. Otto was positively enthusiastic over Law; he used to declare that a barrister " was the finest thing a man could be."

However, he did not succeed in infecting me with his enthusiasm. I took pains, but there was little in the subject that aroused my interest. Christian the Fifth's *Danish Law* attracted me exclusively on account of its language and the perspicuity and pithiness of the expressions occasionally made use of.

With this exception what impressed me most of all that I heard in the lessons was Anders Sandöe Œrsted's *Interpretation of the Law*. When I had read and re-read a passage of law which seemed to me to be easily intelligible, and only capable of being understood in one way, how could I do other than marvel and be seized with admiration, when the coach read out Œrsted's Interpretation, proving that the Law was miserably couched, and could be expounded in three or four different ways, all contradicting one another! But this Œrsted very often did prove in an irrefutable manner.

In my lack of receptivity for legal details, and my want of interest in Positive Law, I flung myself with all the greater fervour into the study of what in olden times was called Natural Law, and plunged again and again into the study of Legal Philosophy.

XIV.

About the same time as my legal studies were thus beginning, I planned out a study of Philosophy and Æsthetics on
a large scale as well. My day was systematically filled up
from early morning till late at night, and there was time
for everything, for ancient and modern languages, for law
lessons with the coach, for the lectures in philosophy which
Professors H. Bröchner and R. Nielsen were holding for
more advanced students, and for independent reading of a
literary, scientific and historic description.

One of the masters who had taught me at school, a very
erudite philologian, now Dr. Oscar Siesbye, offered me gra-
tuitous instruction, and with his help several of the tragedies
of Sophocles and Euripides, various things of Plato's, and
comedies by Plautus and Terence were carefully studied.

Frederik Nutzhorn read the *Edda* and the *Niebelun-
genlied* with me in the originals; with Jens Paludan-Müller
I went through the New Testament in Greek, and with Julius Lange, Æschylus, Sophocles, Pindar, Horace and Ovid,
and a little of Aristotle and Theocritus. Catullus, Martial
and Cæsar I read for myself.

But I did not find any positive inspiration in my studies
until I approached my nineteenth year. In philosophy I had
hitherto mastered only a few books by Sören Kierkegaard.
But now I began a conscientious study of Heiberg's philosophical writings and honestly endeavoured to make myself
familiar with his speculative logic. As Heiberg's *Prose
Writings* came out, in the 1861 edition, they were studied
with extreme care. Heiberg's death in 1860 was a great
grief to me; as a thinker I had loved and revered him. The
clearness of form and the internal obscurity of his adaptation
of Hegel's Teachings, gave one a certain artistic satisfaction,
at the same time that it provoked an effort really to understand.

But in the nature of things, Heiberg's philosophical life-
work could not to a student be other than an admission into
Hegel's train of thought, and an introduction to the master's
own works. I was not aware that by 1860 Europe had long

passed his works by in favour of more modern thinking. With a passionate desire to reach a comprehension of the truth, I grappled with the System, began with the Encyclopædia, read the three volumes of Æsthetics, The Philosophy of Law, the Philosophy of History, the Phenomenology of the Mind, then the Philosophy of Law again, and finally the Logic, the Natural Philosophy and the Philosophy of the Mind in a veritable intoxication of comprehension and delight. One day, when a young girl towards whom I felt attracted had asked me to go and say good-bye to her before her departure, I forgot the time, her journey, and my promise to her, over my Hegel. As I walked up and down my room I chanced to pull my watch out of my pocket, and realised that I had missed my appointment and that the girl must have started long ago.

Hegel's Philosophy of Law had a charm for me as a legal student, partly on account of the superiority with which the substantial quality of Hegel's mind is there presented, and partly on account of the challenge in the attitude of the book to accepted opinions and expressions, " morality " here being almost the only thing Hegel objects to.

But it was the book on Æsthetics that charmed me most of all. It was easy to understand, and yet weighty, superabundantly rich.

Again and again while reading Hegel's works I felt carried away with delight at the new world of thought opening out before me. And when anything that for a long time had been incomprehensible to me, at last after tenacious reflection became clear, I felt what I myself called " an unspeakable bliss." Hegel's system of thought, anticipatory of experience, his German style, overburdened with arbitrarily constructed technical words from the year 1810, which one might think would daunt a young student of another country and another age, only meant to me difficulties which it was a pleasure to overcome. Sometimes it was not Hegelianism itself that seemed the main thing. The main thing was that I was learning to know a world-embracing mind; I was being initiated into an attempt to comprehend the universe which was half wisdom and half poetry; I was obtaining an insight into a method which, if scientifically unsatisfying, and on that ground already abandoned by investigators, was fruitful and based upon a clever, ingenuous, highly intellectual conception of the essence of truth; I felt myself put to school to a great intellectual leader, and in this school I learnt to think.

I might, it is true, have received my initiation in a school built up on more modern foundations; it is true that I should have saved much time, been spared many detours, and have reached my goal more directly had I been introduced to an empirical philosophy, or if Fate had placed me in a school in which historical sources were examined more critically, but not less intelligently, and in which respect for individuality was greater. But such as the school was, I derived from it all the benefit it could afford to my *ego,* and I perceived with delight that my intellectual progress was being much accelerated. Consequently it did not specially take from my feeling of having attained a measure of scientific insight, when I learnt—what I had not known at first—that my teachers, Hans Bröchner, as well as Rasmus Nielsen, were agreed not to remain satisfied with the conclusions of the German philosopher, had " got beyond Hegel." At the altitude to which the study of philosophy had now lifted me, I saw that the questions with which I had approached Science were incorrectly formulated, and they fell away of themselves, even without being answered. Words that had filled men's minds for thousands of years, God, Infinity, Thought, Nature and Mind, Freedom and Purpose, all these words acquired another and a deeper meaning, were stamped with a new character, acquired a new value, and the depurated ideas which they now expressed opposed each other, and combined with each other, until the universe was seen pierced by a plexus of thoughts, and resting calmly within it.

Viewed from these heights, the petty and the every-day matters which occupied the human herd seemed so contemptible. Of what account, for instance, was the wrangling in the Senate and the Parliament of a little country like Denmark compared with Hegel's vision of the mighty march, inevitable and determined by spiritual laws, of the idea of

Freedom, through the world's History! And of what account was the daily gossip of the newspapers, compared with the possibility now thrown open of a life of eternal ideals, lived in and for them!

XV.

I had an even deeper perception of my initiation when I went back from Hegel to Spinoza and, filled with awe and enthusiasm, read the *Ethica* for the first time. Here I stood at the source of modern pantheistic Philosophy. Here Philosophy was even more distinctly Religion, since it took Religion's place. Though the method applied was very artificial, purely mathematical, at least Philosophy had here the attraction of a more original type of mind, the effect being much the same as that produced by primitive painting, compared with a more developed stage. His very expression, *God or Nature,* had a fascinating mysticism about it. The chapter in the book which is devoted to the Natural History of passions, surprised and enriched one by its simple, but profound, explanation of the conditions of the human soul. And although his fight against Superstition's views of life is conducted with a keenness that scouts discussion, whereas in modern Philosophy the contention is merely implied, it seemed as though his thoughts travelled along less stormy paths.

In Hegel, it had been exclusively the comprehensiveness of the thoughts and the mode of the thought's procedure that held my attention. With Spinoza it was different. It was his personality that attracted, the great man in him, one of the greatest that History has known. With him a new type had made its entrance into the world's History; he was the calm thinker, looking down from above on this earthly life, reminding one, by the purity and strength of his character, of Jesus, but a contrast to Jesus, inasmuch as he was a worshipper of Nature and Necessity, and a Pantheist. His teaching was the basis of the faith of the new age. He was a Saint and a Heathen, seditious and pious, at the same time.

XVI.

Still, while I was in this way making a purely mental endeavour to penetrate into as many intellectual domains as I could, and to become master of one subject after another, I was very far from being at peace with regard to my intellectual acquisitions, or from feeling myself in incontestable possession of them. While I was satisfying my desire for insight or knowledge and, by glimpses, felt my supremest happiness in the delight of comprehension, an ever more violent struggle was going on in my emotions.

As my being grew and developed within me and I slowly emerged from the double state of which I had been conscious, in other words, the more I became one and individual and strove to be honest and true, the less I felt myself to be a mere individual, the more I realised that I was bound up with humanity, one link in the chain, one organ belonging to the Universe. The philosophical Pantheism I was absorbed by, itself worked counter to the idea of individualism inherent in me, taught me and presented to me the union of all beings in Nature the All-Divine. But it was not from Pantheism that the crisis of my spiritual life proceeded; it was from the fountains of emotion which now shot up and filled my soul with their steady flow. A love for humanity came over me, and watered and fertilised the fields of my inner world which had been lying fallow, and this love of humanity vented itself in a vast compassion.

This gradually absorbed me till I could hardly bear the thought of the suffering, the poor, the oppressed, the victims of Injustice. I always saw them in my mind's eye, and it seemed to be my duty to work for them, and to be disgraceful of me to enjoy the good things of life while so many were being starved and tortured. Often as I walked along the streets at night I brooded over these ideas till I knew nothing of what was passing around me, but only felt how all the forces of my brain drew me towards those who suffered.

There were warm-hearted and benevolent men among my near relatives. The man whom my mother's younger sister had married had his heart in the right place, so much indeed that he no sooner saw or heard of distress than his hand was in his pocket, although he had little from which to give. My father's brother was a genuinely philanthropic man, who founded one beneficent institution or society after the other, had an unusual power of inducing his well-to-do fellow-townsmen to carry his schemes through, and in the elaboration of them showed a perception and practical sense that almost amounted to genius; this was the more surprising since his intelligence was not otherwise remarkable for its keenness and his reasoning methods were confused.   But what I felt was quite different.   My feelings were not so easily roused as those of the first-mentioned; I was not so good-natured or so quick to act as he.   Neither did they resemble those of my other uncle, who merely represented compassion for those unfortunately situated, but was without the least vestige of rebellious feeling against the conditions or the people responsible for the misery; my uncle was always content with life as it was, saw the hand of a loving Providence everywhere and was fully and firmly convinced that he himself was led and helped by this same Providence, which specially watched over the launching of his projects for the welfare of mankind.   No, my feeling was of quite another kind.   Nothing was farther removed from me than this sometimes quite childish optimism.   It was not enough for me to advertise the sufferings of a few individuals and, when possible, alleviate them; I sought the causes of them in brutality and injustice.   Neither could I recognise the finger of a Universal Ruler in a confusion of coincidences, conversations, newspaper articles, and advice by prudent men, the outcome of all which was the founding of a society for seam-stresses or the erection of a hospital to counteract the misery that the Controlling Power had Itself occasioned.   I was a child no longer, and in that sense never had been childish. But my heart bled none the less with sympathy for society's unfortunates.   I did not as yet perceive the necessity of that selfishness which is self-assertion, and I felt oppressed and tormented by all that I, in my comparatively advantageous position as a non-proletarian, enjoyed, while many others did not.

Then another mood, with other promptings, asserted itself. I felt an impulse to step forward as a preacher to the world around me, to the thoughtless and the hard-hearted. Under the influence of strong emotion I wrote an edifying discourse, *The Profitable Fear*. I began to regard it as my duty, so soon as I was fitted for it, to go out into the town and preach at every street-corner, regardless of whether a lay preacher, like myself, should encounter indifference or harvest scorn.

This course attracted me because it presented itself to me under the guise of the most difficult thing, and, with the perversity of youth, I thought difficulty the only criterion of duty. I only needed to hit upon something that seemed to me to be the right thing and then say to myself: " You dare not do it! " for all the youthful strength and daring that was in me, all my deeper feelings of honour and of pride, all my love of grappling with the apparently insurmountable to unite, and in face of this *You dare not,* satisfy myself that I did dare.

As provisionally, self-abnegation, humility, and asceticism seemed to me to be the most difficult things, for a time my whole spiritual life was concentrated into an endeavour to attain them. Just at this time—I was nineteen—my family was in a rather difficult pecuniary position, and I, quite a poor student, was cast upon my own resources. I had consequently not much of this world's goods to renounce. From a comfortable residence in Crown Prince's Street, my parents had moved to a more modest flat in the exceedingly unaristocratic Salmon Street, where I had an attic of limited dimensions with outlook over roofs by day and a view of the stars by night. Quiet the nights were not, inasmuch as the neighbouring houses re-echoed with screams and shrieks from poor women, whom their late-returning husbands or lovers thrashed in their cups. But never had I felt myself so raised, so exhilarated, so blissfully happy, as in that room. My days slipped by in ecstasy; I felt myself consecrated a combatant in the service of the Highest. I used to test my body, in order to get it wholly under my control, ate as little as possible, slept as little as possible, lay many a night outside my bed on the bare floor, gradually to make myself as hardy as I required to be. I tried to crush the youthful sensuality that was awakening in me, and by degrees acquired complete mastery over myself, so that I could be what I wished to be, a strong and willing instrument in the fight for the victory of Truth. And I plunged afresh into study with a passion and a delight that prevented my perceiving any lack, but month after month carried me along, increasing in knowledge and in mental power, growing from day to day.

XVII.

This frame of mind, however, was crossed by another. The religious transformation in my mind could not remain clear and unmuddied, placed as I was in a society furrowed through and through by different religious currents, issued as I was from the European races that for thousands of years had been ploughed by religious ideas. All the atavism, all the spectral repetition of the thoughts and ideas of the past that can lie dormant in the mind of the individual, leaped to the reinforcement of the harrowing religious impressions which came to me from without.

It was not the attitude of my friends that impressed me. All my more intimate friends were orthodox Christians, but the attempts which various ones, amongst them Julius Lange, and Jens Paludan-Müller, had made to convert me had glanced off from my much more advanced thought without making any impression. I was made of much harder metal than they, and their attempts to alter my way of thinking did not penetrate beyond my hide. To set my mind in vibration, there was needed a brain that I felt superior to my own; and I did not find it in them. I found it in the philosophical and religious writings of Sören Kierkegaard, in such works, for instance, as *Sickness unto Death.*

The struggle within me began, faintly, as I approached my nineteenth year. My point of departure was this: one thing seemed to me requisite, to live in and for *The Idea,* as the expression for the highest at that time was. All

that rose up inimical to *The Idea* or Ideal merited to be
lashed with scorn or felled with indignation. And one day I
penned this outburst: "Heine wept over *Don Quixote*. Yes,
he was right. I could weep tears of blood when I think of
the book." But the first thing needed was to acquire a clear
conception of what must be understood by the Ideal. Heiberg had regarded the uneducated as those devoid of ideals.
But I was quite sure myself that education afforded no criterion. And I could find no other criterion of devotion to the
Ideal than a willingness to make sacrifices. If, I said, I
prove myself less self-sacrificing than any one of the wretches
I am fighting, I shall myself incur well-merited scorn. But
if self-sacrifice were the criterion, then Jesus, according to
the teachings of tradition, was the Ideal, for who as self-
sacrificing as He?

This was an inclined plane leading to the Christian spiritual life, and a year later, when I was nearly twenty, I
had proceeded so far on this plane that I felt myself in all
essentials in agreement with the Christian mode of feeling,
inasmuch as my life was ascetic, and my searching, striving,
incessantly working mind, not only found repose, but rapture, in prayer, and was elated and fired at the idea of being
protected and helped by " God."

But just as I was about to complete my twentieth year,
the storm broke out over again, and during the whole of the
ensuing six months raged with unintermittent violence. Was
I, at this stage of my development, a Christian or not? And
if not, was it my duty to become a Christian?

The first thought that arose was this: It is a great
effort, a constant effort, sometimes a minutely recurring effort, to attain moral mastery over one's self, and though this
certainly need not bring with it a feeling of self-satisfaction,
much less *ought* to do so, it does bring with it a recognition
of the value of this self-mastery. How strange, then, that
Christianity, which commands its attainment, at the same
time declares it to be a matter of indifference to the revealed
God whether a man has lived morally or not, since Faith
or lack of Faith is the one condition upon which so-called
Salvation depends!

The next thought was this: It is only in the writings of Kierkegaard, in his teachings concerning paradox, that Christianity appears so definite that it cannot be confused with any other spiritual trend whatever. But when one has to make one's choice between Pantheism and Christianity, then the question arises, Are Kierkegaard's teachings really historic Christianity, and not rather a rational adaptation? And this question must be answered in the negative, since it is possible to assimilate it without touching upon the question of the revelation of the Holy Ghost in the shape of a dove, to the Voice from the clouds, and the whole string of miracles and dogmas.

The next thought again was this: Pantheism does not place any one unconditional goal in front of man. The unbeliever passes his life interested in the many aims that man, as man, has. The Pantheist will therefore have difficulty in living a perfect ethical life. There are many cases in which, by deviating from the strictly ethic code, you do not harm anyone, you only injure your own soul. The Non-Believer will in this case only hardly, for the sake of impersonal Truth, make up his mind to the step which the God-fearing man will take actuated by his passionate fear of offending God.

Thus was I tossed backwards and forwards in my reflections.

XVIII.

What I dreaded most was that if I reached a recognition of the truth, a lack of courage would prevent me decisively making it my own. Courage was needed, as much to undertake the burdens entailed by being a Christian as to undertake those entailed by being a Pantheist. When thinking of Christianity, I drew a sharp distinction between the cowardice that shrunk from renunciation and the doubt that placed under discussion the very question as to whether renunciation were duty. And it was clear to me that, on the road which led to Christianity, doubt must be overcome before cowardice—not the contrary, as Kierkegaard maintains in his *For Self-Examination,* where he says that none of the martyrs doubted.

But my doubt would not be overcome. Kierkegaard had declared that it was only to the consciousness of sin that Christianity was not horror or madness. For me it was sometimes both. I concluded therefrom that I had no consciousness of sin, and found this idea confirmed when I looked into my own heart. For however violently at this period I reproached myself and condemned my failings, they were always in my eyes weaknesses that ought to be combatted, or defects that could be remedied, never sins that necessitated forgiveness, and for the obtaining of this forgiveness, a Saviour. That God had died for me as my Saviour,—I could not understand what it meant; it was an idea that conveyed nothing to me.

And I wondered whether the inhabitants of another planet would be able to understand how on the Earth that which was contrary to all reason was considered the highest truth.

XIX.

With Pantheism likewise I was on my guard against its being lack of courage, rather than a conviction of its untruth, which held me back from embracing it. I thought it a true postulate that everything seemed permeated and sustained by a Reason that had not human aims in front of it and did not work by human means, a Divine Reason. Nature could only be understood from its highest forms; the Ideal, which revealed itself to the world of men at their highest development, was present, in possibility and intent, in the first germ, in the mist of primeval creation, before it divided itself into organic and inorganic elements. The whole of Nature was in its essence Divine, and I felt myself at heart a worshipper of Nature.

But this same Nature was indifferent to the weal or woe of humans. It obeyed its own laws regardless of whether men were lost thereby; it seemed cruel in its callousness; it took care that the species should be preserved, but the individual was nothing to it.

Now, like all other European children, I had been brought up in the theory of personal immortality, a theory which, amongst other things, is one way of expressing the immense importance, the eternal importance, which is attributed to each individual. The stronger the feeling of his own *ego* that the individual has, the more eagerly he necessarily clings to the belief that he cannot be annihilated. But to none could the belief be more precious than to a youth who felt his life pulsate within, as if he had twenty lives in himself and twenty more to live. It was impossible to me to realise that I could die, and one evening, about a year later, I astonished my master, Professor Bröchner, by confessing as much. " Indeed," said Bröchner, " are you speaking seriously? You cannot realise that you will have to die one day? How young! You are very different from me, who always have death before my eyes."

But although my vitality was so strong that I could not imagine my own death, I knew well enough that my terrestrial life, like all other men's, would come to an end. But I felt all the more strongly that it was impossible everything could be at an end then; death could not be a termination; it could only, as the religions preached and as eighteenth-century Deism taught, be a moment of transition to a new and fuller existence. In reward and punishment after death I could not believe; those were mediæval conceptions that I had long outgrown. But the dream of immortality I could not yet go. And I endeavoured to hold it fast by virtue of the doctrine of the impossibility of anything disappearing. The quantity of matter always remained the same; energy survived every transformation.

Still, I realised that this could not satisfy one, as far as the form which we term individuality was concerned. What satisfaction was it to Alexander that his dust should stop a bung-hole? or to Shakespeare that *Romeo and Juliet* were acted in Chicago? So I took refuge in parallels and images. Who could tell whether the soul, which on earth had been blind to the nature of the other life, did not, in death, undergo the operation which opened its eyes? Who could tell whether death were not, as Sibbern had suggested, to be com-

pared with a birth? Just as the unborn life in its mother's
womb would, if it were conscious, believe that the revolution of birth meant annihilation, whereas it was for the first
time awakening to a new and infinitely richer life, so it was
perhaps for the soul in the dreaded moment of death. . . .

But when I placed before my master these comparisons
and the hopes I built upon them, they were swept away as
meaningless; he pointed out simply that nothing went to
prove a continuation of personality after death, while on the
contrary everything argued against it,—and to this I could
not refuse my assent.

Then I understood that in what I called Pantheism,
the immortality of the individual had no place. And a slow,
internal struggle commenced for renunciation of the importance and value of the individual. I had many a conversation on this point with my teacher, a man tired of life
and thoroughly resigned.

He always maintained that the desire of the individual
for a continuation of personality was nothing but the outcome of vanity. He would very often put the question in a
comical light. He related the following anecdote: In
summer evenings he used to go for a walk along the Philosopher's Avenue (now West Rampart Street). Here he had
frequently met, sitting on their benches, four or five old gentlemen who took their evening ramble at the same time; by
degrees they made each other's acquaintance and got into conversation with one another. It turned out that the old gentlemen were candle-makers who had retired from business
and now had considerable difficulty in passing their time
away. In reality they were always bored, and they yawned
incessantly. These men had one theme only, to which they
always recurred with enthusiasm—their hope in personal immortality for all eternity. And it amused Bröchner that
they, who in this life did not know how to kill so much as one
Sunday evening, should be so passionately anxious to have a
whole eternity to fill up. His pupil then caught a glimpse
himself of the grotesqueness of wishing to endure for millions of centuries, which time even then was nothing in comparison with eternity.

XX.

But in spite of it all, it was a hard saying, that in the pantheistic view of life the absorption of the individual into the great whole took the place of the continued personal existence which was desired by the *ego*. But what frightened me even more was that the divine All was not to be moved or diverted by prayer. But pray I had to. From my earliest childhood I had been accustomed, in anxiety or necessity, to turn my thoughts towards a Higher Power, first forming my needs and wishes into words, and then later, without words, concentrating myself in worship. It was a need inherited from many hundreds of generations of forefathers, this need of invoking help and comfort. Nomads of the plains, Bedouins of the desert, ironclad warriors, pious priests, roving sailors, travelling merchants, the citizen of the town and the peasant in the country, all had prayed for centuries, and from the very dawn of time; the women, the hundreds and hundreds of women from whom I was descended, had centred all their being in prayer. It was terrible, never to be able to pray again. . . . Never to be able to fold one's hands, never to raise one's eyes above, but to live, shut in overhead, alone in the universe!

If there were no eye in Heaven that watched over the individual, no ear that understood his plaint, no hand that protected him in danger, then he was placed, as it were, on a desolate steppe where the wolves were howling.

And in alarm I tried once more the path towards religious quietude that I had recently deemed impracticable,— until the fight within me calmed again, and in renunciation I forced my emotion to bow to what my reason had acknowledged as the Truth.

ADOLESCENCE

I.

AMONG my many good comrades, there was one, Julius Lange, with whom comradeship had developed into friendship, and this friendship again assumed a passionate character. We were the two, who, of them all, were most exactly suited to one another, completed one another. Fundamentally different though we were, we could always teach each other something. We grew indispensable to one another; for years there seldom a day went by that we did not meet. The association with his junior cannot possibly have given Julius Lange a delight corresponding to that which his society gave me. Intellectually equal, we were of temperaments diametrically opposed. Having the same love of Art and the same enthusiasm for Art,—save that the one cared more for its pictorial and the other for its literary expression,—we were of mutual assistance to one another in the interchange of thoughts and information. Entirely at variance in our attitude towards religious tradition, in our frequent collisions we were both perpetually being challenged to a critical inspection of our intellectual furniture. But I was the one who did the worshipping.

When Julius Lange, on December 17, 1861, after having twice been to see me and found me out, the third time

met with me and informed me: " I have received an invitation to go to Italy on Saturday and be away five months,"
was, though surprised, exceedingly glad for my friend's sake,
but at the same time I felt as if I had received a blow
in the face. What would become of me, not only during the
interval, but afterwards? Who could say whether Lange
would ever come back, or whether he would not come back
changed? How should I be able to endure my life! I
should have to work tremendously hard, to be able to bear
the loss of him. I could hardly understand how I should be
able to exist when I could no longer, evening after evening,
slip up to my friend's little room to sit there in calm, quiet
contentment, seeing pictures and exchanging thoughts! It
was as though a nerve had been cut. I only then realised
that I had never loved any man so much. I had had four
eyes; now I had only two again; I had had two brains; now
I had only one; in my heart I had felt the happiness of two
human beings; now only the melancholy of one was left
behind.

There was not a painting, a drawing, a statue or a bas-
relief in the galleries and museums of Copenhagen that we
had not studied together and compared our impressions of.
We had been to Thorwaldsen's Museum together, we went
together to Bissen's studio, where in November, 1861, I met
for the first time my subsequent friends, Vilhelm Bissen and
Walter Runeberg. The memory of Julius Lange was associated in my mind with every picture of Hobbema, Dubbels or
Ruysdael, Rembrandt or Rubens, every reproduction of Ital-
an Renaissance art, every photograph of church or castle.
And I myself loved pictures even more ardently than poetry.
I was fond of comparing my relations with literature to affec-
ion for a being of the same sex; my passion for pictures to
he stormy passion of a youth for a woman. It is true that
I knew much less about Art than about Poetry, but that made
no difference. I worshipped my favourite artists with a more
mpetuous enthusiasm than any of my favourite authors.
And this affection for pictures and statuary was a link between
my friend and myself. When we were sitting in my room
ogether, and another visitor happened to be there, I posi-

tively suffered over the sacrifice of an hour's enjoyment and
when Lange got up to go, I felt as though a window had
been slammed to, and the fresh air shut out.

II.

I had for a long time pursued my non-juridic studie
as well as I could without the assistance of a teacher. Bu
I had felt the want of one. And when a newly appointed
docent at the University, Professor H. Bröchner, offered in
struction in the study of Philosophy to any who cared to
present themselves at his house at certain hours, I had fel
strongly tempted to take advantage of his offer. I hesi
tated for some time, for I was unwilling to give up the leas
portion of my precious freedom; I enjoyed my retirement
the mystery of my modest life of study, but on the othe
hand I could not grapple with Plato and Aristotle withou
the hints of a competent guide as to the why and wherefore
    I was greatly excited. I had heard Professor Bröchne
speak on Psychology, but his diction was handled with suc
painful care, was so monotonous and sounded so strange, tha
it could not fail to alarm. It was only the professor's di
tinguished and handsome face that attracted me, and in pa
ticular his large, sorrowful eyes, with their beautiful expre
sion, in which one read a life of deep research—and tear
Now, I determined to venture up to Bröchner. But I had no
the courage to mention it to my mother beforehand, for fea
speaking of it should frighten me from my resolution, so u
easy did I feel about the step I was taking. When the da
which I had fixed upon for the attempt arrived—it was th
2nd of September, 1861,—I walked up and down in front c
the house several times before I could make up my mind
go upstairs; I tried to calculate beforehand what the profe
sor would say, and what it would be best for me to repl
interminably.
    The tall, handsome man with the appearance of a Spa
ish knight, opened the door himself and received the your
fellow who was soon to become his most intimate pupil, ve
kindly. To my amazement, as soon as he heard my nam

e knew which school I had come from and also that I had
ecently become a student. He vigorously dissuaded me from
going through a course of Plato and Aristotle, saying it
would be too great a strain—said, or implied, that I should
be spared the difficult path he had himself traversed, and
ketched out a plan of study of more modern Philosophy and
Esthetics. His manner inspired confidence and left behind
t the main impression that he wished to save the beginner all
useless exertion. All the same, with my youthful energy, I
felt, as I went home, a shade disappointed that I was not to
begin the History of Philosophy from the beginning.

My visit was soon repeated, and a most affectionate intimacy quickly sprang up between master and pupil, revealed
on the side of the elder, in an attitude of fatherly goodwill to
which the younger had hitherto been a stranger, the teacher,
while instructing his pupil and giving him practical guidance,
constantly keeping in view all that could further his well-
being and assist his future; my attitude was one of reverence
and affection, and of profound gratitude for the care of
which I was the object.

I certainly, sometimes, in face of my master's great thoroughness and his skill in wrestling with the most difficult
thoughts, felt a painful distrust of my own capacity and of
my own intellectual powers, compared with his. I was also
not infrequently vexed by a discordant note, as it were, being
struck in our intercourse, when Bröchner, despite the doubts
and objections I brought forward, always took it for granted
that I shared his pantheistic opinions, without perceiving that
I was still tossed about by doubts, and fumbling after a
firm foothold. But the confidential terms upon which I was
with the maturer man had an attraction for me which my intimacy with undecided and youthfully prejudiced comrades
necessarily lacked; he had the experience of a lifetime behind
him, he looked down from superior heights on the sympathies
and antipathies of a young man.

To me, for instance, Ploug's *The Fatherland* was at
that time Denmark's most intellectual organ, whereas Bille's
Daily Paper disgusted me, more particularly on account of
the superficiality and the tone of finality which distinguished

its literary criticisms. Bröchner, who, with not unmixe
benevolence, and without making any special distinction be
tween the two, looked down on both these papers of the edu
cated mediocrity, saw in his young pupil's bitterness agains
the trivial but useful little daily, only an indication of th
quality of his mind. Bröchner's mere manner, as he re
marked one day with a smile, "You do not read *The Dail
Paper* on principle," made me perceive in a flash the comica
ity of my indignation over such articles as it contained. M
horizon was still sufficiently circumscribed for me to suppos
that the state of affairs in Copenhagen was, in and of itself, o
importance. I myself regarded my horizon as wide. On
day, when making a mental valuation of myself, I wrote, witl
the naïveté of nineteen, "My good qualities, those which wil
constitute my personality, if I ever become of any account, ar
a mighty and ardent enthusiasm, a thorough authority in th
service of Truth, *a wide horizon* and philosophically trainec
thinking powers. These must make up for my lack of hu
mour and facility."

It was only several years after the beginning of our ac
quaintance that I felt myself in essential agreement witl
Hans Bröchner. I had been enraptured by a study of Lud
wig Feuerbach's books, for Feuerbach was the first thinke
in whose writings I found the origin of the idea of God in th
human mind satisfactorily explained. In Feuerbach, too,
found a presentment of ideas without circumlocution anc
without the usual heavy formulæ of German philosophy, a
conquering clarity, which had a very salutary effect on my
own way of thinking and gave me a feeling of security. I
for many years I had been feeling myself more conservative
than my friend and master, there now came a time when ir
many ways I felt myself to be more liberal than he, with hi
mysterious life in the eternal realm of mind of which he fel
himself to be a link.

III.

I had not been studying Jurisprudence much more thar
a year before it began to weigh very heavily upon me. The
mere sight of the long rows of *Schou's Ordinances,* whick

filled the whole of the back of my writing-table, were a daily source of vexation. I often felt that I should not be happy until the Ordinances were swept from my table. And the lectures were always so dreary that they positively made me think of suicide—and I so thirsty of life!—as a final means of escape from the torment of them. I felt myself so little adapted to the Law that I wasted my time with Hamlet-like cogitations as to how I could give up the study without provoking my parents' displeasure, and without stripping myself of all prospects for the future. And for quite a year these broodings grew, till they became a perfect nightmare to me.

I had taken a great deal of work upon myself; I gave lessons every day, that I might have a little money coming in, took lessons myself in several subjects, and not infrequently plunged into philosophical works of the past, that were too difficult for me, such as the principal works of Kant. Consequently when I was nineteen, I begun to feel my strength going. I felt unwell, grew nervous, had a feeling that I could not draw a deep breath, and when I was twenty my physical condition was a violent protest against overwork. One day, while reading Kant's *Kritik der Urteilskraft,* I felt so weak that I was obliged to go to the doctor. The latter recommended physical exercises and cold shower-baths.

The baths did me good, and I grew so accustomed to them that I went on taking them and have done so ever since. I did my gymnastic exercises with a Swede named Nycander, who had opened an establishment for Swedish gymnastics in Copenhagen.

There I met, amongst others, the well-known Icelandic poet and diplomatist, Grimur Thomsen, who bore the title of Counsellor of Legation. His compatriots were very proud of him. Icelandic students declared that Grimur possessed twelve dress shirts, three pairs of patent leather boots, and had embraced a marchioness in Paris. At gymnastics, Grimur Thomsen showed himself audacious and not seldom coarse in what he said and hinted. It is true that by reason of my youth I was very susceptible and took offence at things that an older man would have heard without annoyance.

IV.

I continued to be physically far from strong.   Mentally, I worked indefatigably.   The means of deciding the study question that, after long reflection, seemed to me most expedient, was this: I would compete for one of the University prizes, either the æsthetic or the philosophical, and then, if I won the gold medal, my parents and others would see that if I broke with the Law it was not from idleness, but because I really had talents in another direction.

As early as 1860 I had cast longing eyes at the prize questions that had been set, and which hung up in the Entrance Hall of the University.   But none of them were suited to me.   In 1861 I made up my mind to attempt a reply, even if the questions in themselves should not be attractive.

There was amongst them one on the proper correlation between poetic fiction and history in the historical romances. The theme in itself did not particularly fascinate me; but I was not ignorant of the subject, and it was one that allowed of being looked at in a wide connection, i.e., the claims of the subject as opposed to the imagination of the artist, in general. I was of opinion that just as in sculpture the human figure should not be represented with wings, but the conception of its species be observed, so the essential nature of a past age should be unassailed in historic fiction.   Throughout numerous carefully elaborated abstractions, extending over 120 folio pages, and in which I aimed at scientific perspicuity, I endeavoured to give a soundly supported theory of the limits of inventive freedom in Historical Romance.   The substructure was so painstaking that it absorbed more than half of the treatise.   Quite apart from the other defects of this tyro handiwork, it lauded and extolled an æsthetic direction opposed to that of both the men who were to adjudicate upon it.   Hegel was mentioned in it as " The supreme exponent of Æsthetics, a man whose imposing greatness it is good to bow before."   I likewise held with his emancipated pupil, Fr. Th. Vischer, and vindicated him.   Of Danish thinkers, J. L. Heiberg and S. Kierkegaard were almost the only ones discussed.

Heiberg was certainly incessantly criticised, but was treated with profound reverence and as a man whose slightest utterance was of importance. Sibbern's artistic and philosophical researches, on the other hand, were quite overlooked, indeed sometimes Vischer was praised as being the first originator of psychological developments, which Sibbern had suggested many years before him. I had, for that matter, made a very far from sufficient study of Sibbern's researches, which were, partly, not systematic enough for me, and partly had repelled me by the peculiar language in which they were couched.

Neither was it likely that this worship of Heiberg, which undeniably peeped out through all the proofs of imperfections and self-contradictions in him, would appeal to Hauch.

When I add that the work was youthfully doctrinaire, in language not fresh, and that in its skeleton-like thinness it positively tottered under the weight of its definitions, it is no wonder that it did not win the prize. The verdict passed upon it was to the effect that the treatise was thorough in its way, and that it would have been awarded the prize had the question asked been that of determining the correlation between History and Fiction in general, but that under the circumstances it dwelt too cursorily on Romance and was only deemed deserving of "a very honourable mention."

Favourable as this result was, it was nevertheless a blow to me, who had made my plans for the following years dependent on whether I won the prize or not. Julius Lange, who knocked at my door one evening to tell me the result, was the witness of my disappointment. " I can understand," he said, " that you should exclaim: ' *Oleum et operam perdidi!* ', but you must not give up hope for so little. It is a good thing that you prohibited the opening of the paper giving your name in the event of the paper not winning the prize, for no one will trouble their heads about the flattering criticism and an honourable mention would only harm you in people's eyes; it would stamp you with the mark of mediocrity."

V.

The anonymous recipient of the honourable mention nevertheless determined to call upon his judges, make their acquaintance, and let them know who he was.

I went first to Hauch, who resided at that time at Frederiksberg Castle, in light and lofty rooms. Hauch appeared exaggeratedly obliging, the old man of seventy and over paying me, young man as I was, one compliment after the other. The treatise was " extraordinarily good," they had been very sorry not to give me the prize; but I was not to bear them any ill-will for that; they had acted as their consciences dictated. In eighteen months I should be ready to take my Magister examination; the old poet thought he might venture to prophesy that I should do well. He was surprised at his visitor's youth, could hardly understand how at my age I could have read and thought so much, and gave me advice as to the continuation of my studies.

Sibbern was as cordial as Hauch had been polite and cautious. It was very funny that, whereas Hauch remarked that he himself had wished to give me the prize with an *although* in the criticism, but that Sibbern had been against it, Sibbern declared exactly the reverse; in spite of all its faults he had wanted to award the medal, but Hauch had expressed himself adverse. Apparently they had misunderstood one another; but in any case the result was just, so there was nothing to complain of.

Sibbern went into the details of the treatise, and was stricter than Hauch. He regretted that the main section of the argument was deficient; the premises were too prolix. He advised a more historic, less philosophical study of Literature and Art. He was pleased to hear of the intimate terms I was on with Bröchner, whereas Hauch would have preferred my being associated with Rasmus Nielsen, whom he jestingly designated "a regular brown-bread nature." When the treatise was given back to me, I found it full of apt and instructive marginal notes from Sibbern's hand.

Little as I had gained by my unsuccessful attempt to win this prize, and unequivocally as my conversation with the practical Sibbern had proved to me that a post as master in my mother tongue at a Grammar-school was all that the Magister degree in Æsthetics was likely to bring me, whereas from my childhood I had made up my mind that I would never be a master in a school, this conversation nevertheless ripened my determination to give up my law studies, but of course only when by successfully competing for the prize the next year I had satisfactorily proved my still questionable ability.

VI.

The Meeting of Scandinavian students at Copenhagen in June, 1862, taught me what it meant to be a Scandinavian. Like all the other undergraduates, I was Scandinavian at heart, and the arrangements of the Meeting were well calculated to stir the emotions of youth. Although, an insignificant Danish student, I did not take part in the expedition to North Zealand specially arranged for our guests, consequently neither was present at the luncheon given by Fredderik VII. to the students at Fredensborg (which was interrupted by a heavy shower), I was nevertheless deeply impressed by the Meeting.

It was a fine sight to behold the students from the three other Scandinavian Universities come sailing across the Sound from Malmö to Copenhagen. The Norwegians were especially striking, tall and straight, with narrow faces under tasseled caps, like a wood of young fir trees; the national type was so marked that at first I could hardly see any difference between them.

For me, there were three perfect moments during the festivities. The first was at the meeting of all the students in the Square of Our Lady, after the arrival of the visitors, when the scholars of the Metropolitan School, crowding the windows of the building, greeted them with a shout of delight. There was such a freshness, such a childish enthusiasm about it, that some of us had wet eyes. It was as though the still distant future were acclaiming the young ones now advancing to the assault, and promising them sympathy and conquest.

The second was when the four new flags embroidered
by Danish ladies for the students were consecrated and
handed over.   Clausen's speech was full of grandeur, and
addressed, not to the recipients, but to the flags as living
beings: " Thou wilt cross the Baltic to the sanctuary at
Upsala.   Thou wilt cross the Cattegat to the land of
rocks, . . ." and the address to each of the flags concluded:
" Fortune and Honour attend thee! "   The evening after the
consecration of the flags, there was a special performance
at the Royal Theatre for the members of the Meeting, at
which Heiberg, radiant as she always was, and saluted with
well-merited enthusiasm, played *Sophie* in the vaudeville
" *No*," with a rosette of the Scandinavian colours at her
waist.   Then it was that Paludan-Müller's prologue, recited
by our idolised actor, Michael Wiehe, caused me the third
thrilling moment.   Listening to the words of the poet from
a bad place in the gallery, I was hardly the only one who felt
strangely stirred, as Wiehe, letting his eyes roam round the
theatre, said:

> Oh! that the young of the North might one day worthily play
> Their part! Oh that each one might do his best
> For the party he has chosen! That never there be lack
> Of industry, fidelity, strength and talents!
> And may he firm step forth, the mighty genius
> (*Mayhap, known only to the secret power within him,*
> *Seated amongst us now*), the mighty genius,
> Who, as Fate hath willed it, is to play
> The mighty part and do the mighty things.

Involuntarily we looked round, seeking for the one to whom
the poet's summons referred.

The general spirit of this Meeting has been called flat
in comparison with that pervading former meetings.   It
did not strike the younger participants so.   A breath of Scandinavianism swept over every heart; one felt borne along on
a historic stream.   It seemed like a bad dream that the peoples of the North had for so many centuries demolished and
laid waste each other, tapped one another for blood and gold,
rendered it impossible for the North to assert herself and
spread her influence in Europe.

One could feel at the Meeting, though very faintly, that

the Swedes and Norwegians took more actual pleasure in each other, and regarded themselves as to a greater extent united than either of them looked upon themselves as united with the Danes, who were outside the political Union. I was perhaps the only Dane present who fancied I detected this, but when I mentioned what I thought I observed to a gifted young Norwegian, so far was he from contradicting me that he merely replied: " Have you noticed that, too ?"

Notwithstanding, during the whole of the Meeting, one constantly heard expressed on every hand the conviction that if Germany were shortly to declare war against Denmark— which no one doubted—the Swedes and Norwegians would most decidedly not leave the Danes in the lurch. The promise was given oftener than it was asked. Only, of course, it was childish on the part of those present at the Meeting to regard such promises, given by the leaders of the students, and by the students themselves in festive mood, as binding on the nations and their statesmen.

I did not make any intellectually inspiring acquaintances through the Meeting, although I was host to two Upsala students; neither of them, however, interested me. I got upon a friendly footing through mutual intellectual interests with Carl von Bergen, later so well known as an author, he, like myself, worshipping philosophy and hoping to contribute to intellectual progress. Carl von Bergen was a self-confident, ceremonious Swede, who had read a great many books. At that time he was a new Rationalist, which seemed to promise one point of interest in common; but he was a follower of the Boström philosophy, and as such an ardent Theist. At this point we came into collision, my researches and reflections constantly tending to remove me farther from a belief in any God outside the world, so that after the Meeting Carl von Bergen and I exchanged letters on Theism and Pantheism, which assumed the width and thickness of treatises. For very many years the Swedish essayist and I kept up a friendly, though intermittent intercourse. Meanwhile von Bergen, whose good qualities included neither character nor originality, inclined, as years went on, more and more towards Conservatism, and at forty years old he had attained to a worship of what he had detested, and a detestation of what he had worshipped. His vanity simultaneously assumed extraordinary proportions. In a popular Encyclopædia, which he took over when the letter B was to be dealt with, and, curiously enough, disposed of shortly afterwards, *von Bergen* was treated no less in detail than *Buonaparte*. He did battle with some of the best men and women in Sweden, such as Ellen Key and Knut Wicksell, who did not fail to reply to him. When in 1889 his old friend from the Students' Meeting gave some lectures on Goethe in Stockholm, he immediately afterwards directed some poor opposition lectures against him, which neither deserved nor received any reply. It had indeed become a specialty of his to give "opposition lectures." When he died, some few years later, what he had written was promptly forgotten.

There was another young Swedish student whom I caught a glimpse of for the first time at the Students' Meeting, towards whom I felt more and more attracted, and who eventually became my friend. This was the darling of the gods, Carl Snoilsky. At a fête in Rosenborg Park, amongst the songs was one which, with my critical scent, I made a note of. It was by the then quite unknown young Count Snoilsky, and it was far from possessing the rare qualities, both of pith and form, that later distinguished his poetry; but it was a poet's handiwork, a troubadour song to the Danish woman, meltingly sweet, and the writer of it was a youth of aristocratic bearing, regular, handsome features, and smooth brown hair, a regular Adonis. The following year he came again, drawn by strong cords to Christian Winther's home, loving the old poet like a son, as Swinburne loved Victor Hugo, sitting at Mistress Julie Winther's feet in affectionate admiration and semi-adoration, although she was half a century old and treated him as a mother does a favourite child.

It was several years, however, before there was any actual friendship between the Swedish poet and myself. He called upon me one day in my room in Copenhagen, looking exceedingly handsome in a tight-fitting waistcoat of blue quilted silk. In the absence of the Swedo-Norwegian Ambassador, he was Chargé d'Affaires in Copenhagen, after, in his capacity as diplomatic attaché, having been stationed in various parts of the world and, amongst others, for some time in Paris. He could have no warmer admirer of his first songs than myself, and we very frequently spent our evenings together in Bauer's wine room—talking over everything in Scandinavian, English, or French literature which both of us had enthusiastically and critically read. On many points our verdicts were agreed.

There came a pause in Snoilsky's productive activity; he was depressed. It was generally said, although it sounded improbable, that he had had to promise his wife's relations to give up publishing verse, they regarding it as unfitting the dignity of a noble. In any case, he was at that time suffering under a marriage that meant to him the deprivation of the freedom without which it was impossible to write. Still, he never mentioned these strictly personal matters. But one evening that we were together, Snoilsky was so overcome by the thought of his lack of freedom that tears suddenly began to run down his cheeks. He was almost incapable of controlling himself again, and when we went home together late at night, poured out a stream of melancholy, half-despairing remarks.

A good eighteen months later we met again in Stockholm; Snoilsky was dignified and collected. But when, a few years later, so-called public opinion in Sweden began to rave against the poet for the passion for his second wife which so long made him an exile from his country, I often thought of that evening.

As years passed by, his outward bearing became more and more reserved and a trifle stiff, but he was the same at heart, and no one who had known him in the heyday of his youth could cease to love him.

VII.

A month after the Students' Meeting, at the invitation of my friend Jens Paludan-Müller, I spent a few weeks at his

home at Nykjöbing, in the island of Falster, where his father, Caspar Paludan-Müller, the historian, was at the time
head master of the Grammar-school. Those were rich and
beautiful weeks, which I always remembered later with gratitude.

The stern old father with his leonine head and huge
eyebrows impressed one by his earnestness and perspicacity,
somewhat shut off from the world as he was by hereditary
deafness. The dignified mistress of the house likewise belonged to a family that had made its name known in Danish
literature. She was a Rosenstand-Göiske. Jens was a cordial and attentive host, the daughters were all of them women
out of the ordinary, and bore the impress of belonging to a
family of the highest culture in the country; the eldest was
womanly and refined, the second, with her Roman type of
beauty and bronze-coloured head, lovely in a manner peculiarly her own; the youngest, as yet, was merely an amiable
young girl. The girls would have liked to get away from
the monotony of provincial life, and their release came when
their father was appointed to a professorship at Copenhagen
University. There was an ease of manner and a tone of
mental distinction pervading the whole family. Two young,
handsome Counts Reventlow were being brought up in the
house, still only half-grown boys at that time, but who were
destined later to win honourable renown. One of them, the
editor of his ancestress's papers, kept up his acquaintance
with the guest he had met in the Paludan-Müller home for
over forty years.

There often came to the house a young Dane from Car-
acas in Venezuela, of unusual, almost feminine beauty, with
eyes to haunt one's dreams. He played uncommonly well,
was irresistibly gentle and emotional. After a stay of a few
years in Denmark he returned to his native place. The previously mentioned Grönbeck, with his pretty sister, and other
young people from the town, were frequent guests during the
holidays, and the days passed in games, music, wanderings about the garden, and delightful excursions to the
woods.

On every side I encountered beauty of some description.

I said to Jens one day: "One kind of beauty is the glow
which the sun of Youth casts over the figure, and it vanishes
as soon as the sun sets. Another is stamped into shape from
within; it is Mind's expression, and will remain as long as
the mind remains vigorous. But the supremest beauty of
all is in the unison of the two harmonies, which are contend-
ing for existence. In the bridal night of this supremest
beauty, Mind and Nature melt into one."

A few years later the old historian was called upon to
publish the little book on Gulland, with its short biography
prefixed, as a memorial to his only son, fallen at Sankelmark,
and again, a few years later, to edit Frederik Nutzhorn's
translation of Apuleius in memory of his son's friend, his
elder daughter's fiancé. During the preparation of these two
little books, our relations became more intimate, and our
friendship continued unbroken until in the month of February, 1872, a remark in one of my defensive articles caused
him to take up his pen against me. My remark was to the
effect that there were men of the same opinions as myself even
among the priests of the established church. Caspar Paludan-Müller declared it my public duty to mention of whom I
was thinking at the time, since such a traitor was not to be
tolerated in the lap of the Church. As I very naturally did
not wish to play the part of informer, I incurred, by my silence, the suspicion of having spoken without foundation.
The Danish man whom I had in my thoughts, and who had
confided his opinions to me, was still alive at the time. This
was the late Dean Ussing, at one time priest at Mariager, a
man of an extraordinarily refined and amiable disposition,
secretly a convinced adherent of Ernest Renan. A
Norwegian priest, who holds the same opinions, is still
living.

VIII.

In August, 1863, on a walking tour through North
Sjælland, Julius Lange introduced me to his other celebrated
uncle, Frederik Paludan-Müller, whose Summer residence
was at Fredensborg. In appearance he was of a very differ-

ent type from his brother Caspar. The distinguishing mark
of the one was power, of the other, nobility. For Frederik
Paludan-Müller as a poet I cherished the profoundest admiration. He belonged to the really great figures of Danish
literature, and his works had so fed and formed my inmost
nature that I should scarcely be the same had I not read
them. It was unalloyed happiness to have access to his house
and be allowed to enjoy his company. It was a distinction
to be one of the few he vouchsafed to take notice of and one
of the fewer still in whose future he interested himself. Do
the young men of Denmark to-day, I wonder, admire
creative intellects as they were admired by some few of
us then? It is in so far hardly possible, since there is
not at the present time any Northern artist with such a
hall-mark of refined delicacy as Frederik Paludan-Müller
possessed.

The young people who came to his house might have
wished him a younger, handsomer wife, and thought his
choice, Mistress Charite, as, curiously enough, she was called,
not quite worthy of the poet. Unjustly so, since he himself
was perfectly satisfied with her, and was apparently wholly
absorbed by a union which had had its share in isolating him
from the world. His wife was even more theologically inclined than himself, and appeared anonymously—without
anyone having a suspicion of the fact—as a religious authoress. Still, she was exceedingly kind to anyone, regardless
of their private opinions, who had found favour in the poet's
eyes.

The dry little old lady was the only one of her sex with
whom Paludan-Müller was intimate. He regarded all other
women, however young and beautiful, as mere works of art.
But his delight in them was charming in him, just because
of its freedom from sense. One evening that he was giving
a little banquet in honour of a Swedish lady painter, named
Ribbing, a woman of rare beauty, he asked her to stand by
the side of the bust of the Venus of Milo, that the resem-
blance, which really existed between them, might be apparent. His innocent, enthusiastic delight in the likeness was
most winning.

IX.

Two other celebrated personages whom I met for the first time a little later were Björnstjerne Björnson and Magdalene Thoresen.

I became acquainted with Björnstjerne Björnson at the Nutzhorns, their son, Ditlev, being a passionate admirer of his. His *King Sverre* of 1861 had been a disappointment, but *Sigurd Slembe* of the following year was new and great poetry, and fascinated young people's minds. Björnson, socially, as in literature, was a strong figure, self-confident, loud-voiced, outspoken, unique in all that he said, and in the weight which he knew how to impart to all his utterances. His manner jarred a little on the more subdued Copenhagen style; the impression he produced was that of a great, broad-shouldered, and very much spoilt child. In the press, all that he wrote and did was blazoned abroad by the leading critics of the day, who had a peculiar, challenging way of praising Björnson, although his ability was not seriously disputed by anyone. The National Liberal Leaders, Alfred Hage, Carl Ploug, etc., had opened their hearts and houses to him. It is said that at one time Heiberg had held back; the well-bred old man, a little shocked by the somewhat noisy ways of the young genius, is said to have expressed to his friend Krieger some scruples at inviting him to his house. To Krieger's jesting remark: " What does it matter! He is a young man; let him rub off his corners! " Heiberg is credited with having replied: " Very true! Let him! but not in my drawing-room! That is not a place where people may rub anything off." Heiberg's wife, on the other hand, admired him exceedingly, and was undoubtedly very much fascinated by him.

In a circle of younger people, Björnson was a better talker than conversationalist. Sometimes he came out with decidedly rash expressions of opinion, conclusively dismissing a question, for instance, with severe verdicts over Danish music, Heyse's excepted, judgments which were not supported by sufficient knowledge of the subject at issue. But much of what he said revealed the intellectual ruler, whose self-confi-

dence might now and again irritate, but at bottom was justified. He narrated exceptionally well, with picturesque ad-
jectives, long remembered in correct Copenhagen, spoke of
the *yellow* howl of wolves, and the like. Take it all in all,
his attitude was that of a conqueror.

He upheld poetry that was actual and palpable, consequently had little appreciation for poetry, that, like Paludan-
Müller's, was the perfection of thought and form, and boldly
disapproved of my admiration for it.

X.

It was likewise through Frederik Nutzhorn that I, when
a young beginner in the difficult art of life, became acquainted
with Madame Magdalene Thoresen. Our first conversation took place in the open air one Summer day, at the
Klampenborg bathing establishment. Although Magdalene
Thoresen was at that time at least forty-six years old, her
warm, brownish complexion could well stand inspection in the
strongest light. Her head, with its heavy dark hair, was
Southern in its beauty, her mouth as fresh as a young girl's;
she had brilliant and very striking eyes. Her figure was inclined to be corpulent, her walk a trifle heavy, her bearing
and movements full of youth and life.

She was remarkably communicative, open and warm-
hearted, with a propensity towards considerable extrava-
gance of speech. Originally incited thereto by Björnson's
peasant stories, she had then published her first tales, *The
Student* and *Signe's Story,* which belonged, half to Norwegian, half to Danish literature, and had been well received.
She was the daughter of a fisherman at Fredericia, and after
having known both the buffets and the smiles of Fortune,
had come to be on terms of friendship with many men and
women of importance, now belonging to the recognised personalities of the day. She was also very well received and
much appreciated in the Heiberg circle.

In comparison with her, a woman, I might have been
called erudite and well-informed. Her own knowledge was
very desultory. She was interested in me on account of my

youth, and her warm interest attached me to her for
the next five years,—as long, that is, as she remained in
Denmark. She very soon began to confide in me, and although she scarcely did so unreservedly, still, no woman,
at least no mature and gifted woman, had told me so much
about herself before. She was a woman who had felt
strongly and thought much; she had lived a rich, and eventful life; but all that had befallen her she romanticised. Her
poetic tendency was towards the sublime. She was absolutely veracious, and did not really mean to adorn her tales,
but partly from pride, partly from whimsicality, she saw
everything, from greatest to least, through beautifully coloured magnifying-glasses, so that a translation of her communications into every-day language became a very difficult
matter, and when an every-day occurrence was suspected
through the narrative, the same could not be reproduced in
an every-day light, and according to an every-day standard,
without wounding the narrator to the quick. For these reasons I never ventured to include among my Collected Essays
a little biographical sketch of her (written just as she herself
had idealised its events to me), one of the first articles I
had printed.

She saw strong natures, rich and deep natures, in lives
that were meagre or unsuccessful. Again, from lack of perspicacity, she sometimes saw nothing but inefficiency in people
with wide intellectual gifts; thus, she considered that her son-
in-law, Henrik Ibsen, who at that time had not become either
known or celebrated, had very imperfect poetic gifts.
"What he writes is as flat as a drawing," she would say. Or
she would remark: "He ought to be more than a collaborator
of Kierkegaard." It was only much later that she discovered his genius. Björnson, on the other hand, she worshipped with an enthusiastic love; it was a trouble to her that
just about this time he had become very cool to her.

Vague feelings did not repel her, but all keen and
pointed intelligence did. She was wholly and entirely romantic. Gallicism she objected to; the clarity of the French
seemed to her superficial; she saw depth in the reserved and
taciturn Northern, particularly the Norwegian, nature. She

had groped her way forward for a long time without realising what her gifts really were.   Her husband, who had done
all he could to assist her education, had even for a time imagined, and perhaps persuaded her, that her gifts lay in the
direction of Baggesen's.   Now, however, she had found her
vocation and her path in literature.

On all questions of thought, pure and simple, she was
extremely vague.   She was a Christian and a Heathen with
equal sincerity, a Christian with her overflowing warmheart-
edness, with her honest inclination to believe, a Heathen in
her averseness to any negation of either life or Nature.   She
used to say that she loved Christ and Eros equally, or rather,
that to her, they both meant the same.   To her, Christianity
was the new, the modern, in contrast to the rationalism of a
past age, so that Christianity and modern views of life in general merged in her eyes into one unity.

Hers was a deeply feminine nature, and a productive
nature.   Her fertile character was free from all taint of
over-estimation of herself.   She only revealed a healthy and
pleasing self-satisfaction when she imagined that some person wished to set up himself or herself over her and misjudge
acts or events in her life with respect to which she considered herself the only person qualified to judge.   At such
times she would declare in strong terms that by her own un-
assisted strength she had raised herself from a mean and un-
protected position to the level of the best men and women of
her day.   Herself overflowing with emotion, and of a noble
disposition, she craved affection and goodwill, and gave back
a hundredfold what she received.   If she felt herself the
object of cold and piercing observation, she would be silent
and unhappy, but if she herself were at ease and encountered
no coolness, she was all geniality and enthusiasm, though
not to such an extent that her enthusiasm ceased to be
critical.

She could over-value and under-value people, but was
at the same time a keen, in fact a marvellous psychologist,
and sometimes astonished one by the pertinent things she said,
surprising one by her accurate estimate of difficult psychological cases.   For instance, she understood as few others did the

great artist, the clever coquette, and the old maid in Heiberg's wife, the actress.

She had no moral prejudices, and had written *Signe's Story* as a protest against conventional morality; but she was none the less thoroughly permeated by Christian and humane ideas of morality, and there was no element of rebellion in her disposition.

On the whole, she was more a woman than an authoress. Her nature was tropical in comparison with Mrs. Charite Paludan-Müller's North Pole nature. She lived, not in a world of ideas remote from reality, but in a world of feeling and passion, full of affection and admiration, jealousy and dislike. Being a woman, she was happy at every expression of pleasure over one of her books that she heard or read of, and liked to fancy that the solitary young man who sent her an enthusiastic letter of thanks was only one of hundreds who thought as he did. Like a woman, also, she was hurt by indifference, which, however, her warm heart rarely encountered.

This richly endowed woman made me appear quite new to myself, inasmuch as, in conversations with my almost maternal friend, I began to think I was of a somewhat cold nature, a nature which in comparison with hers seemed rather dry, unproductive and unimaginative, a creature with thoughts ground keen.

Magdalene Thoresen compared me one day to an unlighted glass candelabra, hanging amid several others all lighted up, which had the gleam of the fire on the countless facets of its crystals, but was itself nothing but cold, smooth, polished, prisms.

Thus during my association with Magdalene Thoresen I came to regard myself in a new light, when I saw myself with her eyes, and I was struck more than ever by how different the verdicts over me would be were my various friends and acquaintances each to describe me as I appeared to them. To Magdalene Thoresen I was all mind, to others all passion, to others again all will. At the Nutzhorns' I went by the name of the modest B., elsewhere I was deemed conceitedly ambitious, some people thought me of a mild temper, others saw in me a quarrelsome unbeliever.

All this was a challenge to me to come to a clear understanding about my real nature.   The fruits of my work must
show me what sort of man I was.

XI.

I continued my legal studies with patient persistence,
and gradually, after having made myself master of Civil
Proceedings, I worked my way through the whole of the
juridic system, Roman Law excluded.   But the industry devoted to this was purely mechanical.   I pursued my other
studies, on the contrary, with delight, even tried to produce
something myself, and during the last months of 1862 elaborated a very long paper on *Romeo and Juliet,* chiefly concerning itself with the fundamental problems of the tragedy, as
interpreted in the Æsthetics of the day; it has been lost, like
so much else that I wrote during those years.   I sent it to
Professor Bröchner and asked his opinion of it.

Simultaneously I began to work upon a paper on the
Idea of Fate in Greek Tragedy, a response to the Prize question of the year 1862-1863, and on December 31, 1862,
had finished the Introduction, which was published for the
first time about six years later, under the title *The Idea of
Tragic Fate.*   Appended to this was a laborious piece of
work dealing with the conceptions of Fate recorded in all
the Greek tragedies that have come down to us.   This occupied the greater part of the next six months.

The published Introduction gives a true picture of the
stage of my development then, partly because it shows the
manner in which I had worked together external influences,
the Kierkegaardian thoughts and the Hegelian method,
partly because with no little definiteness it reveals a fundamental characteristic of my nature and a fundamental
tendency of my mind, since it is, throughout, a protest against the ethical conception of poetry and is a proof
of how moral ideas, when they become part of an artistic
whole, lose their peculiar stamp and assume another aspect.

In November, 1862, I joined a very large recently
started undergraduates' society, which met once a fortnight

at Borch's College to hear lectures and afterwards discuss them together. It numbered full fifty members, amongst them most of the men of that generation who afterwards distinguished themselves in Denmark. The later known politician, Octavius Hansen, was Speaker of the Meetings, and even then seemed made for the post. His parliamentary bearing was unrivalled. It was not for nothing he was English on the mother's side. He looked uncommonly handsome on the platform, with his unmoved face, his beautiful eyes, and his brown beard, curled like that of Pericles in the Greek busts. He was good-humoured, just, and well-informed. Of the numerous members, Wilhelm Thomsen the philologist was certainly the most prominent, and the only one whom I later on came to value, that is, for purely personal reasons; in daily association it was only once in a way that Thomsen could contribute anything from his special store of knowledge. One day, when we had been discussing the study of cuneiform inscriptions, the young philologist had said, half in jest, half in earnest: "If a stone were to fall down from the Sun with an inscription in unknown signs, in an unknown language, upon it, we should be able to make it out,"—a remark which I called to mind many years later when Thomsen deciphered the Ancient Turkish inscriptions in the Mountains of Siberia.

A great many political lectures were given. I gave one on Heiberg's Æsthetics.

On January 1, 1863, I received a New Year's letter from Bröchner, in which he wrote that the essay on *Romeo and Juliet* had so impressed him that, in his opinion, no one could dispute my fitness to fill the Chair of Æsthetics, which in the nature of things would soon be vacant, since Hauch, at his advanced age, could hardly continue to occupy it very long.

Thus it was that my eager patron first introduced what became a wearisome tangle, lasting a whole generation, concerning my claims to a certain post, which gradually became in my life what the French call *une scie,* an irritating puzzle, in which I myself took no part, but which attached itself to my name.

That letter agitated me very much; not because at so young an age the prospect of an honourable position in society was held out to me by a man who was in a position to judge of my fitness for it, but because this smiling prospect of an official post was in my eyes a snare which might hold me so firmly that I should not be able to pursue the path of renunciation that alone seemed to me to lead to my life's goal. I felt myself an apostle, but an apostle and a professor were very far apart. I certainly remembered that the Apostle Paul had been a tent-maker. But I feared that, once appointed, I should lose my ideal standard of life and sink down into insipid mediocrity. If I once deviated from my path, I might not so easily find it again. It was more difficult to resign a professorship than never to accept it. And, once a professor, a man soon got married and settled down as a citizen of the state, not in a position to dare anything. To dispose of my life at Bröchner's request would be like selling my soul to the Devil.

So I replied briefly that I was too much attached to Hauch to be able or willing to speculate on his death. But to this Bröchner very logically replied: " I am not speculating on his death, but on his life, for the longer he lives the better you will be prepared to be his successor."

By the middle of June, 1863, the prize paper was copied out. In September the verdict was announced; the gold medal was awarded to me with a laudatory criticism. The gold medal was also won by my friend Jens Paludan-Müller for a historic paper, and in October, at the annual Ceremony at the University, we were presented with the thin medal bearing the figure of Athene, which, for my part, being in need of a Winter overcoat, I sold next day. Clausen, the Rector, a little man with regular features, reserved face and smooth white hair, said to us that he hoped this might prove the first fruits of a far-reaching activity in the field of Danish literature. But what gave me much greater pleasure was that I was shaken hands with by Monrad, who was present as Minister for Education. Although Clausen was well known, both as a theologian and an important National Liberal, I cared nothing for him. But I was a little proud of

Monrad's hand-pressure, for his political liberality, and especially his tremendous capacity for work, compelled respect,
while from his handsome face with its thoughtful, commanding forehead, there shone the evidence of transcendent ability.

XII.

On the morning of November 15th, 1863, Julius Lange
and I went together to offer our congratulations to Frederik
Nutzhorn, whose birthday it was.   His sisters received me
with their usual cheerfulness, but their father, the old doctor,
remarked as I entered: " You come with grave thoughts
in your mind, too," for the general uneasiness occasioned
by Frederik VII.'s state of health was reflected in my face.
There was good reason for anxiety concerning all the future
events of which an unfavourable turn of his illness might be
the signal.

I went home with Julius Lange, who read a few wild
fragments of his " System " to me.   This turned upon the
contrasting ideas of *Contemplation* and *Sympathy,* corresponding to the inhaling and exhaling of the breath; the
resting-point of the breathing was the moment of actual
consciousness, etc.; altogether very young, curious, and
confused.

In the afternoon came the news of the King's death.   In
the evening, at the Students' Union, there was great commotion and much anxiety.   There were rumours of a
change of Ministry, of a Bluhme-David-Ussing Ministry,
and of whether the new King would be willing to sign
the Constitution from which people childishly expected the
final incorporation of Slesvig into Denmark.   That evening I made the acquaintance of the poet Christian Richardt,
who told me that he had noticed my face before he knew my
name.   Julius Lange was exceedingly exasperated and out
of spirits.   Ploug went down the stairs looking like a man
whose hopes had been shattered, and whom the blow had
found unprepared.   His paper had persistently sown distrust of the Prince of Denmark.

The Proclamation was to take place in front of Chris-

tiansborg Castle on December 16th, at 11 o'clock. I was
fetched to it by a student of the same age, the present Bishop
Frederik Nielsen. The latter had made my acquaintance
when a Free-thinker, but fortunately he recognised his errors
only a very few years later, and afterwards the valiant theologian wrote articles and pamphlets against the heretic he
had originally cultivated for holding the same opinions
as himself. There is hardly anyone in Denmark who per-
sists in error; people recognise their mistakes in time, before
they have taken harm to their souls; sometimes, indeed, so
much betimes that they are not even a hindrance to their
worldly career.

The space in front of the Castle was black with people,
most of whom were in a state of no little excitement. Hall,
who was then Prime Minister, stepped out on the balcony
of the castle, grave and upright, and said, first standing with
his back to the Castle, then looking to the right and the left,
these words: " King Frederik VII. is dead. Long live
King Christian IX! "

Then the King came forward. There were loud shouts,
doubtless some cries of " Long live the King," but still more
and louder shouts of: " The Constitution forever! " which
were by no means loyally intended. At a distance, from
the Castle balcony, the different shouts could, of course,
not be distinguished. As the King took them all to be shouts
of acclamation, he bowed politely several times, and as the
shouts continued kissed his hand to right and left. The effect was not what he had intended. His action was not understood as a simple-hearted expression of pure good-will.
People were used to a very different bearing on the part of
their King. With all his faults and foibles, Frederik VII.
was always in manner the Father of his people; always the
graceful superior; head up and shoulders well back, patron-
isingly and affectionately waving his hand: " Thank you,
my children, thank you! And now go home and say ' Good-
morning ' to your wives and children from the King! " One
could not imagine Frederik VII. bowing to the people, much
less kissing his hand to them.

There was a stormy meeting of the Students' Union

that evening.   Vilhelm Rode made the principal speech and
caustically emphasised that it took more than a " Kiss of the
hand and a parade bow " to win the hearts of the Danish
people.   The new dynasty, the head of which had been
abused for years by the National Liberal press, especially
in *The Fatherland,* who had thrown suspicion of German
sympathies on the heir-presumptive, was still so weak that
none of the students thought it necessary to take much notice
of the change of sovereigns that had taken place.   This was
partly because since Frederik VII's time people had been accustomed to indiscriminate free speech concerning the King's
person—it was the fashion and meant nothing, as he was beloved by the body of the people—partly because what had
happened was not regarded as irrevocable.   All depended on
whether the King signed the Constitution, and even the cool-
est and most conservative, who considered that his signing it
would be a fatal misfortune, thought it possible that Christian IX. would be dethroned if he did not.   So it is not difficult to form some idea of how the Hotspurs talked.   The
whole town was in a fever, and it was said that Prince Oscar
was in Scania, ready at the first sign to cross the Sound and
allow himself to be proclaimed King on behalf of Charles
XV.   Men with Scandinavian sympathies hoped for this solution, by means of which the three kingdoms would have been
united without a blow being struck.

In the middle of the meeting, there arrived a message
from Crone, the Head of Police, which was delivered verbally in this incredibly irregular form—that the Head of
Police was as good a Scandinavian as anyone, but he begged
the students for their own sakes to refrain from any
kind of street disturbance that would oblige him to interfere.

I, who had stood on the open space in front of the
Castle, lost in the crowd, and in the evening at the meeting
of the students was auditor to the passionate utterances let
fall there, felt my mood violently swayed, but was altogether
undecided with regard to the political question, the compass
of which I could not fully perceive.   I felt anxious as to
what the attitude of foreign powers would be in the event

of the signing of the Constitution. Old C. N. David had said in his own home that if the matter should depend on him, which, however, he hoped it would not, he would not permit the signing of the Constitution, were he the only man in Denmark of that way of thinking, since by so doing we should lose our guarantee of existence, and get two enemies instead of one, Russia as well as Germany.

The same evening I wrote down: " It is under such circumstances as these that one realises how difficult it is to lead a really ethical existence. I am not far-sighted enough to perceive what would be the results of that which to me seems desirable, and one cannot conscientiously mix one's self up in what one does not understand. Nevertheless, as I stood in the square in front of the Castle, I was so excited that I even detected in myself an inclination to come forward as a political speaker, greenhorn though I be."

XIII.

On the 18th of November, the fever in the town was at its height. From early in the morning the space in front of the Castle was crowded with people. Orla Lehmann, a Minister at the time, came out of the Castle, made his way through the crowd, and shouted again and again, first to one side, then to the other:

" He has signed!   He has signed! "

He did not say: " The King."

The people now endured seven weeks of uninterrupted change and kaleidoscopic alteration of the political situation. Relations with all foreign powers, and even with Sweden and Norway, presented a different aspect to the Danish public every week. Sweden's withdrawal created a very bitter impression; the public had been induced to believe that an alliance was concluded. Then followed the " pressure " in Copenhagen by the emissaries of all the Powers, to induce the Government to recall the November Constitution, then the Czar's letter to the Duke of Augustenborg, finally the occupation of Holstein by German troops, with all the censure and disgrace that the Danish army had to endure, for Hol-

tein was evacuated without a blow being struck, and the
Duke, to the accompaniment of scorn and derision heaped
on the Danes, was proclaimed in all the towns of Holstein.

On Christmas Eve came tidings of the convocation of
the Senate, simultaneously with a change of Ministry which
placed Monrad at the head of the country, and in connection
with this a rumour that all young men of twenty-one were
to be called out at once. This last proved to be incorrect,
and the minds of the young men alternated between com-
posure at the prospect of war and an enthusiastic desire for
war, and a belief that there would be no war at all. The
first few days in January, building on the rumour that the
last note from England had promised help in the event of
the Eider being passed, people began to hope that the war
might be avoided, and pinned their faith to Monrad's
dictatorship.

Frederik Nutzhorn, who did not believe there would be
war, started on a visit to Rome; Jens Paludan-Müller, who
had been called out, was quartered at Rendsborg until the
German troops marched in; Julius Lange, who, as he had
just become engaged, did not wish to see his work interrupted
and his future prospects delayed by the war, had gone to
Eslingen, where he had originally made the acquaintance of
his fiancée. Under these circumstances, as a twenty-one-year-
old student who had completed his university studies, I was
anxious to get my examination over as quickly as possible.
At the end of 1863 I wrote to my teacher, Professor Bröchner, who had promised me a short philosophical summary
as a preparation for the University test: " I shall sit under
conjunction of all the most unfavourable circumstances possible, since for more than a month my head has been so full
of the events of the day that I have been able neither to read
nor think, while the time of the examination itself promises
to be still more disquiet. Still, I dare not draw back, as
I should then risk—which may possibly happen in any
case—being hindered from my examination by being called
out by the conscription and perhaps come to lie in my
grave as *Studiosus* instead of *candidatus magisterii,* which

latter looks infinitely more impressive and is more satisfying to a man as greedy of honour as Your respectful and heartily affectionate, etc."

XIV.

Shortly before, I had paid my first visit to Professor Rasmus Nielsen. He was exceedingly agreeable, recognised me, whom perhaps he remembered examining, and accorded me a whole hour's conversation. He was, as always, alert and fiery, not in the least blasé, but with a slight suggestion of charlatanism about him. His conversation was as lively and disconnected as his lectures; there was a charm in the clear glance of his green eyes, a look of genius about his face. He talked for a long time about Herbart, whose Æsthetics, for that matter, he betrayed little knowledge of, then of Hegel, Heiberg, and Kierkegaard. To my intense surprise, he opened up a prospect, conflicting with the opinions he had publicly advocated, that Science, " when analyses had been carried far enough," might come to prove the possibility of miracles. This was an offence against my most sacred convictions.

Nielsen had recently, from the cathedra, announced his renunciation of the Kierkegaard standpoint he had so long maintained, in the phrase: " The Kierkegaard theory is impracticable"; he had, perhaps influenced somewhat by the Queen Dowager, who about that time frequently invited him to meet Grundtvig, drawn nearer to Grundtvigian ways of thinking,—as Bröchner sarcastically remarked about him: " The farther from Kierkegaard, the nearer to the Queen Dowager."

In the midst of my final preparations for the examination, I wrestled, as was my wont, with my attempts to come to a clear understanding over Duty and Life, and was startled by the indescribable irony in the word by which I was accustomed to interpret my ethically religious endeavours,— *Himmelspræt.*[1]

---

[1] Word implying one who attempts to spring up to Heaven, and of course falls miserably to earth again. The word, in ordinary conversation, is applied to anyone tossed in a blanket.

I handed in, then, my request to be allowed to sit for my Master of Arts examination; the indefatigable Bröchner had already mentioned the matter to the Dean of the University, who understood the examinee's reasons for haste. But the University moved so slowly that it was some weeks before I received the special paper set me, which, to my horror, ran as follows: "Determine the correlation between the pathetic and the symbolic in general, in order by that means to elucidate the contrast between Shakespeare's tragedies and Dante's *Divina Commedia,* together with the possible errors into which one might fall through a one-sided preponderance of either of these two elements."

This paper, which had been set by R. Nielsen, is characteristic of the purely speculative manner, indifferent to all study of history, in which Æsthetics were at that time pursued in Copenhagen. It was, moreover, worded with unpardonable carelessness; it was impossible to tell from it what was to be understood by the correlation on which it was based, and which was assumed to be a given conclusion. Even so speculative a thinker as Frederik Paludan-Müller called the question absolutely meaningless. It looked as though its author had imagined Shakespeare's dramas and Dante's epic were produced by a kind of artistic commingling of pathetic with symbolic elements, and as though he wished to call attention to the danger of reversing the correct proportions, for instance, by the symbolic obtaining the preponderance in tragedy, or pathos in the epopee, or to the danger of exaggerating these proportions, until there was too much tragic pathos, or too much epic symbolism. But a scientific definition of the expressions used was altogether lacking, and I had to devote a whole chapter to the examination of the meaning of the problem proposed to me.

The essay, for the writing of which I was allowed six weeks, was handed in, 188 folio pages long, at the right time. By reason of the sheer foolishness of the question, it was never published.

In a postscript, I wrote: "I beg my honoured examiners to remember the time during which this treatise was written, a time more eventful than any other young men can have been through, and during which I, for my part, have for days at a time been unable to work, and should have been ashamed if I could have done so."

In explanation of this statement, the following jottings, written down at the time on a sheet of paper:

Sunday, Jan. 17th. Received letter telling me I may fetch my leading question to-morrow at 5 o'clock.

Monday, Feb. 1st. Heard to-day that the Germans have passed the Eider and that the first shots have been exchanged.

Saturday, Feb. 6th. Received to-day the terrible, incomprehensible, but only too certain news that the Danevirke has been abandoned without a blow being struck. This is indescribable, overwhelming.

Thursday, Feb. 28th. We may, unfortunately, assume it as certain that my dear friend Jens Paludan-Müller fell at Overs̈o on Feb. 5th.

Feb. 28th. Heard definitely to-day.—At half-past one this night finished my essay.

XV.

I thought about this time of nothing but my desire to become a competent soldier of my country. There was nothing I wanted more, but I felt physically very weak. When the first news of the battles of Midsunde and Bustrup arrived, I was very strongly inclined to follow Julius Lange to the Reserve Officers' School. When tidings came of the abandonment of the Danevirke my enthusiasm cooled; it was as though I foresaw how little prospect of success there was. Still, I was less melancholy than Lange at the thought of going to the war. I was single, and delighted at the thought of going straight from the examination-table into a camp life, and from a book-mad student to become a lieutenant. I was influenced most by the prospect of seeing Lange every day at the Officers' School, and on the field. But my comrades explained to me that even if Lange and I came out of the School at the same time, it did not follow that we should be in the same division, and that the thing, moreover, that was wanted in an officer, was entire self-dependence. They also pointed out to me the improbability of my being able to do the least good, or having the slightest likelihood in front of me of doing anything but quickly find myself in hospital. I did not really think myself that I should be able to stand the fatigue, as the pupils of the military academy went over to the army with an equipment that I could scarcely have carried. I could not possibly suppose that the conscription would select me as a private, on account of my fragile build; but like all the rest, I was expecting every day a general ordering out of the fit men of my age.

All this time I worked with might and main at the development of my physical strength and accomplishments. I went every day to fencing practice, likewise to cavalry sword practice; I took lessons in the use of the bayonet, and I took part every afternoon in the shooting practices conducted by the officers—with the old muzzle-loaders which were the army weapons at the time. I was very delighted one day when Mr. Hagemeister, the fencing-master, one of the many splendid old Holstein non-commissioned officers holding the rank of lieutenant, said I was "A smart fencer."

XVI.

Meanwhile, the examination was taking its course. As real curiosities, I here reproduce the questions set me. The three to be replied to in writing were:

1. To what extent can poetry be called the ideal History?
2. In what manner may the philosophical ideas of Spinoza and Fichte lead to a want of appreciation of the idea of beauty?
3. In what relation does the comic stand to its limitations and its various contrasts?

The three questions which were to be replied to in lectures before the University ran as follows:

1. Show, through poems in our literature, to what extent poetry may venture to set itself the task of presenting the Idea in a form coinciding with the philosophical understanding of it?
2. Point out the special contributions to a philosophical definition of the Idea made by Æsthetics in particular.
3. What are the merits and defects of Schiller's tragedies?

These questions, in conjunction with the main question,

may well be designated a piece of contemporary history; they depict exactly both the Science of the time and the peculiar philosophical language it adopted. Hardly more than one, or at most two, of them could one imagine set to-day.

After the final (and best) lecture, on Schiller, which was given at six hours' notice on April 25th, the judges, Hauch, Nielsen and Bröchner, deliberated for about ten minutes, then called in the auditors and R. Nielsen read aloud the following verdict: " The candidate, in his long essay, in the shorter written tests, and in his oral lectures, has manifested such knowledge of his subject, such intellectual maturity, and such originality in the treatment of his themes, that we have on that account unanimously awarded him the mark: *admissus cum laude præcipua.*"

XVII.

The unusually favourable result of this examination attracted the attention of academical and other circles towards me. The mark *admissus cum præcipua laude* had only very rarely been given before. Hauch expressed his satisfaction at home in no measured terms. His wife stopped my grandfather in the street and informed him that his grandson was the cleverest and best-read young man that her husband had come across during his University experience. When I went to the old poet after the examination to thank him, he said to me (these were his very words) : "I am an old man and must die soon; you must be my successor at the University; I shall say so unreservedly; indeed, I will even say it on my death-bed." Strangely enough, he did say it and record it on his death-bed seven years later, exactly as he had promised to do.

In Bröchner's house, too, there was a great deal said about my becoming a professor. I myself was despondent about it; I thought only of the war, only wished to be fit for a soldier. Hauch was pleased at my wanting to be a soldier. "It is fine of you, if you can only stand it." When Hauch heard for certain that I was only 22 years old (he himself was 73), he started up in his chair and said:

" Why, it is incredible that at your age you can have got so far." Rasmus Nielsen was the only one of the professors who did not entertain me with the discussion of my future academic prospects; but he it was who gave me the highest praise:

" According to our unanimous opinions," said he, " you are the foremost of all the young men."

I was only the more determined not to let myself be buried alive in the flower of my youth by accepting professorship before I had been able to live and breathe freely.—I might have spared myself any anxiety.

XVIII.

A few days later, on May 10th, a month's armistice was proclaimed, which was generally construed as a preliminary to peace, if this could be attained under possible conditions. It was said, and soon confirmed, that at the Conference of London, Denmark had been offered North Slesvig. Most unfortunately, Denmark refused the offer. On June 26th, the war broke out again; two days later Alsen was lost. When the young men were called up to the officers' board for conscription, " being too slight of build," I was deferred till next year. Were the guerilla war which was talked about to break out, I was determined all the same to take my part in it.

But the Bluhme-David Ministry succeeded to Monrad's, and concluded the oppressive peace.

I was very far from regarding this peace as final; for that, I was too inexperienced. I correctly foresaw that before very long the state of affairs in Europe would give rise to other wars, but I incorrectly concluded therefrom that another fight for Slesvig, or in any case, its restoration to Denmark, would result from them.

In the meantime peace, discouraging, disheartening though it was, opened up possibilities of further undisturbed study, fresh absorption in scientific occupations.

When, after the termination of my University studies, I had to think of earning my own living, I not only, as before, gave private lessons, but I gave lectures, first to a circle before whom I lectured on Northern and Greek mythology, then to another, in David's house, to whom I unfolded the inner history of modern literature to interested listeners, amongst them several beautiful young girls.   I finally engaged myself to my old Arithmetic master as teacher of Danish in his course for National school-mistresses.   I found the work horribly dull, but there was one racy thing about it, namely, that I, the master, was three years younger than the youngest of my pupils; these latter were obliged to be at least 25, and consequently even at their youngest were quite old in my eyes.

But there were many much older women amongst them, one even, a priest or schoolmaster's widow, of over fifty, a poor thing who had to begin——at her age!——from the very beginning, though she was anything but gifted.   It was not quite easy for a master without a single hair on his face to make himself respected.   But I succeeded, my pupils being so well-behaved.

It was an exciting moment when these pupils of mine went up for their teacher's examination, I being present as auditor.

I continued to teach this course until the Autumn of 1868.   When I left, I was gratified by one of the ladies rising and, in a little speech, thanking me for the good instruction I had given.

XIX.

Meanwhile, I pursued my studies with ardour and enjoyment, read a very great deal of *belles-lettres,* and continued to work at German philosophy, inasmuch as I now, though without special profit, plunged into a study of Trendelenburg.   My thoughts were very much more stimulated by Gabriel Sibbern, on account of his consistent scepticism.   It was just about this time that I made his acquaintance.   Old before his time, bald at forty, tormented with gout, although he had always lived a most abstemious life, Gabriel Sibbern, with his serene face, clever eyes and independent thoughts, was an emancipating phenomenon.   He had divested himself of all Danish prejudices. " There is still a great deal of phlogiston in our philosophy," he used to say sometimes.

I had long been anxious to come to a clear scientific understanding of the musical elements in speech. I had busied myself a great deal with metrical art. Brücke's *Inquiries* were not yet in existence, but I was fascinated by Apel's attempt to make use of notes (crotchets, quavers, dotted quavers, and semi-quavers) as metrical signs, and by J. L. Heiberg's attempt to apply this system to Danish verse. But the system was too arbitrary for anything to be built up upon it. And I then made up my mind, in order better to understand the nature of verse, to begin at once to familiarise myself with the theory of music, which seemed to promise the opening out of fresh horizons in the interpretation of the harmonies of language.

With the assistance of a young musician, later the well-known composer and Concert Director, Victor Bendix, I plunged into the mysteries of thorough-bass, and went so far as to write out the entire theory of harmonics. I learnt to express myself in the barbaric language of music, to speak of minor scales in fifths, to understand what was meant by enharmonic ambiguity. I studied voice modulation, permissible and non-permissible octaves; but I did not find what I hoped. I composed a few short tunes, which I myself thought very pretty, but which my young master made great fun of, and with good reason. One evening, when he was in very high spirits, he parodied one of them at the piano in front of a large party of people. It was a disconcerting moment for the composer of the tune.

A connection between metrical art and thorough-bass was not discoverable. Neither were there any unbreakable laws governing thorough-bass. The unversed person believes that in harmonics he will find quite definite rules which must not be transgressed. But again and again he discovers that what is, as a general rule, forbidden, is nevertheless, under certain circumstances, quite permissible.

Thus he learns that in music there is no rule binding on genius. And perhaps he asks himself whether, in other domains, there are rules which are binding on genius.

XX.

I had lived so little with Nature. The Spring of 1865, the first Spring I had spent in the country—although quite near to Copenhagen—meant to me rich impressions of nature that I never forgot, a long chain of the most exquisite Spring memories. I understood as I had never done before the inborn affection felt by every human being for the virgin, the fresh, the untouched, the not quite full-blown, just as it is about to pass over into its maturity. It was in the latter half of May. I was looking for anemones and violets, which had not yet gone to seed. The budding beech foliage, the silver poplar with its shining leaves, the maple with its blossoms, stirred me, filled me with Spring rapture. I could lie long in the woods with my gaze fastened on a light-green branch with the sun shining through it, and, as if stirred by the wind, lighted up from different sides, and floating and flashing as if coated with silver. I saw the empty husks fall by the hundred before the wind. I followed up the streams in the wood to their sources. For a while a rivulet oozed slowly along. Then came a little fall, and it began to speak, to gurgle and murmur; but only at this one place, and here it seemed to me to be like a young man or woman of twenty. Now that I, who in my boyhood's days had gone for botanical excursions with my master and schoolfellows, absorbed myself in every plant, from greatest to least, without wishing to arrange or classify any, it seemed as though an infinite wisdom in Nature were being revealed to me for the first time.

As near to Copenhagen as Söndermarken, stood the beech, with its curly leaves and black velvet buds in their silk jackets. In the gardens of Frederiksberg Avenue, the elder exhaled its fragrance, but was soon over; the hawthorn sprang out in all its splendour. I was struck by the loveliness of the chestnut blooms. When the blossom on the cherry-trees had withered, the lilac was out, and the apple and pear-trees paraded their gala dress.

It interested me to notice how the colour sometimes indicated the shape, sometimes produced designs quite inde-

pendently of it.   I loitered in gardens to feast my eyes on the
charming grouping of the rhubarb leaves no less than on the
exuberance of their flowers, and the leaves of the scorzonera
attracted my attention, because they all grew in one plane, but
swung about like lances.

And as my habit was, I philosophised over what I saw
and had made my own, and I strove to understand in what
beauty consisted.   I considered the relations between beauty
and life; why was it that artificial flowers and the imitation of
a nightingale's song were so far behind their originals in
beauty?   What was the difference between the beauty of the
real, the artificial and the painted flower?   Might not Herbart's Æsthetics be wrong, in their theory of form?   The
form itself might be the same in Nature and the imitation,
in the rose made of velvet and the rose growing in the garden.   And I reflected on the connection between the beauty
of the species and that of the individual.   Whether a lily
be a beautiful flower, I can say without ever having seen
lilies before, but whether it be a beautiful lily, I cannot.   The
individual can only be termed beautiful when more like than
unlike to the ideal of the species.   And I mused over the
translation of the idea of beauty into actions and intellectual
conditions.   Was not the death of Socrates more beautiful
than his preservation of Alcibiades' life in battle?—though
this was none the less a beautiful act.

XXI.

In the month of July I started on a walking tour through
Jutland, with the scenery of which province I had not hitherto been acquainted; travelled also occasionally by the old
stage-coaches, found myself at Skanderborg, which, for me,
was surrounded by the halo of mediæval romance; wandered
to Silkeborg, entering into conversation with no end of people,
peasants, peasant boys, and pretty little peasant girls, whose
speech was not always easy to understand.   I studied their
Juttish, and laughed heartily at their keen wit.   The country inns were often over-full, so that I was obliged to sleep
on the floor; my wanderings were often somewhat exhaust-

ing, as there were constant showers, and the night rain had
soaked the roads.   I drove in a peasant's cart to Mariager to
visit my friend Emil Petersen, who was in the office of the
district judge of that place, making his home with his brother-
in-law and his very pretty sister, and I stayed for a few days
with him.   Here I became acquainted with a little out-of-the-
world Danish town.   The priest and his wife were an interesting and extraordinary couple.   The priest, the before-men-
tioned Pastor Ussing, a little, nervous, intelligent and un-
worldly man, was a pious dreamer, whose religion was entirely rationalistic.   Renan's recently published *Life of Jesus*
was so far from shocking him that the book seemed to him
in all essentials to be on the right track.   He had lived in the
Danish West Indies, and there he had become acquainted
with his wife, a lady with social triumphs behind her, whose
charms he never wearied of admiring.   The mere way in
which she placed her hat upon her head, or threw a
shawl round her shoulders, could make him fall into ecstasies,
even though he only expressed his delight in her in half-face-
tious terms.   This couple showed me the most cordial
kindness; to their unpractised, provincial eyes, I seemed to
be a typical young man of the world, and they amazed
me with the way in which they took it for granted that I led
the dances at every ball, was a lion in society, etc.   I was reminded of the student's words in Hostrup's vaudeville
" Goodness!   How innocent they must be to think *me* a
dandy! " and vainly assured them that I lived an exceedingly
unnoticed life in Copenhagen, and had never opened a ball in
my life.

The priest asked us two young men to go and hear his
Sunday sermon, and promised that we should be pleased with
it.   We went to church somewhat expectant, and the sermon
was certainly a most unusual one.   It was delivered with
great rapture, after the priest had bent his head in his hands
for a time in silent reflection.   With great earnestness he addressed himself to his congregation and demanded, after having put before them some of the cures in the New Testament,
generally extolled as miracles, whether they dared maintain
that these so-called miracles could not have taken place ac-

cording to Nature's laws.   And when he impressively called
out: " Darest thou, with thy limited human intelligence,
say, ' This cannot happen naturally? ' " it was in the same
tone and style in which another priest would have shouted
out: " Darest thou, with thy limited human intelligence,
deny the miracle? "   The peasants, who, no doubt, understood his words quite in this latter sense, did not understand
in the least the difference and the contrast, but judged much
the same as a dog to whom one might talk angrily with caress-
ing words or caressingly with abusive words, simply from the
speaker's tone; and both his tone and facial expression were
ecstatic.   They perceived no heresy and felt themselves no
less edified by the address than did the two young Copenhagen
graduates.

XXII.

My first newspaper articles were printed in *The Fatherland* and the *Illustrated Times;* the very first was a notice of
Paludan-Müller's *Fountain of Youth,* in which I had com-
pressed matter for three or four lectures; a commissioned
article on Dante was about the next, but this was of no
value.   But it was a great event to see one's name printed in
a newspaper for the first time, and my mother saw it not without emotion.

About this time Henrik Ibsen's first books fell into my
hands and attracted my attention towards this rising poet,
who, among the leading Danish critics, encountered a reser-
vation of appreciation that scarcely concealed ill-will.   From
Norway I procured Ibsen's oldest dramas, which had appeared there.

Frederik Algreen-Ussing asked me to contribute to a
large biographical dictionary, which he had for a long time
been planning and preparing, and which he had just concluded a contract for with the largest Danish publishing firm
of the time.   A young man who hated the August Association and all its deeds could not fail to feel scruples about engaging in any collaboration with its founder.   But Algreen-
Ussing knew how to vanquish all such scruples, inasmuch as
he waived all rights of censorship, and left it to each author

to write as he liked upon his own responsibility. And he was perfectly loyal to his promise. Moreover, the question here was one of literature only, and not politics.

As the Danish authors were to be dealt with in alphabetical order, the article that had to be set about at once was an account of the only Danish poet whose name began with *Aa*. Thus it was that Emil Aarestrup came to be the first Danish poet of the past of whom I chanced to write. I heard of the existence of a collection of unprinted letters from Aarestrup to his friend Petersen, the grocer, which were of very great advantage to my essay. A visit that I paid to the widow of the poet, on the other hand, led to no result whatever. It was strange to meet the lady so enthusiastically sung by Aarestrup in his young days, as a sulky and suspicious old woman without a trace of former beauty, who declared that she had no letters from her husband, and could not give me any information about him. It was only a generation later that his letters to her came into my hands.

In September, 1865, the article on Aarestrup was finished. It was intended to be quickly followed up by others on the remaining Danish authors in A. But it was the only one that was written, for Algreen-Ussing's apparently so well planned undertaking was suddenly brought to a standstill. The proprietors of the National Liberal papers declared, as soon as they heard of the plan, that they would not on any account agree to its being carried out by a man who took up such a "reactionary" position in Danish politics as Ussing, and in face of their threat to annihilate the undertaking, the publishers, who were altogether dependent on the attitude of these papers, did not dare to defy them. They explained to Algreen-Ussing that they felt obliged to break their contract with him, but were willing to pay him the compensation agreed upon beforehand for failure to carry it out. He fought long to get his project carried through, but his efforts proving fruitless, he refused, from pride, to accept any indemnity, and was thus compelled to see with bitterness many years' work and an infinite amount of trouble completely wasted. Shortly afterwards he succumbed to an attack of illness.

XXIII.

A young man who plunged into philosophical study at the beginning of the sixties in Denmark, and was specially engrossed by the boundary relations between Philosophy and Religion, could not but come to the conclusion that philosophical life would never flourish in Danish soil until a great intellectual battle had been set on foot, in the course of which conflicting opinions which had never yet been advanced in express terms should be made manifest and wrestle with one another, until it became clear which standpoints were untenable and which could be maintained. Although he cherished warm feelings of affection for both R. Nielsen and Bröchner, the two professors of Philosophy, he could not help hoping for a discussion between them of the fundamental questions which were engaging his mind. As Bröchner's pupil, I said a little of what was in my mind to him, but could not induce him to begin. Then I begged Gabriel Sibbern to furnish a thorough criticism of Nielsen's books, but he declined. I began to doubt whether I should be able to persuade the elder men to speak.

A review in *The Fatherland* of the first part of Nielsen's *Logic of Fundamental Ideas* roused my indignation. It was in diametric opposition to what I considered irrefutably true, and was written in the style, and with the metaphors, which the paper's literary criticisms had brought into fashion, a style that was repugnant to me with its sham poetical, or meaninglessly flat expressions (" Matter is the hammer-stroke that the Ideal requires"—" Spontaneity is like food that has once been eaten ").

In an eleven-page letter to Bröchner I condensed all that I had thought about the philosophical study at the University during these first years of my youth, and proved to him, in the keenest terms I could think of, that it was his duty to the ideas whose spokesman he was, to come forward, and that it would be foolish, in fact wrong, to leave the matter alone. I knew well enough that I was jeopardising my precious friendship with Bröchner by my action, but I was willing to take the risk. I did not expect any immediate result

of my letter, but thought to myself that it should fer-
ment, and some time in the future might bear fruit.   The
outcome of it far exceeded my expectations, inasmuch as
Bröchner was moved by my letter, and not only thanked me
warmly for my daring words, but went without delay to
Nielsen and told him that he intended to write a book on his
entire philosophical activity and significance.   Nielsen took
his announcement with a good grace.

However, as Bröchner immediately afterwards lost his
young wife, and was attacked by the insidious consumption
which ravaged him for ten years, the putting of this resolution
into practice was for several years deferred.

At that I felt that I myself must venture, and, as a beginning, Julius Lange and I, in collaboration, wrote a humorous article on Schmidt's review of *The Logic of Fundamental
Ideas,* which Lange was to get into *The Daily Paper,*
to which he had access.   Three days after the article
was finished Lange came to me and told me that to his dismay
it was—gone.   It was so exactly like him that I was just as
delighted as if he had informed me that the article was
printed.   For some time we hoped that it might be on Lange's
table, for, the day before, he had said:

" I am not of a curious disposition, but I *should* like to
know what there really is on that table! "

However, it had irrevocably disappeared.

I then came forward myself with a number of shorter
articles which I succeeded in getting accepted by the *Fatherland.*   When I entered for the first time Ploug's tiny little
office high up at the top of a house behind Höjbro Place, the
gruff man was not unfriendly.   Surprised at the youthful appearance of the person who walked in, he merely burst out:
" How old are you? "   And to the reply: " Twenty-three
and a half," he said smilingly, " Don't forget the half."

The first article was not printed for months; the next
ones appeared without such long delay.   But Ploug was
somewhat uneasy about the contents of them, and cautiously
remarked that there was " not to be any fun made of Religion," which it could not truthfully be said I had done.
But I had touched upon dogmatic Belief and that was enough.

Later on, Ploug had a notion that, as he once wrote, he had excluded me from the paper as soon as he perceived my mischievous tendency. This was a failure of memory on his part; the reason I left the paper was a different one, and I left of my own accord.

Bold and surly, virile and reliable as Ploug seemed, in things journalistic you could place slight dependence on his word. His dearest friend admitted as much; he gave his consent, and then forgot it, or withdrew it. Nothing is more general, but it made an overweening impression on a beginner like myself, inexperienced in the ways of life.

When Ibsen's *Brand* came out, creating an unusual sensation, I asked Ploug if I might review the book and received a definite " Yes " from him. I then wrote my article, to which I devoted no little pains, but when I took it in it was met by him, to my astonishment, with the remark that the paper had now received another notice from their regular reviewer, whom he " could not very well kick aside." Ploug's promise had apparently been meaningless! I went my way with my article, firmly resolved never to go there again.

From 1866 to 1870 I sought and found acceptance for my newspaper articles (not very numerous) in Bille's *Daily Paper,* which in its turn closed its columns to me after my first series of lectures at the University of Copenhagen. Bille as an editor was pleasant, a little patronising, it is true, but polite and invariably good-tempered. He usually received his contributors reclining at full length on his sofa, his head, with its beautifully cut features, resting against a cushion and his comfortable little stomach protruding. He was scarcely of medium height, quick in everything he did, very clear, a little flat; very eloquent, but taking somewhat external views; pleased at the great favour he enjoyed among the Copenhagen bourgeoisie. If he entered Tivoli's Concert Hall in an evening all the waiter's ran about at once like cockroaches. They hurried to know what he might please to want, and fetched chairs for him and his party. Gay, adaptable, and practised, he was the principal speaker at every social gathering. In his editorial capacity he was courteous, decided, and a man of his word; he did not allow himself to be alarmed by trifles. When Björnson attacked me (I was at the time his youngest contributor), he raised my scale of pay, unsolicited. The first hitch in our relations occurred when in 1869 I published a translation of Mill's *Subjection of Women*. This book roused Bille's exasperation and displeasure. He forbade it to be reviewed in his paper, refused me permission to defend it in the paper, and would not even allow the book in his house, so that his family had to read it clandestinely, as a dangerous and pernicious work.

XXIV.

In the beginning of the year 1866 Ludvig David died suddenly in Rome, of typhoid fever. His sorrowing parents founded in memory of him an exhibition for law-students which bears and perpetuates his name. The first executors of the fund were, in addition to his most intimate friend, two young lawyers named Emil Petersen and Emil Bruun, who had both been friends of his. The latter, who has not previously been mentioned in these pages, was a strikingly handsome and clever young man, remarkable for his calm and superior humour, and exceedingly self-confident and virile. His attitude towards Ludvig David in his early youth had been somewhat that of a protector. Unfortunately he was seriously wounded during the first storming of the Dybböl redoubts by the Germans; a bullet crushed one of the spinal vertebræ; gradually the wound brought on consumption of the lungs and he died young.

Ludvig David's death was a great loss to his friends. It was not only that he took such an affectionate interest in their welfare and happiness, but he had a considerable gift for Mathematics and History, and, from his home training, an understanding of affairs of state which was considerably above that of most people. Peculiarly his own was a combination of keen, disintegrating intelligence, and a tendency towards comprehensive, rounded off, summarising. He had strong public antipathies. In his opinion the years of peace that had followed the first war in Slesvig had had an enervating effect; public speakers and journalists had taken the places of brave men; many a solution of a difficulty, announced at first with enthusiasm, had in course of time petrified into a mere set phrase. He thought many of the leading men among the Liberals superficial and devoid of character, and accused them, with the pitilessness of youth, of mere verbiage. Influenced as he was by Kierkegaard, such a man as Bille was naturally his aversion. He considered —not altogether justly—that Bille cloaked himself in false earnestness.

He himself was profoundly and actively philanthropic, with an impulse—by no means universal—to relieve and help. Society life he hated; to him it was waste of time and a torture to be obliged to figure in a ballroom; he cared very little for his appearance, and was by no means elegant in his dress. He was happy, however, in the unconstrained society of the comrades he cared about, enjoyed a merry chat or a frolicsome party, and in intimate conversation he would reveal his inmost nature with modest unpretension, with good-natured wit, directed against himself as much as against others, and with an understanding and sympathetic eye for his surroundings. His warmest outburst had generally a little touch of mockery or teasing about it, as though he were repeating, half roguishly, the feelings of another, rather than unreservedly expressing his own. But a heartfelt, steadfast look would often come into his beautiful dark eyes.

XXV.

His death left a great void in his home. His old father said to me one day:

" Strange how one ends as one begins! I have written no verses since my early youth, and now I have written a poem on my grief for Ludvig. I will read it to you."

There was an Art and Industrial Exhibition in Stockholm, that Summer, which C. N. David was anxious to see. As he did not care to go alone, he took me in his son's place. It was my first journey to a foreign capital, and as such both enjoyable and profitable. I no longer, it is true, had

the same intense boyish impressionability as when I was
in Sweden for the first time, seven years before. The
most trifling thing then had been an experience. In Göteborg I had stayed with a friend of my mother's, whose
twelve-year-old daughter, Bluma Alida, a wondrously charming little maiden, had jokingly been destined by the two mothers for my bride from the child's very birth. And at that
time I had assimilated every impression of people or scenery
with a voracious appetite which rendered these impressions
ineffaceable all my life long. That Summer month, my fancy
had transformed every meeting with a young girl into an adventure and fixed every landscape on my mental retina with
an affection such as the landscape painter generally only feels
for a place where he is specially at home. Then I had
shared for a whole month Göteborg family and social life.
Now I was merely travelling as a tourist, and as the companion of a highly respected old man.

I was less entranced at Stockholm by the Industrial Exhibition than by the National Museum and the Royal Theatre, where the lovely Hyasser captivated me by her beauty
and the keen energy of her acting. I became exceedingly
fond of Stockholm, this most beautifully situated of the
Northern capitals, and saw, with reverence, the places associated with the name of Bellman. I also accompanied my old
friend to Ulriksdal, where the Swedish Queen Dowager expected him in audience. More than an hour before we
reached the Castle he threw away his cigar.

" I am an old courtier," he remarked. He had always
been intimately associated with the Danish Royal family;
for a long time the Crown Prince used to go regularly to his
flat in Queen's Crossway Street, to be instructed by him in political economy. He was consequently used to Court
ceremonial.

Beautiful were those Summer days, lovely the light
nights in Stockholm.

One recollection from these weeks is associated with a
night when the sky was overcast. I had wandered round
the town, before retiring to rest, and somewhere, in a large
square, slipping my hand in my pocket, and feeling it full of

bits of paper, could not remember how they got there, and threw them away. When I was nearly back at the hotel it flashed upon me that it had been small Swedish notes—all the money that I had changed for my stay in Stockholm—that I had been carrying loose in my pocket and had so thoughtlessly thrown away. With a great deal of trouble, I found the square again, but of course not a sign of the riches that in unpardonable forgetfulness I had scattered to the winds. I was obliged to borrow six Rigsdaler (a sum of a little over thirteen shillings) from my old protector. That my requirements were modest is proved by the fact that this sum sufficed.

The Danish Ambassador was absent from Stockholm just at this time, and the Chargé d'Affaires at the Legation had to receive the Danish ex-Minister in his stead. He was very attentive to us, and took the travellers everywhere where C. N. David wished his arrival to be made known. He himself, however, was a most unfortunate specimen of Danish diplomacy, a man disintegrated by hideous debauchery, of coarse conversation, and disposition so brutal that he kicked little children aside with his foot when they got in front of him in the street. Abnormities of too great irregularity brought about, not long afterwards, his dismissal and his banishment to a little Danish island.

This man gave a large dinner-party in honour of the Danish ex-Minister, to which, amongst others, all the Swedish and Norwegian Ministers in Stockholm were invited. It was held at Hasselbakken,[1] and the arrangements were magnificent. But what highly astonished me, and was in reality most out of keeping in such a circle, was the tone that the conversation at table gradually assumed, and especially the obscenity of the subjects of conversation. It was not, however, the Ministers and Diplomats present, but a Danish roué, a professor of Physics, who gave this turn to the talk. He related anecdotes that would have made a sailor blush. Neither Count Manderström, nor any of the other Ministers, neither Malmgren, nor the dignified and handsome Norwegian Minister Bretteville, seemed to be offended. Mander-

[1] A favourite outdoor pleasure resort at Stockholm.

ström's expression, however, changed very noticeably when the professor ventured to make some pointed insinuations regarding the Swedish attitude, and his personal attitude in particular, previous to the Dano-German war and during its course. He suddenly pretended not to understand, and changed the subject of conversation.

It produced an extremely painful impression upon me that not only the Danish Chargé d'Affaires, but apparently several of these fine gentlemen, had determined on the additional amusement of making me drunk. Everybody at table vied one with the other to drink my health, and they informed me that etiquette demanded I should each time empty my glass to the bottom; the contrary would be a breach of good form. As I very quickly saw through their intention, I escaped from the difficulty by asking the waiter to bring me a very small glass. By emptying this I could, without my manners being affected, hold my own against them all.

But,—almost for the first time in my life,—when the company rose from table I felt that I had been in exceedingly bad company, and a disgust for the nominally highest circles, who were so little capable of acting in accordance with the reputation they enjoyed, and the polish imputed to them, remained with me for many years to come.

FIRST LONG SOJOURN ABROAD

I.

I HAD wished for years to see Paris, the city that roused my most devout feelings. As a youth I had felt a kind of reverent awe for the French Revolution, which represented to me the beginning of human conditions for all those who were not of the favoured among men,—and Paris was the city of the Revolution. Moreover, it was the city of Napoleon, the only ruler since Cæsar who had seriously fascinated me, though my feelings for him changed so much that now admiration, now aversion, got the upper hand. And Paris was the city, too, of the old culture, the city of Julian the Apostate, the city of the middle ages, that Victor Hugo had portrayed in *Notre Dame de Paris*—the first book I had read in French, difficult though it was with its many peculiar expressions for Gothic arches and buttresses—and it was the city where Alfred de Musset had written his poems and where Delacroix had painted. The Louvre and the Luxembourg, the Théâtre Français and the Gymnase were immense treasuries that tempted me. In the Autumn of 1866, when Gabriel Sibbern started to Paris, somewhat before I myself could get away, my last words to him: " Till we meet again in the Holy City! " were by no means a jest.

II.

Before I could start, I had to finish the pamphlet which, with Sibbern's help, I had written against Nielsen's adjustment of the split between Protestant orthodoxy and the scientific view of the universe, and which I had called *Dualism*

163

in our Modern Philosophy. I was not troubled with any misgivings as to how I should get the book published. As long ago as 1864 a polite, smiling, kindly man, who introduced himself to me as Frederik Hegel, the bookseller, had knocked at the door of my little room and asked me to let him print the essay which I had written for my Master of Arts examination, and if possible he would also like the paper which had won the University gold medal; and in fact, anything else I might wish published. To my amazed reply that those essays were not worth publishing, and that in general I did not consider what I wrote sufficiently mature for publication, Hegel had first suggested that I should leave that question to the publisher, and then, when he saw that my refusal was honestly meant, had simply asked me to take my work to him when I myself considered that the moment had arrived. On this occasion, as on many others, the acute and daring publisher gave proof of the *flair* which made him the greatest in the North. He accepted the little book without raising any difficulties, merely remarking that it would have to be spread out a little in the printing, that it might not look too thin. Even before the pamphlet was mentioned in the Press, its author was on his way to foreign parts.

III.

On one of the first days of November, I journeyed, in a tremendous storm, to Lübeck, the characteristic buildings of which (the Church of Mary, the Exchange, the Town-hall), together with the remains of the old fortifications, aroused my keen interest. In this Hanse town, with its strongly individual stamp, I found myself carried back three hundred years.

I was amazed at the slave-like dress of the workmen, the pointed hats of the girls, and the wood pavements, which were new to me.

I travelled through Germany with a Portuguese, a little doctor from the University of Coimbra, in whose queer French fifteen was *kouss* and Goethe *Shett*. A practical American, wrapped up in a waterproof, took up three places

to lie down in one evening, pretended to sleep, and never
stirred all night, forcing his inexperienced fellow-travellers to
crowd up into the corners of the carriage, and when the day
broke, chatted with them as pleasantly as if they and he were
the best friends in the world.

At Cologne, where I had stood, reverential, in the noble
forest of pillars in the Cathedral, then afterwards, in my
simplicity, allowed someone to foist a whole case of Eau de
Cologne upon me, I shortened my stay, in my haste to see
Paris. But, having by mistake taken a train which would
necessitate my waiting several hours at Liège, I decided
rather to continue my journey to Brussels and see that city
too. The run through Belgium seemed to me heavenly,
as for a time I happened to be quite alone in my compartment and I walked up and down, intoxicated with the joy of
travelling.

Brussels was the first large French town I saw; it was a
foretaste of Paris, and delighted me.

Never having been out in the world on my own account
before, I was still as inexperienced and awkward as a child.
It was not enough that I had got into the wrong train; I discovered, to my shame, that I had mislaid the key of my box,
which made me think anxiously of the customs officials in
Paris, and I was also so stupid as to ask the boots in the Brussels hotel for "a little room," so that they gave me a miserable little sleeping-place under the roof.

But at night, after I had rambled about the streets of
Brussels, as I sat on a bench somewhere on a broad boulevard, an overwhelming, terrifying, transporting sense of my
solitariness came over me. It seemed to me as though now,
alone in a foreign land, at night time, in this human swarm,
where no one knew me and I knew no one, where no one
would look for me if anything were to happen to me, I was
for the first time thrown entirely on my own resources, and
I recognised in the heavens, with a feeling of reassurance, old
friends among the stars.

With a guide, whom in my ignorance I thought necessary, I saw the sights of the town, and afterwards, for the
first time, saw a French play. So little experience of the

world had I, that, during the interval, I left my overcoat, which I had not given up to the attendant, lying on the seat in the pit, and my neighbour had to explain to me that such great confidence in my fellow-men was out of place.

Everything was new to me, everything fascinated me. I, who only knew " indulgence " from my history lessons at school, saw with keen interest the priest in a Brussels church dispense " *indulgence plénière,*" or, in Flemish, *vollen aflaet.* I was interested in the curious names of the ecclesiastical orders posted up in the churches, marvelled, for instance, at a brotherhood that was called " St. Andrew Avellin, patron saint against apoplexy, epilepsy and sudden death."

In the carriage from Brussels I had for travelling companion a pretty young Belgian girl named Marie Choteau, who was travelling with her father, but talked all the time to her foreign fellow-traveller, and in the course of conversation showed me a Belgian history and a Belgian geography, from which it appeared that Belgium was the centre of the globe, the world's most densely built over, most religious, and at the same time most enlightened country, the one which, in proportion to its size, had the most and largest industries. I gave her some of my bountiful supply of Eau de Cologne.

IV.

The tiring night-journey, with its full four hours' wait at Liège, was all pure enjoyment to me, and in a mood of mild ecstasy, at last, at half-past ten on the morning of November 11th 1866, I made my entry into Paris, and was received cordially by the proprietors of a modest but clean little hotel which is still standing, No. 20 Rue Notre Dame des Victoires, by the proprietors, two simple Lorrainers, François and Müller, to whom Gabriel Sibbern, who was staying there, had announced my arrival. The same morning Sibbern guided my first steps to one of Pasdeloup's great classical popular concerts.

In the evening, in spite of my fatigue after travelling all night, I went to the Théâtre Français for the first time, and there, lost in admiration of the masterly ensemble and the

natural yet passionate acting, with which I had hitherto seen
nothing to compare, I saw Girardin's *Le supplice d'une
femme,* and Beaumarchais' *Le mariage de Figaro,* in one
evening making the acquaintance of such stars as Régnier,
Madame Favart, Coquelin and the Sisters Brohan.

Régnier especially, in his simple dignity, was an unforgettable figure, being surrounded, moreover, in my eyes by
the glory which the well-known little poem of Alfred de
Musset, written to comfort the father's heart, had shed upon
him.   Of the two celebrated sisters, Augustine was all wit,
Madeleine pure beauty and arch, melting grace.

These first days were rich days to me, and as they did
not leave me any time for thinking over what I had seen, my
impressions overwhelmed me at night, till sometimes I could
not sleep for sheer happiness.   This, to me, was happiness,
an uninterrupted garnering of intellectual wealth in association with objects that all appealed to my sympathies, and I
wrote home: " To be here, young, healthy, with alert senses,
keen eyes and good ears, with all the curiosity, eagerness
to know, love of learning, and susceptibility to every impression, that is youth's own prerogative, and to have no wor-
ries about home, all that is so great a happiness that I am
sometimes tempted, like Polycrates, to fling the handsome
ring I had from Christian Richardt in the gutter."

For the rest, I was too fond of characteristic architecture to feel attracted by the building art displayed in the
long, regular streets of Napoleon III., and too permeated
with national prejudices to be able at once to appreciate
French sculpture.   I was justified in feeling repelled by many
empty allegorical pieces on public monuments, but during the
first weeks I lacked perception for such good sculpture as is
to be found in the *foyer* of the Théâtre Français.   " You
feel at every step," I wrote immediately after my arrival,
" that France has never had a Thorwaldsen, and that Denmark possesses an indescribable treasure in him.   We are and
remain, in three or four directions, the first nation in Europe.
This is pure and simple truth."

To my youthful ignorance it was the truth, but it hardly
remained such after the first month.

Being anxious to see as much as possible and not let anything of interest escape me, I went late to bed, and yet got up early, and tried to regulate my time, as one does a blanket that is too short.

I was immensely interested in the art treasures from all over the world collected in the Louvre. Every single morning, after eating my modest breakfast at a *crêmerie* near the château, I paid my vows in the *Salon carré* and then absorbed myself in the other halls. The gallery of the Louvre was the one to which I owe my initiation. Before, I had seen hardly any Italian art in the original, and no French at all. In Copenhagen I had been able to worship all the Dutch masters. Leonardo and the Venetians spoke to me here for the first time. French painting and sculpture, Puget and Houdon, Clouet and Delacroix, and the French art that was modern then, I learnt for the first time to love and appreciate at the Luxembourg.

I relished these works of art, and the old-time art of the Greeks and Egyptians which the Museum of the Louvre contained, in a mild intoxication of delight.

And I inbreathed Paris into my soul. When on the broad, handsome Place de la Concorde, I saw at the same time, with my bodily eyes, the beautifully impressive obelisk, and in my mind's eye the scaffold on which the royal pair met with their death in the Revolution; when in the Latin quarter I went upstairs to the house in which Charlotte Corday murdered Marat, or when, in the highest storey of the Louvre, I gazed at the little gray coat from Marengo and the three-cornered hat, or from the Arc de Triomphe let my glance roam over the city, the life that pulsated through my veins seemed stimulated tenfold by sight and visions.

Yet it was not only the city of Paris, its appearance, its art gems, that I eagerly made my own, and with them much that intellectually belonged to Italy or the Netherlands; it was French culture, the best that the French nature contains, the fragrance of her choicest flowers, that I inhaled.

And while thus for the first time learning to know French people, and French intellectual life, I was unexpectedly admitted to constant association with men and women of the other leading Romance races, Italians, Spaniards, Portuguese, Brazilians.

Bröchner had given me a letter of introduction to Costanza Testa, a friend of his youth, now married to Count Oreste Blanchetti and living in Paris, with her somewhat older sister Virginia, a kind-hearted and amiable woman of the world. The latter had married in Brazil, as her second husband, the Italian banker Pagella, and to their house came, not only Italians and other European Southerners, but members of the South American colony.

So warm a reception as I met with from the two sisters and their husbands I had never had anywhere before. After I had known the two families one hour, these people treated me as though I were their intimate friend; Costanza's younger brother, they called me. I had a seat in their carriage every day, when the ladies drove out in the Bois de Boulogne; they never had a box at the Italian opera, where Adelina Patti's first notes were delighting her countrymen, without sending me a seat. They expected me every evening, however late it often might be when I came from the theatre, in their drawing-room, where, according to the custom of their country, they always received the same circle of friends.

I was sincerely attached to the two sisters, and felt myself at ease in their house, although the conversation there was chiefly carried on in a language of which I understood but little, since French was spoken only on my account. The only shadow over my pleasure at spending my evenings in the Rue Valois du Roule was the fact that this necessitated my missing some acts at the Théâtre Français, for which the Danish Minister, through the Embassy, had procured me a free pass. Certainly no Dane was ever made so happy by the favour. They were enraptured hours that I spent evening after evening in the French national theatre, where I became thoroughly acquainted with the modern, as well as the classical, dramatic repertoire,—an acquaintance which was further fortified during my long stay in Paris in 1870.

I enjoyed the moderation of the best actors, their restraint, and subordination of self to the rôle and the general

effect.   It is true that the word genius could only be applied to a very few of the actors, and at that time I saw none
who, in my opinion, could be compared with the great representatives of the Danish stage, such as Michael Wiehe,
Johanne Luise Heiberg, or Phister.   But I perceived at once
that the mannerisms of these latter would not be tolerated
here for a moment; here, under the influence of this artistic
whole-harmony, they would never have been able to give free
vent to individuality and peculiarity as they did at home.

I saw many hundred performances in these first years
of my youth at the Théâtre Français, which was then at its
zenith.   There, if anywhere, I felt the silent march of the
French muses through Time and Space.

v.

A capable journalist named Grégoire, a sickly, prematurely aged, limping fellow, with alert wits, an Alsatian, who
knew Danish and regularly read Bille's *Daily Paper,* had
in many ways taken me up almost from the first day of my
sojourn on French soil.   This man recommended me, on my
expressing a wish to meet with a competent teacher, to take
instruction in the language from a young girl, a friend of his
sister, who was an orphan and lived with her aunt.   She
was of good family, the daughter of a colonel and the grand-
daughter of an admiral, but her own and her aunt's circumstances were narrow, and she was anxious to give lessons.

When I objected that such lessons could hardly be really
instructive, I was told that she was not only in every way a
nice but a very gifted and painstaking young girl.

The first time I entered the house, as a future pupil, I
found the young lady, dressed in a plain black silk dress,
surrounded by a circle of toddlers of both sexes, for whom
she had a sort of school, and whom on my arrival she sent
away.   She had a pretty figure, a face that was attractive
without being beautiful, a large mouth with good teeth, and
dark brown hair.   Her features were a little indefinite, her
face rather broad than oval, her eyes brown and affectionate.
She had at any rate the beauty that twenty years lends.

We arranged for four lessons a week, to begin with.

The first dragged considerably. My teacher was to correct any mistakes in pronunciation and grammar that I made in conversation. But we could not get up any proper conversation. She was evidently bored by the lessons, which she had only undertaken for the sake of the fees. If I began to tell her anything, she only half listened, and yawned with all her might very often and very loudly, although she politely put her hand in front of her large mouth. There only came a little animation into her expression when I either pronounced as badly as I had been taught by my French master at school, or made some particularly ludicrous mistake, such as *c'est tout égal* for *bien égal*. At other times she was distracted, sleepy, her thoughts elsewhere.

After having tried vainly for a few times to interest the young lady by my communications, I grew tired of the lessons. Moreover, they were of very little advantage to me, for the simple reason that my youthful teacher had not the very slightest scientific or even grammatical knowledge of her own tongue, and consequently could never answer my questions as to *why* you had to pronounce in such and such a way, or by virtue of what *rule* you expressed yourself in such and such a manner. I began to neglect my lessons, sometimes made an excuse, but oftener remained away without offering any explanation.

On my arrival one afternoon, after having repeatedly stayed away, the young lady met me with some temper, and asked the reason of my failures to come, plainly enough irritated and alarmed at my indifference, which after all was only the reflection of her own. I promised politely to be more regular in future. To insure this, she involuntarily became more attentive.

She yawned no more. I did not stay away again.

She began to take an interest herself in this eldest pupil of hers, who at 24 years of age looked 20 and who was acquainted with all sorts of things about conditions, countries, and people of which she knew nothing.

She had been so strictly brought up that nearly all secular reading was forbidden to her, and she had never been

to any theatre, not even the Théâtre Français.   She had not
read Victor Hugo, Lamartine, or Musset, had not even
dared to read *Paul et Virginie,* only knew expurgated editions of Corneille, Racine and Molière.   She was sincerely
clerical, had early been somewhat influenced by her cousin,
later the well-known Roman Catholic author, Ernest Hello,
and in our conversations was always ready to take the part
of the Jesuits against Pascal; what the latter had attacked
were some antiquated and long-abandoned doctrinal books;
even if there were defects in the teaching of certain Catholic
ecclesiastics, their lives at any rate were exemplary, whereas
the contrary was the case with the free-thinking men of science; their teaching was sometimes unassailable, but the lives
they led could not be taken seriously.

When we two young people got into a dispute, we gradually drew nearer to one another.   Our remarks contradicted
each other, but an understanding came about between our
eyes.   One day, as I was about to leave, she called me back
from the staircase, and, very timidly, offered me an orange.
The next time she blushed slightly when I came in.   She
frequently sent me cards of admission to the Athénée, a recently started institution, in which lectures were given by
good speakers.   She began to look pleased at my coming
and to express regret at the thought of my departure.

On New Year's day, as a duty gift, I had sent her a
bouquet of white flowers, and the next day she had tears in
her eyes as she thanked me: " I ask you to believe that I
highly appreciate your attention."   From that time forth
she spoke more and more often of how empty it would be
for her when I was gone.   I was not in love with her, but
was too young for her feelings, so unreservedly expressed, to
leave me unaffected, and likewise young enough to imagine
that she expected me before long to ask for her hand.   So
I soon informed her that I did not feel so warmly towards
her as she did towards me, and that I was not thinking of
binding myself for the present.

" Do you think me so poor an observer? " she replied,
amazed.   "I have never made any claims upon you, even in
my thoughts.   But I owe you the happiest month of my life."

VI.

This was about the state of affairs between Mademoiselle Louise and me, when one evening, at Pagella's, where
there were Southerners of various races present, I was introduced to a young lady, Mademoiselle Mathilde M., who at
first sight made a powerful impression upon me.

She was a young Spanish Brazilian, tall of stature, a
proud and dazzling racial beauty. The contours of her
head were so impeccably perfect that one scarcely understood
how Nature could have made such a being inadvertently,
without design. The rosy hue of her complexion made the
carnation even of a beautiful woman's face look chalky or
crimson by the side of hers. At the same time there was a
something in the colour of her skin that made me understand better the womanish appearance of Zurbaran and Ri-
bera, a warm glow which I had never seen in Nature before.
Her heavy, bluish-black hair hung down, after the fashion
of the day, in little curls over her forehead and fell in thick
ringlets upon her shoulders. Her eyebrows were exquisitely
pencilled, arched and almost met over her delicate nose, her
eyes were burning and a deep brown; they conquered, and
smiled; her mouth was a little too small, with white teeth
that were a little too large, her bust slender and full. Her
manner was distinguished, her voice rich; but most marvellous of all was her hand, such a hand as Parmeggianino might
have painted, all soul, branching off into five delightful
fingers.

Mentally I unhesitatingly dubbed her the most marvel-
ous feminine creature I had ever seen, and that less on account of her loveliness than the blending of the magnificence
of her bearing with the ardour, and often the frolicsomeness,
of her mode of expression.

She was always vigorous and sometimes daring in her
statements, cared only for the unusual, loved only " the impossible," but nevertheless carefully observed every established custom of society. To my very first remark to her,
to the effect that the weakness of women was mostly only
an habitual phrase; they were not weak except when they

wished to be, she replied: "Young as you are, you know women very well!" In that she was quite wrong.

Besides Spanish and Portuguese, she spoke French perfectly and English not badly, sang in a melodious contralto voice, drew well for an amateur, carved alabaster vases, and had all kinds of talents. She did not care to sing ballads, only cared for grand pathos.

She was just twenty years of age, and had come into the world at Rio, where her father represented the Spanish government. The family were descended from Cervantes. As she had early been left motherless, her father had sent her over in her fifteenth year to her aunt in Paris. This latter was married to an old monstrosity of a Spaniard, religious to the verge of insanity, who would seem to have committed some crime in his youth and now spent his whole day in the church, which was next door to his house, imploring forgiveness for his sins. He was only at home at meal-times, when he ate an alarming amount, and he associated only with priests. The aunt herself, however, in spite of her age, was a pleasure-seeking woman, rarely allowed her niece to stay at home and occupy herself as she liked, but dragged her everywhere about with her to parties and balls. In her aunt's company she sometimes felt depressed, but alone she was cheerful and without a care. At the Pagellas' she was like a child of the house. She had the Spanish love of ceremony and magnificence, the ready repartee of the Parisian, and, like a well-brought-up girl, knew how to preserve the balance between friendliness and mirth. She was not in the least prudish, and she understood everything; but there was a certain sublimity in her manner.

While Mademoiselle Louise, the little Parisian, had been brought up in a convent, kept from all free, intelligent, mundane conversation, and all free artistic impressions, the young Spaniard, at the same age, had the education and the style of a woman of the world in her manner.

We two young frequenters of the Pagella salon, felt powerfully drawn to one another. We understood one another at once. Of course, it was only I who was fascinated. When, in an evening, I drove across Paris in the expectation of seeing her, I sometimes murmured to myself Henrik Hertz's verse:

> "My beloved is like the dazzling day,
> Brazilia's Summer!"

My feelings, however, were much more admiration than love or desire. I did not really want to possess her. I never felt myself quite on a level with her even when she made decided advances to me. I rejoiced over her as over something perfect, and there was the rich, foreign colouring about her that there had been about the birds of paradise in my nursery. She seldom disturbed my peace of mind, but I said to myself that if I were to go away then, I should in all probability never see her again, as her father would be taking her the next year to Brazil or Madrid, and I sometimes felt as though I should be going away from my happiness forever. She often asked me to stay with such expressions and with such an expression that I was quite bewildered. And then she monopolised my thoughts altogether, like the queenly being she was.

A Danish poet had once called the beautiful women of the South " Large, showy flowers without fragrance." Was she a large, showy flower? Forget-me-nots were certainly by no means showy, but they were none the more odorous for that.

Now that I was seeing the radiant Mathilde almost every day, my position with regard to Louise seemed to me a false one. I did not yet know how exceedingly rare an undivided feeling is, did not understand that my feelings towards Mathilde were just as incomplete as those I cherished for Louise. I looked on Mademoiselle Mathilde as on a work of art, but I came more humanly close to Mademoiselle Louise. She did not evoke my enthusiastic admiration; that was quite true, but Mademoiselle Mathilde evoked my enthusiastic admiration only. If there were a great deal of compassion mingled with my feelings for the Parisian, there was likewise a slight erotic element.

The young Frenchwoman, in her passion, found expressions for affection and tenderness, in which she forgot all pride. She lived in a commingling, very painful for me, of happiness at my still being in Paris, and of horror at my approaching departure, which I was now about to accelerate, merely to escape from the extraordinary situation in which I found myself, and which I was too young to carry. Although Mathilde, whom I had never seen alone, was always the same, quite the great lady, perfectly self-controlled, it was the thought of saying good-bye to her that was the more painful to me. Every other day, on the other hand, Louise was trembling and ill, and I dreaded the moment of separation.

VII.

I had not left off my daily work in Paris, but had read industriously at the Imperial Library. I had also attended many lectures, some occasionally, others regularly, such as those of Janet, Caro, Lévêque and Taine.

Of all contemporary French writers, I was fondest of Taine. I had begun studying this historian and thinker in Copenhagen. The first book of his that I read was *The French Philosophers of the Nineteenth Century,* in a copy that had been lent to me by Gabriel Sibbern. The book entranced me, and I determined to read every word that I could get hold of by the same author. In the Imperial Library in Paris I read first of all *The History of English Literature,* of which I had hitherto only been acquainted with a few fragments, which had appeared in the *Revue des Deux Mondes.* Taine was to me an antidote to German abstraction and German pedantry. Through him I found the way to my own inmost nature, which my Dano-German University education had covered over.

Shortly after my arrival in Paris, therefore, I had written to Taine and begged for an interview. By a singular piece of ill-luck his reply to me was lost, and it was only at the very end of my stay that I received a second invitation to go to him. Although this one conversation could not be of any vast importance to me, it was nevertheless the first personal link between me and the man who was and remained my greatly loved master and deliverer, even though I mis-

trusted his essential teachings.   I was afraid that I had created a bad impression, as I had wasted the time raising objections; but Taine knew human nature well enough to perceive
the personality behind the clumsy form and the admiration
behind the criticism.   In reality, I was filled with passionate
gratitude towards Taine, and this feeling remained unaltered
until his latest hour.

During this my first stay in Paris I added the impression of Taine's personality to the wealth of impressions that
I took back with me from Paris to Copenhagen.

EARLY MANHOOD

Feud in Danish Literature—Riding—Youthful Longings—On the Rack—My
First Living Erotic Reality—An Impression of the Miseries of Modern
Coercive Marriage—Researches on the Comic—Dramatic Criticism—A
Trip to Germany—Johanne Louise Heiberg—Magdalene Thoresen—
Rudolph Bergh—The Sisters Spang—A Foreign Element—The Woman
Subject—Orla Lehmann—M. Goldschmidt—Public Opposition—A Letter
from Björnstjerne Björnson—Hard Work.

I.

AFTER my return from France to Denmark, in 1867
my thoughts were taken up once more by the feud
that had broken out in Danish literature between
Science and so-called Revelation (in the language of the
time, Faith and Knowledge). More and more had by de
grees entered the lists, and I, who centred my greatest intel
lectual interest in the battle, took part in it with a dual front
against the orthodox theologians, and more especially against
R. Nielsen, the assailant of the theologians, whom I regarded
as no less theologically inclined than his opponents.

I thereby myself became the object of a series of violent
attacks from various quarters. These did not have any ap
preciable effect on my spirits, but they forced me for years
into a somewhat irritating attitude of self-defence. Still I
was now arrived at that period of my youth when philosophy
and art were unable to keep temperament in check.

II.

This manifested itself first in a fresh need for physi
cal exercise. During the first two years after the decision
of 1864, while things were leading up to war between Prus
sia and Austria, and while the young blood of Denmark im
agined that their country would be drawn into this war, I

had taken part, as a member of the Academic Shooting Society, in drill and shooting practice.   After the battle of Königgratz these occupations lost much of their attraction.

I was now going in for an exercise that was new to me and which I had long wished to become proficient in.   This was riding.

Up to that time I had never been able to afford to ride. But just then a captain of the dragoons offered to teach me for a very low fee, and in the Queen's Riding-School I was initiated during the Spring months into the elementary stages of the art, in order that in Summer I might be able to ride out.   These riding-lessons were the keenest possible delight to me.   I, who so seldom felt happy, and still more seldom jubilant, was positively exultant as I rode out in the morning along the Strand Road.   Even if I had had an almost sleepless night I felt fresh on horseback.

It was no pleasure to me to ride the same horse often, if I knew its disposition.   I liked to change as often as possible, and preferred rather difficult horses to mares too well broken in.   I felt the arrogant pride of youth seethe in my veins as I galloped briskly along.

I was still far from an accomplished horseman when an examination of my finances warned me that I must give up my riding lessons.

When I informed my instructor that I could no longer allow myself the pleasure of his lessons, and in reply to his " Why? " had mentioned the reason, the captain answered that it would be very easy to settle that matter: he had a sister, an elderly maiden lady, who was passionately fond of literature and literary history.   Lessons in that subject could to our mutual satisfaction balance the riding lessons, which could thus go on indefinitely.   It is unnecessary to say how welcome the proposition was to me.   It was such a relief!

The captain was a pleasant, good-natured man, quite uneducated in literary matters, who confidingly communicated his bachelor experiences to his pupil.   These were summed up in the reflection that when womenkind fall in love, they dread neither fire nor water; the captain himself, who yet, in his own opinion, only looked well on horse-

back, had once had an affair with a married lady who
bombarded him with letters, and who, in her ardour, began
writing one day without noticing that her husband, who was
standing behind her chair, was looking over her shoulder
Since then the captain had not felt the need of women, so to
speak, preferred to be without them, and found his greatest
pleasure in his horses and his skill as an equestrian.

The sister was a maiden lady of forty, by no means
devoid of intellectual ability, with talent for observation and
an appreciation of good books, but whose development had
been altogether neglected. She now cherished an ambition
to write. She wrote in secret little tales that were not really
stupid but had not the slightest pretensions to style or liter
ary talent. She was very plain and exceedingly stout, which
produced a comical effect, especially as she was inclined to
exaggeration both of speech and gesture.

There was a disproportion between the ages of the mas
ter and the pupil; in my eyes she was quite an old person, in
her eyes, being her intellectual equal, I was likewise her
equal in age. In the natural order of things she felt more
personal sympathy for me than I for her. Consequently, I
involuntarily put a dash of teasing into my instruction, and
occasionally made fun of her sentimentality, and when the
large lady, half angry, half distressed, rose to seize hold of
me and give me a shaking, I would run round the table, pur
sued by her, or shoot out a chair between her and myself,—
which indubitably did not add to the dignity of our lessons

There was no question of thorough or connected in
struction. What the lady wanted more particularly was that
I should go through her literary attempts and correct them
but corrections could not transform them into art. And so
it came about that after no very long time I gave up these
arduous lessons, although obliged to give up my precious
riding lessons at the same time.

Consequently I never became a really expert rider, al
though during the next few years I had a ride now and then
But after a severe attack of phlebitis following upon typhoid
fever, in 1870-71, I was compelled to give up all the physical
exercises that I loved best.

III.

My temperament expressed itself in a profusion of youthful longings, as well as in my love of athletics.

During my University studies, in my real budding manhood, I had voluntarily cut myself away from the usual erotic diversions of youth. Precocious though I was in purely intellectual development, I was very backward in erotic experience. In that respect I was many years younger than my age.

On my return, my Paris experiences at first exercised me greatly. Between the young French lady and myself an active correspondence had sprung up, while the young Spaniard's radiant figure continued to retain the same place in my thoughts.

Then my surroundings claimed their rights, and it was not without emotion that I realised how charming the girls at home were. For I was only then entering upon the Cherubino stage of my existence, when the sight of feminine grace or beauty immediately transports a youth into a mild state of love intoxication.

It was incredible how rich the world was in bewitching creatures, and the world of Copenhagen especially. If you walked down Crown Princess Street, at a window on the ground floor you saw a dark girl with a Grecian-shaped head and two brown eyes, exquisitely set, beneath a high and noble forehead. She united the chaste purity of Pallas Athene with a stern, attractive grace.

If you went out towards the north side of the town, there was a house there on the first floor of which you were very welcome, where a handsome and well-bred couple once a week received young men for the sake of the lady's young niece. The master of the house was a lean and silent man, who always looked handsome, and was always dignified; he had honourably filled an exalted official post. His wife had been very attractive in her youth, had grown white while still quite young, and was now a handsome woman with snow-white curls clustering round her fresh-coloured face. To me she bore, as it were, an invisible mark upon her forehead, for

when quite a young girl she had been loved by a great man.
She was sincerely kind and genuinely pleasant, but the advantage of knowing her was not great; for that she was too
restless a hostess.   When it was her At Home she never
remained long enough with one group of talkers properly to
understand what was being discussed.   After about a minute
she hurried off to the opposite corner of the drawing-room,
said a few words there, and then passed on to look after
the tea.

It was neither to see her nor her husband that many of
the young people congregated at the house.   It was for the
sake of the eighteen-year-old fairy maiden, her niece, whose
face was one to haunt a man's dreams.   It was not from her
features that the witchery emanated, although in shape her
face was a faultless oval, her narrow forehead high and well-
shaped, her chin powerful.   Neither was it from the personality one obtained a glimpse of through her features.   The
girl's character and mental quality seemed much the same as
that of other girls; she was generally silent, or communicative about trifles, and displayed no other coquetry than the
very innocent delight in pleasing which Nature itself would
demand.

But all the same there was a fascination about her, as
about a fairy maiden.   There was a yellow shimmer about
her light hair; azure flames flashed from her blue eyes.
These flames drew a magic circle about her, and the dozen
young men who had strayed inside the circle flocked round
her aunt the evening in the week that the family were " at
home " and sat there, vying with each other for a glance
from those wondrous eyes, hating each other with all their
hearts, and suffering from the ridiculousness of yet meeting
like brothers, week after week, as guests in the same house.
The young girl's male relatives, who had outgrown their
enthusiasm for her, declared that her character was not good
and reliable—poor child! had she to be all that, too?   Others
who did not ask so much were content to enjoy the sound of
her voice.

She was not a Copenhagen girl, only spent a few Win-
ters in the town, then disappeared again.

Some years after, it was rumoured, to everybody's astonishment, that she had married a widower in a provincial town—she who belonged to the realms of Poesy!

Then there was another young girl, nineteen. Whereas the fairy maiden did not put herself out to pretend she troubled her head about the young men whom she fascinated with the rhythm of her movements or the radiation of her loveliness, was rather inclined to be short in her manner, a little staccato in her observations, too accustomed to admiration to attract worshippers to herself by courting them, too undeveloped and impersonal to consciously assert herself— this other girl was of quite another sort. She had no innate irresistibility, but was a shrewd and adaptable human girl. Her face did not attract by its beauty, though she was very much more beautiful than ugly, with a delicately hooked nose, a mouth full of promise, an expression of thoughtfulness and determination. When she appeared at a ball, men's eyes lingered on her neck, and even more on her white back, with its firm, smooth skin, and fine play of the muscles; for if she did not allow very much of her young bust to be seen, her dress at the back was cut down nearly to her belt. Her voice was a deep contralto, and she knew how to assume an expression of profound gravity and reflection. But she captivated most by her attentiveness. When a young man whom she wished to attract commenced a conversation with her, she never took her eyes from his, or rather she gazed into his, and showed such a rapt attention to his words, such an interest in his thoughts and his occupations, that after meeting her once he never forgot her again. Her coquetry did not consist of languishing glances, but of a pretended sympathy, that flattered and delighted its object.

IV.

These Danish girls were likely to appeal to a young man just returned from travels abroad, during which his emotions had been doubly stirred, for the first time, by feminine affection and by enthusiasm for a woman. They influenced me the more strongly because they were Danish, and because I, who loved everything Danish, from the language to the monuments, had, since the war, felt something lacking in everyone, man or woman, who was foreign to Denmark.

But in the midst of all these visitations of calf-love, and their vibrations among undefined sensations, I was pulled back with a jerk, as it were, to my earlier and deepest impression, that of the loveliness and exalted person of the young Spaniard. Letters from Paris furrowed my mind like steamers the waters of a lake, made it foam, and the waves run high, left long streaks across its wake. Not that Mlle. Mathilde sent letters to me herself, but her Italian lady and gentlemen friends wrote for her, apparently in her name, loudly lamenting my unreasonable departure, wishing and demanding my return, telling me how she missed me, sometimes how angry she was.

I was too poor to be able to return at once. I did what I could to procure money, wrote to those of my friends whom I thought could best afford it and on whom I relied most, but met with refusals, which made me think of the messages Timon of Athens received in response to similar requests. Then I staked in the lottery and did not win.

Urged from France to return, and under the high pressure of my own romantic imagination, it seemed clear to me all at once that I ought to unite my lot for good to that of this rare and beautiful woman, whom, it is true, I had never spoken to one minute alone, who, moreover, had scarcely anything in common with me, but who, just by the dissimilarity of her having been born of Spanish parents in Rio, and I of a Danish father and mother in Copenhagen, seemed destined by Fate for me, as I for her. The Palm and the Fir-tree had dreamed of one another, and could never meet; but men and women could, however far apart they might have been born. In the middle of the Summer of 1867 I was as though possessed by the thought that she and I ought to be united.

The simplest objection of all, namely, that I, who was scarcely able to support myself, could not possibly support a wife, seemed to me altogether subordinate. My motives were purely chivalric; I could not leave her in the lurch, as

the miserable hero of Andersen's *Only a Player* did Noomi.
And a vision of her compelling loveliness hovered before my
eyes.

The whole of the month of July and part of the month
of August I was on the rack, now passionately desiring a successful issue of my plans, now hoping just as ardently that
they would be stranded through the opposition of the foreign
family; for I was compelled to admit to myself that the beautiful Spaniard would be very unsuited to Copenhagen, would
freeze there, mentally as well as literally. And I said to
myself every day that supposing the war expected in Denmark were to break out again, and the young men were summoned to arms, the most insignificant little Danish girl would
make me a better Valkyrie; all my feelings would be foreign
to her, and possibly she would not even be able to learn Danish. Any other woman would understand more of my mind
than she. And yet! Yet she was the only one for me.

Thus I was swayed by opposing wishes the whole of the
long time during which the matter was pending and uncertain. I was so exhausted by suspense that I only kept up by
taking cold baths twice a day and by brisk rides. The mere
sight of a postman made my heart beat fast. The scorn
heaped upon me in the Danish newspapers had a curious
effect upon me under these circumstances; it seemed to me
to be strangely far away, like blows at a person who is somewhere else.

I pondered all day on the painful dilemma in which I
was placed; I dreamt of my Dulcinea every night, and began
to look as exhausted as I felt. One day that I went to Fredensborg, in response to an invitation from Frederik Paludan-
Müller, the poet said to me: " Have you been ill lately?
You look so pale and shaken." I pretended not to care;
whatever I said or did in company was incessant acting.

I experienced revulsions of feeling similar to those that
troubled Don Quixote. Now I saw in my distant Spanish
maiden the epitome of perfection, now the picture melted
away altogether; even my affection for her then seemed small,
artificial, whimsical, half-forgotten. And then again she
represented supreme happiness.

When the decision came, when,—as everyone with the
least experience of the world could have foretold,—all the
beautiful dreams and audacious plans collapsed suddenly, I
felt as though this long crisis had thrown me back indescribably; my intellectual development had been at a standstill
for months.   It was such a feeling as when the death of
some loved person puts an end to the long, tormenting anxiety of the foregoing illness.   I, who had centred everything
round one thought, must now start joylessly along new paths.
My outburst,—which astonished myself,—was:
   " How I wanted a heart! "

v.

I could not at once feel it a relief that my fancies had
all been dissipated into thin air.   Physically I was much
broken down, but, with my natural elasticity, quickly recovered.   Yet in my relations towards the other sex I was torn
as I had never been before.   My soul, or more exactly, that
part of my psychical life bordering on the other sex, was like
a deep, unploughed field, waiting for seed.

It was not much more than a month before the field was
sown.   Amongst my Danish acquaintances there was only
one, a young and very beautiful widow, upon whom, placed
as I was with regard to Mlle. Mathilde, I had definitely
counted.   I should have taken the young Spaniard to her;
she alone would have understood her—they would have been
friends.

There had for a long time been warm feelings of sympathy between her and me.   It so chanced that she drew
much closer to me immediately after the decisive word had
been spoken.   She became, consequently, the only one to
whom I touched upon the wild fancies to which I had given
myself up, and confided the dreams with which I had wasted
my time. She listened to me sympathetically, no little amazed
at my being so devoid of practical common sense.   She stood
with both feet on the earth; but she had one capacity that I
had not met with before in any young woman—the capacity
for enthusiasm.   She had dark eyes, with something melan-

choly in their depths; but when she spoke of anything that roused her enthusiasm, her eyes shone like stars.

She pointed out how preposterous it was in me to wish to seek so far away a happiness that perhaps was very close to me, and how even more preposterous to neglect, as I had done, my studies and intellectual aims for a fantastic love. And for the first time in my life, a young woman spoke to me of my abilities and of the impression she had received of them, partly through the reading of the trifles that I had had printed, partly, and more particularly, through her long talks with me. Neither the little French girl nor the young Spanish lady had ever spoken to me of myself, my talents, or my future; this Danish woman declared that she knew me through and through. And the new thing about it all, the thing hitherto unparalleled in my experience, was that she believed in me. More than that: she had the highest possible conception of my abilities, asserted in contradiction to my own opinion, that I was already a man of unusual mark, and was ardently ambitious for me.

Just at this moment, when so profoundly disheartened, and when in idle hopes and plans I had lost sight of my higher goal, by her firm belief in me she imparted to me augmented self-respect. Her confidence in me gave me increasing confidence in myself, and a vehement gratitude awoke in me for the good she thus did me.

Then it happened that one day, without preamble, she admitted that the interest she felt in me was not merely an intellectual one; things had now gone so far that she could think of nothing but me.

My whole nature was shaken to its foundations. Up to this time I had only regarded her as my friend and comforter, had neither felt nor fought against any personal attraction. But she had scarcely spoken, before she was transformed in my eyes. The affection I had thirsted for was offered to me here. The heart I had felt the need of was this heart. And it was not only a heart that was offered me, but a passion that scorned scruples.

In my austere youth hitherto, I had not really had any erotic experiences whatever. I had led the chaste life of the intellectual worker. My thoughts had been the thoughts of a man; they had ascended high and had delved deep, but my love affairs had been the enthusiasms and fancies of a half-grown boy, chimeras and dreams. This young woman was my first living erotic reality.

And suddenly, floodgates seemed to open within me. Streams of lava, streams of molten fire, rushed out over my soul. I loved for the first time like a man.

The next few days I went about as if lifted above the earth; in the theatre, in the evening, I could not follow the performance, but sat in the pit with my face in my hands, full of my new destiny, as though my heart would burst.

And yet it was more a physical state, an almost mechanical outcome of what to me was overwhelmingly new, association with a woman. It was not because it was just this particular woman. For my emotional nature was so composite that even in the first moment of my bliss I did not regard this bliss as unmixed. From the very first hour, I felt a gnawing regret that it was not I who had desired her, but she who had chosen me, so that my love in my heart of hearts was only a reflection of hers.

VI.

About this time it so happened that another woman began to engage my thoughts, but in an altogether different manner. Circumstances resulted in my being taken into the secret of unhappy and disturbing domestic relations in a well-to-do house to which I was frequently invited, and where to all outward seeming all the necessary conditions of domestic happiness were present.

The master of the house had in his younger days been a very handsome man, lazy, not clever, and of an exceedingly passionate temper. He was the son of a man rich, worthy and able, but of a very weak character, and of a kept woman who had been the mistress of a royal personage. Through no fault of his own, he had inherited his mother's professional vices, persistent untruthfulness, a comedian's manner, prodigality, a love of finery and display. He was quite without intellectual interests, but had a distinguished bearing, a winning manner, and no gross vices.

His wife, who, for family reasons, had been married to him much too young, had never loved him, and never been suited to him. As an innocent, ignorant girl, she had been placed in the arms of a man who was much the worse for a reckless life, and suffering from an illness that necessitated nursing, and made him repulsive to her. Every day that passed she suffered more from being bound to a man whose slightest movement was objectionable to her and whose every remark a torture. In the second decade of her marriage the keenest marital repulsion had developed in her; this was so strong that she sometimes had to pull herself together in order, despite her maternal feelings, not to transfer her dislike to the children, who were likewise his, and in whom she dreaded to encounter his characteristics.

Towards her, the man was despotic and cunning, but not unkind, and in so far excusable that, let him have done what he might, she could not have got rid of the hatred that plagued him and consumed her. So dissimilar were their two natures.

Her whole aim and aspiration was to get the bond that united them dissolved. But this he would not hear of, for many reasons, and more especially from dislike of scandal. He regarded himself, and according to the usual conception of the words, justly so, as a good husband and father. He asked for no impossible sacrifice from his wife, and he was affectionate to his children. He could not help her detesting him, and indeed, did not fully realise that she did. And yet, it was difficult for him to misunderstand. For his wife scarcely restrained her aversion even when there were guests in the house. If he told an untruth, she kept silence with her lips, but scarcely with her expression. And she would sometimes talk of the faults and vices that she most abhorred, and then name his.

The incessant agitation in which she lived had made her nervous and restless to excess. As the feminine craving to be able, in marriage, to look up to the man, had never been satisfied, she only exacted the more vehemently veracity, firmness and intellect in men. But undeveloped as she was, and in despair over the dissatisfaction, the drowsiness, and the darkness in which her days glided away, whatever invaded the stagnation and lighted up the darkness: sparkle, liveliness, brilliance and wit, were estimated by her more highly than they deserved to be.

At first when, in the desolation of her life, she made advances to me, this repelled me somewhat. The equestrian performer in Heiberg's Madame Voltisubito cannot sing unless she hears the crack of a whip. Thus it seemed to me that her nature could not sing, save to the accompaniment of all the cart, carriage and riding whips of the mind. But I saw how unhappy she was, and that the intense strain of her manner was only an expression of it.

She could not know the beauty of inward peace, and in spite of her Protestant upbringing she had retained all the unaffectedness and sincerity of the natural human being, all the obstinate love of freedom, unmoved in the least by what men call discipline, ethics, Christianity, convention. She did not believe in it all, she had seen what it resulted in, and what it covered up, and she passed her life in unmitigated despair, which was ordinarily calm to all appearance, but in reality rebellious: what she was enduring was the attempted murder of her soul.

To all that she suffered purely mentally from her life with her husband in the home that was no home at all, there had of late been added circumstances which likewise from a practical point of view made interference and alteration necessary. Her lord and master had always been a bad manager, in fact worse than that; in important matters, thoroughly incapable and fatuous. That had not mattered much hitherto, since others had looked after his affairs; but now the control of them had fallen entirely into his own hands, and he managed them in such a way that expenses increased at a terrific rate, while his income diminished with equal rapidity, and the question of total ruin only seemed a matter of time.

His wife had no outside support. She was an orphan and friendless. Her husband's relations did not like her and

did not understand her. And yet just at this time she required as a friend a man who understood her and could help
her to save her own and the children's fortunes from the ship-
wreck, before it was too late. She felt great confidence in me,
whom she had met, at intervals, from my boyhood, and she
now opened her heart to me in conversation more and more.
She confided in me fully, gave me a complete insight into the
torture of her life, and implored me to help her to acquire
her freedom.

Thus it was that while still quite a young man a powerful, never-to-be-effaced impression of the miseries of modern
coercive marriage was produced upon me. The impression
was not merely powerful, but it waked, like a cry of distress, both my thinking powers and my energy. As through
a chink in the smooth surface of society, I looked down
into the depths of horror. Behind the unhappiness of one,
I suspected that of a hundred thousand, knew that of a
hundred thousand. And I felt myself vehemently called
upon, not only to name the horror by its name, but to step
in, as far as I was able, and prevent the thing spreading
unheeded.

Scales had fallen from my eyes. Under the semblance
of affection and peace, couples were lacerating one another
by the thousand, swallowed up by hatred and mutual aversion. The glitter of happiness among those higher placed
dazzled the thoughtless and the credulous. He who had
eyes to see, observed how the wretchedness due to the arrangement of society, wound itself right up to its pinnacles.

The vices and paltrinesses of the individual could not be
directly remedied; inherited maladies and those brought upon
one's self, stupidity and folly, brutality and malice, undeniably existed. But the institutions of society ought to be so
planned as to render these destructive forces inoperative, or
at least diminish their harmfulness, not so as to give them
free scope and augment their terrors by securing them
victims.

In marriage, the position of the one bound against his or
her will was undignified, often desperate, but worst in the
case of a woman. As a mother she could be wounded in her

most vulnerable spot, and what was most outrageous of all, she could be made a mother against her will.   One single unhappy marriage had shown me, like a sudden revelation, what marriage in countless cases is, and how far from free the position of woman still was.

But that woman should be oppressed in modern society, that the one-half of the human race could be legally deprived of their rights, revealed that justice in society, as it at present stood, was in a sorry state.   In the relations between the strong and the weak, the rich and the poor, the same legalised disproportion would necessarily prevail as between man and woman.

My thought pierced down into the state of society that obtained and was praised so highly, and with ever less surprise and ever greater disquiet, found hollowness everywhere. And this called my will to battle, armed it for the fight.

VII.

From this time forth I began to ponder quite as much over Life as over Art, and to submit to criticism the conditions of existence in the same way as I had formerly done with Faith and Law.

In matters concerning Life, as in things concerning Art, I was not a predetermined Radical.   There was a great deal of piety in my nature and I was of a collecting, retentive disposition.   Only gradually, and step by step, was I led by my impressions, the incidents I encountered, and my development, to break with many a tradition to which I had clung to the last extremity.

It was in the spirit of the Æsthetics of the time, that, after having been engaged upon the Tragic Idea, I plunged into researches on the Comic, and by degrees, as the material ordered itself for me, I tried to write a doctor's thesis upon it. Abstract researches were regarded as much more valuable than historic investigation.   In comic literature Aristophanes in particular delighted me, and I was thinking of letting my general definitions merge into a description of the greatness of the Greek comedian; but as the thread broke for me, I did not get farther than the theory of the Comic in general. It was not, like my previous treatise on the Tragic, treated under three headings, according to the Hegelian model, but written straight ahead, without any subdivision into sections.

Whilst working at this paper I was, of course, obliged constantly to consult the national comedies and lighter plays, till I knew them from cover to cover. Consequently, when Gotfred Rode, the poet, who was connected with a well-known educational establishment for girls, asked me whether I would care to give a course of public lectures for ladies, I chose as my subject *The Danish Comedy.* The lectures were attended in force. The subject was supremely innocent, and it was treated in quite a conservative manner. At that time I cherished a sincere admiration, with only slight reservations, for Heïberg, Hertz, Hostrup and many others as comic playwriters, and was not far short of attributing to their works an importance equal to those of Holberg. And yet I was unable to avoid giving offence. I had, it appears, about Heiberg's *Klister and Malle,* an inseparable betrothed couple, used what was, for that matter, an undoubtedly Kierkegaardian expression, viz., *to beslobber a relation.* This expression was repeated indignantly to the Headmistress, and the thoughtless lecturer was requested to call upon the Principal of the college. When, after a long wait, and little suspecting what was going to be said to me, I was received in audience, it appeared that I had been summoned to receive a polite but decided admonition against wounding the susceptibilities of my listeners by expressions which were not ' good form," and when I, unconscious of wrongdoing, asked which expression she alluded to, the unfortunate word ' beslobber " was alleged; my young hearers were not ' 'Arriets " for whom such expressions might be fitting.

I was not asked again to give lectures for young ladies.

VIII.

Hitherto, when I had appeared before the reading public, it had only been as the author of shorter or longer contributions to the philosophical discussion of the relations between

Science and Faith; when these had been accepted by a dail
paper it had been as its heaviest ballast.   I had never ye
written anything that the ordinary reader could follow wit
pleasure, and I had likewise been obliged to make use of
large number of abstruse philosophical words.

The proprietors of the *Illustrated Times* offered me th
reviewing of the performances at the Royal Theatre in thei
paper, which had not hitherto printed dramatic criticisms.
accepted the offer, because it afforded me a wished-for oppoi
tunity of further shaking off the dust of the schools.
could thus have practice with my pen, and get into touc
with a section of the reading public who, without caring fo
philosophy, nevertheless had intellectual interests; and thes
articles were in reality a vent for what I had at heart abou
this time touching matters human and artistic.   They wer
written in a more colloquial style than anything I had wri
ten before, or than it was usual to write in Denmark at tha
time, and they alternated sometimes with longer essays, suc
as those on Andersen and Goldschmidt.

Regarded merely as dramatic criticisms, they were c
little value.   The Royal Theatre, the period of whose zenit
was nearly at an end, I cared little for, and I was persor
ally acquainted with next to none of the actors, only meetinç
at most, Phister and Adolf Rosenkilde and of ladies, Södrin
in society.

I found it altogether impossible to brandish my car
over the individual actor in his individual part.   But the forr
of it was merely a pretext.   I wanted to show myself as I wa
speak out about dramatic and other literature, reveal how
felt, show what I thought about all the conditions of life r
presented or touched upon on the stage.

My articles were read with so much interest that th
editors of the *Illustrated Times* raised the writer's scale of r
muneration to 10 Kr. a column (about 11s. 3d.), which :
that time was very respectable pay.   Unfortunately, hov
ever, I soon saw that even at that, if I wrote in the paper a
the year round, I could not bring up my yearly income fror
this source to more than 320 kroner of our money, abou
17l. 12s. 6d. in English money; so that, without a Universit

ursary, I should have come badly off, and even with it was
ot rolling in riches.

The first collection of my articles, which I published in
868 under the title of *Studies in Æsthetics,* augmented my in-
ome a little, it is true, but for that, as for the next collection,
Criticisms and Portraits, I only received 20 kroner (22*s.* 6*d.*)
er sheet of sixteen pages. Very careful management was
ecessary.

IX.

With the first money I received for my books, I went
n the middle of the Summer of 1868 for a trip to Germany.
acquired some idea of Berlin, which was then still only the
apital of Prussia, and in population corresponded to the Co-
enhagen of our day; I spent a few weeks in Dresden,
vhere I felt very much at home, delighted in the exquisite
rt collection and derived no small pleasure from the theatre,
t that time an excellent one. I saw Prague for the first
ime, worshipped Rubens in Munich, and, with him specially
n my mind, tried to realise how the greatest painters had
egarded Life. Switzerland added to my store of impres-
ions with grand natural spectacles. I saw the Alps, and a
hunderstorm in the Alps, passed starlit nights on the Swiss
akes, traced the courses of foaming mountain streams such
s the Tamina at Pfäffers, ascended the Rigi at a silly forced
narch, and from the Kulm saw a procession of clouds that
gripped my fancy like the procession of the Vanir in Northern
nythology. Many years afterwards I described it in the
Fourth volume of *Main Currents.* From Interlaken I gazed
n the whiteness of the Jungfrau, but scarcely with greater
emotion than once upon a time when I had gazed at the white
cliffs of Möen. On my homeward journey I saw Heidel-
erg's lovely ruins, to which Charles V.'s castle, near the Alhambra, makes a marvellous pendant, Strassburg's grave
Cathedral, and Goethe's house at Frankfurt.

My travels were not long, but were extraordinarily instructive. I made acquaintance with people from the most
widely different countries, with youthful frankness engaged
n conversation with Germans and Frenchmen, Englishmen

and Americans, Poles and Russians, Dutchmen, Belgians and Swiss, met them as travelling companions, and listened attentively to what they narrated. They were, moreover, marvellously frank towards the young man who, with the curiosity of his age, plied them with questions.

Young Dutchmen, studying music in Dresden, gave me some idea of the ill-will felt in their country towards the Prussians, an ill-will not unmingled with contempt. On the other hand, I was astonished, during a half day's excursion on foot with a few Leipzig students, to learn how strong was the feeling of the unity of Germany and of the necessity of the supremacy of Prussia, even in the states which in the 1866 war had been on the side of Austria. The students felt no grief over having been defeated, the victors were Germans too; everything was all right so long as the German Empire became one. These and similar conversations, which finally brought me to the conclusion that the whole of the bourgeoisie was satisfied with the dominance of Prussia, had for result that in 1870 I did not for a moment share the opinion of the Danes and the French, that the defeated German states would enter into an alliance with France against Prussia.

English undergraduates told me what philosophical and historical works were being most read in the universities of Great Britain; Bohemian students explained to me that in the German philosophical world Kant had quite outshone Hegel and put him in the background.

The lady members of an American family from Boston treated me quite maternally; the wife suggested almost at once, in the railway-carriage, that I should give her when we reached the hotel whatever linen or clothes I had that wanted repairs; she would be very pleased to mend them for me. The husband, who was very pious and good-natured, had all his pockets full of little hymn-books and in his memorandum book a quantity of newspaper cuttings of devotional verse, which he now and then read aloud enthusiastically.

But I also met with Americans of quite a different cast. A young student from Harvard University, who, for that matter, was not in love with the Germans and declared that the United States could with difficulty absorb and digest those who were settled there, surprised me with his view that in the future Bismarck would come to be regarded as no less a figure than Cavour. The admiration of contemporary educated thought was then centred around Cavour, whereas Bismarck had hitherto only encountered passionate aversion outside Germany, and even in Germany was the object of much hatred. This student roused me into thinking about Bismarck for myself.

Having lain down, all bathed in perspiration, during the ascent without a guide of a mountain in Switzerland, I was accosted by a woman, who feared I had come to some harm. I walked on up with her. She turned out to be a young peasant woman from Normandy, who lived half-way up the mountain. She had accompanied her husband to Switzerland, but cursed her lot, and was always longing to be back in France. When I remarked that it must be some consolation to live in so lovely a place, she interrupted me with the most violent protests. A beautiful place! This! The steep mountain, the bristly fir-trees and pine-trees, the snow on the top and the lake deep down below—anything uglier it would be hard to conceive. No fields, no pasture-land, no apple-trees! No indeed! If *she* had to mention a country that really was beautiful, it was Normandy. There was plenty of food for all there, you did not need to go either up or down hill; there, thank God, it was flat. Did I think stones beautiful, perhaps? She had not been down in the valley for five months, and higher than her house she had never been and would never go; no, thank you, not she! She let her husband fetch what they required for the house; she herself sat and fretted all through the Winter; life then was almost more than she could bear.

On one of the steamers on the Lake of Lucerne, I caught, for the first time, a glimpse of Berthold Auerbach, who was very much admired by my comrades in Copenhagen and by myself.

At the hotel table at Lucerne I made the acquaintance of a Dutch captain from Batavia, an acquaintance productive of much pleasure to me. Before the soup was brought round

I had pulled out a letter I had just received, opened it and begun to read it. A voice by my side said in French:

"Happy man! You are reading a letter in a woman's writing!" With that our acquaintance was made.

The captain was a man of forty, who in the course of an active life had had many and varied experiences and met with prosperity, but was suffering from a feeling of great void. His society was exceedingly attractive to me, and he related to me the main events of his life; but after one day's association only, we were obliged to part. All through my trip I had a curious feeling of every farewell on the journey being in all human probability a farewell for life, but had not realised it painfully before. But when next day the brave captain, whose home was far away in another quarter of the globe, held his hand out to say good-bye, I was much affected. "Till we meet again" said the captain.

"And where?"

"Till we meet again all and everywhere, for we live an eternal life; till we meet again in time and space, or outside time and space!"

I reflected sadly that I should never again see this man, who, the last twenty-four hours had shown me, was in extraordinary sympathy and agreement with me.

Separated from those dearest to me, the whole of the journey, for that matter, was a sort of self-torment to me, even though a profitable one. Like every other traveller, I had many a lonely hour, and plenty of time to ponder over my position and vocation in life. I summed up my impressions in the sentence: "The Powers have designated me the champion of great ideas against great talents, unfortunately greater than I."

x.

There was only one distinguished person outside my circle of acquaintance to whom I wished to bring my first descriptive book, as a mark of homage, Johanne Louise Heiberg, the actress. I had admired her on the stage, even if not to the same extent as Michael Wiehe; but to me she was the representative of the great time that would soon sink into the grave. In addition, I ventured to hope that she, being a friend of Frederik Paludan-Müller, Magdalene Thoresen and others who wished me well, would be at any rate somewhat friendly inclined towards me. A few years before, it had been rumoured in Copenhagen after the publication of my little polemical pamphlet against Nielsen, that at a dinner at the Heiberg's there had been a good deal of talk about me; even Bishop Martensen had expressed himself favourably, and it also attracted attention that a short time afterwards, in a note to his book *On Knowledge and Faith,* he mentioned me not unapprovingly, and contented himself with a reminder to me not to feel myself too soon beyond being surprised. When the Bishop of Zealand, one of the actress's most faithful adherents, had publicly spoken thus mildly of the youthful heretic, there was some hope that the lady herself would be free from prejudice. My friends also eagerly encouraged me to venture upon a visit to her home.

I was admitted and asked to wait in a room through the glass doors of which I was attentively observed for some time by the lady's adopted children. Then she came in, in indoor dress, with a stocking in her hand, at which she uninterruptedly continued to knit during the following conversation: She said: " Well! So you have collected your articles." I was simple enough to reply—as if that made any difference to the lady—that the greater part of the book had not been printed before. She turned the conversation upon Björnson's *Fisher Girl,* which had just been published, and which had been reviewed by *The Fatherland* the evening before, declaring that she disagreed altogether with the reviewer, who had admired in the *Fisher Girl* a psychological study of a scenic genius. "It is altogether a mistake," said Mrs. Heiberg, absorbed in counting her stitches, " altogether a mistake that genius is marked by restlessness, refractoriness, an irregular life, or the like. That is all antiquated superstition. True genius has no connection whatever with excesses and caprices, in fact, is impossible without the strict fulfilment of one's duty. (Knitting furiously.) Genius is simple, straightforward, domesticated, industrious."

When we began to speak of mutual acquaintances,

amongst others, Magdalene Thoresen, feeling very uncomfortable in the presence of the lady, I blurted out most tactlessly that I was sure that lady was much interested in me.
It was a mere nothing, but at the moment sounded like conceit and boasting. I realised it the moment the words were
out of my mouth, and instinctively felt that I had definitely displeased her.   But the conversational material was
used up and I withdrew.   I never saw Johanne Louise Heiberg again; henceforth she thought anything but well of me.

XI.

Magdalene Thoresen was spending that year in Copenhagen, and our connection, which had been kept up by correspondence, brought with it a lively mutual interchange of
thoughts and impressions.   Our natures, it is true, were as
much unlike as it was possible for them to be; but Magdalene
Thoresen's wealth of moods and the overflowing warmth of
her heart, the vivacity of her disposition, the tenderness that
filled her soul, and the incessant artistic exertion, which her exhausted body could not stand, all this roused in me a sympathy that the mistiness of her reasoning, and the over-excite-
ment of her intellectual life, could not diminish.   Besides
which, especially when she was away from Copenhagen,
but when she was there, too, she needed a literary assistant
who could look through her MSS. and negotiate over them
with the publishers of anthologies, year-books, and weekly
papers, and for this purpose she not infrequently seized upon
me, innocently convinced, like everybody else for that matter, that she was the only person who made a similar demand
upon me.

Still, it was rather trying that, when my verdict on her
work did not happen to be what she wished, she saw in what
I said an unkindness, for which she alleged reasons that had
nothing whatever to do with Art.

Magdalene Thoresen could not be otherwise than fond
of Rasmus Nielsen; they were both lively, easily enraptured
souls, who breathed most freely in the fog.   That, however,
did not come between her and me, whom she often thought in

the right. With regard to my newspaper activity, she merely urged the stereotyped but pertinent opinion, that I ought not to write so many small things; my nature could not stand this wasting, drop by drop.

I had myself felt for a long time that I ought to concentrate my forces on larger undertakings.

XII.

There were not many of the upper middle class houses in Copenhagen at that time, the hospitality of which a young man with intellectual interests derived any advantage from accepting. One of these houses, which was opened to me, and with which I was henceforward associated, was that of Chief Physician Rudolph Bergh. His was the home of intellectual freedom.

The master of the house was not only a prominent scientist and savant, but, at a time when all kinds of prejudices ruled unassailed, a man who had retained the uncompromising radicalism of the first half of the century. The spirit of Knowledge was the Holy Spirit to him; the profession of doctor had placed him in the service of humanity, and to firmness of character he united pure philanthropy. The most despised outcasts of society met with the same consideration and the same kindness from him as its favoured ones.

His wife was well calculated, by her charm of manner, to be the centre of the numerous circle of talented men who, both from Denmark and abroad, frequented the house. There one met all the foreign natural scientists who came to Copenhagen, all the esteemed personalities Denmark had at the time, who might be considered as belonging to the freer trend of thought, and many neutrals. Actors such as Höedt and Phister went there, favourite narrators such as Bergsöe, painters like Kröyer, distinguished scientists like J. C. Schiödte, the entomologist. This last was an independent and intellectual man, somewhat touchy, and domineering in his manner, a master of his subject, a man of learning, besides, ceremonious, often cordial, ready to listen to anything worth hearing that was said. He had weaknesses, never would admit that he had made a mistake, and was even very unwilling to own he had not read a book that was being spoken of. Besides which, he had spent too great a part of his life in virulent polemics to be devoid of the narrowing of the horizon which is the concomitant of always watching and being ready to attack the same opponent. But he was in the grand style, which is rare in Denmark, as elsewhere.

XIII.

The house of the sisters Spang was a pleasant one to go to; they were two unmarried ladies who kept an excellent girls' school, at which Julius Lange taught drawing. Benny Spang, not a beautiful, but a brilliant girl, with exceptional brains, daughter of the well-known Pastor Spang, a friend of Sören Kierkegaard, adopted a tone of good-fellowship towards me that completely won my affection. She was cheerful, witty, sincere and considerate. Not long after we became acquainted she married a somewhat older man than herself, the gentle and refined landscape painter, Gotfred Rump. The latter made a very good sketch of me.

The poet Paludan-Müller and the Lange family visited at the house; so did the two young and marvellously beautiful girls, Alma Trepka and Clara Rothe, the former of whom was married later to Carl Bloch the painter, the other to her uncle, Mr. Falbe, the Danish Minister in London.

It was hard to say which of the two was the more beautiful. Both were unusually lovely. Alma Trepka was queenly, her movements sedate, her disposition calm and unclouded—Carl Bloch could paint a Madonna, or even a Christ, from her face without making any essential alteration in the oval of its contours. Clara Rothe's beauty was that of the white hart in the legend; her eyes like a deer's, large and shy, timid, and unself-conscious, her movements rapid, but so graceful that one was fascinated by the harmony of them.

XIV.

Just about this time a foreign element entered the circle of Copenhagen students to which I belonged. One day there came into my room a youth with a nut-brown face, short and compactly built, who after only a few weeks' stay in Copenhagen could speak Danish quite tolerably. He was a young Armenian, who had seen a great deal of the world and was of very mixed race. His father had married, at Ispahan, a lady of Dutch-German origin. Up to his seventh year he had lived in Batavia. When the family afterwards moved to Europe, he was placed at school in Geneva. He had there been brought up, in French, to trade, but as he revealed an extraordinary talent for languages, was sent, for a year or eighteen months at a time, to the four German universities of Halle, Erlangen, Göttingen and Leipzig. Now, at the age of 22, he had come to Copenhagen to copy Palahvi and Sanscrit manuscripts that Rask and Westergaard had brought to Europe. He knew a great many languages, and was moreover very many-sided in his acquirements, sang German student songs charmingly, was introduced and invited everywhere, and with his foreign appearance and quick intelligence was a great success. He introduced new points of view, was full of information, and brought with him a breath from the great world outside. Industrious though he had been before, Copenhagen social life tempted him to idleness. His means came to an end; he said that the annual income he was in the habit of receiving by ship from India had this year, for some inexplicable reason, failed to arrive, dragged out a miserable existence for some time under great difficulties, starved, borrowed small sums, and disappeared as suddenly as he had come.

XV.

Knowing this Armenian made me realise how restricted my own learning was, and what a very general field of knowledge I had chosen.

I wrote my newspaper articles and my essays, and I worked at my doctor's thesis on French Æsthetics, which cost

me no little pains; it was my first attempt to construct a consecutive book, and it was only by a vigorous effort that I
completed it at the end of 1869. But I had then been casting
over in my mind for some years thoughts to which I never
was able to give a final form, thoughts about the position of
women in society, which would not let me rest.

A woman whose thought fired mine even further just
about this time, a large-minded woman, who studied society
with an uncompromising directness that was scarcely to be
met with in any man of the time in Denmark, was the wife of
the poet Carsten Hauch. When she spoke of Danish women,
the stage of their development and their position in law,
their apathy and the contemptibleness of the men, whether
these latter were despots, pedants, or self-sufficient Christians,
she made me a sharer of her point of view; our hearts glowed
with the same flame.

Rinna Hauch was not, like certain old ladies of her
circle, a " woman's movement " woman before the name was
invented. She taught no doctrine, but she glowed with ardour for the cause of freedom and justice. She saw through
the weak, petty men and women of her acquaintance and despised them. She too passionately desired a thorough revolution in modern society to be able to feel satisfied merely
by an amelioration of the circumstances of women of the
middle classes; and yet it was the condition of women, especially in the classes she knew well, that she thought most
about.

She began to place some credence in me and cherished
a hope that I should do my utmost to stir up the stagnation
at home, and during the long conversations we had together,
when, in the course of these Summers, I now and again spent
a week at a time with the Hauchs at Hellebæk, she enflamed
me with her ardour.

In September, 1868, after wandering with my old friend
up and down the shore, under the pure, starlit heaven,
and at last finding myself late at night in my room, I was
unable to go to rest. All that had been talked of and discussed in the course of the day made my head hot and
urged me to reflection and action. Often I seized a piece of

paper and scribbled off, disconnectedly, in pencil, remarks corresponding to the internal agitation of my mind, jottings like the following, for example:

S. R., that restive fanatic, has a wife who cannot believe, and wishes for nothing but to be left in peace on religious matters. He *forces her* to go to Communion, though he knows the words of Scripture, that he who partakes unworthily eats and drinks to his own damnation.

There is not one sound, healthy sentiment in the whole of our religious state of being. You frequently hear it said: "Everyone can't be a hypocrite." True enough. But begin, in the middle classes, to deduct hypocrisy, and gross affectation and cowardly dread of Hell, and see what is left!

If we have young people worthy the name, I will tell them the truth; but this band of backboneless creatures blocks up the view.

Women whom Life has enlightened and whom it has disappointed! You I can help.

I see two lovers hand in hand, kissing the tears away from each other's eyes.

I can only rouse the wakeful. Nothing can be done with those who are incapable of feeling noble indignation.

I have known two women prefer death to the infamy of conjugal life.

Open the newspapers!—hardly a line that is not a lie.

And poets and speakers flatter a people like that.

Christianity and Humanity have long wished for divorce. Now this is an accomplished fact.

And the priests are honoured. They plume themselves on not having certain vices, for which they are too weak.

I know that I shall be stoned, that every boy has his balderdash ready against that to which the reflection of years and sleepless nights has given birth. But do you think I am afraid of anyone?

Stupidity was always the bodyguard of Lies.

A people who have put up with the Oldenborgs for four hundred years and made loyalty to them into a virtue!

They do not even understand that here there is no Antichrist but Common Sense.

Abandoned by all, except Unhappiness and me.

When did God become Man? When Nature reached the point in its development at which the first man made his appearance; when Nature became man, then God did.

Women say of the beloved one: "A bouquet he brings smells better than one another brings."

You are weak, dear one, God help you! And you help! and I help!

These thoughts have wrought a man of me, have finally wrought me to a man.

I procured all that was accessible to me in modern French and English literature on the woman subject.

In the year 1869 my thoughts on the subordinate position of women in society began to assume shape, and I attempted a connected record of them. I adopted as my starting point Sören Kierkegaard's altogether antiquated conception of woman and contested it at every point. But all that I had planned and drawn up was cast aside when in 1869 John Stuart Mill's book on the subject fell into my hands. I felt Mill's superiority to be so immense and regarded his book as so epoch-making that I necessarily had to reject my own draft and restrict myself to the translation and introduction of what he had said. In November, 1869, I published Mill's book in Danish and in this manner introduced the modern woman's movement into Denmark.

The translation was of this advantage to me that it brought me first into epistolary communication, and later into personal contact with one of the greatest men of the time.

XVI.

There was one of the political figures of the time whom I often met during these years. This was the man most beloved of the previous generation, whose star had certainly declined since the war, but whose name was still one to conjure with, Orla Lehmann.

I had made his acquaintance when I was little more than a boy, in a very curious way.

In the year 1865 I had given a few lectures in C. N. David's house, on Runeberg, whom I had glorified exceedingly, and as the David and Lehmann houses, despite the political differences between them, were closely related one to the other, and intimately connected, Orla Lehmann had heard these lectures very warmly spoken of. At that time he had just founded a People's Society as a counterpoise to the supremely conservative Society of August, and, looking out for lecturers for it, hit upon the twenty-three-year-old speaker as upon a possibility.

I was then living in a little cupboard of a room on the third floor in Crystal Street, and over my room was one, in the attic, inhabited by my seventeen-year-old brother, who had not yet matriculated.

Orla Lehmann, who had been told that the person he was seeking lived high up, rapidly mounted the four storeys, and knocked, a little out of breath, at the schoolboy's door. When the door opened, he walked in, and said, still standing:

"You are Brandes? I am Lehmann." Without heeding the surprise he read in the young fellow's face, he went on:

"I have come to ask you to give a lecture to the People's Society in the Casino's big room."

As the addressee looked about to speak, he continued, drowning every objection, "I know what you are going to say. That you are too young. Youth is written in your face. But there is no question of seniority here. I am accustomed to accomplish what I determine upon, and I shall take no notice of objections. I know that you are able to give lectures, you have recently given proof of it."

At last there was was a minute's pause, permitting the younger one to interpose:

"But you are making a mistake, it is not I you mean. It must be my elder brother."

"Oh! very likely. Where does your brother live?"

"Just underneath."

A minute later there was a knock at the third-storey door beneath; it was opened, and without even stopping to sit down, the visitor began:

"You are Brandes? I am Lehmann. You recently gave some lectures on Runeberg. Will you kindly repeat one of them before the People's Society in the Casino's big room?"

"Won't you sit down? I thank you for your offer. But my lecture was not good enough to be repeated before

so large a gathering. I do not know enough about Runeberg's life, and my voice, moreover, will not carry. I should
not dare, at my age, to speak in so large a room."

"I expected you to reply that you are too young. Your
youth is written in your face. But there is no question of
seniority about it. I am accustomed to carry through anything that I have determined upon, and I take no notice of
objections. What you do not know about Runeberg's life,
you can read up in a literary history. And if you can give a
successful lecture to a private audience, you can give one in a
theatre hall. I am interested in you, I am depending on you,
I take your promise with me. Good-bye!"

This so-called promise became a regular nightmare to
me, young and absolutely untried as I was. It did not even
occur to me to work up and improve my lecture on Runeberg,
for the very thought of appearing before a large audience
alarmed me and was utterly intolerable to me. During the
whole of my first stay in Paris I was so tormented by the consent that Orla Lehmann had extorted from me, that it was a
shadow over my pleasure. I would go happy to bed and
wake up in the middle of the night with the terror of a debtor
over something far off, but surely threatening, upon me, seek
in my memory for what it was that was troubling me, and
find that this far-off, threatening thing was my promise to
Lehmann. It was only after my return home that I summoned up courage to write to him, pleading my youth and
unfitness, and begging to be released from the honourable
but distasteful duty. Orla Lehmann, in the meantime, had
in all probability not bestowed a thought on the whole matter and long since forgotten all about it.

In any case he never referred to the subject again in
after years, when we frequently met.

Among Bröchner's private pupils was a young student,
Kristian Möller, by name, who devoted himself exclusively
to philosophy, and of whom Bröchner was particularly fond.
He had an unusually keen intelligence, inclined to critical and
disintegrating research. His abilities were very promising,
inasmuch as it seemed that he might be able to establish
destructive verdicts upon much that was confused, or self-

contradicting, but nevertheless respected; in other respects he had a strangely infertile brain. He had no sudden inspirations, no imagination. It could not be expected that he would ever bring forward any specially new thoughts, only that he would penetrate confusion, think out errors to the bottom, and, with the years, carry out a process of thorough cleansing.

But before he had accomplished any independent work his lungs became affected. It was not at once perceived how serious the affection was, and Orla Lehmann, who, with the large-mindedness and open-handedness of a patriot, had taken him up, as well as sundry other young men who promised well or were merely poor, not only invited him to his weekly dinner-parties at Frederiksberg, but sent him to Upsala, that he might study Swedish philosophy there. Möller himself was much inclined to study Boströmianism and write a criticism of this philosophy, which was at that time predominant in Sweden.

He ought to have been sent South, or rather to a sanatorium; Orla Lehmann's Scandinavian sympathies, however, determined his stay in the North, which proved fatal to his health.

In 1868 he returned to Copenhagen, pale, with hollow cheeks, and a stern, grave face, that of a marked man, his health thoroughly undermined. His friends soon learnt, and doubtless he understood himself, that his condition was hopeless. The quite extraordinary strength of character with which he submitted, good-temperedly and without a murmur, to his fate, had for effect that all who knew him vied with each other in trying to lessen the bitterness of his lot and at any rate show him how much they cared for him. As he could not go out, and as he soon grew incapable of connected work, his room became an afternoon and evening meeting-place for many of his comrades, who went there to distract him with whatever they could think of to narrate, or discuss. If you found him alone, it was rarely long before a second and a third visitor came, and the room filled up.

Orla Lehmann, his patron, was also one of Kristian Möller's frequent visitors. But whenever he arrived, gen-

erally late and the last, the result was always the same. The
students and graduates, who had been sitting in the room in
lively converse, were struck dumb, awed by the presence of
the great man; after the lapse of a few minutes, one would
get up and say good-bye; immediately afterwards the next
would remember that he was engaged elsewhere just at that
particular time; a moment later the third would slip noiselessly out of the room, and it would be empty.

There was one, however, who, under such circumstances,
found it simply impossible to go. I stayed, even if I had just
been thinking of taking my leave.

Under the autocracy, Orla Lehmann had been the lyrical figure of Politics; he had voiced the popular hopes and
the beauty of the people's will, much more than the political
poets did. They wrote poetry; his nature was living poetry.
The swing of his eloquence, which so soon grew out of date,
was the very swing of youth in men's souls then. At the
time I first knew him, he had long left the period of his
greatness behind him, but he was still a handsome, well
set-up man, and, at 58 years of age, had lost nothing of
his intellectual vivacity. He had lost his teeth and spoke
indistinctly, but he was fond of telling tales and told them
well, and his enemies declared that as soon as a witty thought
struck him, he took a cab and drove round from house to
house to relate it.

Passionately patriotic though Orla Lehmann was, he
was very far from falling into the then usual error of over-
estimating Denmark's historical exploits and present importance. He related one day that when he was in Paris, as a
young man, speaking under an impression very frequent
among his travelled compatriots, he had, in a conversation
with Sainte-Beuve, reproached the French with knowing so
shamefully little of the Danes. The great critic, as was his
habit, laid his head a little on one side, and with roguish
impertinence replied: *"Eh! bien, faites quelque chose! on
parlera de vous."* He approved of the reply. We younger
ones looked upon him as belonging to another period and living in another plane of ideas, although, being a liberal-
minded man, he was not far removed from us. He was

supposed to be a freethinker, and it was told of him that
when his old housekeeper repeatedly, and with increasing
impatience, requested him to come to table, he would reply,
in the presence of students—a rallying allusion to the lady's
Christian disposition:

" Get help from Religion, little Bech, get help from
Religion ! "—a remark that in those days would be regarded
as wantonly irreligious !

People felt sorry for Lehmann because his politics had
so wholly miscarried, and somewhat sore against him because he wanted to lay all the blame on the old despotism
and the unfavourable circumstances of the time. Take him
altogether, to those who were not intimately associated with
him, and did not share the strong dislike felt against him in
certain circles, he was chiefly a handsome and attractive
antiquity.

Kristian Möller died in 1869, and his death was deeply
lamented. He was one of the few comrades admired by the
younger ones alike for his gifts and his stoicism. With his
death my opportunities of frequently meeting Orla Lehmann
ceased. But that the latter had not quite lost sight of me,
he proved by appearing, at the end of February, 1870, at
my examination upon my doctor's thesis at the University.
As on this occasion Lehmann arrived a little late, he was
placed on a chair in front of all the other auditors, and very
imposing he looked, in a mighty fur coat which showed off
his stately figure. He listened very attentively to everything, and several times during the discussion showed
by a short laugh that some parrying reply had amused
him.

Six months afterwards he was no more.

XVII.

During those years I came into very curious relations
with another celebrity of the time. This was M. Goldschmidt, the author, whose great talent I had considerable
difficulty in properly appreciating, so repelled was I by his
uncertain and calculating personality.

I saw Goldschmidt for the first time, when I was a young man, at a large ball at a club in Copenhagen.

A man who had emigrated to England as a poor boy returned to Copenhagen in the sixties at the age of fifty, after having acquired a considerable fortune. He was un-educated, kind, impeccably honourable, and was anxious to secure acquaintances and associates for his adopted daugh ter, a delicate young girl, who was strange to Copenhagen. With this object in view, he invited a large number of young people to a ball in the rooms of the King's Club, provided good music and luxurious refreshments. This man was a cousin of Goldschmidt's, and as he himself was unable to make more of a speech than a short welcome to table, he begged " his cousin, the poet," to be his spokesman on this occasion.

One would have thought that so polished a writer, such a master of language, as Goldschmidt, would be able, with the greatest ease, to make an after-dinner speech, especially when he had had plenty of time to prepare himself; but the gift of speaking is, as everyone knows, a gift in itself. And a more unfortunate speaker than Goldschmidt could not be. He had not even the art of compelling silence while he spoke.

That evening he began rather tactlessly by telling the company that their host, who was a rich man, had earned his money in a strictly honourable manner; it was always a good thing to know " that one had clear ground to dance upon "; then he dwelt on the Jewish origin of the giver of the feast, and, starting from the assumption that the greater number of the invited guests were young Jews and Jewesses, he formulated his toast in praise of " the Jewish woman, who lights the Sabbath candles." The young Jewesses called out all at once: " The Danish woman! The Danish woman! We are Danish! " They were irritated at the dead Romanticism into which Goldschmidt was trying to push them back. They lighted no Sabbath candles! they did not feel themselves Jewish either by religion or nationality. The day of Antisemitism had not arrived. Consequently there was still no Zionist Movement. They had also often felt vexed at the descriptions that Goldschmidt in his novels frequently gave of modern Jews, whose manners and mode of expression he screwed back fifty years.

These cries, which really had nothing offensive about them, made Goldschmidt lose his temper to such an extent that he shouted, in great exasperation: " Will you keep silence while I speak! What manners are these! I will teach you to keep silence! " and so forth,—which evoked a storm of laughter. He continued for some time to rebuke their exuberant mirth in severe terms, but was so unsuccessful that he broke off his speech and, very much out of humour, sat down.

Not long afterwards, perhaps in the year 1865, I came into contact with Goldschmidt once only, when walking one evening with Magdalene Thoresen. On meeting this lady, whom he knew, he turned round, walking with her as far as her house on the shores of the Lakes, after which his way led towards the town, as did mine. As long as Mrs. Thoresen was present, he naturally addressed his conversation to her and expressed himself, as his habit was, without much ceremony. For instance, he said: " I don't as a rule care for women writers, not even for those we have; but I will concede that, of all the ladies who write, you are the freshest." When Mrs. Thoresen brought the conversation round to her favourite subject, love, he said, banteringly: " My heart is like the flags of the Zouave Regiments, so pierced with holes that it is almost impossible to tell what the material originally looked like."

On the whole, he was animated and polite, but his glance was somewhat stinging.

Goldschmidt had greater difficulty in hitting on the right manner to adopt towards a much younger man. He used expressions which showed that he was standing on his dignity, and was all the time conscious of his own superiority. " People have spoken about you to me," he said, " and I know you by name." The word here rendered *people* had a strangely foreign sound, as though translated, or affected.

" Have you read Taine's History of English Literature? " he asked.

" No, I don't know it."

"Ah, perhaps you are one of those who regard it as superfluous to learn about anything foreign. We have enough of our own, is it not so? It is a very widespread opinion, but it is a mistake."

"You judge too hastily; that is not my opinion."

"Oh,—ah. Yes. Good-bye."

And our ways parted.

I did not like Goldschmidt. He had dared to profane the great Sören Kierkegaard, had pilloried him for the benefit of a second-rate public. I disliked him on Kierkegaard's account. But I disliked him much more actively on my master, Professor Bröchner's account.

Bröchner had an intense contempt for Goldschmidt; intellectually he thought him of no weight, as a man he thought him conceited, and consequently ridiculous. He had not the slightest perception of the literary artist in him. The valuable and unusual qualities of his descriptive talent he overlooked. But the ignorance Goldschmidt had sometimes shown about philosophy, and the incapacity he had displayed with regard to art, his change of political opinion, his sentimentality as a wit, all the weaknesses that one Danish critic had mercilessly dragged into the light, had inspired Bröchner with the strongest aversion to Goldschmidt. Add to this the personal collisions between the two men. At some public meeting Bröchner had gazed at Goldschmidt with such an ironic smile that the latter had passionately called him to account.

"Don't make a scene now!" replied Bröchner.

"I am ready to make a scene anywhere," the answer is reported to have been.

"That I can believe; but keep calm now!"

Shortly afterwards, in *North and South,* Goldschmidt, on the occasion of Bröchner's candidature for parliament, had written that the well-known atheist, H. Bröchner, naturally, as contributor to *The Fatherland,* was supported by the "Party." Now, there was nothing that annoyed Bröchner so much as when anyone called him an atheist, and tried to make him hated for that reason,—the word, it is true, had a hundred times a worse sound then than now,—he always maintaining that he and other so-called atheists were far more religious than their assailants. And although Goldschmidt's sins against Bröchner were in truth but small, although the latter, moreover—possibly unjustifiably—had challenged him to the attack, Bröchner nevertheless imbued me with such a dislike of Goldschmidt that I could not regard him with quite unprejudiced eyes.

Goldschmidt tried to make personal advances to me during my first stay in Paris in 1866.

Besides the maternal uncle settled in France, of whom I have already spoken, I had still another uncle, my father's brother, who had gone to France as a boy, had become naturalised, and had settled in Paris. He was a little older than my father, a somewhat restless and fantastic character, whom Goldschmidt frequently met at the houses of mutual friends. He let me know through this man that he would like to make my acquaintance, gave him his address and mentioned his receiving hours. As I held back, he repeated the invitation, but in vain. Bröchner's influence was too strong. A few years later, in some dramatic articles, I had expressed myself in a somewhat satirical, offhand manner about Goldschmidt, when one day an attempt was made to bring the poet and myself into exceedingly close connection.

One Spring morning in 1869, a little man with blue spectacles came into my room and introduced himself as Goldschmidt's publisher, Bookseller Steen. He had come on a confidential errand from Goldschmidt, regarding which he begged me to observe strict silence, whatever the outcome of the matter might be.

Goldschmidt knew that, as a critic, I was not in sympathy with him, but being very difficultly placed, he appealed to my chivalry. For reasons which he did not wish to enter into, he would be obliged, that same year, to sever his connection with Denmark and settle down permanently in England. For the future he should write in English. But before he left he wished to terminate his literary activity in his native country by an edition of his collected works, or at any rate a very exhaustive selection from them. He would not and could not direct so great an undertaking himself, from another country; he only knew one man who was capable of doing so, and him he requested to undertake the matter. He had drawn up a plan of the edition, a sketch of the order in which the writings were to come out, and what the volume was to contain, and he placed it before me for approval or criticism. · The edition was to be preceded by an account of Goldschmidt as an author and of his artistic development; if I would undertake to write this, I was asked to go to see Goldschmidt, in order to hear what he himself regarded as the main features and chief points of his literary career.

The draft of what the projected edition was to include made quite a little parcel of papers; besides these, Steen gave me to read the actual request to me to undertake the task, which was cautiously worded as a letter, not to me, but to Bookseller Steen, and which Steen had been expressly enjoined to bring back with him. Although I did not at all like this last-mentioned item, and although this evidence of distrust was in very conspicuous variance with the excessive and unmerited confidence that was at the same time being shown me, this same confidence impressed me greatly.

The information that Goldschmidt, undoubtedly the first prose writer in the country, was about to break off his literary activity and permanently leave Denmark, was in itself overwhelming and at once set my imagination actively at work. What could the reason be? A crime? That was out of the question. What else could there be but a love affair, and that had my entire sympathy. It was well known that Goldschmidt admired a very beautiful woman, who was watched the more jealously by her husband, because the latter had for a great number of years been paralysed. He would not allow her to go to the theatre to sit anywhere but in the mirror box[1], where she could not be seen by the public. The husband met with no sympathy from the public; he had always been a characterless and sterile writer, had published only two books, written in a diametrically opposite spirit,

---

[1] The mirror box was a box in the first Royal Theatre, surrounded by mirrors and with a grating in front, where the stage could be seen, reflected in the mirrors, but the occupants were invisible. It was originally constructed to utilise a space whence the performance could not otherwise be seen, and was generally occupied by actresses, etc.

flatly contradicting one another. As long as he was able to go out he had dyed his red hair black. He was an insignificant man in every way, and by his first marriage with an ugly old maid had acquired the fortune which alone had enabled him to pay court to the beautiful woman he subsequently won.

It had leaked out that she was the original of the beautiful woman in *The Inheritance*, and that some of the letters that occur in it were really notes from Goldschmidt to her.

What more likely than the assumption that the position of affairs had at last become unbearable to Goldschmidt, and that he had determined on an elopement to London? In a romantic purpose of the sort Goldschmidt could count upon the sympathy of a hot-blooded young man. I consequently declared myself quite willing to talk the matter over with the poet and learn more particulars as to what was expected of me; meanwhile, I thought I might promise my assistance. It was Easter week, I believe Maunday Thursday; I promised to call upon Goldschmidt on one of the holidays at a prearranged time.

Good Friday and Easter Sunday I was prevented from going to him, and I had already made up my mind to pay my visit on Easter Monday when on Monday morning I received a letter from Bookseller Steen which made me exceedingly indignant. The letter, which exhibited, as I considered, (incorrectly, as it turned out), unmistakably signs of having been dictated to him, bore witness to the utmost impatience. Steen wrote that after undertaking to pay a visit to Goldschmidt I had now let two days elapse without fulfilling my promise. There was " no sense in keeping a man waiting " day after day, on such important business; in Steen's " personal opinion," it had not been at all polite of me, as the younger author, not to inform Goldschmidt which day I would go to see him.

I was very much cooled by reading this letter. I saw that I had wounded Goldschmidt's vanity deeply by not going to him immediately upon receipt of his communication; but my chief impression was one of surprise that Goldschmidt should reveal himself such a poor psychologist in my case. How could he believe that I would allow myself to be terrified by rough treatment or won by tactless reprimands? How could he think that I regarded the task he wished to allot me as such an honour that for that reason I had not refused it? Could not Goldschmidt understand that it was solely the appeal to my better feelings from an opponent, struck by an untoward fate, that had determined my attitude?

Simultaneously, though at first very faintly, a suspicion crossed my mind. Was it possible that the whole touching story which had been confided to me was a hoax calculated to disarm my antagonism, arouse my sympathy and secure Goldschmidt a trumpeting herald? Was it possible that the mysterious information about the flight to London was only an untruth, the sole purpose of which was to get me into Goldschmidt's service?

I dismissed the thought at once as too improbable, but it recurred, for I had learnt from experience that even distinguished authors sometimes did not shrink from very daring means of securing the services of a critic. A critic is like the rich heiress, who is always afraid of not being loved for herself alone. Even then, I was very loth to believe that any recognised author, much less a writer whose position was a vexed question, would make advances to me from pure benevolence, for the sake of my beautiful eyes, as they say in French.

At any rate, I had now made up my mind not to have anything whatever to do with the matter. I replied emphatically:

"Lessons in politeness I take from no one, consequently return you the enclosed papers. Be kind enough to appeal to some one else."

This reply was evidently not the one the letter had been intended to evoke. Steen rushed up to me at once to apologise, but I did not see him. Twice afterwards he came with humble messages from Goldschmidt asking me to "do him the honour" of paying him a visit. But my pride was touchy, and my determination unwavering. Undoubtedly Steen's letter was sent at Goldschmidt's wish, but it is equally undoubted that its form had not been approved by him. That the alliance so cleverly led up to came to nothing was evidently as unexpected by the poet as unpalatable to him.

Not long afterwards, I accidentally had strong confirmation of my suspicion that the story of a flight from Denmark was merely an invention calculated to trap me, and after the lapse of some time I could no longer harbour a doubt that Goldschmidt had merely wished to disarm a critic and secure himself a public crier.

This did not make me feel any the more tenderly disposed towards Goldschmidt, and my feeling lent a sharper tone than it would otherwise have had to an essay I wrote shortly afterwards about him on the production of his play *Rabbi and Knight* at the Royal Theatre.

Three years passed before our paths crossed again and a short-lived association came about between us.

XVIII.

In my public capacity about this time, I had many against me and no one wholly for me, except my old protector Bröchner, who, for one thing, was very ill, and for another, by reason of his ponderous language, was unknown to the reading world at large. Among my personal friends there was not one who shared my fundamental views; if they were fond of me, it was in spite of my views. That in itself was a sufficient reason why I could not expect them, in the intellectual feud in which I was still engaged, to enter the lists on my behalf. I did not need any long experience to perceive that complete and unmixed sympathy with my endeavours was a thing I should not find. Such a sympathy I only met with in reality from one of my comrades, Emil Petersen, a young private individual with no connection whatever with literature, and without influence in other directions.

Moreover, I had learnt long ago that, as a literary beginner in a country on a Liliputian scale, I encountered prompt opposition at every step, and that ill-will against me was always expressed much more forcibly than good-will, was quickly, so to say, organised.

I had against me at once every literary or artistic critic

who already held an assured position, from the influential
men who wrote in *The Fatherland* or the *Berling Times* to
the small fry who snapped in the lesser papers, and if they
mentioned me at all it was with the utmost contempt, or in
some specially disparaging manner. It was the rival that they
fought against. Thus it has continued to be all my life.
Certain " critics," such as Falkman in Denmark and Wirsen
in Sweden, hardly ever put pen to paper for some forty
years without bestowing an affectionate thought upon me.
(Later, in Norway, I became Collin's *idée fixe*.)

Add to these all who feared and hated a train of thought
which in their opinion was dangerous to good old-fashioned
faith and morality.

Definite as were the limits of my articles and longer
contributions to the dispute concerning Faith and Science, and
although, strictly speaking, they only hinged upon an obscure
point in Rasmus Nielsen's philosophy, they alarmed and excited a large section of the ecclesiastics of the country. I
had carefully avoided saying anything against faith or piety;
I knew that Orthodoxy was all-powerful in Denmark. However, I did not meet with refutations, only with the indignation of fanaticism. As far back as 1867 Björnson had
come forward in print against me, had reproached the *Daily
Paper* with giving my contributions a place in their columns, and reported their contents to the Editor, who was
away travelling, on the supposition that they must have been
accepted against his wishes; and although the article did not
bear Björnson's name, this attack was not without weight.
The innocent remark that Sören Kierkegaard was the Tycho
Brahe of our philosophy, as great as Tycho Brahe, but, like
him, failing to place the centre of our solar system in its
Sun, gave Björnson an opportunity for the statement,—
a very dangerous one for a young author of foreign
origin to make,—that the man who could write like that
" had no views in common with other Danes, no Danish
mind."

The year after I was astonished by inflammatory outbursts on the part of the clergy. One day in 1868 the much-
respected Pastor Hohlenberg walked into my friend Benny

Spang's house, reprimanded her severely for receiving such an undoubted heretic and heathen under her roof, and demanded that she should break off all association with me. As she refused to do so and turned a deaf ear to his arguments, losing all self-control, he flung his felt hat on the floor, continued to rage and rail against me, and, no result coming of it, dashed at last, in a towering passion, out through the door, which he slammed behind him. There was a farcical ending to the scene, since he was obliged to ring at the door again for his hat, which, in his exasperation, he had forgotten. This was a kind of private prologue to the ecclesiastical drama which from the year 1871 upwards was enacted in most of the pulpits of the country. Only the parsons instead of flinging their hats upon the floor, beat their hands against the pulpit.

But what surprised me, a literary beginner, still more, was the gift I discovered in myself of hypnotising, by my mere existence, an ever-increasing number of my contemporaries till they became as though possessed by a hatred which lasted, sometimes a number of years, sometimes a whole life long, and was the essential determining factor in their careers and actions. By degrees, in this negative manner, I succeeded in engaging the attentions of more than a score of persons. For the time being, I encountered the phenomenon in the person of one solitary genius-mad individual. For a failure of a poet and philosopher, with whom I had nothing to do, and who did not interest me in the least, I became the one enemy it was his business to attack.

Rudolf Schmidt, who was a passionate admirer of Rasmus Nielsen, in whose examination lectures he coached freshmen, was enraged beyond measure by the objections, perfectly respectful, for that matter, in form, which I had raised against one of the main points in Nielsen's philosophy. In 1866 he published a pamphlet on the subject; in 1867 a second, which, so possessed was he by his fury against his opponent, he signed with the latter's own initials, Gb. And from this time forth, for at least a generation, it became this wretch's task in life to persecute me under every possible pseudonym, and when his own powers were not sufficient, to get up conspiracies against me. In particular, he did all he could against me in Germany.

Meanwhile, he started a magazine in order to bring before the public himself and the ideas he was more immediately serving, viz.: those of R. Nielsen; and since this latter had of late drawn very much nearer to the Grundtvigian way of thinking, partly also those of Grundtvig. The magazine had three editors, amongst them R. Nielsen himself, and when one of them, who was the critic of the *Fatherland,* suddenly left the country, Björnstjerne Björnson took his place. The three names, R. Nielsen, B. Björnson, and Rudolph Schmidt, formed a trinity whose supremacy did not augur well for the success of a beginner in the paths of literature, who had attacked the thinker among them for ideal reasons, and who had been the object of violent attacks from the two others. The magazine *Idea and Reality,* was, as might be expected, sufficiently unfavourable to my cause.

The sudden disappearance of the critic of *The Fatherland* from the literary arena was, under the conditions of the time, an event. He had no little talent, attracted by ideas and fancies that were sometimes very telling, repelled by mannerisms and a curious, far-fetched style, laid chief emphasis, in the spirit of the most modern Danish philosophy, on the will, and always defended ethical standpoints. From the time of Björnson's first appearance he had attached himself so enthusiastically and inviolably to him that by the general public he was almost regarded as Björnson's herald. At every opportunity he emphatically laid down Björnson's importance and as a set-off fell upon those who might be supposed to be his rivals. Ibsen, in particular, received severe handling. His departure was thus a very hard blow for Björnson, but for that matter, was also felt as a painful loss by those he opposed.

XIX.

Not long after this departure, and immediately after the publication of my long article on Goldschmidt, I received one day, to my surprise, a letter of eight closely written pages from Björnstjerne Björnson, dated April 15th, 1869.

What had called it forth was my remark, in that article, that Björnson, like Goldschmidt, sometimes, when talent failed, pretended to have attained the highest, pretended that obscurity was the equivalent of profundity. When writing this, I was thinking of the obscure final speech about God in Heaven in Björnson's *Mary Stuart,* which I still regard as quite vague, pretentious though it be as it stands there; however, it was an exaggeration to generalise the grievance, as I had done, and Björnson was right to reply. He considered that I had accused him of insincerity, though in this he was wrong; but for that matter, with hot-tempered eloquence, he also denied my real contention. His letter began:

Although I seldom read your writings, so that possibly I risk speaking of something you have elsewhere developed more clearly, and thus making a mistake, I nevertheless wish to make a determined protest against its being called a characteristic of mine, in contrast to Oehlenschläger (and Hauch!!), to strain my powers to reach what I myself only perceive unclearly, and then intentionally to state it as though it were clear. I am quite sure that I resemble Oehlenschläger in one thing, namely, that the defects of my book are open to all, and are not glossed over with any sort or kind of lie; anything unclear must for the moment have seemed clear to me, as in his case. My motto has always been: " Be faithful in *small* things, and God shall make you ruler over great things." And never, no, never, have I snatched after great material in order to seem great, or played with words in order to seem clever, or been silent, in order to appear deep. Never. The examples around me have been appalling to me, and I am sure that they have been so because I have from the very beginning been on my guard against lies. There are passages in every work which will not yield immediately what one impatiently demands of them;—and then I have always waited, never tried; the thing has had to come itself unforced, and it is possible that what I have received has been a deception; but I have believed in it; to me it has been no deception. Before I finally conclude, I always, it is true, go over again what I have written (as in the case of *Synnöve,* and *A Happy Boy, Between the Fights, etc.* I wish to have the advantage of a better perception. Thus far, in what I have gone through, I have seen weak places which I can no longer correct. Lies I have never found.

Unfortunately one is often exposed to the danger of being untrue; but it is in moments of surprise and absolute passion, when something happens to one's eye or one's tongue, that one feels is half mad, but when the beast of prey within one, which shrinks at nothing, is the stronger. Untrue in one's beautiful, poetic calm, one's confessional silence, at one's work, I think very few are.

This summing up, which does honour to Björnson and is not only a striking self-verdict, but a valuable contribution to poetic psychology in general, in its indication of the strength of the creative imagination and its possibilities of error, was followed by a co-ordinate attempt at a characterisation and appreciation of Goldschmidt:

You are likewise unjust to Goldschmidt on this point, that I know with certainty. Goldschmidt is of a naïve disposition, susceptible of every noble emotion. It is true that he often stages these in a comic manner, and what you say about that is true; he does the same in private life, but you have not recognised the source of this. In the last instance, it is not a question of what we think, but of what we do. Just as this, on the whole, is an error that you fall persistently into, it is in particular an error here, where, for instance, his two brothers, with the same qualifications and with the same dual nature, have both developed into characters, the one indeed into a remarkable personality. But Goldschmidt began as a corsair captain at seventeen; his courage was the courage behind a pen that he fancied was feared, his happiness that of the flatterer, his dread that of being vapid; and there were many other unfavourable circumstances, for that matter. . . . He is now striving hard towards what he feels has, during his life, been wasted in his ability, both moral and intellectual qualities, and for my part, I respect this endeavour more than his decisive success within narrow limits.

In this passage the distinction and contrast between contemplative life and actual existence was quite in the Rasmus Nielsen spirit; the use that was made of it here was strange. One would suppose that the example adduced established that similar natural qualifications, similar family and other conditions, in other words, the actual essential conditions of life, were of small importance compared with one's mode of thought, since the brothers could be so different; Björnson wished to establish, hereby, that the mode of life was more important than the mode of thought, although the former must depend on the latter. For the rest, he alluded to Goldschmidt's weak points, even if in somewhat too superior a manner, and without laying stress upon his great artistic importance, with leniency and good-will.

But if, in other things he touched upon, he had an eye for essentials, this failed him sadly when the letter proceeded to a characterisation of the addressee, in which he mixed up true and false in inextricable confusion. Amongst other things, he wrote:

Here, I doubtless touch upon a point that is distinctive of your criticism. It is an absolute beauty worship. With that you can quickly traverse our little literature and benefit no one greatly; for the poet is only benefited by the man who approaches him with affection and from his own standpoint; the other he does not understand, and the public will, likely enough, pass with you through this unravelling of the thousand threads, and believe they are growing; but no man or woman who is sound and good lays down a criticism of this nature without a feeling of emptiness.

I chanced to read one of your travel descriptions which really became a pronouncement upon some of the greatest painters. It was their nature in their works (not their history or their lives so much as their natural dispositions) that you pointed out,—also the influence of their time upon them, but this only in passing; and you compared these painters, one with another. In itself, much of this mode of procedure is correct, but the result is merely racy. A single one of them, seized largely and affectionately, shown in such manner that the different paintings and figures became a description of himself, but were simultaneously the unfolding of a culture, would have been five times as understandable. A contrast can be drawn in when opportunity arises, but that is not the essential task. Yes, this is an illustration of the form of your criticism. It is an everlasting, and often very painful, juxtaposition of things appertaining and contrasting, but just as poetry itself is an absorption in the one thing that it has extracted from the many, so comprehension of it is dependent on the same conditions. The individual work or the individual author whom you have treated of, you have in the same way not brought together, but disintegrated, and the whole has become merely a piquant piece of effectiveness. Hitherto one might have said that it was at least good-natured; but of late there have supervened flippant expressions, paradoxical sentences, crude definitions, a definite contumacy and disgust, which is now and again succeeded by an outburst of delight over the thing that is peculiarly Danish, or peculiarly beautiful. I cannot help thinking of P. L. Möller, as I knew him in Paris.

There are a thousand things between Heaven and Earth that you understand better than I. But for that very reason you can listen to me. It seems to me now as if the one half of your powers were undoing what the other half accomplishes. I, too, am a man with intellectual interests, but I feel no cooperation. Might there not be other tasks that you were more fitted for than that of criticism? I mean, that would be less of a temptation to you, and would *build* up on your personality, at the same time as you yourself were building? It strikes me that even if you do choose criticism, it should be more strongly in the direction of our educating responsibilities and less as the arranger of technicalities, the spyer out of small things, the dragger together of all and everything which can be brought forward as a witness for or against the author, which is all frightfully welcome in a contemporary critical epidemic in Copenhagen, but, God help me, is nothing and accomplishes nothing.

This part of the letter irritated me intensely, partly by the mentor's tone assumed in it, partly by a summing up of my critical methods which was founded simply and solely on the reading of three or four articles, more especially those on Rubens and Goldschmidt, and which quite missed the point. I was far from feeling that I had been understood, and for that reason warned against extremes; on the contrary, I saw myself only caricatured, without even wit or humour, and could not forget that the man who had sketched this picture of me had done his utmost to injure me. And he compared me with P. L. Möller!

The fact that the conclusion of the letter contained much that was conciliatory and beautiful consequently did not help matters. Björnson wrote:

When you write about the Jews, although I am not in agreement with you, *altogether* in agreement, you yet seem to me to touch upon a domain where you might have much to offer us, many beautiful prospects to open to

us. In the same way, when you interpret Shakespeare (not when you make
poetry by the side of him), when you tranquilly expound, I seem to see the
beginnings of greater works, in any case of powers which I could imagine
essentially contributing to the introduction into our culture of greater breadth
of view, greater moral responsibility, more affection.

When I now read these words, I am obliged to transport myself violently back, into the feelings and to the intellectual standpoint that were mine at the time, in order
to understand how they could to such a pitch incense me.   It
was not only that, like all young people of any account, I
was irritable, sensitive and proud, and unwilling to be treated
as a pupil; but more than that, as the way of youth is, I confused what I knew myself capable of accomplishing with
what I had already accomplished; felt myself rich, exuber-
antly rich, already, and was indignant at perceiving myself
deemed still so small.

But the last straw was a sentence which followed:

I should often have liked to talk all this over with you, when last I was
in Copenhagen, but I noticed I was so pried after by gossips that I gave it up.

The last time Björnson was in Copenhagen he had written that article against me.   Besides, I had been told that
some few times he had read my first articles aloud in public
in friends' houses, and made fun of their forced and tyro-like
wording.   And now he wanted me to believe that he had at
that time been thinking of visiting me, in order to come to
an understanding with me.   And worse still, the fear of gossip had restrained him!   This hero of will-power so afraid
of a little gossip!   He might go on as he liked now, I had
done with him.   He did go on, both cordially and gracefully, but condescendingly, quite incapable of seeing how
wounding the manner of his advances was.   He wished to
make advances to me and yet maintain a humiliating attitude
of condescension:

There are not many of us in literature who are in earnest; the few who
are ought not to be daunted by the accidental separation that opposed opinions
can produce, when there is a large field for mutual understanding and
co-operation.   I sometimes get violently irate for a moment; if this in
lesser men, in whom there really is something base, brings about a lifelong
separation, it does not greatly afflict me.   But I should be very sorry if it
should influence the individuals in whom I feel there are both ability and

will. And as far as you are concerned, I have such a strong feeling that you must be standing at a parting of the ways, that, by continuing your path further, you will go astray, that I want to talk to you, and consequently am speaking from my heart to you now. If you do not understand, I am sorry; that is all I can say.

In the Summer I am going to Finmark, and involuntarily, as I write this, the thought occurs to me what a journey it would be for you; away from everything petty and artificial to a scenery which in its magnificent loneliness is without parallel in the world, and where the wealth of birds above us and fish beneath us (whales, and shoals of herrings, cod and capelans often so close together that you can take them up in your hands, or they press against the sides of the boat) are marvel upon marvel, in the light of a Sun that does not set, while human beings up there live quiet and cowed by Nature. If you will come with me, and meet me, say, at Trondhjem, I know that you would not regret it. And then I should get conversation again; here there are not many who hit upon just that which I should like them to. Think about it.

A paragraph relating to Magdalene Thoresen followed. But what is here cited is the essential part of the letter. Had its recipient known Björnson better, he would in this have found a foundation to build upon. But as things were, I altogether overlooked the honestly meant friendliness in it and merely seized upon the no small portion of it that could not do other than wound. My reply, icy, sharp and in the deeper sense of the word, worthless, was a refusal. I did not believe in Björnson, saw in the letter nothing but an attempt to use me as a critic, now that he had lost his former advocate in the Press. The prospect of the journey to the North did not tempt me; in Björnson's eyes it would have been Thor's journey with Loki, and I neither was Loki nor wished to be.

But even had I been capable of rising to a more correct and a fuller estimate of Björnson's character, there was too much dividing us at this time for any real friendship to have been established. Björnson was then still an Orthodox Protestant, and in many ways hampered by his youthful impressions; I myself was still too brusque to be able to adapt myself to so difficult and masterful a personality.

Eight years elapsed before the much that separated me from Björnson crumbled away. But then, when of his own accord he expressed his regret on a public occasion at the rupture between us, and spoke of me with unprejudiced comprehension and good-will, I seized with warmth and gratitude the hand stretched out to me. A hearty friendship, bringing with it an active and confidential correspondence, was established between us and remained unshaken for the next ten years, when it broke down, this time through no fault of mine, but through distrust on Björnson's part, just as our intimacy had been hindered the first time through distrust on mine.

The year 1869 passed in steady hard work. Among the many smaller articles I wrote, one with the title of *The Infinitely Small and the Infinitely Great in Poetry,* starting with a re-presentment of Shakespeare's Harry Percy, contained a criticism of the hitherto recognised tendency of Danish dramatic poetry and pointed out into the future. The paper on H. C. Andersen, which came into being towards midsummer, and was read aloud in a clover field to a solitary listener, was representative of my critical abilities and aims at that date. I had then known Andersen socially for a considerable time. My cordial recognition of his genius drew us more closely together; he often came to see me and was very ready to read his new works aloud to me. It is hardly saying too much to declare that this paper secured me his friendship.

The fundamental principles of the essay were influenced by Taine, the art philosopher I had studied most deeply, and upon whom I had written a book that was to be my doctor's thesis. Lightly and rapidly though my shorter articles came into being, this larger task was very long in hand. Not that I had little heart for my work; on the contrary, no question interested me more than those on which my book hinged; but there were only certain of them with which, as yet, I was equal to dealing.

First and foremost came the question of the nature of the producing mind, the possibility of showing a connection between its faculties and deriving them from one solitary dominating faculty, which would thus necessarily reveal itself in every aspect of the mind. It puzzled me, for example, how I was to find the source whence Pascal's taste, both for mathematics and religious philosophy, sprang. Next came the question of the possibility of a universally applicable scientific method of criticism, regarded as intellectual optics. If one were to define the critic's task as that of under-

standing, through the discovery and elucidation of the dependent and conditional contingencies that occur in the intellectual world, then there was a danger that he might approve
everything, not only every form and tendency of art that
had arisen historically, but each separate work within each
artistic section. If it were no less the critic's task to distinguish between the genuine and the spurious, he must at any
rate possess a technical standard by which to determine
greater or lesser value, or he must be so specially and extraordinarily gifted that his instinct and tact estimate infallibly.

Further, there was the question of genius, the point on
which Taine's theory roused decisive opposition in me. He
regarded genius as a summing up, not as a new starting-
point; according to him it was the assemblage of the
original aptitudes of a race and of the peculiarities of a
period in which these aptitudes were properly able to display
themselves. He overlooked the originality of the man of
genius, which could not be explained from his surroundings,
the new element which, in genius, was combined with the
summarising of surrounding particles. Before, when studying Hegel, I had been repelled by the suggestion that what
spoke to us through the artist was only the universally valid,
the universal mind, which, as it were, burnt out the originality of the individual. In Taine's teaching, nation and
period were the new (although more concrete) abstractions
in the place of the universally valid; but here, too, the par-
ticularity of the individual was immaterial. The kernel of
my work was a protest against this theory.

I was even more actively interested in the fundamental
question raised by a scientific view of history. For some
years I had been eagerly searching Comte and Littré, Buckle,
Mill and Taine for their opinions on the philosophy
of History. Here, too, though in another form, the question of the importance of the individual *versus* the masses
presented itself. Statistics had proved to what extent conscious actions were subordinated to uniform laws. We
could foresee from one year to another how many murders
would be committed and how many with each kind of instrument. The differences between men and men neutralised

each other, if we took the average of a very large number.
But this did not prove that the individual was not of considerable importance.   If the victory of Salamis depended on
Themistocles, then the entire civilisation of Europe henceforth depended on him.

Another aspect of the question was: Did the consistent determinism of modern Science, the discovery of an un-
alterable interdependency in the intellectual, as in the physical worlds, allow scope for actions proceeding otherwise than
merely illusorily from the free purpose or determination of
the individual?   Very difficult the question was, and I did
not feel confident of solving it; but it was some consolation
to reflect that the doubt as to the possibility of demonstrat-
ing a full application of the law in the domain in which chance
has sway, and Ethics its sphere, was comparatively infinitesi-
mal in the case of those domains in which men make themselves felt by virtue of genius or talent as producers of literary and artistic works.   Here, where natural gifts and their
necessary deployment were of such extraordinary weight,
the probability of a demonstration of natural laws was, of
course, much greater.

The general fundamental question was: Given a literature, a philosophy, an art, or a branch of art, what is the
attitude of mind that produces it?   What are its sufficing
and necessary conditions?   What, for instance, causes England in the sixteenth century to acquire a dramatic poetry of
the first rank, or Holland in the seventeenth century a painting art of the first rank, without any of the other branches
of art simultaneously bearing equally fine fruit in the same
country?

My deliberations resulted, for the time being, in the conviction that all profound historical research was psychical
research.

That old piece of work, revised, as it now is, has certainly none but historic interest; but for a doctor's thesis,
it is still a tolerably readable book and may, at any rate, introduce a beginner to reflection upon great problems.

After the fundamental scientific questions that engaged
my attention, I was most interested in artistic style.   There

was, in modern Danish prose, no author who unreservedly appealed to me; in German Heinrich Kleist, and in French Mérimée, were the stylists whom I esteemed most. The latter, in fact, it seemed to me was a stylist who, in unerring sureness, terseness and plasticism, excelled all others. He had certainly not much warmth or colour, but he had a sureness of line equal to that of the greatest draughtsmen of Italian art. His aridity was certainly not winning, and, in reading him, I frequently felt a lack of breadth of view and horizon, but the compelling power of his line-drawing captivated me. When my doctor's thesis was finished, towards the middle of December, 1869, both it and the collection of articles bearing the name *Criticisms and Portraits* were placed in the printer's hands. In the beginning of 1870 two hitherto unprinted pieces were added, of which one was a paper written some time before on Kamma Rahbek, which had been revised, the other, a new one on Mérimée, which in general shows what at that time I admired in style.

It had long been settled that as soon as I had replied to the critics of my thesis I should start on prolonged travels, the real educational travels of a young man's life. I had a little money lying ready, a small bursary, and a promise of a travelling allowance from the State, which promise, however, was not kept. This journey had for a long time been haunting my fancy. I cherished an ardent wish to see France again, but even more especially to go to Italy and countries still farther South. My hope of catching a glimpse of Northern Africa was only fulfilled thirty-five years later; but I got as far as Italy, which was the actual goal of my desires. I knew enough of the country, its history from ancient days until then, and was sufficiently acquainted with its Art from Roman times upwards and during the Renaissance, to be regarded as passed for intellectual consecration in the South.

When the thesis was done with and the printing of the second book was nearing completion, not anxiety to travel, but melancholy and heavy-heartedness at the thought of my departure, gained the upper hand. It had been decided that I was to remain away at least a year, and it was less to myself than to others whom I must necessarily leave behind, that the time seemed immeasurably long. Professor Schiödte advised me rather to take several short journeys than one long one; but that was impracticable. I wanted to get quite away from the home atmosphere. As, however, there were some who thought of my journey with disquiet and dread, and from whom it was difficult for me to tear myself, I put off my departure as long as I could. At last the remnant of work that still bound me to Copenhagen was finished, and then all the new and enriching prospects my stay in foreign countries was to bring me shone in a golden light. Full of undaunted hope, I set out on my travels at the beginning of April, 1870.

SECOND LONGER STAY ABROAD

I.

THE first thing that impressed me was Hamburg, and by that I mean the European views prevalent there. At that time, doubtless mainly for national reasons, Denmark hated Hamburg. Different Danish authors had recently written about the town, and in as depreciatory a strain as they could. The description of one amounted to an assertion that in Hamburg people only talked of two things, money and women; that of another commenced: "Of all the places I have ever seen in my life, Hamburg is the most hideous."

The situation of the town could not be compared with that of Copenhagen, but the Alster quarter was attractive, the architecture and the street life not uninteresting. What decided me, however, was not the externals of the town, but the spirit I noticed pervading the conversation. The idea underlying things was that a young man must first and foremost learn to keep himself well and comfortably; if he could not do this in Hamburg, then as soon as possible he must set off to some place across the sea, to Rio, or New York, to the Argentine, or Cape Colony, and there make his way and earn a fortune. The sons of the families I was invited to visit, or heard talked about, had long been away; in the houses I went to, the head of the family had seen other parts of the world. The contrast with Copenhagen was obvious; there the young sons of the middle classes were a burden on their families sometimes until they were thirty, had no enterprise, no money of their own to dispose of, were often glued, as it were, to the one town, where there was no promotion to look forward to and no wide prospect of any sort.

It was a long time since I had been so much struck by anything as by an expression that a Hamburg lady, who had been to Copenhagen and had stayed there some time, used about the young Danish men, namely, that they had *l'apparence chétive*. I tried to persuade her that life in Copenhagen had only accidentally appeared so wretched to her; but I did not convince her in the least. She demonstrated to me, by numerous examples, to what an extent enterprise was lacking in Denmark, and I was obliged to restrict myself to explaining that the tremendous pressure of political pettiness and weakness had brought a general slackness with it, without people feeling or suspecting it, and had robbed nearly every one of daring and success. The result of the conversation was that Denmark was shown to me in a fresh light.

A Hamburg merchant who had lived for a long time in Mexico invited me to dinner, and at his house I had the same impression of apparent happiness, comfort, enterprise and wide outlook, in contrast to the cares and the narrowness at home, where only the few had travelled far or collected material which might by comparison offer new points of view and give one a comprehensive experience of life. My psychological education in Danish literature, with its idolising of " thoroughness " had imprinted on my mind that whoever thoroughly understood how to observe a man, woman and child in a Copenhagen backyard had quite sufficient material whence to brew a knowledge of human nature. It now dawned upon me that comparative observation of a Mexican and a North German family, together with their opinions and prejudices, might nevertheless considerably advance one's knowledge of human nature, should such comparisons constantly obtrude themselves upon one.

The same man let fall an observation which set me think-ing. When the conversation turned upon the strained rela-tions between France and Prussia since the battle of König-gratz, and I expressed myself confident that, in the event of a war, France would be victorious, as she generally was victo-rious everywhere, he expressed well-supported doubts. Prus-sia was a comparatively young state, extremely well organ-ised and carefully prepared for war; antiquated routine held great sway in the French army; the Emperor himself, the esteem in which he was held, and his management were on the down grade. These were words that I had never heard in Denmark. The possibility of France being defeated in a war with Prussia was not even entertained there.

This merchant showed me an original photograph of the execution of the Emperor Maximilian, taken on the spot a moment before the word to fire was given, and a second taken immediately afterwards. The calm bearing of the Emperor and the two generals compelled admiration. This was the first time I had seen photography taken into the ser-vice of history.

In the Hamburg Zoological Gardens I was fascinated by the aquarium, with its multitudes of aquatic animals and fish. There, for the first time in my life, I saw an elephant, and did not tire of gazing at the mighty beast. I was struck by the strange caprice with which the great Being we call Nature goes to work, or, more correctly, by the contrast between the human point of view and Nature's mode of operations. To us, the elephant's trunk was burlesque, its walk risibly clumsy; the eagle and the kite seemed to us, as they sat, to have a severe appearance and a haughty glance; the apes, picking lice from one another and eating the vermin, were, to our eyes, contemptible and ridicu-lous at the same time; but Nature took everything equally seriously, neither sought nor avoided beauty, and to her one being was not more central than another. That must be deemed Nature's central point which is equidistant from the lowest and from the highest being; it was not impossible, for instance, that the *harefish*, a great, thick, odd-looking creature, was the real centre of terrestrial existence, in the same way as our celestial sphere has its centre, through which a line reaches the pole of the zodiac in the constellation of the Dragon. And I smiled as I thought of R. Nielsen and his pupils always speaking as if they stood on the most intimate footing with the " central point " of existence, and pouring contempt on others who, it was to be supposed, could not approach it.

I was very unfavourably impressed in Hamburg by German drama and German dramatic art.

At the town theatre, Hebbel's *Judith* was being performed, with Clara Ziegler in the leading part. At that time this lady enjoyed a considerable reputation in Germany, and was, too, a tall, splendid-looking female, with a powerful voice, a good mimic, and all the rest of it, but a mere word-machine. The acting showed up the want of taste in the piece. Holofernes weltered knee-deep in gore and bragged incessantly; Judith fell in love with his " virility," and when he had made her " the guardian of his slumbers " murdered him, from a long disremembered loyalty to the God of Israel.

At the Thalia Theatre, Raupach's *The School of Life* was being produced, a lot of silly stuff, the theme of it, for that matter, allied to the one dealt with later by Drachmann in *Once upon a Time*. A Princess is hard-hearted and capricious. To punish her, the King, her father, shuts a man into her bedroom, makes a feigned accusation against her, and actually drives her out of the castle. She becomes a waiting-maid, and passes through various stages of civil life. The King of Navarra, whose suit she had haughtily rejected, disguised as a goldsmith, marries her, then arrays himself in silks and velvets, to tempt her to infidelity. When she refuses, he allows every possible injustice to be heaped upon her, to try her, makes her believe that the King, on a false accusation, has had her husband's eyes put out, and then himself goes about with a bandage before his eyes, and lets her beg. She believes everything and agrees to everything, until at last, arrived at honour and glory, she learns that it has all been only play-acting, trial, and education.

This nonsense was exactly on a par with taste in Germany at the time, which was undeniably considerably below the level of that in France and Denmark, and it was acted by a group of actors, some very competent, at the chief theatre of Hamburg. Slowly though business life pulsated in Denmark, we were superior to Germany in artistic perception.

The low stage of artistic development at which Hamburg had then arrived could not, however, efface the impression its superiority over Copenhagen in other respects had made upon me. Take it all together, my few days in Hamburg were well spent.

II.

And then I set foot once more in the country which I regarded as my second fatherland, and the overflowing happiness of once more feeling French ground under my feet returned undiminished and unchanged. I had had all my letters sent to Mlle. Louise's address, so fetched them shortly after my arrival and saw the girl again. Her family invited me to dinner several times during the very first week, and I was associated with French men and women immediately upon my arrival.

They were well-brought-up, good-natured, hospitable bourgeois, very narrow in their views. Not in the sense that they took no interest in politics and literature, but in that questions for them were decided once and for all in the clerical spirit. They did not regard this as a party standpoint, did not look upon themselves as adherents of a party; their way of thinking was the right one; those who did not agree with them held opinions they ought to be ashamed of, and which they probably, in private, were ashamed of holding and expressing.

Mlle. Louise had a cousin whom she used to speak of as a warm-hearted man with peculiar opinions, eager and impetuous, who would like to make the acquaintance of her friend from the North. The aunts called him a passionate Catholic, and an energetic writer in the service of the Church Militant. Shortly after my arrival, I met him at dinner. He was a middle-aged, pale, carelessly dressed man with ugly, irregular features, and a very excitable manner. With him came his wife, who though pale and enthusiastic like himself, yet looked quite terrestrial. He introduced himself as Ernest Hello, contributor to Veuillot's then much talked of Romish paper, *L'Univers,* which, edited with no small talent by a noted stylist, adopted all sorts of abusive methods as weapons in every feud in which the honour of the Church was involved. It was against Veuillot that Augier had just aimed the introduction to his excellent comedy, *Le Fils de Giboyer,* and he made no secret of the fact that in the Déodat mentioned in the piece he had had this writer of holy abuse in his mind. Hello was in everything Veuillot's vassal.

He was one of the martial believers who despised and hated the best free research men, and who knew himself in a position to confute them. He possessed some elements of culture, and had early had thoroughly drilled into him what, in comparison with the views of later times on History and Religion, was narrow and antiquated in Voltaire's education, and for this reason regarded, not only Voltaire's attack on the Church, but all subsequent philosophy inimical to the Church, as belonging to a bygone age. He was a fanatic, and there was a sacristy odour about all that he said. But there was in his disposition an enthusiastic admiration for weakness in fighting against external strength, and for courage that expressed itself in sheer defiance of worldly prudence, that made him feel kindly towards the young Dane. Denmark's taking up arms, with its two million inhabitants, against a great power like Prussia, roused his enthusiasm. " It is great, it is Spartan ! " he exclaimed. It must certainly be admitted that this human sympathy was not a prominent characteristic, and he wearied me with his hateful verdicts over all those whom I, and by degrees, all Europe, esteemed and admired in France.

As an instance of the paradoxicalness to which Huysmans many years later became addicted, the latter tried to puff up Hello as being a man of remarkable intellect; and an instance of the want of independence with which the new Catholic movement was carried on in Denmark is to be found in the fact that the organ of Young Denmark, *The Tower,* could declare: " Hello is one of the few whom all men of the future are agreed to bow before. . . . Hello was,—not only a Catholic burning with religious ardour,—but a genius; these two things explain everything."

When Hello invited me to his house, I regarded it as my duty to go, that I might learn as much as possible, and although his circle was exceedingly antipathetic to me, I did not regret it; the spectacle was highly instructive.

Next to Hello himself, who, despite his fanaticism and restlessness, impressed one as very inoffensive at bottom, and not mischievous if one steered clear of such names as Voltaire or Renan, the chief member of his circle was the black doctor, (*le Docteur noir,*) so much talked of in the last years of the Empire, and who is even alluded to in Taine's *Graindorge.* His real name was Vries. He was a negro from the Dutch West Indies, a veritable bull, with a huge body and a black, bald physiognomy, made to stand outside a tent at a fair, and be his own crier to the public. His conversation was one incessant brag, in atrocious French. Although he had lived seventeen years in France, he spoke almost unintelligibly.

He persuaded himself, or at least others, that he had discovered perpetual motion, vowed that he had made a machine which, " by a simple mechanism," could replace steam power and had been declared practicable by the first engineers in Paris; but of course he declined to speak freely about it. Columbus and Fulton only were his equals; he knew all the secrets of Nature. He had been persecuted—in 1859 he had been imprisoned for eleven months, on a charge of quackery—because all great men were persecuted; remember our Lord Jesus Christ! He himself was the greatest man living. *Moi vous dire le plus grand homme d'universe.* Hello and the ladies smiled admiringly at him, and never grew tired of listening to him. This encouraged him to monopolise the conversation: He, Vries, was a man possessed of courage and wisdom; he understood Phrenology, Allopathy, Homœopathy, Engineering Science, Metereology— like Molière's doctors and Holberg's Oldfux. His greatest

and most special gift was that of curing cancer. Like writing-
masters, who hang out specimens of how people wrote when
they came to them, and of their caligraphy after they
had benefited by their instruction, he had his cancer patients
photographed before and after his treatment, looking
ghastly the first time, and as fresh as a flower the second,
and these pictures hung on view in his house. No wonder,
therefore, that Napoleon III—so Vries said—had his portrait in an album containing, besides, only portraits of European sovereigns.

He pretended that he had made many important proph-
ecies. This was a bond between him and Hello, who
claimed the same extraordinary power, and had foretold all
sorts of singular events. He performed miraculous cures;
this appealed to Hello, who was suspicious of all rational
Science and ready to believe any mortal thing. He could
read everybody's characters in their faces. This was a pretext for the most barefaced flattery of Hello, his wife, and
their friends of both sexes, and of course everything was
swallowed with alacrity. To me he said: "Monsieur is
gentle, very calm, very indulgent, and readily forgives an
injury."

Hideous though he was, his powerful brutality had a
great effect on the ladies of the circle. They literally hung
upon his words. He seized them by the wrists, and slid his
black paws up their bare arms. The married women whispered languishingly: "You have a marvellous power over
women." The husbands looked on smilingly.

Now when Hello and he and their friends and the ladies began to talk about religious matters and got steam up,
it was a veritable witches' Sabbath, and no mistake, every
voice being raised in virulent cheap Jack denunciation of
freedom, and common sense. Satan himself had dictated
Voltaire's works; now Voltaire was burning in everlasting
fire. Unbelievers ought to be exterminated; it would serve
them right. Renan ought to be hanged on the first tree that
would bear him; the Black Doctor even maintained that in
Manila he would have been shot long ago. It was always
the Doctor who started the subject of the persecution of

heretics. Hello himself persecuted heretics with patronising scorn, but was already ready to drop into a hymn of praise to the Madonna.

I had then read two of Hello's books, *Le Style* and *M. Renan, L'Allemagne et l'Athéisme au 19me Siècle*. Such productions are called books, because there is no other name for them. As a matter of fact, idle talk and galimatias of the sort are in no wise literature. Hello never wrote anything but Roman Catholic sermons, full of theological sophistries and abuse of thinking men. In those years his books, with their odour of incense, made the small, flat inhabitants of the sacristy wainscotting venture out of their chinks in the wall in delight; but they obtained no applause elsewhere.

It was only after his death that it could occur to a morbid seeker after originality, with a bitter almond in place of a heart, like Huysmans, to make his half-mad hero, Des Esseintes, who is terrified of the light, find satisfaction in the challenges to common sense that Hello wrote. Hello was a poor wretch who, in the insane conviction that he himself was a genius, filled his writings with assertions concerning the marvellous, incomprehensible nature of genius, and always took up the cudgels on its behalf. During the Empire, his voice was drowned. It was only a score of years later that the new Catholic reaction found it to their advantage to take him at his word and see in him the genius that he had given himself out to be. He was as much a genius as the madman in the asylum is the Emperor.

III.

A few days after my arrival, I called upon Taine and was cordially received. He presented me with one of his books and promised me his great work, *De l'Intelligence,* which was to come out in a few days, conversed with me for an hour, and invited me to tea the following evening. He had been married since I had last been at his house, and his wife, a young, clear-skinned lady with black plaits, brown eyes and an extremely graceful figure, was as fresh as a rose, and talked with the outspoken freedom of youth, though expressing herself in carefully selected words.

After a few days, Taine, who was generally very formal with strangers, treated me with conspicuous friendliness. He offered at once to introduce me to Renan, and urgently advised me to remain six months in Paris, in order to master the language thoroughly, so that I might enlighten Frenchmen on the state of things in the North, as well as picture the French to my fellow-countrymen. Why should I not make French my auxiliary language, like Turgenieff and Hillebrandt!

Taine knew nothing of German belles lettres. As far as philosophy was concerned, he despised German Æsthetics altogether, and laughed at me for believing in " Æsthetics " at all, even one day introducing me to a stranger as " A young Dane who does not believe in much, but is weak enough to believe in Æsthetics." I was not precisely overburdened by the belief. But a German Æsthetic, according to Taine's definition, was a man·absolutely devoid of artistic perception and sense of style, who lived only in definitions. If you took him to the theatre to see a sad piece, he would tear his hair with delight, and exclaim: " *Voilà das Tragische!* "

Of the more modern German authors, Taine knew only Heine, of whom he was a passionate admirer and whom, by reason of his intensity of feeling, he compared with Dante. A poem like the *Pilgrimage to Kevlaar* roused his enthusiasm. Goethe's shorter poems, on the other hand, he could not appreciate, chiefly no doubt because he did not know German sufficiently well. He was not even acquainted with the very best of Goethe's short things, and one day that I asked him to read one poem aloud, the words in his mouth rang very French.

Lieber dur Laydénn möcht ee mee schlag'e, als so feel Frödenn des Laybengs airtrah'ge, was intended to be—

> Lieber durch Leiden,
> Möcht ich mich schlagen
> Als so viel Freuden
> Des Lebens ertragen.

Goethe's prose he did not consider good, but heavy and

prolix, and lacking in descriptive power. He would praise
Voltaire's prose at his expense. " You perceive the figure
and its movements far more clearly," he said. The German
romanticists disgusted him; their style, also, was too inartistic for him (*ils ne savent pas écrire, cela me dègoûte
d'eux*).

I frequently met friends at his house, amongst others,
Marcelin, who had been his friend from boyhood, and upon
whom, many years later, he wrote a melancholy obituary.
This man, the proprietor of that supremely worldly paper,
La Vie Parisienne, was a powerful, broad-shouldered, ruddy-
cheeked man, who looked the incarnation of health and very
unlike one's preconception of the editor of the most frivolous and fashionable weekly in Paris. He was a draughts-
man and an author, had studied the history of the last few
centuries in engravings, and himself owned a collection of no
fewer than 300,000. What Taine had most admired in him
was the iron will with which, left, at nineteen years of age,
penniless, and defectively educated, as head of his family,
he had kept his mother and brothers and sisters by his work.
Next to that Taine admired his earnestness. Marcelin, who
was generally looked upon as belonging to gay Paris, was a
solitary-minded man, an imaginative re-creator of the peoples of the past, as they were and went about, of their
ways and customs. He it was who opened Taine's eyes
to the wealth of contributions to history locked up in
collections of engravings, more especially perhaps as regarded people's external appearance, and what the exte-
rior revealed.

Another friend who came to Taine at all sorts of times
was Gleyre, the old painter, who had been born in French
Switzerland, but was otherwise a Parisian. And he was not
the only deeply idealistic artist with whom Taine was connected in the bonds of friendship. Although a fundamental
element of Taine's nature drew him magnetically to the art
that was the expression of strength, tragic or carnal strength,
a swelling exuberance of life, there was yet room in his soul
for sympathy with all artistic endeavour, even the purely
emotional. That which drew him to the idealistic painters

was, at bottom, the same quality as drew him to Beethoven and Chopin.

Gleyre's best-known picture is the painting in the Louvre, somewhat weak in colouring, but showing much feeling, a Nile subject representing a man sitting on the banks of the river and watching the dreams of his youth, represented as beautiful women, fleeing from him on a decorated dahabeah, which is disappearing. The title is *Lost Illusions*. There is more strength in the painting, much reproduced in engraving, of a Roman army, conquered by Divico the Helvetian, passing under the yoke—a picture which, as an expression of the national pride of the Swiss, has been placed in the Museum at Lausanne.

Still, it was the man himself, rather than his pictures, that Taine thought so much of. Intellectually, Taine was in his inmost heart an admirer of the Italian and the English Renaissance, when most pagan and most unrestrained; his intellectual home was the Venice of the sixteenth century; he would have been in his right place at one of the festivals painted by Veronese, and should have worn the rich and tasteful costume of that period. But socially, and as a citizen, he was quite different, was affectionate and subdued and calm, excessively conventional; temperate in all his judgments, as in his life.

If I succeeded in winning his good-will, it was most emphatically not because I had written a book about him, which, for that matter, he could not understand; he barely glanced through it; he read, at most, the appreciative little review that Gaston Paris did me the honour to write upon it in the *Revue Critique*. But it appealed to him that I had come to France from pure love of knowledge, that I might become acquainted with men and women and intellectual life, and that I had spent my youth in study.

He grew fond of me, advised me as a father or an elder brother might have done, and smiled at my imprudences— as for instance when I almost killed myself by taking too strong a sleeping draught—(*vous êtes imprudent, c'est de votre âge*). He sometimes reproached me with not jotting down every day, as he did, whatever had struck me; he talked

to me about his work, about the projected Essay on Schiller
that came to nothing on account of the war, of his *Notes sur
l'Angleterre,* which he wrote in a little out-of-the-way summer-house containing nothing save the four bare white-
washed walls, but a little table and a chair. He introduced
into the book a few details that I had mentioned to him after
my stay in England.

When we walked in the garden at his country-house at
Châtenay, he sometimes flung his arm round my neck—an
act which roused great astonishment in the Frenchmen present, who could scarcely believe their eyes. They knew how
reserved he usually was.

It quite irritated Taine that the Danish Minister did
nothing for me, and introduced me nowhere, although he
had had to procure me a free pass to the theatre. Again
and again he reverted to this, though I had never mentioned
either the Minister or the Legation to him. But the revolutionary blood in him was excited at what he regarded as a
slight to intellectual aristocracy. " What do you call a man
like that? A Junker? " I said no. " Never mind! it is
all the same. One feels that in your country you have had
no revolution like ours, and know nothing about equality.
A fellow like that, who has not made himself known in any
way whatever, looks down on you as unworthy to sit at his
table and does not move a finger on your behalf, although
that is what he is there for. When I am abroad, they come
at once from the French Embassy to visit me, and open to
me every house to which they have admittance. I am a person of very small importance in comparison with Benedetti,
but Benedetti comes to see me as often as I will receive him.
We have no lording of it here."

These outbursts startled me, first, because I had never
in the least expected or even wished either to be received
by the Danish Minister or to be helped by him; secondly,
because it revealed to me a wide difference between the point
of view in the Romance countries, in France especially, and
that in the North. In Denmark, I had never had the entrée
to Court or to aristocratic circles, nor have I ever acquired it
since, though, for that matter, I have not missed it in the

least. But in the Romance countries, where the aristocratic world still occasionally possesses some wit and education, it is taken as a matter of course that talent is a patent of nobility, and, to the man who has won himself a name, all doors are open, indeed, people vie with one another to secure him. That a caste division like that in the North was quite unknown there, I thus learnt for the first time.

IV.

Through Taine, I very soon made the acquaintance of Renan, whose personality impressed me very much, grand and free of mind as he was, without a trace of the unctuousness that one occasionally meets in his books, yet superior to the verge of paradox.

He was very inaccessible, and obstinately refused to see people. But if he were expecting you, he would spare you several hours of his valuable time.

His house was furnished with exceeding simplicity. On one wall of his study hung two Chinese water-colours and a photograph of Gérôme's *Cleopatra before Cæsar;* on the opposite wall, a very beautiful photograph of what was doubtless an Italian picture of the Last Day. That was all the ornamentation. On his table, there always lay a Virgil and a Horace in a pocket edition, and for a long time a French translation of Sir Walter Scott.

What surprised me most in Renan's bearing was that there was nothing solemn about it and absolutely nothing sentimental. He impressed one as being exceptionally clever and a man that the opposition he had met with had left as it found him. He enquired about the state of things in the North. When I spoke, without reserve, of the slight prospect that existed of my coming to the front with my opinions, he maintained that victory was sure. (*Vous l'emporterez! vous l'emporterez!*) Like all foreigners, he marvelled that the three Scandinavian countries did not try to unite, or at any rate to form an indissoluble Union. In the time of Gustavus Adolphus, he said, they had been of some political importance; since then they had retired completely from the historical stage. The reason for it must very probably be sought for in their insane internecine feuds.

Renan used to live, at that time, from the Spring onwards, at his house in the country, at Sèvres. So utterly unaffected was the world-renowned man, then already forty-seven years of age, that he often walked from his house to the station with me, and wandered up and down the platform till the train came.

His wife, who shared his thoughts and worshipped him, had chosen her husband herself, and, being of German family, had not been married after the French manner; still, she did not criticise it, as she thought it was perhaps adapted to the French people, and she had seen among her intimate acquaintances many happy marriages entered into for reasons of convenience. They had two children, a son, Ary, who died in 1900 after having made a name for himself as a painter, and written beautiful poems (which, however, were only published after his death), and a daughter, Noémi (Madame Psichari) who, faithfully preserving the intellectual heritage she has received from her great father, has become one of the centres of highest Paris, a soul of fire, who fights for Justice and Truth and social ideas with burning enthusiasm.

v.

A source of very much pleasure to me was my acquaintance with the old author and Collège de France Professor, Philarète Chasles. Grégoire introduced me to him and I gradually became at home, as it were, in his house, was always a welcome visitor, and was constantly invited there. In his old age he was not a man to be taken very seriously, being diffusive, vague and vain. But there was no one else so communicative, few so entertaining, and for the space of fifty years he had known everybody who had been of any mark in France. He was born in 1798; his father, who was a Jacobin and had been a member of the Convention, did not have him baptised, but brought him up to believe in Truth, (hence the name Philarète,) and apprenticed him to a printer. At the Restoration of the Royal Family, he was imprisoned, together with his father, but released through the influence of Châteaubriand; he then went to England, where he remained for full seven years (1819-1826), working as a typographer, and made a careful study of English literature, then almost unknown in France. After having spent some further time in Germany, he returned to Paris and published a number of historical and critical writings.

Philarète Chasles, as librarian to the Mazarin Library, had his apartments in the building itself, that is, in the very centre of Paris; in the Summer he lived in the country at Meudon, where he had had his veranda decorated with pictures of Pompeian mosaic. He was having a handsome new house with a tower built near by. He needed room, for he had a library of 40,000 volumes.

His niece kept house for him; she was married to a German from Cologne, Schulz by name, who was a painter on glass. The pair lived apart. Madame Schulz was pretty, caustic, spiteful, and blunt. Her daughter, the four-teen-year-old Nanni, was enchantingly lovely, as developed and mischievous as a girl of eighteen. Everyone who came to the house was charmed with her, and it was always full of guests, young students from Alsace and Provence, young negroes from Hayti, young ladies from Jerusalem, and poet-esses who would have liked to read their poems aloud and would have liked still better to induce Chasles to make them known by an article.

Chasles chatted with everyone, frequently addressing his conversation to me, talking incessantly about the very men and women that I most cared to hear about, of those still living whom I most admired, such as George Sand, and Mérimée, and, in fact, of all the many celebrities he had known. As a young man, he had been taken to the house of Madame Récamier, and had there seen Châteaubriand, an honoured and adored old man, and Sainte-Beuve an eager and attentive listener, somewhat overlooked on ac-count of his ugliness, in whom there was developing that lurk-ing envy of the great, and of those women clustered round, which he ought to have combatted, to produce just criticism.

Chasles had known personally Michelet and Guizot, the elder Dumas and Beyle, Cousin and Villemain, Musset and Balzac; he knew the Comtesse d'Agoult, for so many years the friend of Liszt, and Madame Colet, the mistress, first of Cousin, then of Musset, and finally of Flaubert, of whom my French uncle, who had met her on his travels, had drawn me a very unattractive picture. Chasles was on terms of daily intimacy with Jules Sandeau; even as an old man he could not forget George Sand, who had filched the greater part of his name and made it more illustrious than the whole became. Sandeau loved her still, forty years after she had left him.

Chasles was able, in a few words, to conjure up very vividly the images of the persons he was describing to his listener, and his anecdotes about them were inexhaustible. He took me behind the scenes of literature and I saw the stage from all its sides. The personal history of his contemporaries was, it is quite true, more particularly its chronicle of scandals, but his information completed for me the severe and graceful restraint of all Taine said. And side by side with his inclination for gay and malicious gossip, Chasles had a way of sketching out great synopses of intellectual history, which made one realise, as one reflected, the progress of development of the literatures with which one was familiar. Those were pleasant evenings, those moonlight Spring evenings in the open veranda out there at Meudon, when the old man with the sharp-pointed beard and the little skull-cap on one side of his head, was spokesman. He had the aptest and most amusing way of putting things. For instance, to my question as to whether Guizot had really been as austere by nature as he was in manner, he replied: " It is hard to say; when one wishes to impress, one cannot behave like a harlequin."

Although I had a keen enough eye for Philarète Chasles' weaknesses, I felt exceedingly happy in his house. There I could obtain without difficulty the information I wished for, and have the feeling of being thoroughly " in Paris." Paris was and still is the only city in the world that is and wishes to be the capital not only of its own country but of Europe; the only one that takes upon itself as a duty, not merely to meet the visitor half-way by opening museums, collections, buildings, to him, but the only one where people habitually, in conversation, initiate the foreigner in search of knowledge into the ancient, deep culture of the nation, so that its position with regard to that of other races and countries is made clear to one.

VI.

I had not let a single day elapse before I took my seat again in the *Théâtre Français,* to which I had free admission for an indefinite period. The first time I arrived, the door-keeper at the theatre merely called the sub-officials together; they looked at me, noted my appearance, and for the future I might take my seat wherever I liked, when the man at the entrance had called out his *Entrée.* They were anything but particular, and in the middle of the Summer, after a visit of a month to London, I found my seat reserved for me as before.

The first evening after my arrival, I sat, quietly enjoying *Hernani* (the lyric beauty of which always rejoiced my heart), with Mounet-Sully in the leading rôle, Bressant as Charles V, and as Doña Sol, Mlle. Lloyd, a minor actress, who, however, at the conclusion of the piece, rose to the level of the poetry. The audience were so much in sympathy with the spirit of the piece that a voice from the gallery shouted indignantly: *"Le roi est un lâche!"* Afterwards, during the same evening, I saw, in a transport of delight, Mme. de Girardin's charming little piece, *La Joie fait Peur.* A certain family believe that their son, who is a young naval officer, fallen in the far East, has been cruelly put to death. He comes back, unannounced, to his broken-hearted mother, his despairing bride, his sister, and an old man-servant. This old, bent, faithful retainer, a stock dramatic part, was played by Régnier with the consummate art that is Nature itself staged. He has hidden the returned son behind a curtain for fear that his mother, seeing him unexpectedly, should die of joy. The sister comes in. Humming, the servant begins to dust, to prevent her going near the curtain; but unconsciously, in his delight, his humming grows louder and louder, until, in a hymn of jubilation, tratara-tratara! he flings the broom up over his head, then stops short suddenly, noticing that the poor child is standing there, mute with astonishment, not knowing what to think. Capital, too, was the acting of a now forgotten actress, Mlle. Dubois, who played the young girl. Her exclamation, as she suddenly sees her brother, "*Je n' ai pas peur, va!*" was uttered so lightly and gaily, that all the people round me, and I myself, too, burst into tears.

I was much impressed by Edmond Thierry, then director of the *Théâtre Français.* I thought him the most refined man I had so far met, possessed of all the old French courtesy, which seemed to have died out in Paris. A conversation with him was a regular course in Dramaturgy, and although a young foreigner like myself must necessarily have been troublesome to him, he let nothing of this be perceptible. I was so charmed by him that nearly two years later I introduced a few unimportant words of his about Molière's *Misanthrope* into my lectures on the first part of *Main Currents in European Literature,* simply for the pleasure of mentioning his name.

It was, moreover, a very pleasant thing to pay him a visit, even when he was interrupted. For actors streamed in and out of his house. One day, for instance, the lovely Agar burst into the room to tell her tale of woe, being dissatisfied with the dress that she was to wear in a new part. I saw her frequently again when war had been declared, for she it was who, every evening, with overpowering force and art, sang the *Marseillaise* from before the footlights.

The theatrical performances were a delight to me. I had been charmed as much only by Michael Wiehe and Johanne Luise Heiberg in my salad days when they played together in Hertz's *Ninon.* But my artistic enjoyment went deeper here, for the character portrayal was very much more true to life. The best impressions I had brought with me of Danish art were supremely romantic, Michael Wiehe as Henrik in *The Fairies,* as the Chevalier in *Ninon,* as Mortimer in Schiller's *Mary Stuart*.　But this was the real, living thing.

One evening I saw *Ristori* play the sleep-walking scene in *Macbeth* with thrilling earnestness and supreme virtuosity.　You felt horror to the very marrow of your bones, and your eyes filled with tears of emotion and anxiety.　Masterly was the regular breathing that indicated slumber, and the stiff fingers when she washed her hands and smelt them to see if there were blood upon them.　But Mme. Favart, who with artistic self-restraint co-ordinated herself into the whole, without any virtuosity at all, produced no less an effect upon me.　As the leading character in Feuillet's *Julie*, she was perfection itself; when I saw her, it seemed to me as though no one at home in Denmark had any idea of what feminine characterisation was.　What had been taken for such (Heiberg's art, for instance,) only seemed like a graceful and brilliant convention, that fell to pieces by the side of this.

The performances at the *Théâtre Français* lasted longer than they do now.　In one evening you could see Gozlan's *Tempête dans un verre d'Eau,* Augier's *Gabrielle,* and Banville's *Gringoire.*　When I had seen Mme. Favart and Régnier in *Gabrielle,* Lafontaine as Louis XI, his wife as Loyse, Mlle. Ponsin as Nicole, and Coquelin, at that time still young and fresh, as Gringoire, I felt that I had enjoyed one of the greatest and most elevating pleasures the world had to offer.　I went home, enraptured and enthusiastic, as much edified as the believer returning from his church.　I could see *Gringoire* a dozen times in succession and find only one expression for what I felt:　" This is holy."

The piece appealed to me so much, no doubt, because it was more in agreement than the rest with what in Denmark was considered true poetry.　But during the three years since I had last seen him, Coquelin had made immense strides in this rôle. He rendered it now with an individuality, a heartfelt sincerity and charm, that he had not previously attained; in contrast to harsh King Louis and unfeeling Loyse, was so poor, and hungry, and ill and merry and tender and such a hero and such a genius—that I said to myself: "Who, ever has seen this, has lived."

Quite a short while after my arrival—April 12, 1870 —I saw for the first time Sarah Bernhardt, who had just begun to make a name at the Odéon. She was playing in George Sand's beautiful and mutinous drama *L'autre,* from which the great-grandmother in Björnson's *Leonarda* is derived. The piece is a plea for the freedom of love, or rather, for indulgence with regard to what are branded by society as the sins of love. Sarah Bernhardt was the young girl who, in her innocence, judges all moral irregularities with the utmost severity, until her eyes are opened to what the world really is. She is, without knowing it, the child of unlawful love, and the father's curse is that of not daring to be anything to his child—whom he has educated and over whom he watches—not daring to claim his right to her affection, as he would otherwise stain her mother's memory. In his presence, the young girl utters all the hard words that society has for those who break her laws; she calls her unknown father false and forsworn. George Sand has collected all the justified protests and every prejudice for this young girl to utter, because in her they inspire most respect, and are to their best advantage.—So far her father has not revealed himself. Then at last it dawns upon her that it is he, her benefactor, who is the *other one* whom she has just condemned, and as the curtain falls she flings herself, melted, into his arms.

Sarah played the part with great modesty, with what one might assume to be the natural melancholy of the orphan, and the enthusiasm of the young virgin for strict justice, and yet in such wise that, through all the coldness, through the expressive uncertainty of her words, and especially through the lovely, rich ring of her voice, one suspected tenderness and mildness long held back.

VII.

I tried, while I was in Paris, to understand something of the development of French literature since the beginning of the century, to arrange it in stages, and note the order of their succession; I wanted, at the same time, to form for myself a similar general view of Danish literature, and institute parallels between the two, being convinced beforehand that the spirit of the age must be approximately the same in two European countries that were, so to speak, intellectually allied. This was my first naïve attempt to trace The Main Currents in Nineteenth Century Literature.

The French poetry of the nineteenth century seemed to me to fall into three groups: Romanticism, the School of Common Sense, the Realistic Art. I defined them as follows:

I. What the French call *Romanticism* has many distinguishing marks. It is, firstly, a *break with Græco-Roman antiquity*. It therefore harks back to the Gallic, and to the Middle Ages. It is a resurrection of the poets of the sixteenth century. But the attempt is a failure, for Ronsard and the Pleiad[1] are also Greek-taught, are Anacreontics. If we except the *Chanson de Roland,* there is no original mediæval literature that can be compared with the Icelandic. For that reason the choice of subjects is extended from the Middle Ages in France to the Middle Ages in other countries, for instance, Germany, whence Victor Hugo derives his drama *Les Burgraves.* The poets select foreign matter, Alfred de Vigny treats Chatterton and Musset Italian and Spanish themes. Mérimée harks back to the French Middle Ages (The Peasant Rising), but as he there finds too little originality, he flees, as a poet, to less civilised nationalities, Spaniards, South Americans, Corsicans, Russians, etc. Romanticism becomes ethnographical.

Its second distinguishing mark is *tempestuous violence.* It is connected with the 1830 revolution. It attacks society and the conditions of property (Saint Simon, Fourier, Proudhon), attacks marriage and the official verdict upon sexual relations (Dumas' *Antony,* the preface to Victor Hugo's *Angelo,* George Sand's *Indiana, Valentine, Jacques*). Everywhere Passion is deified.

Its third distinguishing mark is its *Continuation of Rousseauism.* Even the attacks on society descend from

---

[1] The poets who formed the first and greater Pleiad were, besides Ronsard, Dubellay, Remi, Belleau, Jodelle, Dorat, Baïf and Pontus de Thiard.

Rousseau's old doctrine that Nature is good, the natural state the right one, and that society alone has spoilt everything. George Sand in particular worships Rousseau, and writes in essential agreement with him.

In the later French literature the influence of Voltaire and that of Rousseau are alternately supreme. Voltaire rules until 1820, Rousseau again until 1850, then Voltaire takes the reins once more with About, Taine, and Sarcey. In Renan Voltaire is merged with Rousseau, and now, later still, Diderot has taken the place of both.

II. The *School of Common Sense* (*l'école de bon sens*) follows upon Romanticism. As the latter worshipped passion, so the School of Common Sense pays homage to sound human intelligence. In certain individuals it is possible to trace the transition—Musset's *Un Caprice* in contrast with the wanton works of his youth. George Sand's village novels, in contrast with her novels on Marriage. The popular tone and the landscape drawing here, which, for that matter, are all derived from Rousseau, lead on into a tranquil idyl. Works like Ponsard's *Lucrèce* and Augier's *Gabrielle* show the reaction from Romanticism. In the tragedy it is Lucrèce, in the modern play, Gabrielle, upon whom the action hinges. In Ponsard and Augier common sense, strict justice, and a conventional feeling of honour, are acclaimed. Marriage is glorified in all of Ponsard, Augier and Octave Feuillet's dramas. Literature has no doubt been influenced in some degree by the ruling orders of the monarchy of July. Louis Philippe was the bourgeois King. An author like Scribe, who dominates the stages of Europe, is animated by the all-powerful bourgeois spirit, educated and circumscribed as it was. Cousin, in his first manner, revolutionary Schellingism, corresponded to romanticism; his eclecticism as a moralising philosopher corresponds to the School of Common Sense. The distinctive feature which they have in common becomes a so-called Idealism. Ponsard revives the classical traditions of the seventeenth century. In criticism this endeavour in the direction of the sensible and the classical, is represented by Nisard, Planche, and Sainte-Beuve in his second manner.

III. The third tendency of the century is *Realistic Art,* with physiological characteristics. It finds its support in positivist philosophy; Herbart in Germany, Bentham and Mill in England, Comte and Littré in France. In criticism, Sainte-Beuve's third manner. On the stage, the younger Dumas. In novels, the brothers Goncourt, and Flaubert. In Art, a certain brutality in the choice of subject, Gérôme and Régnault. In politics, the accomplished fact (*le fait accompli*), the Empire, the brutal pressure from above and general levelling by universal suffrage from below. In lyric poetry, the strictly technical artists of form of the *Parnasse,* Coppée, who describes unvarnished reality, and the master workmen (*les maîtres de la facture*), Leconte Delisle, Gautier and his pupils, who write better verse than Lamartine and Hugo, but have no new thoughts or feelings—the poetic language materialists.

In conclusion, a great many indistinct beginnings, of which it is as yet impossible to say whither they are tending.

This, my first attempt to formulate for myself a general survey of one of the great literatures of the nineteenth century, contained much that was true enough, but revealed very plainly the beginner's lack of ability to estimate the importance of phenomena, an inclination to over-estimate purely evanescent apparitions, and a tendency to include that which was merely externally similar, under one heading. The insignificant School of Common Sense could not by any means be regarded as marking an epoch. Neither, with any justice, could men like Augier and Dumas be placed in different groups. The attempt to point out realism in the lyric art was likewise exceedingly audacious.

However, this division and grouping seemed to me at that time to be a great discovery, and great was my disappointment when one day I consulted Chasles on the subject and he thought it too forced, and another day submitted it to Renan, who restricted himself to the reply:

"No! no! Things do not proceed so systematically!"

As this survey of the literature of France was also intended to guide me with regard to the Danish, I groped my way forward in the following manner:

I. *Romanticism.* Oehlenschläger's attitude towards the past corresponds exactly to Victor Hugo's; only that the resurrection of the Middle Ages in poetry is much more successful (*Earl Hakon, The Gods of the North*), by reason of the fresh originality in Snorre and the *Edda.* Grundtvig's *Scenes from the Lives of the Warriors of the North* likewise owes all its value to the Edda and the Sagas. Oehlenschläger's *Aladdin* is the Northern pendant to Hugo's *Les Orientales.* Gautier, as a poet, Delacroix as a painter, affect the East, as Oehlenschläger does in *Ali and Gulhyndi.* Steffens and Sibbern, as influenced by Schelling, correspond to Cousin. Hauch not infrequently seeks his poetic themes in Germany, as do Nodier and Gérard de Nerval. Ingemann's weak historical novels correspond to the French imitations of Sir Walter Scott (Alfred de Vigny's *Cinq-Mars,* Dumas' *Musketeers*). Oehlenschläger's tragedies correspond to the dramas of Victor Hugo. With the Danes, as with the French, hatred of intelligence, as cold; only that the Danes glorify imagination and enthusiasm, the French, passion. Romanticism lasts in Denmark (without Revolutions and Restorations) until about 1848, as in France.

II. The *School of Common Sense* is in Denmark partly a worship of the sound sense of the people, partly a moralising tendency. Grundtvig, with his popular manner, his appreciation of the unsophisticated peasant nature, had points of contact with the pupils of Rousseau. Moralising works are Heiberg's *A Soul after Death,* Paludan-Müller's *Adam Homo,* and Kierkegaard's *Either-Or.* The funny thing about the defence of marriage contained in this last book is that it defends what no one in Denmark attacks. It can only be understood from the contemporary movement in the intellectual life of Europe, which is now asserting the universal validity of morality, as it formerly did the right of passion. Its defence of Protestantism corresponds to Octave Feuillet's defence of Catholicism, only that Feuillet is conciliatory, Kierkegaard vehement. Björnson's peasant novels, which are a continuation of Grundtvig and Blicher, are, by their harmony and their peaceable relations to all that is, an outcome of love of common sense; they have the same anti-Byronic stamp as the School of Common Sense. The movement comes to us ten years later. But Björnson has simultaneously something of Romanticism and something of Realism. We have not men to place separately in the various frames.

III. *Realistic Art.* There is so far only an attempt at a realistic art.

Thus, in Björnson's *Arne* and *Sigurd Slembe.* Note also an attempt in Bergsöe's clumsy use of realistic features, and in his seeking after effect. Richardt corresponds in our lyric art as an artist in language to the poets of the *Parnasse,* while Heiberg's philosophy and most of his poetry may be included in the School of Common Sense. Bröchner's *Ideal Realism* forms the transitional stage to the philosophy of Reality. Ibsen's attack upon the existing state of things corresponds to realism in the French drama. He is Dumas on Northern soil. In the *Love Comedy,* as a scoffer he is inharmonious. In *Peer Gynt,* he continues in the moralising tendency with an inclination to coarse and brutal realistic effects (relations with Anitra).

In Germany we find ourselves at the second stage still, sinking deeper and deeper into dialect and popular subjects (from Auerbach to Claus Groth and Fritz Reuter).

It is unnecessary to point out to readers of the present day how incomplete and arbitrary this attempt at a dissection of Danish literature was. I started from the conviction that modern intellectual life in Europe, in different countries, must necessarily in all essentials traverse the same stages, and as I was able to find various unimportant points of similarity in support of this view, I quite overlooked the fact that the counterbalancing weight of dissimilarities rendered the whole comparison futile.

IX.

As, during my first stay in Paris, I had frequently visited Madame Victorine, the widow of my deceased uncle, and her children, very cordial relations had since existed between us, especially after my uncle's faithless friend had been

compelled to disgorge the sums sent from Denmark for her
support, which he had so high-handedly kept back. There
were only faint traces left of the great beauty that had once
been hers; life had dealt hardly with her. She was good
and tender-hearted, an affectionate mother, but without other
education than was usual in the Parisian small bourgeois
class to which she belonged. All her opinions, her ideas of
honour, of propriety, of comfort and happiness, were typical of her class.

Partly from economy, partly from a desire not to waste
the precious time, I often, in those days, restricted my mid-
day meal. I would buy myself, at a provision-dealer's, a
large veal or ham pie and eat it in my room, instead of going
out to a restaurant. One day Victorine surprised me at a
meal of this sort, and exclaimed horrified: *"Comment? vous
vous nourrissez si mal!"* To her, it was about the same as
if I had not had any dinner at all. To sit at home without
a cloth on the table, and cut a pie in pieces with a paper
knife, was to sink one's dignity and drop to poor man's fare.

Her thoughts, like those of most poor people in France
and elsewhere, centred mostly on money and money anx-
ieties, on getting on well in the world, or meeting with ad-
versity, and on how much this man or the other could earn,
or not earn, in the year. Her eldest son was in St. Peters-
burg, and he was doing right well; he was good and kind
and sent his mother help when he had a little to spare. He
had promised, too, to take charge of his next brother. But
she had much anxiety about the little ones. One of them
was not turning out all that he should be, and there were
the two youngest to educate.

There was a charming celebration in the poor
home when little Emma went to her first communion, dressed
all in white, from head to foot, with a long white veil and
white shoes, and several other little girls and boys came
just as smartly dressed, and presents were given and good
wishes offered. Little Henri looked more innocent than any
of the little girls.

Victorine had a friend whom she deemed most happy;
this was Jules Clarétie's mother, for, young though her son

was, he wrote in the papers, wrote books, too, and earned money, so that he was able to maintain his mother altogether. He was a young man who ought to be held in high estimation, an author who was all that he should be. There was another author whom she detested, and that was P. L. Möller, the Dane:

" Jacques, as you know, was always a faithful friend of Monsieur Möller; he copied out a whole book for him,[1] when he himself was very busy. But then when Jacques died—*pauvre homme!*—he came and paid visits much too often and always at more and more extraordinary times, so that I was obliged to forbid him the house."

X.

In a students' hotel near the Odéon, where a few Scandinavians lived, I became acquainted with two or three young lawyers and more young abbés and priests. If you went in when the company were at table in the dining-room, the place rang again with their noisy altercations. The advocates discussed politics, literature and religion with such ardour that the air positively crackled. They were apparently practising to speak one day at the Bar or in the Chamber. It was from surroundings such as these that Gambetta emerged.

The young abbés and priests were very good fellows, earnest believers, but so simple that conversations with them were only interesting because of their ignorance and lack of understanding. Scandinavians in Paris who knew only Roman Catholic priests from *Tartuffe* at the theatre, had very incorrect conceptions regarding them. Bressant was the cold, elegant hypocrite, Lafontaine the base, coarse, but powerful cleric, Leroux the full-blooded, red-faced, voluptuary with fat cheeks and shaking hands, whose expression was now angry, now sickly sweet. Northern Protestants were very apt to classify the black-coated men whom they saw in the streets and in the churches, as belonging to one

---

[1] *The Modern Drama in France and Denmark,* which won the University Gold Medal for Möller.

of these three types.   But my ecclesiastical acquaintances
were as free from hypocrisy as from fanaticism.   They
were good, honest children of the commonalty, with, not the
cunning, but the stupidity, of peasants.

Many a day I spent exploring the surroundings of Paris
in their company.   We went to St. Cloud and Sèvres, to
Versailles and St. Germain, to Saint Denis, to Montmorency
and Enghien, or to Monthléry, a village with an old tower
from the thirteenth century, and then breakfasted at Long-
jumeau, celebrated for its postillion.   There Abbé Leboul-
leux declared himself opposed to cremation, for the reason
that it rendered the resurrection impossible, since God himself could not collect the bones again when the body had
been burnt.   It was all so amiable that one did not like
to contradict him.   At the same meal another was giving
a sketch of the youth of Martin Luther; he left the church
—*on se demande encore pourquoi*.   In the innocence of his
heart this abbé regarded the rebellion of Luther less as an
unpermissible than as an inexplicable act.

XI.

The society of the Italian friends of my first visit gave
me much pleasure.   My first call at the Pagellas' was a blank;
at the next, I was received like a son of the house and heaped
with reproaches for not having left my address; they had
tried to find me at my former hotel, and endeavoured in vain
to learn where I was staying from Scandinavians whom they
knew by name; now I was to spend all the time I could with
them, as I used to do in the old days.   They were delighted
to see me again, and when I wished to leave, drove me home
in their carriage.   I resumed my former habit of spending
the greater part of my spare time with Southerners; once
more I was transported to Southern Europe and South
America.   The very first day I dined at their house I met a
jovial old Spaniard, a young Italian, who was settled in
Egypt, and a very coquettish young Brazilian girl.   The
Spaniard, who had been born in Venezuela, was an engineer
who had studied conditions in Panama for eleven years, and

had a plan for the cutting of the isthmus. He talked a great deal about the project, which Lesseps took up many years afterwards.

Pagella, too, was busy with practical plans, setting himself technical problems, and solving them. Thus he had discovered a new method of constructing railway carriages on springs, with a mechanism to prevent collisions. He christened this the *Virginie-ressort,* after his wife, and had had offers for it from the Russian government.

An Italian engineer, named Casellini, who had carried out the construction for him, was one of the many bold adventurers that one met with among the Southerners in Paris. He had been sent to Spain the year before by Napoleon III to direct the counter-revolution there. Being an engineer, he knew the whole country, and had been in constant communication with Queen Isabella and the Spanish Court in Paris. He gave illuminating accounts of Spanish corruptibility. He had bribed the telegraph officials in the South of Spain, where he was, and saw all political telegrams before the Governor of the place. In Malaga, where he was leading the movement against the Government, he very narrowly escaped being shot; he had been arrested, his despatches intercepted and 1,500 rifles seized, but he bribed the officials to allow him to make selection from the despatches and destroy those that committed him. In Madrid he had had an audience of Serrano, after this latter had forbidden the transmission from the town of any telegrams that were not government telegrams; he had taken with him a telegram drawn up by the French party, which sounded like an ordinary business letter, and secured its being sent off together with the government despatches. Casellini had wished to pay for the telegram, but Serrano had dismissed the suggestion with a wave of his hand, rung a bell and given the telegram to a servant. It was just as in Scribe's *Queen Marguerite's Novels,* the commission was executed by the enemy himself.

Such romantic adventures did not seem to be rare in Spain. Prim himself had told the Pagellas how at the time of the failure of the first insurrection he had always, in his flight, (in spite of his defective education, he was more magnanimous and noble-minded than any king), provided for the soldiers who were sent out after him, ordered food and drink for them in every inn he vacated, and paid for everything beforehand, whereas the Government let their poor soldiers starve as soon as they were eight or ten miles from Madrid.

I often met a very queer, distinguished looking old Spaniard named Don José Guell y Rente, who had been married to a sister of King Francis, the husband of King Isabella, but had been separated from her after, as he declared, she had tried to cut his throat. As witness to his connubial difficulties, he showed a large scar across his throat. He was well-read and, amongst other things, enthusiastically admired Scandinavian literature because it had produced the world's greatest poet, Ossian, with whom he had become acquainted in Cesarotti's Italian translation. It was useless to attempt to explain to him the difference between Scandinavia and Scotland. They are both in the North, he would reply.

XII.

A young American named Olcott, who visited Chasles and occasionally looked me up, brought with him a breath from the universities of the great North American Republic. A young German, Dr. Goldschmidt, a distinguished Sanscrit scholar, a man of more means than I, who had a pretty flat with a view over the Place du Châtelet, and dined at good restaurants, came, as it were, athwart the many impressions I had received of Romance nature and Romance intellectual life, with his violent German national feeling and his thorough knowledge. As early as the Spring, he believed there would be war between Germany and France and wished in that event to be a soldier, as all other German students, so he declared, passionately wished. He was a powerfully built, energetic, well-informed man of the world, with something of the rich man's habit of command. He seemed destined to long life and quite able to stand fatigue. Nevertheless, his life was short. He went through the whole of the war in France without a scratch, after the conclusion of peace was appointed professor of Sanscrit at the University of conquered Strasburg, but died of illness shortly afterwards.

A striking contrast to his reticent nature was afforded by the young Frenchmen of the same age whom I often met. A very rich and very enthusiastic young man, Marc de Rossiény, was a kind of leader to them; he had 200,000 francs a year, and with this money had founded a weekly publication called "*L'Impartial*," as a common organ for the students of Brussels and Paris. The paper's name, *L'Impartial,* must be understood in the sense that it admitted the expression of every opinion with the exception of defence of so-called revealed religion. The editorial staff was positivist, Michelet and Chasles were patrons of the paper, and behind the whole stood Victor Hugo as a kind of honorary director. The weekly preached hatred of the Empire and of theology, and seemed firmly established, yet was only one of the hundred ephemeral papers that are born and die every day in the Latin quarter. When it had been in existence a month, the war broke out and swept it away, like so many other and greater things.

XIII.

Of course I witnessed all that was accessible to me of Parisian public life. I fairly often found my way, as I had done in 1866, to the Palais de Justice to hear the great advocates plead. The man I enjoyed listening to most was Jules Favre, whose name was soon to be on every one's lips. The younger generation admired in him the high-principled and steadfast opponent of the Empire in the Chamber, and he was regarded as well-nigh the most eloquent man in France. As an advocate, he was incomparable. His unusual handsomeness,—his beautiful face under a helmet of grey hair, and his upright carriage,—were great points in his favour. His eloquence was real, penetrating, convincing, inasmuch as he

piled up fact upon fact, and was at the same time, as the
French manner is, dramatic, with large gesticulations that
made his gown flutter restlessly about him like the wings of a
bat.   It was a depressing fact that afterwards, as the Minister
opposed to Bismarck, he was so unequal to his position.

I was present at the *Théâtre Français* on the occasion
of the unveiling of Ponsard's bust.   To the Romanticists,
Ponsard was nothing less than the ass's jawbone with which
the Philistines attempted to slay Hugo.   But Emile Chasles,
a son of my old friend, gave a lecture upon him, and afterwards *Le lion amoureux* was played, a very tolerable little
piece from the Revolutionary period, in which, for one thing,
Napoleon appears as a young man.   There are some very fine
revolutionary tirades in it, of which Princess Mathilde, after
its first representation, said that they made her *Republican*
heart palpitate.   The ceremony in honor of this little anti-
pope to Victor Hugo was quite a pretty one.

Once, too, I received a ticket for a reception at the
French Academy.   The poet Auguste Barbier was being
inaugurated and Silvestre de Sacy welcomed him, in academic fashion, in a fairly indiscreet speech.   Barbier's *Jamber*
was one of the books of poems that I had loved for years, and
I knew many of the strophes by heart, for instance, the celebrated ones on Freedom and on Napoleon; I had also noticed
how Barbier's vigour had subsided in subsequent collections
of poems; in reality, he was still living on his reputation from
the year 1831, and without a doubt most people believed him
to be dead.   And now there he stood, a shrivelled old man in
his Palm uniform, his speech revealing neither satiric power
nor lofty intellect.   It was undoubtedly owing to his detestation of Napoleon (*vide* his poem *L'Idole*) that the Academy,
who were always agitating against the Empire, had now, so
late in the day, cast their eyes upon him.   Bald little Silvestre
de Sacy, the tiny son of an important father, reproached him
for his verses on Freedom, as the bold woman of the people
who was not afraid to shed blood.

" That is not Freedom as I understand it," piped the
little man,—and one believed him,—but could not refrain
from murmuring with the poet:

C'est que la Liberté n'est pas une comtesse
Du noble Faubourg St. Germain,
Une femme qu'un cri fait tomber en faiblesse,
Qui met du blanc et du carmin;
C'est une forte femme.

XIV.

A very instructive resort, even for a layman, was the
Record Office, for there one could run through the whole history of France in the most entertaining manner with the
help of the manuscripts placed on view, from the most ancient papyrus rolls to the days of parchment and paper.
You saw the documents of the Feudal Lords' and Priests'
Conspiracies under the Merovingians and the Capets, the
decree of divorce between Philip Augustus and Ingeborg, and
letters from the most notable personages of the Middle Ages
and the autocracy. The period of the Revolution and the
First Empire came before one with especial vividness. There
was Charlemagne's monogram stencilled in tin, and that of
Robert of Paris, reproduced in the same manner, those of
Louis XIV. and Molière, of Francis the Catholic and Mary
Stuart. There were letters from Robespierre and Danton,
requests for money and death-warrants from the Reign of
Terror, Charlotte Corday's last letters from prison and the
original letters of Napoleon from St. Helena.

In June I saw the annual races at Longchamps for the
first time. Great was the splendour. From two o'clock in
the afternoon to six there was an uninterrupted stream of
carriages, five or six abreast, along the Champs Elysées;
there were thousands of *lorettes* (as they were called at that
time) in light silk gowns, covered with diamonds and precious stones, in carriages decorated with flowers. Coachmen and footmen wore powdered wigs, white or grey, silk
stockings and knee-breeches and a flower in the button-
hole matching the colour of their livery and the flowers
which hung about the horses' ears. Some of the carriages
had no coachman's box or driver, but were harnessed to four
horses ridden by postillions in green satin or scarlet velvet,
with white feathers in their caps.

The only great *demi-mondaine* of whom I had hitherto caught a glimpse was the renowned Madame de Païva, who had a little palace by the side of the house in which Frölich the painter lived, in the Champs Elysées. Her connection with Count Henckel v. Donnersmark permitted her to surround herself with regal magnificence, and, to the indignation of Princess Mathilde, men like Gautier and Renan, Sainte-Beuve and Goncourt, Saint-Victor and Taine, sat at her table. The ladies here were younger and prettier, but socially of lower rank. The gentlemen went about among the carriages, said *tu* without any preamble to the women, and squeezed their hands, while their men-servants sat stolid, like wood, seeming neither to hear nor see.

This race-day was the last under the Empire. It is the one described in Zola's *Nana*. The prize for the third race was 100,000 francs. After English horses had been victorious for several years in succession, the prize was carried off in 1870—as in *Nana*—by a native-born horse, and the jubilation was great; it was a serious satisfaction to national vanity.

At that time, the Tuileries were still standing, and I was fond of walking about the gardens near closing time, when the guard beat the drums to turn the people out. It was pleasant to hear the rolling of the drums, which were beaten by two of the Grenadier Guard drummers and a Turco. Goldschmidt had already written his clever and linguistically very fine piece of prose about this rolling of the drums and what it possibly presaged: Napoleon's own expulsion from the Tuileries and the humiliation of French grandeur before the Prussians, who might one day come and drum this grandeur out. But Goldschmidt had disfigured the pretty little piece somewhat by relating that one day when, for an experiment, he had tried to make his way into the gardens after the signal for closing had sounded, the Zouave had carelessly levelled his bayonet at him with the words: "*Ne faites pas des bêtises!*" This levelling of the bayonet on such trivial provocation was too tremendous, so I made up my mind one evening to try myself. The soldier on guard merely remarked politely: "*Fermé, monsieur, on va sortir.*"

I little dreamed that only a few months later the Empress would steal secretly out of the palace, having lost her crown, and still less that only six months afterwards, during the civil war, the Tuileries would be reduced to ashes, never to rise again.

XV.

At that time the eyes of the Danes were fixed upon France in hope and expectation that their national resuscitation would come from that quarter, and they made no distinction between France and the Empire. Although the shortest visit to Paris was sufficient to convince a foreigner not only that the personal popularity of the Emperor was long since at an end, but that the whole government was despised, in Denmark people did not, and would not, know it. In the Danish paper with the widest circulation, the *Daily Paper,* foreign affairs were dealt with by a man of the name of Prahl, a wildly enthusiastic admirer of the Empire, a pleasant man and a brainy, but who, on this vital point, seemed to have blinkers on. From all his numerous foreign papers, he deduced only the opinions that he held before, and his opinions were solely influenced by his wishes. He had never had any opportunity of procuring information at first hand. He said to me one day:

"I am accused of allowing my views to be influenced by the foreign diplomatists here, I, who have never spoken to one of them. I can honestly boast of being unacquainted with even the youngest attaché of the Portuguese Ministry." His remarks, which sufficiently revealed this fact, unfortunately struck the keynote of the talk of the political wiseacres in Denmark.

Though the Danes were so full of the French, it would be a pity to say that the latter returned the compliment. It struck me then, as it must have struck many others, how difficult it was to make people in France understand that Danes and Norsemen were not Germans. From the roughest to

the most highly educated, they all looked upon it as an understood thing, and you could not persuade them of anything
else.   As soon as they had heard Northerners exchange a
few words with each other and had picked up the frequently
recurring *Ja,* they were sufficiently edified.   Even many
years after, I caught the most highly cultured Frenchmen
(such as Edmond de Goncourt), believing that, at any rate on
the stage, people spoke German in Copenhagen.

One day in June I began chatting on an omnibus with
a corporal of Grenadiers.   When he heard that I was Danish, he remarked: " German, then." I said: " No."
He persisted in his assertion, and asked, cunningly, what *oui*
was in Danish.   When I told him he merely replied, philosophically, " Ah! then German is the mother tongue."   It
is true that when Danes, Norwegians and Swedes met abroad
they felt each other to be compatriots; but this did not prevent them all being classed together as Germans; that they
were not Englishmen, you saw at a glance.   Even when
there were several of them together, they had difficulty in
asserting themselves as different and independent; they were
a Germanic race all the same, and people often added, " of
second-class importance," since the race had other more pronounced representatives.

The only strong expression of political opinion that
was engineered in France then was the so-called plebiscite of
May, 1870; the government challenged the verdict of the
entire male population of France upon the policy of Napoleon III. during the past eighteen years, and did so with the
intention, strangely enough not perceived by Prime Minister
Ollivier, of re-converting the so-called constitutional Empire
which had been in existence since January 1, 1870, into an
autocracy.   Sensible people saw that the plebiscite was only
an objectionable comedy; a favourable reply would be obtained all over the country by means of pressure on the voters
and falsification of votes; the oppositionist papers showed
this up boldly in articles that were sheer gems of wit.   Dis-
turbances were expected in Paris on the 9th of May, and
here and there troops were collected.   But the Parisians,
who saw through the farce, remained perfectly indifferent.

The decision turned out as had been expected; the huge majority in Paris was *against,* the provincial population voted *for,* the Emperor.

XVI.

On July 5th I saw John Stuart Mill for the first time. He had arrived in Paris the night before, passing through from Avignon, and paid a visit to me, unannounced, in my room in the Rue Mazarine; he stayed two hours and won my affections completely. I was a little ashamed to receive so great a man in so poor a place, but more proud of his thinking it worth his while to make my acquaintance. None of the French savants had ever had an opportunity of conversing with him; a few days before, Renan had lamented to me that he had never seen him. As Mill had no personal acquaintances in Paris, I was the only person he called upon.

To talk to him was a new experience. The first characteristic that struck me was that whereas the French writers were all assertive, he listened attentively to counter-arguments; it was only when his attitude in the woman question was broached that he would not brook contradiction and overwhelmed his adversaries with contempt.

At that time Mill was without any doubt, among Europe's distinguished men, the greatest admirer of French history and French intellectual life to be found outside of France; but he was of quite a different type from the French, even from those I esteemed most highly. The latter were comprehensive-minded men, bold and weighty, like Taine, or cold and agile like Renan, but they were men of intellect and thought, only having no connection with the practical side of life. They were not adapted to personal action, felt no inclination to direct interference.

Mill was different. Although he was more of a thinker than any of them, his boldness was not of the merely theoretic kind. He wished to interfere and re-model. None of those Frenchmen lacked firmness; if, from any consideration, they modified their utterances somewhat, their fundamental views, at any rate, were formed independently; but their firm-

ness lay in defence, not in attack; they wished neither to rebuke nor to instigate; their place was the lecturer's platform,
rather than the tribune.   Mill's firmness was of another kind,
hard as steel; both in character and expression he was relent-
less, and he went to work aggressively.   He was armed, not
with a cuirass, but a glaive.

Thus in him I met, for the first time in my life, a figure
who was the incarnation of the ideal I had drawn for myself
of the great man.   This ideal had two sides; talent and
character: great capacities and inflexibility.   The men of
great reputation whom I had met hitherto, artists and scientists, were certainly men richly endowed with talents; but
I had never hitherto encountered a personality combining
talents with gifts of character.   Shortly before leaving home,
I had concluded the preface to a collection of criticisms with
these words: " My watchword has been: " As flexible as
possible, when it is a question of understanding, as inflexible
as possible, when it is a question of speaking," and I had
regarded this watchword as more than the motto of a little
literary criticism.   Now I had met a grand inflexibility of
ideas in human form, and was impressed for my whole life
long.

Unadapted though I was by nature to practical politics,
or in fact to any activity save that of ideas, I was far
from regarding myself as mere material for a scholar, an
entertaining author, a literary historian, or the like.   I
thought myself naturally fitted to be a man of action.   But
the men of action I had hitherto met had repelled me by
their lack of a leading principle.   The so-called practical
men at home, lawyers and parliamentarians, were not men
who had made themselves masters of any fund of new
thoughts that they wished to reduce to practical effect; they
were dexterous people, well-informed of conditions at their
elbow, not thinkers, and they only placed an immediate goal
in front of themselves.   In Mill I learnt at last to know a
man in whom the power of action, disturbance, and accom-
plishment were devoted to the service of modern sociological
thought.

He was then sixty-four years old, but his skin was as

fresh and clear as a child's, his deep blue eyes young. He stammered a little, and nervous twitches frequently shot over his face; but there was a sublime nobility about him.

To prolong the conversation, I offered to accompany him to the Windsor Hotel, where he was staying, and we walked the distance. As I really had intended to go over to England at about that time, Mill proposed my crossing with him. I refused, being afraid of abusing his kindness, but was invited to visit him frequently when I was in England, which I did not fail to do. A few days afterwards I was in London.

XVII.

My French acquaintances all said the same thing, when I told them I wanted to go over to England: "What on earth do you want there?" Though only a few hours' journey from England, they had never felt the least curiosity to see the country. "And London! It was said to be a very dull city; it was certainly not worth putting one's self out to go there." Or else it was: "If you are going to London, be careful! London is full of thieves and rascals; look well to your pockets!"

Only a few days later, the Parisians were shaken out of their calm, without, however, being shaken out of their self-satisfaction. The Duc de Grammont's speech on the 6th of July, which amounted to the statement that France was not going to stand any Hohenzollern on the throne of Spain, made the people fancy themselves deeply offended by the King of Prussia, and a current of martial exasperation ran through the irritable and misled people, who for four years had felt themselves humiliated by Prussia's strong position. All said and believed that in a week there would be war, and on both sides everything was so ordered that there might be. There was still hope that common sense might get the better of warlike madness in the French Government; but this much was clear, there was going to be a sudden downfall of everything.

Between Dover and Calais the waves beat over the ship. From Dover, the train went at a speed of sixty miles an hour,

and made one think him a great man who invented the
locomotive, as great as Aristotle and Plato together.   It
seemed to me that John Stuart Mill was that kind of man.
He opened, not roads, but railroads; his books were like
iron rails, unadorned, but useful, leading to their goal.   And
what *will* there was in the English locomotive that drew our
train,—like the driving instinct of England's character!

Two things struck me on my journey across, a type of
mechanical Protestant religiosity which was new to me, and
the knowledge of the two languages along the coasts.   A
pleasant English doctor with whom I got into conversation
sat reading steadily in a little Gospel of St. John that he
carried with him, yawning as he read.   The seamen on the
ship and the coast dwellers both in England and France spoke
English and French with about equal ease.   It is probably
the same in all border countries, but it occurred to me that
what came about here quite naturally will in time be a possibility all over the world, namely, the mastery of a second and
common language, in addition to a people's own.

I drove into London through a sea of houses.   When
I had engaged a room, changed my clothes, and written a
letter that I wanted to send off at once, the eighteen-year-old
girl who waited on me informed me that no letters were
accepted on Sundays.   As I had some little difficulty in making out what she said, I supposed she had misunderstood my
question and thought I wanted to speak to the post-official.
For I could not help laughing at the idea that even the letter-
boxes had to enjoy their Sabbath rest.   But I found she was
right.   At the post-office, even the letter-box was shut, as it
was Sunday; I was obliged to put my letter in a pillar-box in
the street.

In Paris the Summer heat had been oppressive.   In
London, to my surprise, the weather was fresh and cool, the
air as light as it is in Denmark in Autumn.   My first visit
was to the Greek and Assyrian collections in the British Museum.   In the Kensington Museum and the Crystal Palace
at Sydenham, I added to my knowledge of Michael Angelo,
to whom I felt drawn by a mighty affection.   The admiration for his art which was to endure undiminished all my life

was even then profound. I early felt that although Michael Angelo had his human weaknesses and limitations, intellectually and as an artist he is one of the five or six elect the world has produced, and scarcely any other great man has made such an impression on my inner life as he.

In the British Museum I was accosted by a young Dane with whom I had sometimes ridden out in the days of my riding lessons; this was Carl Bech, now a landed proprietor, and in his company I saw many of the sights of London and its environs. He knew more English than I, and could find his way anywhere. That the English are rigid in their conventions, he learnt one day to his discomfort; he had put on a pair of white trousers, and as this was opposed to the usual precedent and displeased, we were stared at by every man, woman and child we met, as if the young man had gone out in his underclothing. I had a similar experience one day as I was walking about the National Gallery with a young German lady whose acquaintance I had made. An Englishwoman stopped her in one of the rooms to ask: "Was it you who gave up a check parasol downstairs?" and receiving an answer in the affirmative, she burst out laughing in her face and went off.

On July 16th came the great daily-expected news. War was declared, and in face of this astounding fact and all the possibilities it presented, people were struck dumb. The effect it had upon me personally was that I made up my mind to return as soon as possible to France, to watch the movement there. In London, where Napoleon III. was hated, and in a measure despised, France was included in the aversion felt for him. Everywhere, when I was asked on which side my sympathies were, they broke in at once: "We are all for Prussia."

XVIII.

As often as I could, I took the train to Blackheath to visit John Stuart Mill. He was good and great, and I felt myself exceedingly attracted by his greatness. There were fundamental features of his thought and mode of feeling that coincided with inclinations of my own; for instance, the

Utilitarian theory, as founded by Bentham and his father and developed by him. I had written in 1868 : " What we crave is no longer to flee from society and reality with our thoughts and desires. On the contrary, we wish to put our ideas into practice in society and life. That we may not become a nation of poetasters, we will simply strive towards actuality, the definite goal of Utility, which the past genera- tion mocked at. Who would not be glad to be even so little useful?"

Thus I found myself mentally in a direction that led me towards Mill, and through many years' study of Comte and Littré, through an acquaintance with Mill's correspond- ence with Comte, I was prepared for philosophical conver- sations concerning the fundamental thoughts of empiric phi- losophy as opposed to speculative philosophy, conversations which, on Mill's part, tended to represent my entire Univer- sity philosophical education at Copenhagen as valueless and wrong.

But what drew me the most strongly to Mill was not similarity of thought, but the feeling of an opposed rela- tionship. All my life I had been afraid of going further in a direction towards which I inclined. I had always had a passionate desire to perfect my nature—to make good my de- fects. Julius Lange was so much to me because he was so unlike me. Now I endeavoured to understand Mill's nature and make it my own, because it was foreign to mine. By so doing I was only obeying an inner voice that perpetually urged me. When others about me had plunged into a subject, a language, a period, they continued to wrestle with it to all eternity, made the thing their speciality. That I had a hor- ror of. I knew French well; but for fear of losing myself in French literature, which I could easily illustrate, I was always wrestling with English or German, which presented greater difficulties to me, but made it impossible for me to grow nar- row. I had the advantage over the European reading world that I knew the Northern languages, but nothing was further from my thoughts than to limit myself to opening up North- ern literature to Europe. Thus it came about that when the time in my life arrived that I felt compelled to settle outside

Denmark I chose for my place of residence Berlin, the city with which I had fewest points in common, and where I could consequently learn most and develop myself without one-sidedness.

Mill's verbally expressed conviction that empiric philosophy was the only true philosophy, made a stronger impression upon me than any assertion of the kind that I had met with in printed books. The results of empiric philosophy seemed to me much more firmly based than those of the newer German philosophy. At variance with my teachers, I had come to see that Hume had been right rather than Kant. But I could not conform to the principle of empiric philosophy. After all, our knowledge is not ultimately based merely on experience, but on that which, prior to experience, alone renders experience possible. Otherwise not even the propositions of Mathematics can be universally applicable. In spite of my admiration for Mill's philosophical works, I was obliged to hold to the rationalistic theory of cognition; Mill obstinately held to the empiric. " Is not a reconciliation between the two possible? " I said. " I think that one must *choose* between the theories," replied Mill. I did not then know Herbert Spencer's profoundly thoughtful reconciliation of the teachings of the two opposing schools. He certainly maintains, as does the English school, that all our ideas have their root in experience, but he urges at the same time, with the Germans, that there are innate ideas. The conscious life of the individual, that cannot be understood from the experience of the individual, becomes explicable from the inherited experience of the race. Even the intellectual form which is the condition of the individual's apprehension is gradually made up out of the experience of the race, and consequently innate without for that reason being independent of foregoing experiences. But I determined at once, incited thereto by conversations with Mill, to study, not only his own works, but the writings of James Mill, Bain, and Herbert Spencer; I would endeavour to find out how much truth they contained, and introduce this truth into Denmark.

I was very much surprised when Mill informed me that

he had not read a line of Hegel, either in the original or in translation, and regarded the entire Hegelian philosophy as sterile and empty sophistry.   I mentally confronted this with the opinion of the man at the Copenhagen University who knew the history of philosophy best, my teacher, Hans Bröchner, who knew, so to speak, nothing of contemporary English and French philosophy, and did not think them worth studying.   I came to the conclusion that here was a task for one who understood the thinkers of the two directions, who did not mutually understand one another.

I thought that in philosophy, too, I knew what I wanted, and saw a road open in front of me.

However, I never travelled it.   The gift for abstract philosophical thought which I had possessed as a youth was never developed, but much like the tendency to verse-making which manifested itself even earlier, superseded by the historio-critical capacity, which grew strong in me.   At that time I believed in my natural bent for philosophy, and did so even in July, 1872, when I sketched out and began a large book: " *The Association of Ideas, conceived and put forward as the fundamental principle of human knowledge,*" but the book was never completed.   The capacity for abstraction was too weak in me.

Still, if the capacity had no independent development, it had a subservient effect on all my criticism, and the conversations with Mill had a fertilising and helpful influence on my subsequent intellectual life.

XIX.

Some weeks passed in seeing the most important public buildings in London, revelling in the treasures of her museums and collections, and in making excursions to places in the neighbourhood and to Oxford.   I was absorbed by St. Paul's, saw it from end to end, and from top to bottom, stood in the crypt, where Sir Christopher Wren lies buried,— *Si monumentum requiris, circumspice*—mentally compared Wellington's burial-place here with that of Napoleon on the other side of the Channel, then went up to the top of the building and looked out to every side over London, which I was already so well acquainted with that I could find my way everywhere alone, take the right omnibuses, and the right trains by the underground, without once asking my way. I spent blissful hours in the National Gallery. This choice collection of paintings, especially the Italian ones, afforded me the intense, overwhelming delight which poetry, the masterpieces of which I knew already, could no longer offer me. At the Crystal Palace I was fascinated by the tree-ferns, as tall as fruit-trees with us, and by the reproductions of the show buildings of the different countries, an Egyptian temple, a house from Pompeii, the Lions' den from the Alhambra. Here, as everywhere, I sought out the Zoological Gardens, where I lingered longest near the hippopotami, who were as curious to watch when swimming as when they were on dry land. Their clumsiness was almost captivating. They reminded me of some of my enemies at home.

Oxford, with the moss-grown, ivy-covered walls, with all the poetry of conservatism, fascinated me by its dignity and its country freshness; there the flower of the English nature was expressed in buildings and trees. The antiquated and non-popular instruction, however, repelled me. And the old classics were almost unrecognisable in English guise, for instance, the anglicised *veni, vidi, vici,* which was quoted by a student.

The contrast between the English and the French mind was presented to me in all its force when I compared Windsor Castle with Versailles. The former was an old Northern Hall, in which the last act of Oehlenschläger's *Palnatoke* would have been well staged.

I saw all that I could: the Houses of Parliament, Westminster Hall and Abbey, the Tower and the theatres, the Picture Gallery at Dulwich with Rembrandt's *Girl at the Window,* the one at Hampton Court, with the portrait of Loyola ascribed to Titian, sailed down the river to Greenwich and lingered in the lovely Gardens at Kew, which gave me a luxuriant impression of English scenery. I also saw the Queen's model farm. Every animal was as splendid a specimen as if it had been intended for an agricultural show, the dairy walls were tiled all over. The bailiff regretted that Prince Albert, who had himself made the drawings for a special kind of milk containers, had not lived to see them made. It was not without its comic aspect to hear him inform you sadly, concerning an old bullock, that the Queen herself had given it the name of *Prince Albert*

For me, accustomed to the gay and grotesque life deployed in an evening at the dancing-place of the Parisian students in the *Closerie des lilas,* it was instructive to compare this with a low English dancing-house, the Holborn Casino, which was merely sad, stiff, and repulsive.

Poverty in London was very much more conspicuous than in Paris; it spread itself out in side streets in the vicinity of the main arteries in its most pitiable form. Great troops, regular mobs of poor men, women and children in rags, dispersed like ghosts at dawn, fled away hurriedly and vanished, as soon as a policeman approached and made sign to them to pass on. There was nothing corresponding to it to be seen in Paris. Crime, too, bore a very different aspect here. In Paris, it was decked out and audacious, but retained a certain dignity; here, in the evening, in thickly frequented streets, whole swarms of ugly, wretchedly dressed, half or wholly drunken women could be seen reeling about, falling, and often lying in the street.

Both the tendency of the English to isolate themselves and their social instincts were quite different from those of the French. I was permitted to see the comfortably furnished Athenæum Club in Pall Mall, membership of which was so much desired that people of high standing would have their names on the list for years beforehand, and these clubs corresponded to the cafés in Paris, which were open to every passer-by. I noticed that in the restaurants the tables were often hidden behind high screens, that the different parties who were dining might not be able to see one another.

XX.

The house in London where I was happiest was Antonio Gallenga's.   A letter from the Hauchs was my introduction there, and I was received and taken up by them as if they had known me and liked me for years.

Antonio Gallenga, then a man of seventy, who nevertheless gave one an impression of youthfulness, had a most eventful life behind him.   He had been born at Parma, was flung into prison at the age of twenty as a conspirator under Mazzini, was banished from Piedmont, spent some time at Malta, in the United States and in England, where he earned his living as a journalist and teacher of languages, and in 1848 returned to Italy, where he was active as a liberal politician.   After the battle of Novara, he was again obliged to take refuge in London; but he was recalled to Piedmont by Cavour, who had him elected deputy for Castellamonte.   He wrote an Italian Grammar in English, and, likewise in English, the *History of Piedmont*, quarrelled with Mazzini's adherents, withdrew from parliamentary life, and in preference to settling down permanently in Italy elected to be war correspondent to the *Times*.   In that capacity he took part from 1859 onwards in the campaigns in Italy, in the North American States, in Denmark, and in Spain.   His little boy was still wearing the Spanish national costume.   Now he had settled down in London, on the staff of the *Times,* and had just come into town from the country, as the paper wished him to be near, on account of the approaching war. Napoleon III., to whom Gallenga had vowed an inextinguishable hatred, had been studied so closely by him that the Emperor might be regarded as his specialty.   He used the energetic, violent language of the old revolutionary, was with all his heart and soul an Italian patriot, but had, through a twenty years' connection with England, acquired the practical English view of political affairs.   Towards Denmark, where he had been during the most critical period of the country's history, he felt kindly; but our war methods had of course not been able to excite his admiration; neither had our diplomatic negotiations during the war.

Gallenga was a well-to-do man; he owned a house in the best part of London and a house in the country as well. He was a powerful man, with passionate feelings, devoid of vanity. It suited him well that the *Times,* as the English custom is, printed his articles unsigned; he was pleased at the increased influence they won thereby, inasmuch as they appeared as the expression of the universal paper's verdict. His wife was an Englishwoman, pleasant and well-bred, of cosmopolitan education and really erudite. Not only did she know the European languages, but she wrote and spoke Hindustani. She was a splendid specimen of the English housekeeper, and devoted herself enthusiastically to her two exceedingly beautiful children, a boy of eleven and a little girl of nine. The children spoke English, Italian, French, and German with equal facility and correctness.

Mrs. Gallenga had a more composite and a deeper nature than her husband, who doubted neither the truth of his ideas, nor their salutary power. She shared his and my opinions without sharing our confidence in them. When she heard me say that I intended to assert my ideas in Denmark, and wage war against existing prejudices, she would say, in our long conversations:

" I am very fond of Denmark; the people there seem to me to be happy, despite everything, and the country not to be over-populated. In any case, the population finds ample means of outlet in sea-life and emigration. Denmark is an idyllic little country. Now you want to declare war there. My thoughts seek down in dark places, and I ask myself whether I really believe that truth does any good, whether in my secret heart I am convinced that strife is better than stagnation? I admire Oliver Cromwell, but I sympathise with Falkland, who died with ' Peace! Peace! '[1] on his lips. I am afraid that you will have to bear a great deal. You will learn that the accoutrements of truth are a grievously heavy coat of mail. You will call forth reaction. Even that is the least. But reaction will come about in your own mind; after a long time, I mean. Still, you are

---

[1] Sir Lucius Cary, second Viscount Falkland, who fell at Newbury, Sept. 20, 1643.

strong; it will be a reaction of the kind that keeps aloof in order to spring farther and better. Your unity will not go to pieces. You are a kind of cosmos."

When the conversation turned upon England and English conditions, she protested against the opinion prevalent on the continent since Byron's day, that English society was infested with hypocrisy.

"I do not think that hypocrisy is characteristic of English thought. We have, of course, like every serious people, our share of hypocrites; in a frivolous nation hypocrisy has no pretext for existence. But its supremacy amongst us is over. Apathetic orthodoxy, and superficial ideas of the correct thing, ruled England during the first half of the century. The intellectual position of the country is different now. No one who has not lived in England has any idea how serious and real the belief here is in the tough doctrine of the Trinity, who, in human form, walked about in Galilee. Good men, noble men, live and work for this dogma, perform acts of love for it. We, you and I, have drunk from other sources; but for these people it is the fountain of life. Only it is depressing to see this doctrine in its Roman Catholic form winning greater power everywhere every day. In Denmark, intellectual stagnation has hindered it hitherto; you have political, but not yet religious, freedom. Belgium has both, and Belgium is at the present time the most fiery Catholic power there is. France is divided between extreme materialism and Madonna worship. When European thought—between 1820 and 1860, let us say— rebelled against every kind of orthodoxy, and, as always happens with rebellion, made mistakes and went too far, France played a wretched rôle. It is a Celtic land, and Celtic it will remain; it desires, not personal freedom, but a despotic levelling, not equality before the law, but the base equality which is inimical to excellence, not the brotherhood that is brotherly love, but that which gives the bad the right to share with the good. That is why the Empire could be victorious in France, and that is why the Roman Catholic Church, even in its most modern, Byzantine form, is triumphant there."

So thoroughly English was Anna Gallenga's way of looking at things, in spite of an education which had included the chief countries in Europe. So blindly did she share the prejudice that the French are essentially Celtic. And so harshly did she judge, in spite of a scepticism, feminine though it was, that was surprising in a woman.

XXI.

Don Juan Prim, Count of Reus, Marques de los Castillejos, would now be forgotten outside Spain were it not that Régnault's splendid equestrian picture of him, as he is receiving the homage of the people (on a fiery steed, reminding one of Velasquez), keeps his memory green in everyone who visits the Gallery of the Louvre. At that time his name was on every tongue. The victorious general and revolutionary of many years' standing had since 1869 been Prime Minister of Spain, and had eagerly endeavoured to get a foreign prince for the throne who would be dependent upon him and under whom he would be able to keep the power in his own hands. He had now offered the throne of Spain to Leopold of Hohenzollern, but without having assured himself of the consent of the Powers. That of Prussia was of course safe enough, and for six weeks Napoleon had looked on benevolently at the negotiations, and acted as though the arrangement had his approval, which Prim had the more reason to suppose since Leopold was related to the Murat family, and the Emperor had raised no objection to a Hohenzollern ascending the throne of Roumania. Consequently, Prim was thunderstruck when France suddenly turned round and seized upon this trivial pretext for a breach of the peace.

He was in regular correspondence with the Gallengas, whom he had seen a good deal of during the years, after the unsuccessful rebellion against Queen Isabella, that he had spent in London. At that time he had been a man of fifty, and, with his little body and large head, had looked very strange among Englishmen. He was of modest birth, but denied the fact. He was now a Spanish grandee of the first class, but this was through a patent bestowed on him for courage in the war with Morocco; he had little education, did not know a word of English, wrote French with a purely fantastic orthography, but had excellent qualities as a Liberal, an army chief, and a popular leader. Still, he was not pleased that Régnault had painted him greeted by the enthusiastic cheers of an untidy, ragged mob of rebels; he would have preferred to be receiving the acclamations of regular troops, and of the highest men and women in the nation, as now, at the conclusion of his career, he really was. Only a few months later (in December, 1870), he was shot by an assassin in the streets of Madrid.

In Prim's communications to Gallenga, the attitude of the French government appeared to me in a most unfavourable light. Ollivier, the Premier, I had long despised; it did not need much political acumen to see that he was an ambitious and conceited phrase-monger, who would let himself be led by the nose by those who had disarmed him. The Emperor himself was a wreck. I had had no doubt of that since I had one day seen him at very close quarters in the Louvre, where he was inspecting some recently hung, decorative paintings. It was quite evident that he could not walk alone, but advanced, half-sliding, supported by two tall chamberlains, who each gave him an arm. His eyes were half-closed and his gaze absolutely dulled. The dressed and waxed moustache, which ran to a needle-like point, looked doubly tasteless against his wax mask of a face. He was the incarnation of walking decrepitude, vapid and slack. Quite evidently he had committed the blunder of trusting to a split in Germany. In his blindness he explained that he had come to free the Germans, who had, against their will, been incorporated into Prussia, and all Germany rose like one man against him. And in his foolish proclamation he declared that he was waging this war for the sake of the civilising ideals of the first Republic, as if Germany were now going to be civilised for the first time, and as if he, who had made an end of the second Republic by a *coup d'état,* could speak in the name of Republican freedom. His whole attitude was mendacious and mean, and the wretched pretext under which he declared war could not but prejudice Europe against him. In addition to this, as they knew very well in England, from the earlier wars of the Empire, he had no generals; his victories had been soldier victories.

I was very deeply impressed, in the next place, by the suicide of Prévost-Paradol. I had studied most carefully his book, *La France Nouvelle;* I had seen in this friend and comrade of Taine and of Renan the political leader of the future in France. No one was so well acquainted with its resources as he; no one knew better than he what policy ought to be followed. If he had despaired, it was because he foresaw that the situation was hopeless. He had certainly made mistakes; first, in believing that in January it had been Napoleon's serious intention to abrogate personal control of the state, then that of retaining, despite the long hesitation so well known to me, his position as French Envoy to North America, after the plebiscite. That he should now have turned his pistol against his own forehead told me that he regarded the battle as lost, foresaw inevitable collapse as the outcome of the war. When at first all the rumours and all the papers announced the extreme probability of Denmark's taking part in the war as France's ally, I was seized with a kind of despair at the thought of the folly she seemed to be on the verge of committing. I wrote to my friends, would have liked, had I been permitted, to write in every Danish paper a warning against the martial madness that had seized upon people. It was only apparently shared by the French. Even now, only a week after the declaration of war, and before a single collision had taken place, it was clear to everyone who carefully followed the course of events that in spite of the light-hearted bragging of the Parisians and the Press, there was deep-rooted aversion to war. And I, who had always counted Voltaire's *Microm-égas* as one of my favourite tales, thought of where Sirius, the giant, voices his supposition that the people on the earth are happy beings who pass their time in love and thought, and of the philosopher's reply to him: "At this moment there are a hundred thousand animals of our species, who wear hats, engaged in killing a hundred thousand more, who wear turbans, or in being killed by them. And so it has been all over the earth from time immemorial." Only that this time not a hundred thousand, but some two million men were being held in readiness to exterminate each other.

What I saw in London of the scenic art at the Adelphi Theatre, the Prince of Wales' Theatre and the Royal Strand Theatre was disheartening. Molière was produced as the lowest kind of farce, Sheridan was acted worse than would be permitted in Denmark at a second-class theatre; but the scenic decorations, a greensward, shifting lights, and the like, surpassed anything that I had ever seen before.

More instructive and more fascinating than the theatres were the parliamentary debates and the trials in the Law Courts. I enjoyed in particular a sitting of the Commons with a long debate between Gladstone and Disraeli, who were like representatives of two races and two opposed views of life. Gladstone was in himself handsomer, clearer, and more open, Disraeli spoke with a finer point, and more elegantly, had a larger oratorical compass, more often made a witty hit, and evoked more vigorous response and applause. Their point of disagreement was the forthcoming war; Disraeli wished all the documents regarding it to be laid before parliament; Gladstone declared that he could not produce them. In England, as elsewhere, the war that was just breaking out dominated every thought.

XXII.

The Paris I saw again was changed. Even on my way from Calais I heard, to my astonishment, the hitherto strictly forbidden *Marseillaise* hummed and muttered. In Paris, people went arm in arm about the streets singing, and the *Marseillaise* was heard everywhere. The voices were generally harsh, and it was painful to hear the song that had become sacred through having been silenced so long, profaned in this wise, in the bawling and shouting of half-drunken men at night. But the following days, as well, it was hummed, hooted, whistled and sung everywhere, and as the French are one of the most unmusical nations on earth, it sounded for the most part anything but agreeable.

In those days, while no collision between the masses of troops had as yet taken place, there was a certain cheerfulness over Paris; it could be detected in every conversation; people were more lively, raised their voices more, chatted more than at other times; the cabmen growled more loudly, and cracked their whips more incessantly than usual.

Assurance of coming victory was expressed everywhere, even among the hotel servants in the Rue Racine and on the lips of the waiters at every restaurant. Everybody related how many had already volunteered; the number grew from day to day; first it was ten thousand, then seventy-five thousand, then a hundred thousand. In the Quartier Latin, the students sat in their cafés, many of them in uniform, surrounded by their comrades, who were bidding them good-bye. It was characteristic that they no longer had their womenfolk with them; they had flung them aside, now that the matter was serious. Every afternoon a long stream of carriages, filled with departing young soldiers, could be seen moving out towards the Gare du Nord. From every carriage large flags waved. Women, their old mothers, work-women, who sat in the carriages with them, held enormous bouquets on long poles. The dense mass of people through which one drove were grave; but the soldiers for the most part retained their gaiety, made grimaces, smoked and drank.

Nevertheless, the Emperor's proclamation had made a very poor impression. It was with the intention of producing an effect of sincerity that he foretold the war would be long and grievous, (*longue et pénible*) ; with a people of the French national character it would have been better had he been able to write " terrible, but short." Even now, when people had grown accustomed to the situation, this proclamation hung like a nightmare over them. I was all the more astonished when an old copy of the *Daily Paper* for the 30th of July fell into my hands, and I read that their correspondent (Topsöe, recently arrived in Paris) had seen a bloused workman tear off his hat, after reading the proclamation, and heard him shout, " *Vive la France!* " So thoughtlessly

did people continue to feed the Danish public with the food
to which it was accustomed.

Towards the 8th or 9th of August I met repeatedly
the author of the article. He told me that the Duc de Cadore
had appeared in Copenhagen on a very indefinite errand,
but without achieving the slightest result. Topsöe, for that
matter, was extraordinarily ignorant of French affairs, had
only been four weeks in France altogether, and openly admitted that he had touched up his correspondence as well as
he could. He had never yet been admitted to the *Corps
législatif,* nevertheless he had related how the tears had
come into the eyes of the members and the tribunes the
day when the Duc de Grammont "again lifted the flag of
France on high." He said: " I have been as unsophisticated as a child over this war," and added that Bille had been
more so than himself.

XXIII.

One could hardly praise the attitude of the French papers between the declaration of war and the first battles.
Their boasting and exultation over what they were going to
do was barely decent, they could talk of nothing but the victories they were registering beforehand, and, first and last,
the entry into Berlin. The insignificant encounter at Saar-
brücken was termed everywhere the *première victoire!* The
caricatures in the shop-windows likewise betrayed terrible
arrogance. One was painfully reminded of the behaviour
of the French before the battle of Agincourt in Shakespeare's
Henry V.

It was no matter for surprise that a populace thus excited should parade through the streets in an evening, shouting " *A Berlin!   A Berlin!* "

National enthusiasm could vent itself in the theatres,
in a most convenient manner, without making any sacrifice.
As soon as the audience had seen the first piece at the Théâtre Français, the public clamoured for *La Marseillaise,* and
brooked no denial. A few minutes later the lovely Mlle.

Agar came in, in a Greek costume.   Two French flags were
held over her head.   She then sang, quietly, sublimely, with
expression at the same time restrained and inspiring, the
Marseillaise.   The countless variations of her voice were in
admirable keeping with her animated and yet sculptural
gesticulation, and the effect was thrilling, although certain
passages in the song were hardly suitable to the circumstances
of the moment, for instance, the invocation of Freedom,
the prayer to her to fight for her defenders.   When
the last verse came, she seized the flag and knelt down;
the audience shouted, *"Debout!"*   All rose and listened
standing to the conclusion, which was followed by mad
applause.

People seized upon every opportunity of obtruding
their patriotism.   One evening *Le lion amoureux* was given.
In the long speech which concludes the second act, a young
Republican describes the army which, during the Revolution,
crossed the frontier for the first time and utterly destroyed
the Prussian armies.   The whole theatre foamed like the sea.

XXIV.

Those were Summer days, and in spite of the political
and martial excitement, the peaceful woods and parks in the
environs of Paris were tempting.   From the Quartier Latin
many a couple secretly found their way to the forests of St.
Germain, or the lovely wood at Chantilly.   In the morning
one bought a roast fowl and a bottle of wine, then spent
the greater part of the day under the beautiful oak-trees,
and sat down to one's meal in the pleasant green shade.   Now
and again one of the young women would make a wreath
of oak leaves and twine it round her companion's straw hat,
while he, bareheaded, lay gazing up at the tree-tops.   For
a long time I kept just such a wreath as a remembrance, and
its withered leaves roused melancholy reflections some years
later, for during the war every tree of the Chantilly wood had
been felled; the wreath was all that remained of the magnificent oak forest.

XXV.

The news of the battle of Weissenburg on August 4th was a trouble, but this chiefly manifested itself in profound astonishment. What? They had suffered a defeat? But one did not begin to be victorious at once; victory would soon follow now. And, indeed, next morning, the news of a victory ran like lightning about the town. It had been so confidently expected that people quite neglected to make enquiries as to how and to what extent it was authenticated. There was bunting everywhere; all the horses had flags on their heads, people went about with little flags in their hats. As the day wore on it turned out to be all a false report, and the depression was great.

Next evening, as I came out of the *Théâtre Français*, there stood the Emperor's awful telegram to read, several copies of it posted up on the columns of the porch: "Macmahon has lost a battle. Frossard is retreating. Put Paris in a condition of defence as expeditiously as possible!" Then, like everyone else, I understood the extent of the misfortune. Napoleon had apparently lost his head; it was very unnecessary to publish the conclusion of the telegram.

Immediately afterwards was issued the Empress' proclamation, which was almost silly. "I am with you," it ran —a charming consolation for the Parisians.

Astonishment produced a kind of paralysis; anger looked round for an object on which to vent itself, but hardly knew whom to select. Besides, people had really insufficient information as to what had happened. The *Siècle* printed a fairly turbulent article at once, but no exciting language in the papers was required. Even a foreigner could perceive that if it became necessary to defend Paris after a second defeat, the Empire would be at an end.

The exasperation which had to vent itself was directed at first against the Ministers, and ridiculously enough the silence imposed on the Press concerning the movements of the troops (*le mutisme*) was blamed for the defeat at Weissenburg; then the exasperation swung back and was directed against the generals, who were dubbed negligent and incapable, until, ponderously and slowly, it turned against the Emperor himself.

But with the haste that characterises French emotion, and the rapidity with which events succeeded one another, even this exasperation was of short duration. It raged for a few days, and then subsided for want of contradiction of its own accord, for the conviction spread that the Emperor's day was irrevocably over and that he continued to exist only in name. A witness to the rapidity of this *volte face* were three consecutive articles by Edmond About in *Le Soir*. The first, written from his estate in Saverne, near Strassburg, was extremely bitter against the Emperor; it began: "*Napoleone tertio feliciter regnante,* as people said in the olden days, I have seen with my own eyes, what I never thought to see: Alsace overrun by the enemy's troops." The next article, written some days later, in the middle of August, when About had come to Paris, called the Emperor, without more ado, " The last Bonaparte," and began: " I see that I have been writing like a true provincial; in the provinces at the moment people have two curses on their lips, one for the Prussians, and one for those who began the war; in Paris, they have got much farther; there they have only one curse on their lips, one thought, and one wish; there are names that are no more mentioned in Paris than if they belonged to the twelfth century."

What he wrote was, at the moment, true and correct. I was frequently asked in letters what the French now said about the government and the Emperor. The only answer was that all that side of the question was antiquated in Paris. If I were to say to one of my acquaintances: "*Eh! bien, que dites-vous de l'empereur?*" the reply would be: "*Mais, mon cher, je ne dis rien de lui. Vous voyez si bien que moi, qu'il ne compte plus. C'est un homme par terre. Tout le monde le sait; la gauche même ne l'attaque plus.*" Even General Trochu, the Governor of the capital, did not mention Napoleon's name in his proclamation to Paris. He himself hardly dared to send any messages. After having been obliged to surrender the supreme command, he followed the army, like a mock emperor, a kind of onlooker, a superfluous piece on the board.   People said of him :   " *On croit qu'il se promène un peu aux environs de Châlons.*"

As can be seen from this, the deposition of the Emperor had taken place in people's consciousness, and was, so to speak, publicly settled, several weeks before the battle of Sedan brought with it his surrender to the King of Prussia and the proclamation of the French Republic.   The Revolution of September 4th was not an overturning of things; it was merely the ratification of a state of affairs that people were already agreed upon in the capital, and had been even before the battle of Gravelotte.

In Paris preparations were being made with the utmost energy for the defence of the city.   All men liable to bear arms were called up, and huge numbers of volunteers were drilled.   It was an affecting sight to see the poor workmen drilling on the Place du Carrousel for enrolment in the volunteer corps.   Really, most of them looked so bloodless and wretched that one was tempted to think they went with the rest for the sake of the franc a day and uniform.

XXVI.

Anyone whose way led him daily past the fortifications could see, however technically ignorant he might be, that they were exceedingly insignificant.   Constantly, too, one heard quoted Trochu's words :   " I don't delude myself into supposing that I can stop the Prussians with the matchsticks that are being planted on the ramparts." Strangely enough, Paris shut herself in with such a wall of masonry that in driving through it in the Bois de Boulogne, there was barely room for a carriage with two horses.   They bored loop-holes in these walls and ramparts, but few doubted that the German artillery would be able to destroy all their defences with the greatest ease.

Distribute arms to the civil population, as the papers unanimously demanded, from readily comprehensible reasons, no one dared to do.   The Empress' Government had to hold out for the existing state of things ; nevertheless, in Paris,—certainly from about the 8th August,—people were under the impression that what had been lost was lost irrevocably.

I considered it would be incumbent upon my honour to return to Denmark, if we were drawn into the war, and I lived with this thought before my eyes. I contemplated with certainty an approaching revolution in France; I was vexed to think that there was not one conspicuously great and energetic man among the leaders of the Opposition, and that such a poor wretch as Rochefort was once more daily mentioned and dragged to the front. Of Gambetta no one as yet thought, although his name was respected, since he had made himself felt the last season as the most vehement speaker in the Chamber. But it was not speakers who were wanted, and people did not know that he was a man of action.

The Ministry that followed Ollivier's inspired me with no confidence. Palikao, the Prime Minister, was termed in the papers an *iron man* (the usual set phrase). It was said that he " would not scruple to clear the boulevards with grape "; but the genius needed for such a performance was not overwhelming. What he had to do was to clear France of the Germans, and that was more difficult.

Renan had had to interrupt the journey to Spitzbergen which he had undertaken in Prince Napoleon's company; the Prince and his party had only reached Tromsöe, when they were called back on account of the war, and Renan was in a state of the most violent excitement. He said: " No punishment could be too great for that brainless scoundrel Ollivier, and the Ministry that has followed his is worse. Every thinking man could see for himself that the declaration of this war was madness. (*A-t-on jamais vu pareille folie, mon Dieu, mon Dieu, c'est navrant. Nous sommes un peuple désarçonné.*)" In his eyes, Palikao was no better than a robber, Jérôme David than a murderer. He considered the fall of Strasburg imminent. He was less surprised than I at the unbounded incapacity shown by the French fleet under the difficult conditions; all plans for a descent on Northern Germany had already been given up, and the French fleet was unable to set about even so much as a blockade of the ports, such as the Danes had successfully carried out six years before.

Taine was as depressed as Renan. He had returned from Germany, where he had gone to prepare a treatise on Schiller, on account of the sudden death of Madame Taine's mother. As early as August 2d, when no battle had as yet been fought, he felt exceedingly anxious, and he was the first Frenchman whom I heard take into consideration the possibility of the defeat of France; he expressed great sorrow that two nations such as France and Germany should wage national war against each other as they were doing. " I have just come from Germany," he remarked, " where I have talked with many brave working-men. When I think of what it means for a man to be born into the world, nursed, brought up, instructed, and equipped; when I think what struggling and difficulties he must go through himself to be fit for the battle of life, and then reflect how all that is to be flung into the grave as a lump of bleeding flesh, how can I do other than grieve ! With two such statesmen as Louis Philippe, war could certainly have been averted, but with two quarrelsome men like Bismarck and Napoleon at the head of affairs, it was, of course, inevitable."

Philarète Chasles saw in the defeats a confirmation of the theory that he proclaimed, day in, day out, namely: that the Latin races were on the rapid down-grade; Spain and Portugal, Italy, Roumania, the South American republics, were, in his opinion, in a state of moral putrefaction, France a sheer Byzantium. It had been a piece of foolhardiness without parallel to try to make this war a decisive racial struggle between the nation that, as Protestant, brought free research in its train and one which had not yet been able to get rid of the Pope and political despotism. Now France was paying the penalty.

Out in the country at Meudon, where he was, there had —probably from carelessness—occurred repeated explosions, the last time on August 20th. Twenty cases of cartridges had just been sent to Bazaine; a hundred still remained, which were to start the day that they were urgently required. They blew up, and no one in the town doubted that the ex-

plosion was the work of Prussian spies. For things had
come to such a pass that people saw Prussian spies everywhere. (During the first month of the war all Germans
were called Prussians.) Importance was attached to the
fact that General Frossard's nephew, a young lieutenant who
lay wounded in Chasles' tower-house, from a sword-thrust
in the chest, and was usually delirious, at the crash had
jumped up and come to his senses, crying out: "It is
treachery! It is Chamber No. 6 blowing up!" As a matter of fact, that was where the cartridges were. It was said
that at Meudon traces had been found of the same explosive
as had been used in bombs against the Emperor during the
first days of May (a plot that had probably been hatched by
the police). The perpetrator, however,—doubtless for good
reasons—was not discovered.

Whatever vanity there was about old Philarète Chasles
left him altogether during this critical time, which seemed
to make good men better still. His niece, too, who used to
be loud-voiced and conceited, was quite a different person.
One day that I was at their house at Meudon, she sat in a
corner for a long time crying quietly. Out there, they were
all feverishly anxious, could not rest, craved, partly to hear
the latest news, partly to feel the pulse of Paris. One day
after dinner, Chasles invited me to go into town with him,
and when we arrived he took a carriage and drove about
with me for two hours observing the prevailing mood. We
heard countless anecdotes, most of them apocryphal, but
reflecting the beliefs of the moment: The Empress had sent
three milliards (!) in French gold to the Bank of England.
The Emperor, who was jealous of Macmahon since the latter had rescued him at Magenta, had taken the command of
the Turcos from the Marshal, although the latter had said in
the Council of War: "The Turcos must be given to me, they
will not obey anyone else." And true it was that no one else
had any control over them. If one had committed theft,
or misbehaved himself in any other way, and Macmahon,
whom they called only "Our Marshal," rode down the
front of their lines and scolded them, they began to cry,
rushed up and kissed his feet, and hung to his horse, like

children asking for forgiveness. And now someone had made the great mistake of giving them to another general. And, the commander being anxious to dazzle the Germans with them, they and the Zouazes had been sent first into the fire, in spite of Bazaine's very sensible observation: "When you drive, you do not begin at a galop." And so these picked troops were broken up in their first engagement. It was said that of 2,500 Turcos, only 29 were left.

An anecdote like the following, which was told to us, will serve to show how popular legends grow up, in virtue of the tendency there is to reduce a whole battle to a collision between two generals, just as in the Homeric age, or in Shakespeare: The Crown Prince of Prussia was fighting very bravely at Wörth, in the front ranks. That he threw the Turcos into confusion was the result of a ray of sunlight falling on the silver eagle on his helmet. The Arabs thought it a sign from Heaven. Macmahon, who was shooting in the ranks, was so near the Crown Prince that the latter shouted to him in French: "*Voilà un homme!*" but the Frenchman surpassed him in chivalrous politeness, for he saluted, and replied: "*Voilà un héros!*"

XXVII.

After my return to Paris, I had taken lessons from an excellent language teacher, Mademoiselle Guémain, an old maid who had for many years taught French to Scandinavians, and for whom I wrote descriptions and remarks on what I saw, to acquire practise in written expression. She had known most of the principal Northerners who had visited Paris during the last twenty years, had taught Magdalene Thoresen, amongst others, when this latter as a young woman had stayed in Paris. She was an excellent creature, an unusual woman, intellectual, sensitive, and innocent, who made an unforgettable impression upon one. Besides the appointed lesson-times, we sometimes talked for hours together. How sad that the lives of such good and exceptional women should vanish and disappear, without any special thanks given to them in their life-times, and with no one of the many whom they have benefitted to tell publicly of their value. She possessed all the refinement of the French, together with the modesty of an old maid, was both personally inexperienced, and by virtue of the much that she had seen, very experienced in worldly things. I visited her again in 1889, after the lapse of nineteen years, having learned her address through Jonas Lie and his wife, who knew her.   I found her older, but still more charming, and touchingly humble. It cut me to the heart to hear her say: " *C'est une vraie charité que vous me faites de venir me voir.*"

Mlle. Guémain was profoundly affected, like everyone else, by what we were daily passing through during this time of heavy strain. As a woman, she was impressed most by the seriousness which had seized even the most frivolous people, and by the patriotic enthusiasm which was spreading in ever wider circles. She regarded it as deeper and stronger than as a rule it was.

XXVIII.

The temper prevailing among my Italian friends was very different. The Italians, as their way was, were just like children, laughed at the whole thing, were glad that the Prussians were " drubbing " the French, to whom, as good patriots, they wished every misfortune possible. The French had behaved like tyrants in Italy; now they were being paid out. Besides which, the Prussians would not come to Paris. But if they did come, they would be nice to them, and invite them to dinner, like friends. Sometimes I attempted to reply, but came off badly. One day that I had ventured a remark to a large and ponderous Roman lady, on the ingratitude of the Italians towards the French, the good lady jumped as if a knife had been stuck into her, and expatiated passionately on the infamy of the French. The Romans were,—as everyone knew,—the first nation on earth. The French had outraged them, had dared to prevent them making their town the capital of Italy, by garrisoning it with French soldiers who had no business there, so that they had themselves asked for the Nemesis which was now overtaking

them, and which the Italians were watching with flashing
eyes.   She said this, in spite of her anger, with such dignity,
and such a bearing, that one could not but feel that, if she
were one day called upon to adorn a throne, she would seat
herself upon it as naturally, and as free from embarrassment,
as though it were nothing but a Roman woman's birthright.

XXIX.

In the meantime, defeats and humiliations were beginning to confuse the good sense of the French, and to lead
their instincts astray.   The crowd could not conceive that
such things could come about naturally.   The Prussians
could not possibly have won by honourable means, but must
have been spying in France for years.   Why else were so
many Germans settled in Paris!   The French were paying
now, not for their faults, but for their virtues, the good faith,
the hospitality, the innocent welcome they had given to
treacherous immigrants.   They had not understood that the
foreigner from the North was a crafty and deceitful enemy.
It gradually became uncomfortable for a foreigner in
Paris.   I never went out without my passport.   But even
a passport was no safeguard.   It was enough for someone to make some utterly unfounded accusation, express
some foolish, chance suspicion, for the non-Frenchman to be
maltreated as a " spy."   Both in Metz and in Paris, in the
month of August, people who were taken for " Prussians "
were hanged or dismembered.   In the latter part of August
the papers reported from the Dordogne that a mob there
had seized a young man, a M. de Moneys, of whom a gang
had asserted that he had shouted " *Vive la Prusse!* " had
stripped him, bound him with ropes, carried him out into a
field, laid him on a pile of damp wood, and as this would not
take fire quick enough, had pushed trusses of straw underneath all round him, and burnt him alive.   From the *Quartier La Vilette* in Paris, one heard every day of similar
slaughter of innocent persons who the people fancied were
Prussian spies.   Under such circumstances, a trifle might become fatal.   One evening at the end of August I had been

hearing *L'Africaine* at the grand opera, and at the same time
Marie Sass' delivery of the *Marseillaise*—she sang as though
she had a hundred fine bells in her voice, but she sang the
national anthem like an aria.   Outside the opera-house I
hailed a cab.   The coachman was asleep; a man jogged him
to wake him, and he started to drive.   I noticed that during the drive he looked at his watch and then drove on for
all that he was worth, as fast as the harness and reins would
stand.   When I got to the hotel I handed him his fare and a
four sous' tip.   He bawled out that it was not enough; he
had been *de remise;* he had taken me for someone else, being
waked so suddenly; he had been bespoken by another gentleman.   I laughed and replied that that was his affair, not
mine; what had it got to do with me?   But as all he could
demand, if he had really been *de remise,* was two sous more,
and as, under the ordinances prevailing, it was impossible to
tell whether he was or not, I gave him the two sous, but no
tip with it, since he had no right to claim it, and I had not
the slightest doubt that he was lying.   Then he began
to croak that it was a shame not to give a *pourboire,* and, seeing that did not help matters, as I simply walked up the hotel
steps, he shouted in his ill-temper, first *" Vous n'êtes pas
Français! "* and then *" Vous êtes Prussien! "*   No sooner had
he said it than all the hotel servants who were standing in the
doorway disappeared, and the people in the street listened,
stopped, and turned round.   I grasped the danger, and flew
into a passion.   In one bound I was in the road, I rushed
at the cabman, seized him by the throat and shook my hand,
with its knuckle-duster upon it, threateningly at his head.
Then he forgot to abuse me and suddenly whined: *" Ne
frappez pas, monsieur! "* mounted his box, and drove very
tamely away.   In my exasperation I called the hotel waiters
together and poured scorn on them for their cowardice.

In spite of the season, it was uncomfortable weather,
and the temper of the town was as uncomfortable as the
weather.   As time went on, few people were to be seen about
the streets, but there was a run on the gunmakers' and sword-
smiths'.   By day no cheerful shouts or songs rang out, but
children of six or seven years of age would go hand in hand

in rows down the street in the evenings, singing " *Mourir pour la patrie,*" to its own beautiful, affecting melody. But these were the only gentle sounds one heard. Gradually, the very air seemed to be reeking with terror and frenzy. Exasperation rolled up once more, like a thick, black stream, against the Emperor, against the ministers and generals, and against the Prussians, whom people thought they saw everywhere.

xxx.

Foreigners were requested to leave Paris, so that, in the event of a siege, the city might have no unnecessary mouths to feed. Simultaneously, in Trochu's proclamation, it was announced that the enemy might be outside the walls in three days. Under such circumstances, the town was no longer a place for anyone who did not wish to be shut up in it.

One night at the end of August, I travelled from Paris to Geneva. At the departure station the thousands of German workmen who had been expelled from Paris were drawn up, waiting, herded together like cattle,—a painful sight. These workmen were innocent of the war, the defeats, and the spying service of which they were accused; now they were being driven off in hordes, torn from their work, deprived of their bread, and surrounded by inimical lookers-on.

As it had been said that trains to the South would cease next day, the Geneva train was overfilled, and one had to be well satisfied to secure a seat at all. My travelling companions of the masculine gender were very unattractive: an impertinent and vulgar old Swiss who, as it was a cold night, and he had no travelling-rug, wrapped himself up in four or five of his dirty shirts—a most repulsive sight; a very precise young Frenchman who, without a vestige of feeling for the fate of his country and nation, explained to us that he had long had a wish to see Italy, and had thought that now, business being in any case at a standstill, the right moment had arrived.

The female travellers in the compartment were a Parisian, still young, and her bright and charming fifteen-year-old daughter, whose beauty was not unlike that of Mlle. Massin, the lovely actress at the *Théâtre du Gymnase*. The mother was all fire and flame, and raved, almost to tears, over the present pass, cried shame on the cowardice of the officers for not having turned out the Emperor; her one brother was a prisoner at Königsberg; all her male relations were in the field. The daughter was terror-struck at the thought that the train might be stopped by the enemy—which was regarded as very likely—but laughed at times, and was divided between fear of the Prussians and exceeding anxiety to see them: "*J'aimerais bien pouvoir dire que j'aie vu des Prussiens!*"

At one station some soldiers in rout, with torn and dusty clothes, got into our carriage; they looked repulsive, bespattered with mud and clay; they were in absolute despair, and you could hear from their conversation how disorganised discipline was, for they abused their officers right and left, called them incapable and treacherous, yet themselves gave one the impression of being very indifferent soldiers. The young sergeant major who was leading them was the only one who was in anything like spirits, and even he was not much to boast of. It was curious what things he believed: Marshal Lebœuf had had a Prussian officer behind his chair, disguised as a waiter, at Metz, and it had only just been discovered. Russia had lent troops to Prussia, and put them into Prussian uniforms; otherwise there could not possibly be so many of them. But Rome, too, was responsible for the misfortunes of France; the Jesuits had planned it all, because the country was so educated; they never liked anybody to learn anything.

After Culoz commenced the journey through the lovely Jura mountains. On both sides an immense panorama of high, wooded mountain ridges, with poverty-stricken little villages along the mountain sides. At Bellegarde our passports were demanded; no one was allowed to cross the frontier without them—a stupid arrangement. The Alps began to bound our view. The train went on, now through long tunnels, now between precipices, now again over a rocky ridge, whence you looked down into the valley where the blue-green Rhone wound and twined its way between the rocks like a narrow ribbon. The speed seemed to be accelerating more and more. The first maize-field. Slender poplars, without side-branches, but wholly covered with foliage, stood bent almost into spirals by the strong wind from the chinks of the rocks. The first Swiss house.

XXXI.

There was Geneva, between the Alps, divided by the southern extremity of Lake Leman, which was spanned by many handsome bridges. In the centre, a little isle, with Rousseau's statue. A little beyond, the Rhone rushed frothing and foaming out of the lake. From my window I could see in the distance the dazzling snow peak of Mont Blanc.

After Paris, Geneva looked like a provincial town. The cafés were like servants' quarters or corners of cafés. There were no people in the streets, where the sand blew up in clouds of dust till you could hardly see out of your eyes, and the roads were not watered. In the hotel, in front of the mirror, the New Testament in French, bound in leather; you felt that you had come to the capital of Calvinism.

The streets in the old part of the town were all up and down hill. In the windows of the booksellers' shops there were French verses against France, violent diatribes against Napoleon III. and outbursts of contempt for the nation that had lost its virility and let itself be cowed by a tyrant. By the side of these, portraits of the Freethinkers and Liberals who had been driven from other countries and found a refuge in Switzerland.

I sailed the lake in every direction, enraptured by its beauty and the beauty of the surrounding country. Its blueness, to which I had never seen a parallel, altogether charmed me in the changing lights of night and day. On the lake I made the acquaintance of a very pleasant Greek family, the first I had encountered anywhere. The eldest daughter, a girl of fourteen, lost her hat. I had a new silk handkerchief packed amongst my things, and offered it to her. She accepted it and bound it round her hair. Her name was Maria

Kumelas. I saw for the first time an absolutely pure Greek profile, such as I had been acquainted with hitherto only from statues. One perfect, uninterrupted line ran from the tip of her nose to her hair.

XXXII.

I went for excursions into Savoy, ascended La Grande Salève on donkey-back, and from the top looked down at the full length of the Leman.

I drove to the valley of Chamounix, sixty-eight miles, in a diligence and four; about every other hour we had relays of horses and a new driver. Whenever possible, we went at a rattling galop. Half-way I heard the first Italian. It was only the word *quattro;* but it filled me with delight. Above the high, wooded mountains, the bare rock projected out of the earth, at the very top. The wide slopes up which the wood ascended, until it looked like moss on stone, afforded a view miles in extent. The river Arve, twisting itself in curves, was frequently spanned by the roadway; it was of a greyish white, and very rapid, but ugly. Splendid wooden bridges were thrown over it, with abysms on both sides. Midway, after having for some time been hidden behind the mountains, Mont Blanc suddenly appeared in its gleaming splendour, positively tiring and paining the eye. It was a new and strange feeling to be altogether hemmed in by mountains. It was oppressive to a plain-dweller to be shut in thus, and not to be able to get away from the immutable sheet of snow, with its jagged summits. Along the valley of the stream, the road ran between marvellously fresh walnut-trees, plane-trees, and avenues of apple trees; but sometimes we drove through valleys so narrow that the sun only shone on them two or three hours of the day, and there it was cold and damp. Savoy was plainly enough a poor country. The grapes were small and not sweet; soil there was little of, but every patch was utilised to the best advantage. In one place a mountain stream rushed down the rocks; at a sharp corner, which jutted out like the edge of a sloping roof, the stream was split up and transformed into such fine spray that one could perceive no water at all; afterwards the stream united again at the foot of the mountain, and emptied itself with frantic haste into the river, foaming greyish white, spreading an icy cold around. The changes of temperature were striking. Under shelter, hot Summer, two steps further, stern, inclement Autumn, air that penetrated to the very marrow of your bones. You ran through every season of the year in a quarter of an hour.

The other travellers were English people, all of one pattern, unchangeable, immovable. If one of them had buttoned up his coat at the beginning of the drive, he did not unbutton it on the way, were he never so warm, and if he had put leather gloves on, for ten hours they would not be off his hands. The men yawned for the most part; the young ladies jabbered. The English had made the whole country subservient to them, and at the hotels one Englishman in this French country was paid more attention to than a dozen Frenchmen.

Here I understood two widely different poems: Hauch's *Swiss Peasant,* and Björnson's *Over the Hills and Far Away.* Hauch had *felt* this scenery and the nature of these people, by virtue of his Norwegian birth and his gift of entering into other people's thought; Björnson had given unforgettable expression to the feeling of imprisoned longing. But for the man who had been breathing street dust and street sweepings for four months, it was good to breathe the strong, pure air, and at last see once more the clouds floating about and beating against the mountain sides, leaning, exhausted, against a declivity and resting on their journey. Little children of eight or ten were guarding cattle, children such as we know so well in the North, when they come with their marmots; they looked, without exception, like tiny rascals, charming though they were.

I rode on a mule to Montanvert, and thence on foot over the *Mer de Glace,* clambered up the steep mountain side to Chapeau, went down to the crystal Grotto and rode from there back to Chamounix. The ride up in the early hours of the morning was perfect, the mountain air so light; the mists parted; the pine-trees round the fresh mountain path ex-

haled a penetrating fragrance. An American family with
whom I had become acquainted took three guides with them
for four persons. One worthy old gentleman who was
travelling with his young daughter, would not venture upon
this feat of daring, but his daughter was so anxious to
accompany us that when I offered to look after her she was
entrusted to my care. I took two mules and a guide, thinking that sufficient. From Montanvert and down to the glacier, the road was bad, a steep, rocky path, with loose, rolling
stones. When we came to the Ice Sea, the young lady, as
was natural, took the guide's hand, and I, the last of the car-
avan, strode cautiously along, my alpenstock in my hand,
over the slippery, billow-like ice. But soon it began to split
up into deep crevasses, and farther on we came to places
where the path you had to follow was no wider than a few
hands' breadth, with yawning precipices in the ice on both
sides. I grew hot to the roots of my hair, and occasionally
my heart stood still. It was not that I was actually afraid.
The guide shouted to me: " Look neither to right nor left;
look at your feet, and turn out your toes! " I had only one
thought—not to slip!—and out on the ice I grew burningly
hot. When at last I was across, I noticed that I was shaking.
Strangely enough, I was trembling at the *thought* of the blue,
gaping crevasses on both sides of me, down which I had
barely glanced, and yet I had passed them without a shudder.
The beginning of the crossing had been comparatively easy;
it was only that at times it was very slippery. But in the
middle of the glacier, progress was very uncomfortable; mo-
raines, and heaps of gigantic blocks lay in your path, and all
sorts of stone and gravel, which melted glaciers had brought
down with them, and these were nasty to negotiate. When
at last you had them behind you, came *le Mauvaus Pas,* which
corresponded to its name. You climbed up the precipitous
side of the rock with the help of an iron railing drilled into it.
But foothold was narrow and the stone damp, from the number of rivulets that rippled and trickled down. Finally it
was necessary at every step to let go the railing for a few
seconds. The ascent then, and now, was supposed to be quite
free from danger, and the view over the glaciers which one

gained by it, was a fitting reward for the inconvenience. Even more beautiful than the summit of Mont Blanc itself, with its rounded contours, were the steep, gray, rocky peaks, with ice in every furrow, that are called *l'Aiguille du Dru*. These mountains, which as far as the eye could range seemed to be all the same height, although they varied from 7,000 to 14,800 feet, stretched for miles around the horizon.

The ice grotto here was very different from the sky-blue glacier grotto into which I had wandered two years earlier at Grindelwald. Here the ice mass was so immensely high that not the slightest peep of daylight penetrated through it into the excavated archway that led into the ice. It was half-dark inside, and the only light proceeded from a row of little candles stuck into the crevices of the rock. The ice was jet black in colour, the light gleaming with a golden sheen from all the rounded projections and jagged points. It was like the gilt ornamentation on a velvet pall.

When I returned from Chamounix to Geneva, the proprietor of the hotel was standing in the doorway and shouted to me: "The whole of the French army, with the Emperor, has been taken prisoner at Sedan!"—"Impossible!" I exclaimed. "It is quite certain," he replied; "it was in the German telegrams, and so far there has not come a single unveracious telegram from the Germans."

The next day a Genevese paper published the news of the proclamation of the Republic in France.

Simultaneously arrived a letter from Julius Lange, attacking me for my "miserly city politics," seriously complaining that "our declaration of war against Prussia had come to nothing," and hoping that my stay in France had by now made me alter my views.

In his opinion, we had neglected "an opportunity of rebellion, that would never recur."

XXXIII.

Lake Leman fascinated me. All the scenery round looked fairy-like to me, a dream land, in which mighty mountains cast their blue-black shadows down on the turquoise water, beneath a brilliant, sparkling sunshine that saturated the air with its colouring. My impressions of Lausanne, Chillon, Vevey, Montreux, were recorded in the first of my lectures at the University the following year. The instruments of torture at Chillon, barbaric and fearsome as they were, made me think of the still worse murderous instruments being used in the war between France and Germany. It seemed to me that if one could see war at close quarters, one would come to regard the earth as peopled by dangerous lunatics. Political indifference to human life and human suffering had taken the place of the premeditated cruelty of the Middle Ages. Still, if no previous war had ever been so frightful, neither had there ever been so much done to mitigate suffering. While fanatic Frenchwomen on the battlefields cut the noses off wounded Germans, and mutilated them when they could, and while the Germans were burning villages and killing their peaceful inhabitants, if one of them had so much as fired a shot, in all quietness the great societies for the care of the wounded were doing their work. And in this Switzerland especially bore the palm. There were two currents then, one inhuman and one humane, and of the two, the latter will one day prove itself the stronger. Under Louis XIV. war was still synonymous with unlimited plundering, murder, rape, thievery and robbery. Under Napoleon I. there were still no such things as ambulances. The wounded were carted away now and again in waggons, piled one on the top of each other, if any waggons were to be had; if not, they were left as they lay, or were flung into a ditch, there to die in peace. Things were certainly a little better.

XXXIV.

In Geneva, the news reached me that—in spite of a promise Hall, as Minister, had given to Hauch, when the latter asked for it for me—I was to receive no allowance from the Educational Department. To a repetition of the request, Hall had replied: " I have made so many promises and half-promises, that it has been impossible to re-

member or to keep them." This disappointment hit me
rather hard; I had in all only about £50 left, and could not
remain away more than nine weeks longer without getting
into debt, I, who had calculated upon staying a whole year
abroad. Circumstances over which I had no control later
obliged me, however, to remain away almost another year.
But that I could not foresee, and I had no means whatever
to enable me to do so. Several of my acquaintances had
had liberal allowances from the Ministry; Krieger and Martensen had procured Heegaard £225 at once, when he had
been anxious to get away from Rasmus Nielsen's influence.
It seemed to me that this refusal to give me anything augured
badly for the appointment I was hoping for in Denmark.
I could only earn a very little with my pen: about 11s. 3d.
for ten folio pages, and as I did not feel able, while travelling, to write anything of any value, I did not attempt it.
It was with a sort of horror that, after preparing for long
travels that were to get me out of the old folds, I thought
of the earlier, narrow life I had led in Copenhagen. All
the old folds seemed, at this distance, to have been the folds
of a strait-waistcoat.

XXXV.

With abominable slowness, and very late, " on account
of the war," the train crawled from Geneva, southwards.
Among the travellers was a rhetorical Italian master-mason,
from Lyons, an old Garibaldist, the great event of whose
life was that Garibaldi had once taken lunch alone with him
at Varese. He preserved in his home as a relic the glass
from which the general had drunk. He was talkative, and
ready to help everyone; he gave us all food and drink from
his provisions. Other travellers told that they had had to
stand in queue for fully twelve hours in front of the ticket
office in Paris, to get away from the town.

The train passed the place where Rousseau had lived,
at Madame de Warens'. In an official work on Savoy, written by a priest, I had recently read a summary dismissal of
Rousseau, as a calumniator of his benefactress. According

to this author, it certainly looked as though, to say the least of it, Rousseau's memory had failed him amazingly sometimes. The book asserted, for instance, that the Claude of whom he speaks was no longer alive at the time when he was supposed to be enjoying Madame de Warens' favours.

We passed French volunteers in blouses bearing a red cross; they shouted and were in high good humour; passed fen districts, where numbers of cretins, with their hideous excrescences, sat by the wayside. At last we arrived,—several hours behind time,—at St. Michel, at the foot of Mont Cenis; it was four o'clock in the afternoon, and I was beginning to feel tired, for I had been up since four in the morning. At five o'clock we commenced the ascent, to the accompaniment of frightful groanings from the engine; all the travellers were crowded together in three wretched little carriages, the small engine not being able to pull more. Gay young French girls exulted at the idea of seeing "Italy's fair skies." They were not particularly fair here; the weather was rough and cloudy, in keeping with abysms and mountain precipices. But late at night the journey over Mont Cenis was wonderful. High up on the mountain the moonlight gleamed on the mountain lake. And the way was dominated, from one rocky summit, by the castle of Bramans with its seven imposing forts.

The locomotive stopped for an hour, for want of water. We were thus obliged to sleep at the little Italian town of Susa (in a glorious valley under Mont Cenis), the train to Turin having left three hours before. Susa was the first Italian town I saw. When the train came in next morning to the station at Turin, a crowd of Italian soldiers, who were standing there, shouted: " The Prussians for ever! " and winked at me. " What are they shouting for? " I asked a young Turin fellow with whom I had had some long conversations. " It is an ovation to you," he replied. " People are delighted at the victory of the Prussians, and they think you are a Prussian, because of your fair moustache and beard."

XXXVI.

An overwhelming impression was produced upon me by the monuments of Turin, the River Po, and the lovely glee-singing in the streets. For the first time, I saw colonnades, with heavy curtains to the street, serve as pavements, with balconies above them. Officers in uniforms gleaming with gold, ladies with handkerchiefs over their heads instead of hats, the mild warmth, the brown eyes, brought it home to me at every step that I was in a new country.

I hurried up to Costanza Blanchetti. *Madame la comtesse est à la campagne. Monsieur le comte est sorti.* Next morning, as I was sitting in my room in the Hotel Trombetta, Blanchetti rushed in, pressed me to his bosom, kissed me on both cheeks, would not let me go, but insisted on carrying me off with him to the country.

We drove round the town first, then went by rail to Alpignano, where Costanza was staying with a relative of the family, Count Buglioni di Monale. Here I was received like a son, and shown straight to my room, where there stood a little bed with silk hangings, and where, on the pillow, there lay a little, folded-up thing, likewise of white silk, which was an enigma to me till, on unfolding it, I found it was a night-cap, the classical night-cap, tapering to a point, which you see at the theatre in old comedies. The Buglionis were gentle, good-natured people, rugged and yet refined, an old, aristocratic country gentleman and his wife. Nowhere have I thought grapes so heavy and sweet and aromatic as there. The perfume from the garden was so strong and fragrant. Impossible to think of a book or a sheet of paper at Alpignano. We walked under the trees, lay among the flowers, enjoyed the sight and the flavour of the apricots and grapes, and chatted, expressing by smiles our mutual quiet, deep-reaching sympathy.

One evening I went into Turin with Blanchetti to see the play. The lover in *La Dame aux Camélias* was played by a young Italian named Lavaggi, as handsome as an Antinous, a type which I often encountered in Piedmont. With his innate charm, restful calm, animation of movement and the fire of his beauty, he surpassed the acting of all the young lovers I had seen on the boards of the French theatres. The very play of his fingers was all grace and expression.

XXXVII.

On my journey from Turin to Milan, I had the mighty Mont Rosa, with its powerful snow mass, and the St. Bernard, over which Buonaparte led his tattered troops, before my eyes. We went across maize fields, through thickets, over the battlefield of Magenta. From reading Beyle, I had pictured Milan as a beautiful town, full of free delight in life. Only to see it would be happiness. And it was,— the cupola gallery, the dome, from the roof of which, immediately after my arrival, I looked out over the town, shining under a pure, dark-blue sky. In the evening, in the public gardens, I revelled in the beauty of the Milanese women. Italian ladies at that time still wore black lace over their heads instead of hats. Their dresses were open in front, the neck being bare half-way down the chest. I was struck by the feminine type. Upright, slender-waisted women; delicate, generally bare hands; oval faces, the eyebrows of an absolutely perfect regularity; narrow noses, well formed, the nostrils curving slightly upwards and outwards—the models of Leonardo and Luini.

The *Last Supper,* in the church of St. Maria delle Grazie, and the drawings in the Ambrose Library, brought me closer to Leonardo than I had ever been able to get before, through reproductions; I saw the true expression in the face of the Christ in the *Last Supper,* which copies cannot avoid distorting.

XXXVIII.

A violent affection for Correggio, and a longing to see his works where they are to be found in greatest number, sent me to Parma.

I reached the town at night; no gas, no omnibus from any hotel. An out-porter trotted with my portmanteau on his back through wide, pitch-dark, deserted, colonnaded streets, past huge palaces, until, after half an hour's rapid walk, we arrived at the hotel. The day before my arrival dall 'Ongaro had unveiled the beautiful and beautifully situated statue of Correggio in the Market Square. I first investigated the two domes in the Cathedral and San Giovanni Evangelista, then the ingratiating pictorial decoration of the convent of San Paolo. In the Museum, where I was pretty well the only visitor, I was so eagerly absorbed in studying Correggio and jotting down my impressions, that, in order to waste no time, I got the attendant to buy my lunch, and devoured it,—bread, cheese, and grapes,—in the family's private apartments. They were pleasant, obliging people, and as I bought photographs for a considerable amount from them, they were very hospitable. They talked politics to me and made no secret of their burning hatred for France.

There were other things to see at Parma besides Correggio, although for me he dominated the town. There was a large exhibition of modern Italian paintings and statuary, and the life of the people in the town and round about. In the streets stood carts full of grapes. Four or five fellows with bare feet would stamp on the grapes in one of these carts; a trough led from the cart down to a vat, into which the juice ran, flinging off all dirt in fermentation.

It was pleasant to walk round the old ramparts of the town in the evening glow, and it was lively in the ducal park. One evening little knots of Italian soldiers were sitting there. One of them sang in a superb voice, another accompanied him very nicely on the lute; the others listened with profound and eager attention.

XXXIX.

After this came rich days in Florence. Everything was a delight to me there, from the granite paving of the streets, to palaces, churches, galleries, and parks. I stood in reverence before the Medici monuments in Michael Angelo's sanctuary. The people attracted me less; the women seemed to me to have no type at all, compared with the

lovely faces and forms at Milan and Parma. The fleas attracted me least of all.

Dall 'Ongaro received every Sunday evening quite
an international company, and conversation consequently
dragged. With the charming Japanese wife of the English consul, who spoke only English and Japanese, neither
of her hosts could exchange a word. There were Dutchmen
and Swiss there with their ladies; sugar-sweet and utterly
affected young Italian men; handsome young painters and a
few prominent Italian scientists, one of whom, in the future, was to become my friend.

I had a double recommendation to the Danish Minister
at Florence, from the Ministry of Foreign Affairs, and from
an old and intimate friend of his in Copenhagen. When I
presented my letters, he exclaimed, in annoyance: "These
special recommendations again! How often must I explain
that they are unnecessary, that all Danes, as such, are welcome to my house!"—This was the delicate manner in
which he let me understand that he was not inclined to do
anything whatever for me. Moreover, he began at once
with regrets that his family were absent, so that he was not
in housekeeping, and could not entertain anyone.

At a production of Emile Augier's *Le Fils de Giboyer,*
at which all the foreign diplomatists were present, he, too,
turned up. While the other diplomatists greeted each other
silently with a nod, he made more of the meeting than any
one else did, went from place to place in the stalls, shook
hands, spoke French, German, English and Italian by turns,
was all things to all men, then came and sat down by me,
made himself comfortable, and in a moment was fast asleep.
When he began to snore, one after another of his colleagues
turned their heads, and smiled faintly. He slept through
two acts and the intervals between them, in spite of the
voices from the stage and the loud talking between the acts,
and woke up in the middle of the third act, to mumble in my
ear, "It is not much pleasure to see the piece played like
this."

At my favourite restaurant, *Trattoria dell' antiche car-
rozze,* I was one day witness to a violent dispute between a

Polish noble who, for political reasons, had fled from Russian Poland, and Hans Semper, a Prussian, author of a book on Donatello. The latter naturally worshipped Bismarck, the former warmly espoused the cause of Denmark. When I left, I said politely to him:

"I thank you for having so warmly defended my country; I am a Dane." The next day the Pole came to look for me at the restaurant, and a closer acquaintance resulted. We went for many walks together along the riverside; he talking like a typical Polish patriot, I listening to his dreams of the resuscitated Poland that the future was to see. I mention this only because it affords an example of the remarkable coincidences life brings about, which make one so easily exclaim: "How small the world is!" This Pole became engaged several years afterwards to a young Polish girl and left her, without any explanation, having got entangled with a Russian ballet dancer. I made her acquaintance at Warsaw fifteen years after I had met him at Florence. She was then twenty-six years of age, and is one of the women who have taught me most; she told me the story of her early youth and of the unengaging part my acquaintance of 1870 had played in it.

At Florence I saw Rossi as Hamlet. The performance was a disappointment to me, inasmuch as Rossi, with his purely Italian nature, had done away with the essentially English element in Hamlet. The keen English humour, in his hands, became absurd and ridiculous. Hamlet's hesitation to act, he overlooked altogether. Hamlet, to him, was a noble young man who was grieved at his mother's ill-behaviour. The details he acted like a virtuoso. For instance, it was very effective during the mimic play, when, lying at Ophelia's feet, he crushes her fan in his hands at the moment when the King turns pale. I derived my chief enjoyment, not from the acting, but from the play. It suddenly revealed itself to me from other aspects, and I fell prostrate in such an exceeding admiration for Shakespeare that I felt I should never rise again. It was touching to hear the Italians' remarks on *Hamlet*. The piece was new to them. You frequently heard the observation: "It is a very philosophical piece." As people changed from place to place, and sat wherever they liked, I overheard many different people's opinions of the drama. The suicide monologue affected these fresh and alert minds very powerfully.

That evening, moreover, I had occasion to observe human cowardice, which is never accounted so great as it really is. There was a noise behind the scene during the performance, and immediately afterwards a shout of *Fuoco!* The audience were overmastered by terror. More than half of them rushed to the doors, pulled each other down, and trampled on the fallen, in their endeavours to get out quickly enough; others rushed up on the stage itself. As there was not the least sign of fire visible, I of course remained in my seat. A few minutes later one of the actors came forward and explained that there had been no fire; a fight between two of the scene-shifters had been the cause of all the alarm. The good-humoured Italians did not even resent the fellows having thus disturbed and interrupted the performance.

John Stuart Mill had given me an introduction to Pasquale Villari, who, even at that time, was *commendatore professore,* and held a high position on the Board of Education, but was still far from having attained the zenith of his fame and influence. When the reserve of the first few days had worn off, he was simply splendid to me. When anything I said struck him as being to the point, he pressed my hands with all the ardour of youth, and he applauded every joke I attempted with uproarious laughter.

Some twenty years were to elapse before I saw him again. Then he called upon me in Copenhagen, wishing to make my acquaintance, without in the least suspecting that I was the young man who, so long before, had come to him from Mill. He looked with amazement at books in which he had written with his own hand, and at old letters from himself which I produced. I visited him again in 1898. His books on Machiavelli and Savonarola entitle him to rank among the foremost students and exponents of Italy.

I went one day to the great annual fair at Fiesole.

Shouting and shrieking, the people drove down the unspeakably dusty road with such haste, carelessness and high spirits
that conveyances struck against each other at every moment.   It was the life represented in Marstrand's old-time
pictures.   In crowded Fiesole, I saw the regular Tuscan
country type, brown eyes, yellow or clear, white skin, thin,
longish face, brown or fair, but never black hair, strong,
healthy bodies.   The masculine type with which I was acquainted from the soldiers, was undeniably handsomer than
our own, in particular, was more intelligent; the young
women were modest, reserved in their manner, seldom entered into conversation with the men, and despite the fire
in their eyes, manifested a certain peasant bashfulness, which
seems to be the same everywhere.

XL.

Vines twine round the fruit-trees; black pigs and their
families make their appearance in tribes; the lake of Thrasy-
mene, near which Hannibal defeated the Romans, spreads
itself out before us.   The train is going from Florence to
Rome.   Towards mid-day a girl enters the carriage, apparently English or North American, with brown eyes and
brown hair, that curls naturally about her head; she has her
guitar-case in her hand, and flings it up into the net.   Her
parents follow her.   As there is room in the compartment
for forty-eight persons without crowding, she arranges places
for her parents, and after much laughter and joking the
latter settle off to sleep.   The Italians stare at her; but not
I.   I sit with my back to her.   She sits down, back to
back with me, then turns her head and asks me, in Italian,
some question about time, place, or the like.   I reply as best
I can.   *She* (in English): " You are Italian? "   On my
reply, she tells me: " I hardly know twenty words in Italian; I only speak English, although I have been living in
Rome for two years."
        She then went on to relate that she was an American,
born of poor parents out on the Indian frontier; she was
twenty-six years old, a sculptor, and was on her way from

Carrara, where she had been superintending the shipment of
one of her works, a statue of Lincoln, which the Congress at
Washington had done her the honour of ordering from
her.   It was only when she was almost grown up that her
talent had been discovered by an old sculptor who happened
to pay a visit and who, when he saw her drawing, had, half
in jest, given her a lump of clay and said: " Do a portrait
of me! "   She had then never seen a statue or a painting,
but she evinced such talent that before long several distinguished men asked her to do busts of them, amongst others,
Lincoln.   She was staying at his house that 14th April,
1865, when he was murdered, and was consequently selected
to execute the monument after his death.   She hesitated for
a long time before giving up the modest, but certain, position
she held at the time in a post-office; but, as others believed
in her talent, she came to Europe, stayed first in Paris, where,
to her delight, she made the acquaintance of Gustave Doré,
and where she modelled a really excellent bust of Père Hya-
cinthe, visited London, Berlin, Munich, Florence, and settled down in Rome.   There she received plenty of orders,
had, moreover, obtained permission to execute a bust of
Cardinal Antonelli, was already much looked up to, and
well-to-do.   In a few weeks she was returning to America.

As she found pleasure in talking to me, she exclaimed
without more ado: "I will stay with you," said a few polite things to me, and made me promise that I would travel
with her to Rome from the place where we were obliged to
leave the train, the railway having been broken up to prevent the Italian troops entering the Papal States.   At Treni
a Danish couple got into the train, a mediocre artist and his
wife, and with national astonishment and curiosity watched
the evident intimacy between the young foreigner and myself, concerning which every Scandinavian in Rome was informed a few days later.

From Monte Rotondo, where the bridge had been
blown up, we had to walk a long distance, over bad roads,
and were separated in the throng, but she kept a place for
me by her side.   Thus I drove for the first time over the
Roman Campagna, by moonlight, with two brown eyes gaz-

ing into mine.   I felt as though I had met one of Sir Walter Scott's heroines, and won her confidence at our first
meeting.

XLI.

Vinnie Ream was by no means a Scott heroine, however,
but a genuine American, and doubly remarkable to me as being the first specimen of a young woman from the United
States with whom I became acquainted.   Even after I had
seen a good deal of her work, I could not feel wholly attracted
by her talent, which sometimes expressed itself rather in a pictorial than a plastic form, and had a fondness for emotional
effects.   But she was a true artist, and a true woman, and I
have never, in any woman, encountered a will like hers.   She
was uninterruptedly busy.   Although, now that the time of
her departure was so near, a few boxes were steadily being
packed every day at her home, she received every day visits
from between sixteen and twenty-five people, and she had so
many letters by post that I often found three or four un-
opened ones amongst the visiting cards that had been left.
Those were what she had forgotten, and if she had read
them, she had no time to reply to them.   Every day she sat
for a few hours to the clever American painter Healy, who
was an admirer of her talent, and called her abilities genius.
Every day she worked at Antonelli's bust.   To obtain permission to execute it, she had merely, dressed in her most
beautiful white gown, asked for an audience of the dreaded
cardinal, and had at once obtained permission.   Her intrepid
manner had impressed the hated statesman of the political
and ecclesiastical reaction, and in her representation of him
he appeared, too, in many respects nobler and more refined
than he was.   But besides modelling the cardinal's bust, she
put the finishing touches to two others, saw to her parents'
household affairs and expenses, and found time every day
to spend a few hours with me, either in a walk or wandering
about the different picture-galleries.

She maintained the family, for her parents had nothing
at all.   But when the statue of Lincoln had been ordered
from her, Congress had immediately advanced ten thou-

sand dollars.   So she was able to live free from care, though
for that matter she troubled not at all about money.   She
was very ignorant of things outside her own field, and
the words *my work* were the only ones that she spoke
with passion.   What she knew, she had acquired prac-
tically, through travel and association with a multiplicity
of people.   She hardly knew a dozen words of any language
besides English, and was only acquainted with English and
American writers; of poets, she knew Shakespeare and Byron
best; from life and books she had extracted but few general
opinions, but on the other hand, very individual personal
views.   These were based upon the theory that the lesser
mind must always subordinate itself to the higher, and that
the higher has a right to utilise freely the time and strength
of the lesser, without being called to account for doing so.
She herself was abjectly modest towards the artists she looked
up to.   Other people might all wait, come again, go away
without a reply.

Rather small of stature, strong and healthy,—she had
never been ill, never taken medicine,—with white teeth
and red cheeks, quick in everything, when several people
were present she spoke only little and absently, was as cold,
deliberate and composed as a man of strong character; but
at the same time she was unsuspecting and generous, and in
spite of her restlessness and her ambitious industry, ingrati-
atingly coquettish towards anyone whose affection she wished
to win.   It was amusing to watch the manner in which she
despatched the dutifully sighing Italians who scarcely crossed
the threshold of her studio before they declared themselves.
She replied to them with a superabundance of sound sense
and dismissed them with a jest.

One day that I went to fetch her to the Casino
Borghese, I found her dissolved in tears.   One of the two
beautiful doves who flew about the house and perched on her
shoulders, and which she had brought with her from Washington, had disappeared in the night.   At first I thought
that her distress was half jest, but nothing could have been
more real; she was beside herself with grief.   I realised
that if philologians have disputed as to how far Catullus'

poem of the girl's grief over the dead sparrow were jest or earnest, it was because they had never seen a girl weep over a bird. Catullus, perhaps, makes fun a little of the grief, but the grief itself, in his poem too, is serious enough.

In the lovely gardens of the Villa Borghese, Vinnie Ream's melancholy frame of mind was dispersed, and we sat for a long time by one of the handsome fountains and talked, among other things, of our pleasure in being together, which pleasure was not obscured by the prospect of approaching parting, because based only on good-fellowship, and with no erotic element about it. Later in the evening, she had forgotten her sorrow altogether in the feverish eagerness with which she worked, and she kept on, by candle-light, until three o'clock in the morning.

A poor man, an Italian, who kept a little hotel, came in that evening for a few minutes; he sometimes translated letters for Vinnie Ream. As he had no business with me, I did not address any of my remarks to him; she, on the contrary, treated him with extreme kindness and the greatest respect, and whispered to me: "Talk nicely to him, as you would to a gentleman, for that he is; he knows four languages splendidly; he is a talented man. Take no notice of his plain dress. We Americans do not regard the position, but the man, and he does honour to his position." I had not been actuated by the prejudices she attributed to me, nevertheless entered into conversation with the man, as she wished, and listened with pleasure to his sensible opinions. (He spoke, among other things, of Northern art, and warmly praised Carl Bloch's *Prometheus*.)

XLII.

Vinnie Ream's opinion of me was that I was the most impolitic man that she had ever known. She meant, by that, that I was always falling out with people (for instance, I had at once offended the Danes in Rome by some sharp words about the wretched Danish papers), and in general made fewer friends and more enemies all the time. She herself won the affection of everyone she wished, and

made everyone ready to spring to do her bidding. She
pointed out to me how politic she had had to be over
her art. When she had wished to become a sculptor,
everyone in her native place had been shocked at the un-
femininity of it, and people fabled behind her back about
her depraved instincts. She, for her part, exerted no more
strength than just enough to carry her point, let people
talk as much as they liked, took no revenge on those who
spread calumnies about her, showed the greatest kindliness
even towards the evil-disposed, and so, she said, had not an
enemy. There was in her a marvellous commingling of determination to progress rapidly, of self-restraint and of real
good-heartedness.

On October 20th there was a great festival in Rome
to celebrate the first monthly anniversary of the entry of the
Italians into the town. Young men went in the evening
with flags and music through the streets. Everybody rushed
to the windows, and the ladies held out lamps and candles.
In the time of the popes this was only done when the Host
was being carried in solemn procession to the dying;
it was regarded therefore as the greatest honour that could
be paid. Everyone clapped hands and uttered shouts of delight at the improvised illumination, while the many beautiful women looked lovely in the flickering lamplight. The
23d again was a gala day, being the anniversary of the death
of Enrico Cairoli—one of the celebrated brothers; he fell
at Mentana;—and I had promised Vinnie Ream to go to
see the fête with her; but she as usual having twenty call-
ers just when we ought to have started, we arrived too late.
Vinnie begged of me to go with her instead to the American chapel; she must and would sing hymns, and really did
sing them very well.

The chapel was bare. On the walls the ten commandments and a few other quotations from Holy Writ, and
above a small altar, " Do this in remembrance of me," in
Gothic lettering. I had to endure the hymns, the sermon
(awful), and the reading aloud of the ten commandments,
with muttered protestations and Amens after each one from
the reverent Americans. When we went out I said noth-

ing, as I did not know whether Vinnie might not be somewhat moved, for she sang at the end with great emotion.   However, she merely took my arm and exclaimed:
"That minister was the most stupid donkey I have ever
heard in my life; but it is nice to sing."   Then she began a
refutation of the sermon, which had hinged chiefly on the
words: "Thy sins are forgiven thee," and of the unspeakable delight it should be to hear this.   Vinnie thought that
no rational being would give a fig for forgiveness, unless
there followed with it a complete reinstatement of previous
condition.   What am I benefitted if ever so many heavenly
beings say to me: "I pretend you have not done it" if I
know that I have!

The last week in October we saw marvellous Northern
Lights in Rome.   The northern half of the heavens, about
nine o'clock in the evening, turned a flaming crimson, and
white streaks traversed the red, against which the stars shone
yellow, while every moment bluish flashes shot across the
whole.   When I discovered it I went up to the Reams' and
fetched Vinnie down into the street to see it.   It was an incredibly beautiful atmospheric phenomenon.   Next evening
it manifested itself again, on a background of black clouds,
and that was the last beautiful sight upon which Vinnie and
I looked together.

Next evening I wrote:

Vinnie Ream leaves to-morrow morning; I said goodbye to her this
evening.   Unfortunately a great many people were there.   She took my
hand and said: "I wish you everything good in the world, and I know
that you wish me the same."   And then: Good-bye.   A door opens, and a
door closes, and people never meet again on this earth, never again, never—
and human language has never been able to discover any distinction between
good-bye for an hour, and good-bye forever.   People sit and chat, smile and
jest.   Then you get up, and the story is finished.   Over! over!   And that is
the end of all stories, says Andersen.

All one's life one quarrels with people as dear to one as Ploug is to me.
I have a well-founded hope that I may see Rudolph Schmidt's profile again
soon, and a hundred times again after that; but Vinnie I shall never see
again.

I did not understand her at first; I had a few unpleasant conjectures
ready.   I had to have many conversations with her before I understood her
ingenuousness, her ignorance, her thorough goodness, in short, all her simple
healthiness of soul.   Over!

When I was teasing her the other day about all the time I had wasted
in her company, she replied: "People do not waste time with their friends,"
and when I exclaimed: "What do I get from you?" she answered, laugh-

ing: "*Inspiration.*" And that was the truth. Those great brown eyes, the firm eyebrows, the ringleted mass of chestnut brown hair and the fresh mouth—all this that I still remember, but perhaps in three months shall no longer be able to recall, the quick little figure, now commanding, now deprecating, is to me a kind of inspiration. I have never been in love with Vinnie; but most people would think so, to hear the expressions I am now using. But I love her as a friend, as a mind akin to my own. There were thoughts of our brains and strings of our hearts, which always beat in unison. Peace be with her! May the cursed world neither rend her nor devour her; may she die at last with the clear forehead she has now! I am grateful to her. She has communicated to me a something good and simple that one cannot see too much of and that one scarcely ever sees at all. Finally, she has shown me again the spectacle of a human being entirely happy, and good because happy, a soul without a trace of bitterness, an intellect whose work is not a labour.

It is not that Vinnie is—or rather was, since she is dead for me—an educated girl in the Copenhagen sense of the word. The verdict of the Danish educational establishments upon her would be that she was a deplorably uneducated girl. She was incomprehensibly dull at languages. She would be childishly amused at a jest or joke or compliment as old as the hills (such as the Italians were fond of using), and think it new, for she knew nothing of the European storehouse of stereotyped remarks and salted drivel. Her own conversation was new; a breath of the independence of the great Republic swept through it. She was no fine lady, she was *an American girl,* who had not attained her rank by birth, or through inherited riches, but had fought for it herself with a talent that had made its way to the surface without early training, through days and nights of industry, and a mixture of enthusiasm and determination.

She was vain; she certainly was that. But again like a child, delighted at verses in her honour in the American papers, pleased at homage and marks of distinction, but far more ambitious than vain of personal advantages. She laughed when we read in the papers of Vinnie Ream, that, in spite of the ill-fame creative lady artists enjoy, far from being a monster with green eyes, she ventured to be beautiful.

She was a good girl. There was a certain deep note about all that her heart uttered. She had a mind of many colours. And there was the very devil of a rush and Forward! March! about her, *always in a hurry.*

And now—no Roman elegy—I will hide her away in my memory:

Here lies
VINNIE REAM
Sculptor
of Washington, U. S. A.
Six-and-twenty years of age
This recollection of her is retained by
One who knew her
for seventeen days
and will never forget her.

I have really never seen Vinnie Ream since. We exchanged a few letters after her departure, and the rest was silence.

Her statue of Abraham Lincoln stands now in a rotunda on the Capitol, for which it was ordered. Later, a Congress Commitee ordered from her a statue of Admiral

Farragut, which is likewise erected in Washington. These are the only two statues that the government of the United States has ever ordered from a woman. Other statues of hers which I have seen mentioned bear the names of *Miriam, The West, Sappho, The Spirit of Carnival,* etc. Further than this, I only know that she married Richard L. Hoxie, an engineer, and only a few years ago was living in Washington.

XLIII.

It was a real trouble to me that the Pope, in his exasperation over the conquest of Rome—in order to make the accomplished revolution recoil also on the heads of the foreigners whom he perhaps suspected of sympathy with the new order of things—had closed the Vatican and all its collections. Rome was to me first and foremost Michael Angelo's Sistine Chapel, Raphael's Stanzas and Loggias, and now all this magnificent array, which I had travelled so far to see, was closed to me by an old man's bad temper.

But there was still enough to linger over in Rome. The two palaces that seemed to me most deserving of admiration were the Farnese and the Cancellaria, the former Michael Angelo's, the latter Bramante's work, the first a perpetuation in stone of beauty and power, the second, of grace and lightness. I felt that if one were to take a person with no idea of architecture and set him in front of these buildings, there would fall like scales from his eyes, and he would say: " Now I know what the building art means."

Luini's exquisite painting, *Vanity and Modesty,* in the Galleria Sciarra, impressed me profoundly. It represented two women, one nun-like, the other magnificently dressed. The latter is Leonardo's well-known type, as a magically fascinating personality. Its essential feature is a profoundly serious melancholy, but the beauty of the figure is seductive. She is by no means smiling, and yet she looks as though a very slight alteration would produce a smile, and as though the heavens themselves would open, if smile she did. The powerful glance of the dark blue eyes is in harmony with the

light-brown hair and the lovely hands. " It would be terrible to meet in real life a woman who looked like that," I
wrote; " for a man would grow desperate at his inability
to win her and desperate because the years must destroy
such a marvel. That is why the gracious gods have willed
it otherwise; that is why she does not exist. That is why
she is only a vision, a revelation, a painting, and that is why
she was conceived in the brain of Leonardo, the place on
earth most favoured by the gods, and executed by Luini, that
all generations might gaze at her without jealousy, and without dread of the molestations of Time."

One day, at the Museo Kircheriano, where I was looking at the admirable antiquities, I made acquaintance with a
Jesuit priest, who turned out to be exceedingly pleasant and
refined, a very decent fellow, in fact. He spoke Latin to
me, and showed me round; at an enquiry of mine, he fetched
from his quarters in the Collegio Romano a book with reproductions from the pagan section of the Lateran Museum,
and explained to me some bas-reliefs which I had not understood. His obligingness touched me, his whole attitude
made me think. Hitherto I had only spoken to one solitary
embryo Jesuit,—a young Englishman who was going to
Rome to place himself at the service of the Pope, and who
was actuated by the purest enthusiasm; I was struck by the
fact that this second Jesuit, too, seemed to be a worthy man.
It taught me how independent individual worth is of the
nature of one's convictions.

Most of the Italians I had so far been acquainted with
were simple people, my landlord and his family, and those
who visited them, and I sometimes heard fragments of conversation which revealed the common people's mode of
thought to me. In one house that I visited, the mistress discovered that her maid was not married to her so-called husband, a matter in which, for that matter, she was very blame-
less, since her parents had refused their consent, and she had
afterwards allowed herself to be abducted. Her mistress
reproached her for the illegal relations existing. She replied,
" If God wishes to plunge anyone into misery, that person
is excused."—" We must not put the blame of everything

upon God," said the mistress.—" Yes, yes," replied the girl unabashed; " then if the Devil wishes to plunge a person into misery, the person is excused."—" Nor may we put the blame of our wrongdoing on the Devil," said the mistress.— " Good gracious," said the girl, " it must be the fault of one or other of them, everybody knows that. If it is not the one, it is the other."

At the house of the Blanchettis, who had come to Rome, I met many Turin and Roman gentlemen. They were all very much taken up by an old Sicilian chemist of the name of Muratori, who claimed that he had discovered a material which looked like linen, but was impervious to bullets, sword-cuts, bayonet-thrusts, etc. Blanchetti himself had fired his revolver at him at two paces, and the ball had fallen flat to the ground. There could be no question of juggling; Muratori was an honourable old Garibaldist who had been wounded in his youth, and now went about on crutches, but, since we have never heard of its being made practical use of, it would seem that there was nothing in it.

I did not care to look up all the Italians to whom I had introductions from Villari. But I tried my luck with a few of them. The first was Dr. Pantaleoni, who had formerly been banished from the Papal States and who left the country as a radical politician, but now held almost conservative views. He had just come back, and complained bitterly of all the licentiousness. " Alas ! " he said, " we have freedom enough now, but order, order ! " Pantaleoni was a little, eager, animated man of fifty, very much occupied, a politician and doctor, and he promised to introduce me to all the scholars whose interests I shared. As I felt scruples at taking up these gentlemen's time, he exclaimed wittily : " My dear fellow, take up their time ! To take his time is the greatest service you can render to a Roman; he never knows what to do to kill it ! "

The next man I went to was Prince Odescalchi, one of the men who had then recently risen to the surface, officially termed the hero of the Young Liberals. Pantaleoni had dubbed him a blockhead, and he had not lied. He turned out to be a very conceited and frothy young man with a parting all over his head, fair to whiteness, of strikingly Northern type, with exactly the same expressionless type of face as certain of the milksops closely connected with the Court in Denmark.

XLIV.

There were a great many Scandinavians in Rome; they foregathered at the various eating-houses and on a Saturday evening at the Scandinavian Club. Some of them were painters, sculptors and architects, with their ladies, there were some literary and scientific men and every description of tourists on longer or shorter visits to the Eternal City. I held myself aloof from them. Most of them had their good qualities, but they could not stand the test of any association which brought them into too close contact with one another, as life in a small town does. They were divided up into camps or hives, and in every hive ruled a lady who detested the queen bee of the next one. So it came about that the Scandinavians lived in perpetual squabbles, could not bear one another, slandered one another, intrigued against one another. When men got drunk on the good Roman wine at the *osterie,* they abused one another and very nearly came to blows. Moreover, they frequently got drunk, for most of them lost their self-control after a few glasses. Strangely enough, in the grand surroundings, too much of the Northern pettiness came to the surface in them. One was continually tempted to call out to the ladies, in Holberg's words: " Hold your peace, you good women! " and to the men: " Go away, you rapscallions, and make up your quarrels! "

There were splendid young fellows among the artists, but the painters, who were in the majority, readily admitted that technically they could learn nothing at all in Rome, where they never saw a modern painting; they said themselves that they ought to be in Paris, but the authorities in Christiania and Copenhagen were afraid of Paris: thence all bad and dangerous influences proceeded, and so the painters still journey to Rome, as their fathers did before them.

XLV.

Towards the middle of November the Pope opened the Vatican. But in face of the enormous conflux of people, it was not easy to get a *permesso* from the consul, and that could not be dispensed with. I had just made use of one for the Vatican sculpture collection, one day, when I felt very unwell. I ascribed my sensations at first to the insufferable weather of that month, alternately sirocco and cold sleet, or both at once; then I was seized with a dread of the climate, of Rome, of all these strange surroundings, and I made up my mind to go home as quickly as possible. The illness that was upon me was, without my knowing it, the cause of my fear. The next day I was carried downstairs by two vile-smelling labourers and taken by Vilhelm Rosenstand the painter, who was one of the few who had made friends with me and shown me kindness, to the Prussian hospital on the Tarpeian Rock, near the Capitol.

Here a bad attack of typhoid fever held me prisoner in my bed for some few months, after a compatriot, who had no connection whatever with me, had been so inconsiderate as to inform my parents by telegraph how ill I was, and that there was little hope for me.

The first month I was not fully conscious; I suffered from a delusion of coercion. Thus it seemed to me that the left side of my bed did not belong to me, but to another man, who sometimes took the place; and that I myself was divided into several persons, of which one, for instance, asked my legs to turn a little to the one side or the other. One of these persons was Imperialist, and for that reason disliked by the others, who were Republicans; nevertheless, he performed great kindnesses for them, making them more comfortable, when it was in his power. Another strangely fantastic idea that held sway for a long time was that on my head, the hair of which had been shorn by the hospital attendant rather less artistically than one cuts a dog's, there was a clasp of pearls and precious stones, which I felt but could not see.

Afterwards, all my delusions centred on food.

I was very much neglected at the hospital.   The attendance was wretched.   The highly respected German doctor, who was appointed to the place, had himself an immense practice, and moreover was absolutely taken up by the Franco-Prussian war.   Consequently, he hardly ever came, sometimes stayed away as long as thirteen days at a stretch, during all which time a patient who might happen to be suffering, say, from constipation, must lie there without any means of relief.   My bed was as hard as a stone, and I was waked in the night by pains in my body and limbs; the pillow was so hard that the skin of my right ear was rubbed off from the pressure.   There were no nurses.   There was only one custodian for the whole hospital, a Russian fellow who spoke German, and who sometimes had as many as fourteen patients at a time to look after, but frequently went out to buy stores, or visit his sweetheart, and then all the patients could ring at once without any one coming.   After I had passed the crisis of my illness, and consequently began to suffer terribly from hunger, I was ordered an egg for my breakfast; I sometimes had to lie for an hour and a half, pining for this egg.   Once, for three days in succession, there were no fresh eggs to be had.   So he would bring for my breakfast nothing but a small piece of dry bread.   One day that I was positively ill with hunger, I begged repeatedly for another piece of bread, but he refused it me.   It was not malice on his part, but pure stupidity, for he was absolutely incapable of understanding how I felt.   And to save fuel, he let me suffer from cold, as well as from hunger; would never put more than one wretched little stick at a time into the stove.   Everything was pinched to an incredible extent.   Thus it was impossible for me to get a candle in the evening before it was absolutely dark, and then never more than one, although it made my eyes water to try to read.   Candles and firing, it appears, were not put down in the bill.   And yet this hospital is kept up on subscriptions from all the great Powers, so there must be someone into whose pockets the money goes. Most of us survived it; a few died who possibly might have been kept alive; one was preserved for whom the Danish newspapers have beautiful obituaries ready.

Over my head, in the same building, there lived a well-known German archæologist, who was married to a Russian princess of such colossal physical proportions that Roman popular wits asserted that when she wished to go for a drive she had to divide herself between two cabs. This lady had a great talent for music. I never saw her, but I became aware of her in more ways than one: whenever she crossed the floor on the third story, the ceiling shook, and the boards creaked, in a manner unbearable to an invalid. And just when I had settled myself off, and badly wanted to sleep, towards eleven o'clock at night, the heavy lady above would sit down at her grand piano, and make music that would have filled a concert hall resound through the place.

After a month had passed, the doctor declared that I had " turned the corner," and might begin to take a little food besides the broth that up till then had been my only nourishment. A little later, I was allowed to try to get up. I was so weak that I had to begin to learn to walk again; I could not support myself on my legs, but dragged myself, with the help of the custodian, the four or five steps from the bed to a sofa.

Just at this time I received two letters from Copenhagen, containing literary enquiries and offers. The first was from the editor of the *Illustrated Times,* and enquired whether on my return home I would resume the theatrical criticisms in the paper; in that case they would keep the position open for me. I gave a negative reply, as I was tired of giving my opinion on the Danish drama. The second letter, which surprised me more, was from the editor of the, at that time, powerful *Daily Paper,* Steen Bille, offering me the entire management of the paper after the retirement of Molbech, except so far as politics were concerned, the editor naturally himself retaining the latter. As Danish things go, it was a very important offer to a young man. It promised both influence and income, and it was only my profound and ever-increasing determination not to give myself up to journalism that made me without hesitation dictate a polite refusal. I was still too weak to write. My motive was simply and solely that I wished to devote my life to knowledge. But Bille, who knew what power in a little country like Denmark his offer would have placed in my hands, hardly understood it in this way, and was exceedingly annoyed at my refusal. It gave the first impulse to his altered feeling toward me. I have sometimes wondered since whether my fate in Denmark might not have been different had I accepted the charge. It is true that the divergence between what the paper and I, in the course of the great year 1871, came to represent, would soon have brought about a split. The Commune in Paris caused a complete *volte face* of the liberal bourgeoisie in Denmark, as elsewhere.

XLVI.

While I was still too weak to write, I received a letter from Henrik Ibsen (dated December 20, 1870), which impressed me greatly. Henrik Ibsen and I had been on friendly terms with one another since April, 1866, but it was only about this time that our intimacy began to emit sparks, an intimacy which was destined to have a very widening influence upon me, and which is perhaps not without traces on the stages of his poetical progress.

Ibsen thought I had already recovered, and wrote to me as to a convalescent. He complained bitterly of the conquest of Rome by the Italians: Rome was now taken from " us men " and given over to the " politicians "; it had been a spot sacred to peace, and was so no longer.—This assertion was at variance with my religion. It seemed to me unpermissible to desire, for æsthetic reasons, to see the restoration of an ecclesiastical régime, with its remorseless system of oppression. Human happiness and intellectual progress were worth more than the retention of the idylls of naiveté. I replied to him by declaring my faith in freedom and soon he outdid me in this, as in other domains.

But there was one other part of the letter that went to my heart and rejoiced me. It was where Ibsen wrote that what was wanted was a revolt in the human mind, and in that I ought to be one of the leaders. These words, which were

in exact agreement with my own secret hope, fired my imagination, ill though I was.   It seemed to me that after having
felt myself isolated so long, I had at last met with the mind
that understood me and felt as I did, a real fellow-fighter.
As soon as I was once more fit to use my pen, I wrote a flaming reply in verse (headed, The Hospital in Rome, the night
of January 9, 1871).   In it I described how solitary I had
been, in my intellectual fight and endeavour, and expressed
my contentment at having found a brother in him.

XLVII.

Among the Danes, and there were not many of them,
who frequently came to see me at the hospital, I must mention the kind and tactful musician Niels Ravnkilde, whom I
had known when I was a child.   He had been living in
Rome now for some twenty years.   He was gentle and
quiet, good-looking, short of stature, modest and unpre-
tending, too weak of character not to be friends with
everyone, but equipped with a natural dignity.   When a
young music master in Copenhagen, he had fallen in love
with a young, wealthy girl, whose affections he succeeded in
winning in return, but he was turned out of the house by her
harsh, purse-proud father, and in desperation had left Denmark to settle down in Rome.   As his lady-love married
soon after and became a contented wife and mother, he remained where he was.   He succeeded in making his
way.

He gradually became a favourite teacher of music
among the ladies of the Roman aristocracy, who sometimes
invited him to their country-houses in the Summer.   He was
on a good footing with the native maestros most in request,
who quickly understood that the modest Dane was no dangerous rival.   Graceful as Ravnkilde was in his person, so he was
in his art; there was nothing grand about him.   But he was
clever, and had a natural, unaffected wit.   His difficult position as a master had taught him prudence and reserve.   He
was obligingness personified to travelling Scandinavians, and
was proud of having, as he thought, made the acquaintance

in Rome of the flower of the good society of the Northern
countries. Even long after he had come to the front, he
continued to live in the fourth storey apartment of the Via
Ripetta, where he had taken up his abode on his arrival in
Rome, waited upon by the same simple couple. His circumstances could not improve, if only for the reason that he
sent what he had to spare to relatives of his in Copenhagen,
who had a son who was turning out badly, and lived by wasting poor Ravnkilde's savings. After having been the providence of all Danish travellers to Rome for thirty years, certain individuals who had influence with the government succeeded in obtaining a distinction for him. The government
then gave him, not even the poor little decoration that he
ought to have had twenty years before, but—brilliant idea!
—awarded him the title of *Professor,* which in Italian, of
course, he had always been, and which was a much more insignificant title than *Maestro,* by which he was regularly
called.

Ravnkilde wrote my letters at the hospital for me, and
the day I came out we drove away together to the French
restaurant to celebrate the occasion by a dinner.

I went from there up to Monte Pincio in a glorious
sunshine, rejoiced to see the trees again, and the people in
their Sunday finery, and the lovely women's faces, as well
as at being able to talk to people once more. It was all like
new life in a new world. I met a good many Scandinavians,
who congratulated me, and a young savant, Giuseppe Saredo,
who, as professor of law, had been removed from Siena to
Rome, and with whom, at the house of dall'Ongaro at Florence, I had had some delightful talks. We decided that we
would keep in touch with one another.

XLVIII.

It was only this one day, however, that happiness and
the sun shone upon me. On the morrow pains in my right
leg, in which there was a vein swollen, made me feel very
unwell. So ignorant was the doctor that he declared this
to be of no importance, and gave me a little ointment with

which to rub my leg.   But I grew worse from day to day,
and after a very short time my leg was like a lump of lead.
I was stretched once more for some months on a sick-bed,
and this weakened me the more since very heroic measures
were used in the treatment of the complaint, a violent attack
of phlebitis.   The leg was rubbed every day from the sole
of the foot to the hip with mercury ointment, which could
not be without its effect on my general health.

Still, I kept up my spirits finely.   Among the Scandinavians who showed me kindness at this time I gratefully
remember the Danish painters Rosenstand and Mackeprang,
who visited me regularly and patiently, and my friend Walter Runeberg, the Finnish sculptor, whose cheerfulness did
me good.

Other Scandinavians with whom I was less well acquainted came to see me now and again, but they had one
very annoying habit.   It was customary at that time for all
letters to be addressed, for greater security, to the Danish
consulate, which served the purpose of a general Scandinavian consulate.   Anyone who thought of coming to see me
would fetch what letters had arrived for me that day and put
them in his pocket to bring me.   The letters I ought to have
had at ten o'clock in the morning I generally received at
seven in the evening.   But these gentlemen often forgot to
pay their visit at all, or did not get time, and then it would
happen that after having gone about with the letters in their
pockets for a few days, they took them back to the consulate,
whence they were sent to me, once, three days late.   As my
whole life on my sick-bed was one constant, painful longing for letters from home, the more so as my mother,
all the time I was in bed, was lying dangerously ill, I
felt vexed at the thoughtless behaviour of my compatriots.

However, I had not travelled so far to meet Northmen,
and I learnt far more from the one Italian who sat by
my bedside day after day, Giuseppe Saredo.   It was amusing to note the difference between his ways and the Northmen's.   He did not come in; he exploded.   At six o'clock
in the evening, he would rush in without knocking at the

door, shouting at one and the same time Italian to the people
of the house, and French to me. He talked at a furious
rate, and so loudly that people who did not know might have
fancied we were quarrelling, and he changed his seat once a
minute, jumped up from the easy chair and seated himself
half in the window, began a sentence there and finished it
sitting on my bed. And every second or third day he either
himself brought books to entertain me or sent large parcels
by a messenger.

He had risen to be professor at the University of the
the capital, without ever having been either student or grad-
uate. His family were too poor for him to study. For
many years, when a lad, he had never eaten dinner. His
occupation, when at last he began to get on, was that of
proof-reader in a printing establishment, but he tried to add
to his income by writing melodramas for the boulevard theatres in Turin.

He thought he had written over fifty. He told me:
" The manager generally came to me on a Sunday, when
we were at liberty, and said: ' We must have a new play
for next Sunday.' On Monday the first act was finished, on
Tuesday the second, etc.; and every act was delivered as it
was written, and the parts allotted. Sometimes the last
act was only finished on Saturday morning, which, however,
would not prevent the piece being played on Sunday evening." In a number of the *Revue des deux Mondes* for 1857
we found Saredo mentioned among the melodramatists of
Italy. This must have been ferreted out privately, since he
always wrote these melodramas anonymously, he having determined, with naïve conceit, " not to stain his future reputation." When he was twenty-one, he tried to raise himself from this rank to that of a journalist, and succeeded;
he sent all sorts of articles to three newspapers. From his
twenty-first to his twenty-fourth year he wrote for the daily
papers, and wrote gay accounts of the volatile lives of
young Italian journalists with the ladies of the theatres.
Then he fell in love with the lady who later became his
wife (known as a novelist under the pseudonym of Ludo-
vico de Rosa), and from that time forth never looked at an-

other woman. All his life he cherished a great admiration for his wife and gratitude towards her.

When he had commenced his legal work, he strained every nerve to the utmost, and obtained his professorships in the various towns through competition, without having followed the usual University path. " I have always had the most unshaken faith in my star," he said one day, "even when, from hunger or despair, thoughts of suicide occurred to me. When I broke my black bread, I said to myself: 'The day will come when I shall eat white.' "

Like all Italians at that time, Saredo detested and despised modern France. As far as reconquered Rome was concerned, he regarded her with sorrowful eyes. " There are only nobility, ecclesiastics, and workmen here," he said; " no middle classes, no industry and no trade. Absurd tariff laws have up till now shut off the Papal States from the surrounding world. And what a government! A doctor, who after his second visit did not make his patient confess to a priest, lost his official post, if he happened to hold one, and was in any case sent to prison for five months. A doctor who did not go to Mass a certain number of times during the week was prohibited practising. The huge number of tied-up estates made buying and selling very difficult. The new government has struck the nobility a fatal blow by abolishing entailed property and lands. The calling in of the ecclesiastical property by the State is giving the towns a chance to breathe."

Whenever I revisited Italy, I saw Saredo. His heroism during the inquiries into the irregularities in Naples in 1900-1901 made his name beloved and himself admired in his native country. He died in 1902, the highest life official in Italy; since 1897 he had been President of the Council.

XLIX.

I came under an even greater debt of gratitude than to Saredo, to the good-natured people in whose house I lay ill. I was as splendidly looked after as if I had made it a specified condition that I should be nursed in case of illness.

My landlady, Maria, especially, was the most careful nurse, and the best creature in the world, although she had the physiognomy of a regular Italian criminal, when her face was in repose. The moment she spoke, however, her features beamed with maternal benevolence. After the hospital, it was a decided change for the better. I was under no one's tyranny and did not feel as though I were in prison; I could complain if my food was bad, and change *trattoria,* when I myself chose. Everything was good.

As long as I was well, I had taken hardly any notice of the people in the house, hardly exchanged a word with them; I was out all day, and either hastily asked them to do my room, or to put a little on the fire. It was only when I fell ill that I made their acquaintance.

Let me quote from my notes at the time:

Maria is forty, but looks nearly sixty. Her husband is a joiner, a stout, good-looking man, who works all day for his living, and has a shop. Then there is Maria's niece, the nineteen-year-old Filomena, a tall, handsome girl. Every evening they have fine times, laugh, sing, and play cards. On Sunday evening they go out to the fair (*alla fiera*) and look at the things without buying. Others have to pay a *lire* to go in, but they go in free, as they know some of the people. On festival occasions Maria wears a silk dress.

There is a crucifix over my bed, an oleograph of the Madonna and child and a heart, embroidered with gold on white, horribly pierced by the seven swords of pain, which were supposed to be nails; on the centre of the heart, you read, partly in Latin, partly in Greek letters:

JESU XPI PASSIO.

All the same, Maria is very sceptical. Yesterday, on the evening of my birthday, we had the following conversation:

Myself: " Here you celebrate your saints' day, not your birthday; but, you know, up in the North we have not any saints "—and, thinking it necessary to add a deep-drawn religious sigh, I continued: " We think it enough to believe in God." "Oh! yes," she said slowly, and then, a little while after: "That, too, is His own business." "How?" "Well," she said, "You know that I am dreadfully ignorant; I know nothing at all, but I think a great deal. There are these people now who are always talking about the *Lord*. I think it is all stuff. When I married, they said to me: 'May it please the Lord that your husband be good to you.' I thought: If I had not been sensible enough to choose a good husband, it would not help me much what should please the Lord. Later on they said: 'May it please the Lord to give you sons.' I had some, but they died when they were little ones. Then I thought to myself: 'If my husband and I do not do something in the matter, it won't be much use for the Lord to be pleased to give them to us. Nature, too, has something to say to it. (*Anche la natura è una piccola cosa.*) You have no idea, sir, how we have suffered from priests here in the Papal State. Everyone had to go to Confession, and as of course they did not wish to confess their own sins, they confessed other people's,—and told lies, too,—and in that way the priests knew everything. If the priest had heard anything about a person, he or she would get a little ticket from him: 'Come to me at such and such a time!' Then, when the person went, he would say: 'Are you mad to live with such and such a person without being married!'— and all the while he himself had a woman and a nest full of children. Then he would say: 'I won't have you in my parish,' and he would publish the poor thing's secret to the whole world. Or, if he were more exasperated, he would say: 'Out of the Pope's country!' and send for a few carabineers; they would take one to a cart and drive one to the frontier; there, there were fresh carabineers, who took one farther— and all without trial, or any enquiry. Often the accusation was false. But we were ruled by spies, and all their power was based on the confessional, which is nothing but spying. Shortly before Easter, a priest came and counted how many there were in the house. If afterwards there were one who did not go to mass, then his name was stuck up on the church door as an infidel, in disgrace. It is many years now since I have been to any confessor. When I die, I shall say: ' God, forgive me my sins and my mistakes,' and shall die in peace without any priest."

Whatever we talk about, Maria always comes back to her hatred of the priests. The other day, we were speaking of the annoyance I had been subjected to by a compatriot of mine, K. B., who came to see me, but looked more particularly at a large *fiasco* I had standing there, containing four bottles of Chianti. He tasted the wine, which was very inferior, declared it ' nice,' and began to drink, ten glasses straight off. At first he was very polite to me, and explained that it was impossible to spend a morning in a more delightful manner than by visiting the Sistine Chapel first, and me in my sick-room afterwards, but by degrees he became ruder and ruder, and as his drunkenness increased I sank in his estimation. At last he told me that I was intolerably conceited, and started abusing me thoroughly. Lying defenceless in bed, and unable to move, I was obliged to ring for Maria, and whisper to her to fetch a few gentlemen from the Scandinavian Club, who could take the drunken man home, after he had wasted fully six hours of my day. I managed in this way to get him out of the door. He was hardly gone than Maria burst out: " *Che porcheria!* " and then added, laughing, to show me her knowledge of languages: " *Cochonnerie, Schweinerei!* " She has a remarkable memory for the words she has heard foreigners use. She knows a number of French words, which she pronounces half like Italian, and she also knows a little Russian and a little German, having, when a young girl, kept house for a Russian prince and his family.

" I feel," she said to me, " that I could have learnt both French and German easily, if I could have *compared* them in a book. But I can neither read nor write. These wretched priests have kept us in ignorance. And now I am old and good for nothing. I was forty a little while ago, and that is too old to learn the alphabet. Do you know, signore, how it originally came about that I did not believe, and despised the priests? I was twelve years old, and a tall girl, and a very good-looking girl, too, though you cannot see that, now that I am old and ugly. (You can see it very plainly, for her features are haughty and perfectly pure of line; it is only that her expression, when she sits alone, is sinister.) " I lost my father when I was five years old. About that time my mother married again, and did not trouble herself any more about me, as she had children with her new husband. So I was left to myself, and ran about the streets, and became absolutely ungovernable, from vivacity, life, and mischief, for I was naturally a very lively child. Then one day I met a mule, alone; the man had left it; I climbed up, and seated myself upon it, and rode about, up and down the street, until a dog came that frightened the mule and it kicked and threw me over its head. There I lay, with a broken collar-bone, and some of the bone stuck out through the skin. Then a doctor came and wanted to bind it up for me, but I was ashamed for him to see my breast, and would not let him. He said: ' Rubbish! I have seen plenty of girls.' So I was bound up and for six weeks had to lie quite still. In the meantime a priest, whom they all called *Don Carlo*—I do not know why they said Don—came to see me, and when I was a little better and only could not move my left arm, he said to me one day, would I go and weed in his garden, and he would give me money for it. So I went every day into the garden, where I could very well do the work with one arm. He came down to me, brought me sweets and other things, and asked me to be his friend. I pretended not to understand. He said, too, how pretty I was, and such things. Then at last one day, he called me into his bedroom, and first gave me sweets, and then set me on his knee. I did not know how to get away. Then I said to him: ' It is wrong, the Madonna would not like it.' Do you know, sir, what he replied? He said: ' Child! there is no Madonna (*non c'è Madonna*) she is only a bridle for the common people ' (*è un freno per il populo basso*). Then I was anxious to run away, and just then my mother passed by the garden, and as she did not see me there, called, ' Anna Maria! Anna Maria!' I said: ' Mother is calling me,' and ran out of the room. Then mother said to me: ' What did the priest say to you, and what did he do to you? You were in his bedroom.' I said: 'Nothing'; but when my mother went to confession, instead of confessing her sins, she said over and over again to him: 'What have you done to my daughter? I will have my daughter examined, to see what sort of a man you are.' He declared: 'I will have you shot if you do' (*una buona schioppettata*). So mother did not dare to go farther in the matter. But she would not believe me."

Here we were interrupted by the Russian woman from next door coming in; she is married, more or less, to a waiter, and she complained of his volatility, and cried with jealousy. "Once I was just as weak," said Maria. "When I was newly married I was so jealous of my husband, that I could neither eat nor drink if any one came to me and said: 'This evening he is with such and such a one.' If I tried to eat, I was sick at once. I am just as fond of him as I was then, but I am cured now. If I saw his infidelity with my own eyes, I should not feel the least bit hurt about it. Then, I could have strangled him."

FILOMENA

FILOMENA sings lustily from early morning till late at night, and her name suits her. The Greek Philomela has acquired this popular form, and in use is often shortened to Filomé.

The other day I made her a present of a bag of English biscuits. Her face beamed as I have never besides seen anything beam but the face of my *cafetière*—he is a boy of twelve—when now and again he gets a few *soldi* for bringing me my coffee or tea. Anyone who has only seen the lighting up of Northern faces has no conception,—as even painters admit,—of such transfiguration. Yes, indeed! Filomena's tall figure and fresh mountain blood would freshen up the Goldschmidtian human race to such an extent that they would become better men and women in his next books.

I have seen a little of the Carnival. This morning Filomena came to my room, to fetch a large Italian flag which belongs there. " I am going to wave it on Thursday," she said, and added, with blushing cheeks, " then I shall have a mask on." But this evening she could not restrain herself. For the first time during the five months I have lived here, and for the first time during the month I have been ill, she came in without my having called or rung for her. She had a red silk cap on, with a gold border. " What do you say to that, sir! " she said, and her clear laughter rang through the room. It revived my sick self to gaze at ease at so much youth, strength and happiness; then I said a few kind words to her, and encouraged by them she burst into a stream of eloquence about all the enjoyment she was promising herself. This would be the first carnival she had seen; she came from the mountains and was going

342

back there this Spring. She was in the seventh heaven over her cap. She always reminds me, with her powerful frame, of the young giantess in the fairy tale who takes up a peasant and his plough in the hollow of her hand.

Filomena is as tall as a moderately tall man, slenderly built, but with broad shoulders. She impresses one as enjoying life thoroughly. She has herself made all she wears—a poor little grey woollen skirt with an edging of the Italian colours, which has been lengthened some nine inches at the top by letting in a piece of shirting. A thin red-and-black-striped jacket that she wears, a kind of loose Garibaldi, is supposed to hide this addition, which it only very imperfectly does. Her head is small and piquant; her hair heavy, blue-black; her eyes light brown, of exquisite shape, smiling and kind. She has small, red lips, and the most beautiful teeth that I remember seeing. Her complexion is brown, unless she blushes; then it grows darker brown. Her figure is unusually beautiful, but her movements are heavy, so that one sees at once she is quite uneducated. Still, she has a shrug of the shoulders, ways of turning and twisting her pretty head about, that are absolutely charming.

I have sent Filomena into the town to buy a pound of figs for me and one for herself. While she is away, I reflect that I cannot sufficiently congratulate myself on my excellent landlady, and the others. As a rule, these Roman lodging-house keepers are, judging by what one hears, perfect bandits. When F., the Norwegian sculptor, lay dangerously ill, the woman in whose house he was did not even speak to him; she went out and left him alone in the house. When the Danish dilettante S. was at death's door, his landlady did not enter his room once a day, or give him a drink of water, and he was obliged to keep a servant. V.'s landlady stole an opera-glass, a frock-coat, and a great deal of money from him. Most foreigners are swindled in a hundred different ways; if they make a stain on the carpet, they must pay for a new one. Maria looks after me like a mother. Every morning she rubs me with the ointment the doctor has prescribed. When I have to have a bath, she takes me in her arms, without any false shame, and puts me in the water; then takes me up and puts me to bed again; after my sojourn in the hospital, I am not very heavy. What I am most astonished at is the indulgent delicacy of these people. For instance, Maria has forbidden her good-natured husband, whom, like Filomena, I like to call *Zio* (uncle), to eat garlic (the favourite food of the Romans) while I am ill, that I may not be annoyed in my room by the smell. I have only to say a word, and she and her niece run all my errands for me. Indeed, the other day, Maria exclaimed, quite indignantly: " Sir, do not say ' *when* you go into the town, will you buy me this or that?' Are we robbers, are we scoundrels? Only say, ' go,' and I will go." I never say to her: " Will you do me a favour?" without her replying: " Two, sir." Yes, and she heaps presents upon me; she and Filomena bring me, now a bundle of firewood, now a glass of good wine, now macaroni, etc. All the Danes who come here are astonished, and say: " You have got deucedly good people to look after you."

Maria's greatest pleasure is talking. She has no time for it in the day. In the evening, however, she tidies my room slowly, entertaining me all the time. When she has quite finished, at the time of day when others are drowsy or go to bed, she still likes to have just a little more conversation, and she knows that when I see she has put the last thing into its place, her task for the day is ended, and I shall dismiss her with a gracious *Buona sera, bon riposo!* To put off this moment as long as possible, she will continue to hold some object in her hand, and, standing in the favourite position of the Romans, with her arms akimbo, and some toilet article under her arm, will hold a long discourse. She sometimes looks so indescribably comic that I almost choke with suppressed laughter as we talk.

To-day is the first day of the Carnival. So even Filomena has been out this evening in tri-coloured trousers. . . . I am interrupted by the inmates of all the floors returning from the Carnival, all talking at once, and coming straight in to me to show me their dress. Amongst them are guests from the mountains, tall, dark men, in exceedingly fantastic garb. They tell me how much they have enjoyed themselves. Filomena has naïvely made me a present of a few burnt almonds with sugar upon them, that she has had in her trouser pockets, and informs me with impetuous volubility how she has talked to all the people she met, "who do not know her and whom she does not know." She has had one of my white shirts on, which she had embroidered all over with ribbons till it looked like a real costume. She is beaming with happiness. The tambourine tinkles all the evening in the street; they are dancing the tarantella to it down below, and it is difficult to go to sleep. Maria stays behind, when the others have gone, to finish her day's work. It is a sight for the gods to see her doing it with a gold brocade cap on her head, and in red, white and green trousers!

None of them guess what a torment it is to me to lie and hear about the Carnival, which is going on a few streets from where I am lying, but which I cannot see. When shall I spend a Winter in Rome again? And no other Carnival will be to compare with this one after the Romans for ten years have held altogether aloof from it, and one hardly even on *Moccoli Eve* saw more than two carriages full of silly Americans pelting one another with confetti, while the porters and the French soldiers flung jibes and dirt at each other. Now Rome is free, jubilation breaks out at all the pores of the town, and I, although I am in Rome, must be content to see the reflection of the festival in a few ingenuous faces.

It is morning. I have slept well and am enjoying the fresh air through the open windows. Heavens! what a lovely girl is standing on the balcony nearly opposite, in a chemise and skirt! I have never seen her there before. Olive complexion, blue-black hair, the most beautiful creature; I cannot see her features distinctly. Now they are throwing something across to her from the house next door to us, on a piece of twine; I think they are red flowers. They almost touch her, and yet she cannot catch them, and laughing stretches out both hands a second, a third and fourth time, equally unsuccessfully. Why, it is our Filomena, visiting the model the other side the street. She gives up the attempt with a little grimace, and goes in.

Loud voices are singing the Bersagliere hymn as a duet under my window. Verily, things are alive in *Purificazione* to-day. The contagion of example affects a choir of little boys who are always lying outside the street door, and they begin to sing the Garibaldi march for all they are worth. Our singers at the theatre at home would be glad of such voices. The whole street is ringing now; all are singing one of Verdi's melodies.

I am sitting up in bed. At the side of my bed, Filomena, with her black, heavy hair well dressed, and herself in a kind of transitional toilette; her under-garment fine, the skirt that of a festival gown, on account of the preparations for the Carnival; her top garment the usual red jacket. She is standing with her hand on her hip, but this does not make her look martial or alarming.

I—You ate *magro* today? (It was a fast day.)

She—Good gracious! *Magro* every day just now!

I—Do you know, Filomena, that I eat *grasso?*

She—Yes, and it is your duty to do so.

I—Why?

She—Because you are ill, and you *must* eat meat; the Pope himself ate meat when he was ill. Religion does not mean that we are to injure our health.

I—How do you know, Filomena, what Religion means?

She—From my Confessor. I had a little headache the other day, and he ordered me at once to eat meat.

I—The worst of it is that I have no Confessor and do not go to church. Shall I be damned for that?

She—Oh! no, sir, that does not follow! Do you think I am so stupid as not to see that you others are far better Christians than we? You are good; the friends who come to see you are good. The Romans, on the other hand, who go to church one day, kill people the next, and steal, and will not let us poor girls go about the streets in peace."

I am quite sorry that she is to go home at Easter; I shall miss her face about the house. But I have missed more.

Late evening. They have come back from the Carnival. Filomena came in and presented me with an object the
use of which is an enigma to me. A roll of silver paper.
Now I see what it is, a Carnival cap. My Danish friend
R. declares she has got it into her head that when I am better
I shall marry her, or rather that Maria has put it into her
head. I thought I would see how matters stood. I began
talking to Maria about marriages with foreigners. Maria
mentioned how many girls from Rome and Capri had married foreigners, but added afterwards, not without significance, addressing me: " It is not, as you believe, and as
you said once before, that a girl born in a warm country
would complain of being taken to a cold one. If she did,
she would be stupid. But a Roman girl will not do for a
foreign gentleman. The Roman girls learn too little."

Much, the lower classes certainly do not learn. Before I
came, Filomena did not know what ink was. Now I have
discovered that she does not know what a watch is. She
reckons time by the dinner and the Ave Maria. Not long
ago her uncle spent a week in trying to teach this great child
to make and read figures, but without success. Not long
ago she had to write to her mother in the mountains, so went
to a public writer, and had it done for her. She came in to
me very innocently afterwards to know whether the right
name and address were upon it. I told her that she could
very well have let me write the letter. Since then, all the
people in the house come to me when there is anything they
want written, and ask me to do it for them.

The news of my skill has spread. Apropos of letters,
I have just read the four letters that I received to-day. Filomena is perpetually complaining of my sweetheart's uncon-
trollable passion as revealed in this writing madness. She
imagines that all the letters I receive from Denmark are from
one person, and that person, of course, a woman. She herself hardly receives one letter a year.

I have (after careful consideration) committed a great
imprudence, and escaped without hurt. I had myself carried down the stairs, drove to the Corso, saw the Carnival,

and am back home again. I had thought first of driving up and down the Corso in a carriage, but did not care to be wholly smothered with confetti, especially as I had not the strength to pelt back. Nor could I afford to have the horses and carriage decorated. So I had a good seat in a first-floor balcony engaged for me, first row. At 3 o'clock I got up, dressed, and was carried down. I was much struck by the mild Summer air out of doors (about the same as our late May), and I enjoyed meeting the masked people in the streets we passed through. The few but rather steep stairs up to the balcony were a difficulty. But at last I was seated, and in spite of sickness and weakness, enjoyed the Carnival in Rome on its most brilliant day. I was sitting nearly opposite to the high box of Princess Margharita, from which there was not nearly so good a view as from my seat. This was what I saw: All the balconies bedecked with flags; red, white and green predominating. In the long, straight street, the crowd moving in a tight mass. In between them, an up and a down stream of carriages, drawn at a walking pace by two horses, and forced at every moment to stop. The streets re-echoed with the jingle of the horses' bells, and with shouts of glee at a magnificently decorated carriage, then at some unusually beautiful women, then at a brisk confetti fight between two carriages, or a carriage and a balcony. And this air, re-echoing with the ring of bells, with shouting, and with laughter, was no empty space. Anyone reaching the Corso, as I had done, after the play had only been going on for an hour and a half, found themselves in the midst of a positive bombardment of tiny little aniseed balls, or of larger plaster balls, thrown by hand, from little tin cornets, or half-bushel measures, and against which it is necessary to protect one's self by a steel wire mask before the face. For whilst some gentle young ladies almost pour the confetti down from their carriages, so that it falls like a soft shower of rain, many of the Romans fling it with such force that without a mask the eyes might suffer considerably. The brim of one's hat, and every fold in one's clothes, however, are full of little balls. Most people go about with a huge, full bag by their side, others on the bal-

conies have immense baskets standing, which are hardly
empty before they are re-filled by eager sellers. All the ladies
standing in the windows, who were disguised as Turkish ladies, or workwomen from the port, had a deep wooden
trough, quite full, brought outside their windows, and
into this supply dipped continually—in the street, which
had been covered with soil for the sake of the horse-racing,
was a crowd of people in fancy dress, many of them having
great fun, and being very amusing. One old woman in a
chemise was amongst the best. A young fellow, dressed entirely in scarlet, more particularly amused himself by putting
the officers of the National Guard, who were walking about
to keep order, out of countenance. When they were looking especially stern, he would go up to them and tickle them
on the cheeks, and talk baby talk to them, and they had to
put the best face they could on it. The street life and the
pedestrians, however, did not attract much attention. All the
interest was centred on the carriages, and the games between
them and the windows and balconies. The people in carriages were all in fancy dress. Amongst them one noticed
charming groups of Roman ladies in light cloaks of red silk
with a red steel wire mask before their faces, through which
one could catch a glimpse of their features; there was a
swarm of delightful figures, certainly half of them in men's
clothes, armed young sailors, for instance. Fine, happy
faces! And the young men, how handsome! Not flashing
eyes, as people affectedly say, but happy eyes; a good, healthy
physique, an expression which seemed to say that they had
breathed in sunshine and happiness and all the beatitude of
laziness, all the mild and good-humoured comfort of leisure,
all their lives long. One party had a colossal cart with out-
riders and postilions, and hung in the yards and stood on the
thwarts of a large cutter poised upon it, in becoming naval
officers' dress, flinging magnificent bouquets to all the beautiful ladies who drove past. The bouquets would have cost
several lire each, and they flung them by the hundred, so they
must have been young fellows of means. The throwing of
confetti is merely bellicose and ordinary. Infinitely more
interesting is the coquettish, ingratiating, genuinely Italian

flinging backwards and forwards of bouquets. The grace and charm of the manner in which they are flung and caught, nothing can surpass; there may be real passion in the way in which six or seven bouquets in succession are flung at one and the same lady, who never omits to repay in similar coin. One carriage was especially beautiful; it had a huge square erection upon it, entirely covered with artificial roses and greenery, which reached almost to the second storey of the houses, and upon it, in two rows, facing both sides of the streets, stood the loveliest Roman girls imaginable, flinging bouquets unceasingly. Most of the carriages have tall poles sticking up with a crossway bar at the top, and there are bouquets on every bar, so there is a constant supply to draw from. Beautiful Princess Margharita was, of course, the object of much homage, although her balcony was on the second floor. One form this took was very graceful. A few young gentlemen in blue and white drove slowly past; one of them had a large flat basket filled with lovely white roses; he stuck a long halberd through the handle and hoisted the basket up to the Princess, being richly rewarded with bouquets. One wag hit upon an idea that was a brilliant success. At five o'clock he sent a bladder, in the shape of a huge turkey, up in the flickering sunlight. It was so fixed up as to move its head about, with an expression of exceedingly ridiculous sentimentality, now to the right, now caressingly to the left, as it ascended. The whole Corso rang again with laughter and clapping. The horse-racing at the end was not of much account. The horses start excited by the rocket let off at their tails, and by all the sharp pellets hanging around about them, to say nothing of the howling of the crowd. At six o'clock I was at home and in bed.

K. B. has been here to see me; Filomena hates and despises him from the bottom of her heart since the day that he got drunk on my wine. When he was gone she said: "*Brutta bestia,* I forgot to look whether he was clean to-day." She and Maria declare that he is the only one of all my acquaintances who does not wear clean linen. This point

of cleanliness is a mild obsession of Filomena's just now.
She prides herself greatly on her cleanliness, and asks me
every day whether she is clean or not. She is a new convert
to cleanliness, and renegades or newly initiated people are
in all religions the most violent. When I came to the house,
her face was black and she washed her hands about once a
day. R. then remarked about her—which was a slight exaggeration—that if one were to set her up against the wall,
she would stick fast. She noticed with unfeigned astonishment how many times I washed myself, and asked for fresh
water, how often I had clean shirts, etc. This made a profound impression on her young mind, and after I came back
from the hospital she began in earnest to rub her face with
a sponge and to wash herself five or six times a day, likewise to wash the handkerchiefs she wears round her neck.
Maria looks on at all this with surprise. She says, like the
old woman in *Tonietta,* by Henrik Hertz: "A great,
strong girl like that does not need to wash and splash
herself all over like an Englishwoman." The lectures
she has given me every time I have wanted to wash
myself, on the harm water does an invalid, are many
and precious. Whenever I ask for water I might
be wanting to commit suicide; it is only after repeated requests that she brings it, and then with a quiet, resigned expression, as if to say: " I have done my best to prevent
this imprudence: I wash my hands of all responsibility."
Filomena, in her new phase of development, is quite different. She looks at my shirt with the eyes of a connoisseur,
and says: " It will do for to-morrow; a clean one the
day after to-morrow! " or, " Did you see what beautiful
cuffs the tall, dark man (M. the painter) had on yesterday? " or, " Excuse my skirt being so marked now, I am
going to have a clean one later in the day," or, " Is my cheek
dirty? I don't think so, for I have washed myself twice
to-day; you must remember that I am very dark-complex-
ioned, almost like a Moor." Or else there will be a triumphal entry into my room, with a full water-can in her hand,
one of the very large ones that are used here. " What is
that, Filomena? What am I to do with that?" "Look,

sir, it is full." "Well, what of that?" "It is the waiter's
water-can; it has been standing there full for ten days
(scornfully) : he is afraid of water; he only uses it for his
coffee." She has forgotten how few months it is since she
herself was afraid of water.

She came in while I was eating my supper, and remarked: "You always read at your meals; how can you
eat and read at the same time? I do not know what reading is like, but I thought it was more difficult than that. It
is a great misfortune for me that I can neither read nor write.
Supposing I were to be ill like you, how should I pass away
the time! There was no school at Camarino, where I was
born, and I lived in the country till I was eighteen, and
learnt nothing at all. We were nine brothers and sisters;
there was seldom any food in the house; sometimes we
worked; sometimes we lay on the ground. It is unfortunate
that I cannot read, for I am not at all beautiful; if I could
only do something, I should be able to get a husband."
"Don't you know any of the letters, Filomena?"
"No, sir." "Don't trouble about that. You are happier
than I, who know a great deal more than you. You laugh
and sing all day long; I neither laugh nor sing." "Dear
sir, you will laugh, and sing as well, when you get home.
Then your little girl (*ragazza*) who is so *appassionata* that
she writes four letters a day, will make fête for you, and I
think that when you go to the *osteria* with your friends you
laugh. It is enough now for you to be patient." As she had
spoken about getting a husband, I asked: "Are your sisters
married?" "They are all older than I, and married."
(Saving her pride in the first part of her reply.) After a
few minutes' reflection she went on: "I, for my part, will
not have a husband under thirty; the young ones all beat
their wives." Shortly afterwards, I put an end to the audience. We had had a few short discussions, and I had
been vanquished, apparently by her logic, but chiefly by reason of her better mastery of the language, and because I defended all sorts of things in joke. At last I said: "Have
you noticed, Filomena, that when we argue it is always you

who silence me? So you can see, in spite of all my reading, that you have better 'brains than I." This compliment pleased her; she blushed and smiled, without being able to find a reply.

She realises the Northern ideal of the young woman not spoilt by novel-reading. Nor does she lack intelligence, although she literally does not know what North and South mean; she is modest, refined in her way, and happy over very little. For the moment she is engaged in making the little dog bark like mad by aggravatingly imitating the mewing of a cat.

Later. The boy from the café brings me my supper. What has become of Filomena? I wonder if she is out? I cannot hear her having her evening fight with the boy in the passage. She likes to hit him once a day for exercise.

Maria comes in. "Do you hear the cannon, sir? What do you think it is?" I reply calmly: "It is war; the Zouaves (papal troops) are coming." Maria goes out and declares the reply of the oracle in the next room. Some cannon salutes really were being fired. Maria hurries down into the street to hear about it and Filomena comes in to me. "I am afraid," she says. "Do you mean it?" She was laughing and trembling at the same time. I saw that the fear was quite real. "Is it possible that you can be so afraid? There is not really any war or any Zouaves, it was only a joke." That pacified her. "I was afraid, if you like," said she, "when the Italians (the Romans never call themselves Italians) marched into Rome. One shell came after another; one burst on the roof of the house opposite." "Who are you for, the Pope or Vittorio?" "For neither. I am a stupid girl; I am for the one that will feed and clothe me. But I have often laughed at the Zouaves. One of them was standing here one day, taking pinch after pinch of snuff, and he said to me: 'The Italians will never enter Rome.' I replied: 'Not if they take snuff, but they will if they storm the town.'" "Do you think that the Pope will win?" "No, I think his cause is lost. Perhaps there will even come a time when no

one goes to churches here." *She:* "Who goes to church!
The girls to meet their lovers; the young men to see a pretty
shop-girl. We laugh at the priests." "Why?" "Because they are ridiculous: if it thunders, they say at once that
it is a sign from God. The sky happens to be flaming red,
like it was last October. That was because the Italians entered Rome in September. Everything is a sign from God,
a sign of his anger, his exasperation. He is not angry, that
is clear enough. If he had not wanted the Italians to come
in, they would not have come, but would all have died at
once." She said this last with great earnestness and pathos,
with an upward movement of her hand, and bowed her head,
like one who fears an unknown power. Maria returned, saying people thought the shots meant that Garibaldi had come.
Said I: "There, he is a brave man. Try to be like him,
Filomena. It is not right for a big strong girl to tremble."
She: "I am not strong, but still, I am stronger than you,
who have been weakened so much by your illness,—and yet,
who knows, you have been much better the last few days.
Shall we try?" I placed my right hand in hers, first tested
her strength a little, and then found to my surprise that her
arm was not much stronger than that of an ordinary lady;
then I bent my fingers a little, and laid her very neatly on the
floor. I was sitting in bed; she was on her knees in front
of the bed, but I let her spring up. It was a pretty sight;
the blue-black hair, the laughing mouth with the fine, white
teeth, the brown, smiling eyes. As she got up, she said:
"You are well now; I am not sorry to have been conquered."

Have taken my *second* flight. I have been at the Moccoli fête, had myself carried and driven there and back, like
last time. Saredo had taken a room on the Corso; I saw
everything from there, and now I have the delightful impressions of it all left. What exuberant happiness! What
jubilation! What childlike gaiety! It is like going into a
nursery and watching the children play, hearing them shout
and enjoy themselves like mad, as one can shout and enjoy
things one's self no longer.

I arrived late and only saw the end of the processions;

far more carriages, wilder shouting, more madness,—bac-
chantic, stormy,—than last time. The whole length of the
Corso was one shriek of laughter. And how many lovely
faces at the windows, on the balconies and verandas! Large
closed carriages with hidden music inside and graceful ladies
on the top. As *i preti* (the Catholic papers) had said that
all who took part in the Carnival were paid by the government, a number of men and women, in the handsomest carriages—according to the *Nuova Roma* for to-day, more than
20,000—had the word *pagato* (paid) fastened to their caps,
which evoked much amusement. Then the lancers cleared
the street at full galop for the horse races (*barberi*), and at
once an immense procession of Polichinelli and ridiculous
equestrians in Don Quixote armour organised itself and rode
down the Corso at a trot in parody. Then came the mad,
snorting horses. Then a few minutes,—and night fell over
the seven heights of Rome, and the Corso itself lay in darkness. Then the first points of light began to make their
appearance. Here below, one little shimmer of light, and
up there another, and two there, and six here, and ten down
there to the left, and hundreds on the right, and then thousands, and many, many thousands. From one end of the
great long street to the other, from the first floor to the roof
of every house and every palace, there is one steady twinkling of tiny flames, of torches, of large and small lights; the
effect is surprising and peculiar. As soon as the first light
appeared, young men and girls ran and tried to blow each
other's candles out. Even the children took part in the
game; I could see into several houses, where it was going
on briskly. Then, from every side-street decorated carriages began to drive on to the Corso again, but this time
every person held a candle in his hand. Yes, and that
was not all! at least every other of the large waggons—they
were like immense boxes of flowers—had, on poles, or made
fast, Bengal fire of various colours, which lighted up every
house they went past, now with a red, now with a green
flare. And then the thousands of small candles, from every
one in the throng, from carriages, balconies, verandas,
sparkled in the great flame, fighting victoriously with the

last glimmer of daylight. People ran like mad down the
Corso and fanned out the lights in the carriages. But many
a Roman beauty found a better way of lighting up her
features without exposing herself to the risk of having her
light put out. Opposite me, for instance, on the second
floor, a lovely girl was standing in a window. In the shut-
ter by her side she had fixed one of those violent red flares
so that she stood in a bright light, like sunlight seen through
red glass, and it was impossible not to notice her. Meanwhile, the people on the balconies held long poles in
their hands, with which they unexpectedly put out the small
candles in the carriages. You heard incessantly, through
the confusion, the shouts of individuals one to another, and
their jubilation when a long-attempted and cleverly foiled ex-
tinguishing was at length successful, and the clapping and
shouts of *bravo!* at an unusually brightly lighted and decorated carriage. The pickpockets meanwhile did splendid
business; many of the Danes lost their money.

At eight o'clock I was in bed again, and shortly afterwards the people of the house came home for a moment.
Filomena looked splendid, and was very talkative. "*Lei é
ingrassato,*" she called in through the door. It is her great
pleasure that the hollows in my cheeks are gradually disappearing. She was now ascribing a special efficacy in this
direction to Moccoli Eve.

At half-past ten in the morning, there is a curious spectacle in the street here. At that time Domenico comes and
the lottery begins. Lotteries are forbidden in Rome, but
Domenico earns his ten lire a day by them. He goes about
this and the neighbouring streets bawling and shouting until
he has disposed of his ninety tickets.

Girls and women lean out through the windows and call
out the numbers they wish to have—in this respect they are
boundlessly credulous. They do not believe in the Pope;
but they believe that there are numbers which they must become possessed of that day, even at the highest price, which
is two *soldi*. The *soldi* are thrown out through the window,
and each one remembers her own number. Then Domen-

ico goes through all the numbers in a loud voice, that there may be no cheating. A child draws a number out of the bag, and Domenico shouts: "Listen, all Purificazione, No. 34 has won, listen, Purificazione, 34 . . . 34." The disappointed faces disappear into the houses. All those who have had 33, 35 and 36 rail against unjust Fate, in strong terms.

At the first rattle of the lottery bag, Filomena rushes in here, opens the window, and calls for a certain number. If anyone else wants it, she must manage to find two *soldi* in her pocket. If I fling a few *soldi* from my bed towards the window, this facilitates the search. However, we never win. Filomena declares that I have indescribable ill-luck in gambling, and suggests a reason.

She was again singing outside. I called her, wanting to know what it was she kept singing all the time. "They are songs from the mountains," she replied, "all *canzone d'amore*." "Say them slowly, Filomena. I will write them down." I began, but was so delighted at the way she repeated the verses, her excellent declamatory and rhythmic sense, that I was almost unable to write. And to my surprise, I discovered that they were all what we call ritornellos. But written down, they are dull larvæ, compared with what they are with the proper pronunciation and expression. What is it Byron says?:

> I love the language, that soft bastard Latin,
> Which melts like kisses from a female mouth,
> And sounds as if it should be writ on satin.

I shall really feel a void when Filomena goes away. The unfortunate part of it is that her dialect pronunciation is so difficult to make out, and that she swallows so many syllables in order to make the metre right, as there are generally too many feet, and it is only the delicacy of her declamation that makes up for the incorrectness of the rhymes and the verses. For instance, she constantly says *lo* instead of *il* (*lo soldato*), and she can never tell me how many words there are in a line, since neither she nor Maria knows what a single word, as opposed to several, is, and because it is no use spelling the word to her and asking: " Is that right? " since she cannot spell, and does not recognise the letters.   Saredo tells me that a driver who once drove him and his wife about for five days in Tuscany sang all day long like Filomena, and improvised all the time. This is what she, too, does continually; she inserts different words which have about the same meaning, and says: " It is all the same " (*c'è la stessa cosa*).   On the other hand, she always keeps to the metre, and that with the most graceful intonation; never a faulty verse:

> Fior di giacinto!
> La donna che per l'uomo piange tanto—
> Il pianto delle donne è pianto finto.

> Amore mio!
> Non prendite le fiori di nessuno,
> Se vuoi un garofletto, lo do io.

> Fior di limone!
> Limone è agra, e le fronde son' amare,
> Ma son' più' amare le pene d'amor'.

> Lo mi' amore che si chiama Peppe,
> Lo primo giuocatore delle carte
> Prende 'sto cuore e giuoca a tre-sette.[1]

In this way I wrote out some scores.

Spent an hour teaching Filomena her large letters up to N, and making her say them by rote, and with that end in view have divided them into three portions—ABCD—EFG—ILMN. She manages all right, except that she al-

[1] Flower of the hyacinth!
The woman who weeps so much for the man's sake—
Yet, the complaint of women is a feigned one,

My love!
Do not accept flowers from anyone.
If thou wilt have a wall-flower, I will give it thee.

Flower of the lemon!
The lemon is sharp, and its leaves are bitter;
But more bitter are the torments of love.

My beloved, whose name is Peppe,
He is the first to play cards,
He has taken this heart and is playing a game of Three to Seven with it.

ways jumps E and L. Lesson closed: "Were you at church to-day, Filomena?" "No, I have nothing to confess." "Did you go to church last Sunday?" "No, I have not been for six weeks now. I have committed no sin. What wrong do I do? I have no love affair, nothing." "What used you to confess?" "A few bad words, which had slipped out. Now I do nothing wrong." "But one can go wrong, without committing any sin, when one is high-minded, for instance." "I am not high-minded. If you, on the other hand, were to imagine yourself better than the friends who come to visit you, that would be quite natural; for you are better."

The day has been long. This evening the girl had errands to do for me. She came in here after her Sunday walk in the Campagna. I said: "Shall we read?" (Just then a band of young people passed along the street with a harmonica and a lot of castanets, and commenced a song in honour of Garibaldi. With all its simplicity, it sounded unspeakably affecting; I was quite softened.) She replied: "With pleasure." I thought to myself: "Now to see whether she remembers a word of what I said to her yesterday." But she went on at once: "Signore, I have been industrious." She had bought herself an ABC and had taught herself alone not only all the large letters, but also all the little ones, and had learnt them all off by heart as well. I was so astonished that I almost fell back in the bed. "But what is this, Filomena? Have you learnt to read from someone else?" "No, only from you yesterday. But for five years my only wish has been to learn to read, and I am so glad to be able to." I wanted to teach her to spell. "I almost think I can a little." And she was already so far that—without spelling first—she read a whole page of two-letter spellings, almost without a mistake. She certainly very often said: "Da—ad," or read *fo* for *of,* but her progress was amazing. When she spells, she takes the words as a living reality, not merely as words, and adds something to them, for instance, *s—a, sa; l—i, li; r—e, re; salire alle scale,* (jump down the stairs.) "Filomena, I could teach you to read in three weeks." *She:* "I have always thought it the greatest shame for a man or woman not to be able to read." I told her something about the progress of the human race, that the first men and women had been like animals, not at all like Adam and Eve. "Do you think I believe that Eve ate an apple and that the serpent could speak? *Non credo niente.* Such things are like *mal'occhi* (belief in the evil eye)." And without any transition, she begins, *sempre allegra,* as she calls herself—to sing a gay song. Just now she is exceedingly delighted with a certain large red shawl. There came a pedlar to the door; she sighed deeply at the sight of the brilliant red; so I gave it her.

She is a great lover and a connoisseur of wine, like myself. We taste and drink together every dinner-time. As she always waits upon me, I often give her a little cake and wine while I am eating. Now we have begun a new wine, white Roman muscat. But I change my wine almost every other day. Filomena had taken the one large bottle and stacked up newspapers round it on the table, so that if K. B. came he should not see it. It so happened that he came to-day, whilst I was dining and she eating with me. There was a ring; she wanted to go. "Stay; perhaps it is not for me at all; and in any case, I do not ask anyone's permission for you to be here." He came in, and said in Danish, as he put his hat down: "Oh, so you let the girl of the house dine with you; I should not care for that." Filomena, who noticed his glance in her direction, and his gesture, said, with as spiteful a look, and in as cutting a voice as she could muster: "*Il signore prende il suo pranzo con chi lui pare e piace.*" (The gentleman eats with whomsoever he pleases.) "Does she understand Danish?" he asked, in astonishment. "It looks like it," I replied. When he had gone, her *furia* broke loose. I saw her exasperated for the first time, and it sat very comically upon her. "Did you ask him whom *he* eats with? Did he say I was ugly? Did you ask him whether his *ragazza* was prettier?" (She meant a Danish lady, a married woman, with whom she had frequently met K. B. in the street.)

She said to me yesterday: " There is one thing I can do, sir, that you cannot. I can carry 200 pounds' weight on my head. I can carry two *conchas,* or, if you like to try me, all that wood lying there." She has the proud bearing of the Romans.

Read with Filomena for an hour and a half. She can now spell words with three letters fairly well. This language has such a sweet ring that her spelling is like music. And to see the innocent reverence with which she says *g-r-a, gra,*—it is what a poet might envy me. And then the earnest, enquiring glance she gives me at the end of every line. It is marvellous to see this complete absorption of a grown-up person in the study of *a-b, ab,* and yet at the same time there is something almost great in this ravenous thirst for knowledge, combined with incredulity of all tradition. It is a model such as this that the poets should have had for their naïve characters. In Goethe's *Roman Elegies,* the Roman woman's figure is very inconspicuous; she is not drawn as a genuine woman of the people, she is not naïve. He knew a Faustina, but one feels that he afterwards slipped a German model into her place. Filomena has the uncompromising honesty and straightforwardness of an unspoilt soul. Her glance is not exactly pure, but free —how shall I describe it? Full, grand, simple. With a *concha* on her head, she would look like a caryatid. If I compare her mentally with a feminine character of another poet, Lamartine's Graziella, an Italian girl of the lower classes, like herself, I cannot but think Graziella thin and poetised, down to her name. The narrator, if I remember rightly, teaches her to read, too; but Graziella herself does not desire it; it is he who educates her. Filomena, on the contrary, with her anxiety to learn, is an example and a symbol of a great historic movement, the poor, oppressed Roman people's craving for light and knowledge. Of Italy's population of twenty-six millions, according to the latest, most recent statistics, seventeen millions can neither read nor write. She said to me to-day: " What do you really think, sir, do you not believe that the Holy Ghost is *una virtù* and cannot be father of the child? " " You are right, Filomena." "That is why I never pray." "Some day, when you are very unhappy, perhaps you will pray." "I have been very unhappy; when I was a child I used to suffer horribly from hunger. I had to get up at five o'clock in the morning to work and got eight *soldi* for standing all day long in a vineyard in the sun and digging with a spade, and as corn was dear and meat dear, we seven children seldom had a proper meal. Last year, too, I was hungry often, for it was as the proverb says: ' If I eat, I cannot dress myself, and if I dress myself I cannot eat.' (What a sad and illuminating proverb!) Sir, if there were any Paradise, you would go there, for what you do for me. If I can only read and write, I can earn twice as much as I otherwise could. Then I can be a *cameriera,* and bring my mistress a written account of expenditure every week."

Filomena knows that Saredo is a professor at the University. But she does not know what a professor or a University is. She puts her question like this: " Probably my idea of what a university is, may not be quite correct? "

No one comes now. An invalid is very interesting at first, and arouses sympathy. If he continue ill too long, people unconsciously think it impossible for him to get well, and stay away. So the only resource left me all day is to chat with Filomena, to whom Maria has entrusted the nursing of me. Every evening I read with her; yesterday she had her fourth lesson, and could almost read straight off. Her complexion and the lower part of her face are like a child's; her undeveloped mental state reveals itself, thus far, in her appearance. I told her yesterday, as an experiment, that there were five continents and in each of them many countries, but she cannot understand yet what I mean, as she has no conception of what the earth looks like. She does not even know in what direction from Rome her native village, Camerino, lies. I will try to get hold of a map, or a globe. Yesterday, we read the word *inferno.* She said: " There is no hell; things are bad enough on earth; if we are to burn afterwards, there would be two hells." " Good gracious! Filomena, is life so bad? Why, you sing all day long." " I sing because I am well; that is perfectly natural, but how can I be content?" "What do you wish for then?" "So much money (*denari*) that I should be sure of never being hungry again. You do not know how it hurts. Then there is one other thing I should like, but it is impossible. I should like not to die; I am so horribly afraid of death. I should certainly wish there were a Paradise. But who can tell! Still, my grandmother lived to be a hundred all but three years, and she was never ill for a day; when she was only three years from being a hundred she still went to the fields like the rest of us and worked, and was like a young woman (*giovanotta*). Mother is forty-two, but although she is two years older than my aunt, she looks quite young. *Chi lo sa!* Perhaps I may live to be a hundred too, never be ill—I never have been yet, one single day,—and then go in and lie down on the bed like she did and be dead at once."

"She really is sweet!" said R. this evening. The word does not fit. Her laugh, her little grimaces, her witticisms, quaint conceits and gestures are certainly very attractive, but her mode of expression, when she is talking freely, is very unreserved, and if I were to repeat some of her remarks to a stranger, he would perhaps think her coarse or loose. "We shall see what sort of a girl you bring home to us when you are well again, and whether you have as good taste as our Frenchman. Or perhaps you would rather visit her? I know how a fine gentleman behaves, when he visits his friend. She is often a lady, and rich. He comes, knocks softly at the door, sits down, and talks about difficult and learned things. Then he begs for a kiss, she flings her arms round his neck; *allora, il letto rifatto, va via.*" She neither blushes nor feels the slightest embarrassment when she talks like this. "How do you know such things, when you have no experience?" "People have told me; I know it from hearsay. I myself have never been in love, but I believe that it is possible to love one person one's whole life long, and never grow tired of him, and never love another. You said the other day (for a joke?) that people ought to marry for a year or six months; but I believe that one can love the same person always."

In such chat my days pass by. I feel as though I had

dropped down somewhere in the Sabine Mountains, been well received in a house—Maria is from Camarino, too,—and were living there hidden from the world among these big children.

Yesterday, Uncle had his National Guard uniform on for the first time. He came in to show himself. I told him that it suited him very well, which delighted him. Filomena exhibited him with admiration. When Maria came home later on, she asked the others at once: "Has the *signore* seen him? What did he say? Does not he want to see him again?"

Written down a score of ritornellos; I have chosen the best of them. Many of them are rather, or very, indecent. But, as Filomena says: "You do not go to Hell for singing *canzone;* you cannot help what they are like." The indecent ones she will only say at a terrific rate, and not a second time. But if one pay attention, they are easy to understand. They are a mixture of audacity and simple vulgarity. They all begin with flowers. She is too undeveloped to share the educated girl's abhorrence of things that are in bad taste; everything natural, she thinks, can be said, and she speaks out, quite unperturbed. Still, now she understands that there are certain things—impossible things—that I do not like to hear her say.

I was sitting cutting a wafer (to take powders with) into oblates. *She:* "You must not cut into consecrated things, not even put the teeth into it. The priest says: 'Thou shalt not bite Christ.'" Unfortunately, she has not any real impression of religion, either of its beauty or its underlying truth. None of them have any idea of what the New Testament is or contains; they do not know its best-known quotations and stories. Religion, to them, is four or five rigmaroles, which are printed in our *Abecedario,* the Creed, the Ave Maria, the various Sacraments, etc., which they know by heart. These they reject, but they have not the slightest conception of what Christianity is. If I quote a text from the New Testament, they have never heard it.

But they can run the seven cardinal virtues, and the seven other virtues, off by rote. One of these last, that of instructing the ignorant, is a virtue which the priesthood (partly for good reasons) have not practised to any remarkable extent in this country.

Yesterday Maria came home in a state of great delight, from a *trattoria,* where a gentleman had spoken *tanto bene, tanto bene* against religion and the Pope and the priests; there were a few *Caccialepri* present (a derogatory expression for adherents of the priests), who had just had to come down a peg or two. When she had finished, to my astonishment, she said to me, *exactly this:* " It is Nature that is God, is it not so? "

An expression almost symbolical of the ignorance and credulity of the Romans is their constant axiom, *Chi lo sa?* (Who knows?) I said to Maria the other day, after she had said it for the fourth time in a quarter of an hour: " My good Maria! The beginning of wisdom is not to fear God, but to say *Perche?* (why?), instead of *Chi lo sa?* "

Yesterday, while I was eating my dinner, I heard Filomena's story. She came to Rome last December: " You think I came because Maria wanted to help mother. I came to Rome because there was a man who wanted to marry me." " What was his name? " " His name was Peppe." *" Lo mi' amore, che si chiama Peppe."* . . . " Ah, I do not love him at all. No, the thing is that at Camerino all the men beat their wives. My sister, for instance, has always a black eye, and red stripes on her back. My friend Marietta always gets beaten by her husband, and the more he beats her, the more she loves him: sometimes she goes away from him for a few days to her sister, but she always goes back again." " What has that to do with our friend Peppe? " " Well, you see, mother knew that Peppe's brother beat his wife all day and all night; so she would not give me to him." " Yes, it was bad, if it were a family failing." " So one evening father said to me: ' Your aunt has written to us from Rome, to ask whether you will pay her a visit of a few days.' And he showed me a false letter. Aunt cannot write and knew nothing about any letter. I did not want to, much, said I would not, but came here all the same, and found that I was to stay here, and that mother did not want me to have Peppe. So I began to cry, and for five whole days I cried all the time and would neither eat nor drink. Then I thought to myself: It is all over between Peppe and me. Shall I cry myself to death for a man? So I left off crying, and very soon forgot all about him. And after a week's time I did not care anything about the whole matter, and sang and was happy, and now I want to stay in Rome always."

Last night I got up for a little, read with Filomena, and determined to go in and have supper with the family in their little room. Filomena opened the door wide, and called out along the corridor: " *Eccolo!* " and then such a welcome as there was for the invalid, now that he had at last got up! and I was obliged to drink two large beer-glasses of the home-grown wine. First Maria told how it was that I had always had everything so punctually whilst I was ill. It was because Filomena had made the little boy from the *café* believe that I was going to give him my watch when I got well, if he never let anything get cold. So the boy ran as though possessed, and once fell down the stairs and broke everything to atoms. " He is delirious," said Filomena one day, " and talks of nothing but of giving you his watch." " How can he be so ill," said the boy suspiciously, " when he eats and drinks? " " Do you want the watch or not? " said Filomena, and off the lad ran. I let the others entertain me. Maria said: " You told Filomena something yesterday about savages; I know something about them, too. Savage people live in China, and the worst of all are called Mandarins. Do you know what one of them did to an Italian lady? She was with her family over there; suddenly there came a Mandarin, carried her off, and shut her up in his house. They never found her again. Then he had three children by her; but one day he went out and forgot to shut the door; she ran quickly out of the house, down to the water, and saw a ship far away. Do you know what the mandarin did, sir, when he came home and found that

his wife was gone? He took the three children, tore them
through the middle, and threw the pieces out into the street."
It reminded one of Lucidarius, and other mediæval legends.
Then our good *zio*, the honest uncle, began, and told Maria
and Filomena the history of Napoleon I., fairly correctly.
He had heard it from his master Leonardo, who taught him
his trade; the man had taken part in five of the campaigns.
The only egregious mistake he made was that he thought
the Austrians had gradually poisoned the Duke of Reich-
stadt, because he threatened to become even more formid-
able than his father. But that the old grenadier might easily
have believed. The thing that astonished me was that the
narrative did not make the slightest impression upon either
Maria or Filomena. I asked Filomena if she did not think
it was very remarkable. But she clearly had a suspicion
that it was all lies, besides, what has happened in the world
before her day is of as little importance to her as what goes
on in another planet; finally, she abominates war. *Zio* concluded his story with childlike self-satisfaction: "When I
learnt about all this, I was only an apprentice; now I am
mastro Nino."

These last few days that I have been able to stumble
about the room a little, I have had a feeling of delight and
happiness such as I have hardly experienced before. The
very air is a fête. The little black-haired youngsters, running about this picturesquely steep street, are my delight,
whenever I look out of the window. All that is in front of
me: the splendours of Rome, the Summer, the art of Italy,
Naples in the South, Venice in the North, makes my heart
beat fast and my head swim. I only need to turn round
from the window and see Filomena standing behind me,
knitting, posed like a living picture by Küchler to feel, with
jubilation: I am in Rome. Saredo came to-'day at twelve
o'clock, and saw me dressed for the first time. I had put on
my nicest clothes. I called Filomena, had three dinners
fetched, and seated between him and her, I had my banquet.
I had just said: "I will not eat any soup to-day, unless it
should happen to be *Zuppa d'herba*. Filomena took the

lid off and cried: " *A punto.*" This is how all my wishes are fulfilled now. I had a fine, light red wine. It tasted so good that if the gods had known it they would have poured their nectar into the washtub. Filomena poured it out, singing:

> L'acqua fa mare,
>   Il vino fa cantare;
> Il sugo della gresta
>   Fa gira' la testa.
>
> (Water is bad for one;
>   Wine makes one sing;
> The juice of the grape
>   Makes the head swim.)

To-morrow I may go out. After Sunday, I shall leave off dining at home. On Sunday Filomena goes to Camerino.

SECOND LONGER STAY ABROAD

(*Continued*)

I

SAREDO said to me one day: " I am not going to flatter you—I have no interest in doing so; but I am going to give you a piece of advice, which you ought to think over. Stay in Italy, settle down here, and you will reach a far higher position than you can possibly attain in your own country. The intellectual education you possess is exceedingly rare in Italy; what I can say, without exaggeration, is that in this country it is so extraordinary that it might be termed an active force. Within two years you would be a power in Italy, at home, you will never be more than a professor at a University. Stay here! Villari and I will help you over your first difficulties. Write in French, or Italian, which you like, and as you are master of the entire range of Germanic culture, which scarcely any man in Italy is, you will acquire an influence of which you have not the least conception. A prophet is never honoured in his own country. We, on the other hand, need you. So stay here! Take Max Müller as an example. It is with individuals as with nations; it is only when they change their soil that they attain their full development and realise their own strength."

I replied: " I am deaf to that sort of thing. I love the Danish language too well ever to forsake it. Only in the event of my settlement in Denmark meeting with opposition, and being rendered impossible, shall I strap on my knapsack, gird up my loins, and hie me to France or Italy; I am glad to hear that the world is not so closed to me as I had formerly believed."

My thoughts were much engaged on my sick-bed by reflections upon the future of Denmark. The following entry is dated March 8, 1871:

What do we mean by *our national future,* which we talk so much about? We do not purpose to extend our borders, to make conquests, or play any part in politics. For that, as is well comprehensible, we know we are too weak. I will leave alone the question as to whether it is possible to live without, in one way or another, growing, and ask: What do we want? *To continue to exist.* How exist? We want to get Slesvig back again, for as it is we are not *existing;* we are sickening, or else we are living like those lower animals who even when they are cut in pieces, are quite nimble; but it is a miserable life. We are in a false position with regard to Germany. The centripetal force that draws the individual members of one nationality together, and which we in Denmark call Danishness, that which, further, draws nationalities of the same family together, and which in Denmark is called *Scandinavianism,* must logically lead to a sympathy for the merging of the entire race, a kind of *Gothogermanism.* If we seek support from France, we shall be behaving like the Poles, turning for help to a foreign race against a nation of our own. I accuse us, not of acting imprudently, but of fighting against a natural force that is stronger than we. We can only retard, we cannot annihilate, the attraction exerted by the greater masses on the lesser. We can only hope that we may not live to feel the agony.

Holland and Denmark are both threatened by Germany, for in this geography is the mighty ally of Germany. The most enlightened Dane can only cherish the hope that Denmark, conquered, or not conquered, will brave it out long enough for universal civilisation, by virtue of the level it has reached, to bring our independence with it. As far as the hope which the majority of Danes cherish is concerned (including the noble professors of philosophy), of a time when Nemesis (reminiscence of theology!), shall descend on Prussia, this hope is only an outcome of foolishness. And even a Nemesis upon Prussia will never hurt Germany, and thus will not help us.

But the main question is this: If we—either through a peaceable restoration of Slesvig, or after fresh wars, or through the dawning of an era of peace and civilisation—regain our integrity and independence, shall we exist then? Not at all. Then we shall sicken again. A country like Denmark, even including Slesvig, is nowadays no country at all. A tradesman whose whole capital consists of ten rigsdaler is no tradesman. The large capitals swallow up the small. The small must seek their salvation in associations, partnerships, joint-stock companies, etc.

Our misfortune lies in the fact that there is no other country with which we can enter into partnership except Sweden and Norway, a little, unimportant state. By means of this association, which for the time being, is our sheet-anchor, and which, by dint of deploying enormous energy, might be of some importance, we can at best retard our destruction by a year or two. But the future! Has Denmark any future?

It was France who, to her own unspeakable injury, discovered, or rather, first proclaimed, the principle of nationality, a principle which at most could only give her Belgium and French Switzerland, two neutral countries, guaranteed by Europe, but which gave Italy to Piedmont, Germany to Prussia, and which one day will give Russia supremacy over all the Slavs. Even before the war, France was, as it were, squeezed between bucklers; she had no possible chance of gaining anything through her own precious principle, and did not even dare to apply it to the two above-mentioned points. While she fearfully allowed herself to be awarded Savoy and Nice, Prussia grew from nineteen million inhabitants to fifty millions; and probably in a few years the Germans of Austria will fall to Germany as well. Then came the war, and its outcome was in every particular what Prévost-Paradol, with his keen foresight, had predicted: "Afterwards," he wrote, "France, with Paris, will take up in Europe the same position as Hellas with Athens assumed in the old Roman empire; it will become the city of taste and the noble delights; but it will never be able to regain its power." It has, in fact, been killed by this very theory of nationality; for the only cognate races, Spain and Italy, are two countries of which the one is rotten, the other just entered upon the convalescent stage. Thus it is clear that Germany will, for a time, exercise the supreme sway in Europe. But the future belongs neither to her nor to Russia, but, if not to England herself, at any rate to the Anglo-Saxon race, which has revealed a power of expansion in comparison with which that of other nations is too small to count. Germans who go to North America, in the next generation speak English. The English have a unique capacity for spreading themselves and introducing their language, and the power which the Anglo-Saxon race will acquire cannot be broken in course of time like that of ancient Rome; for there are no barbarians left, and their power is based, not on conquest, but on assimilation, and the race is being rejuvenated in North America.

How characteristic it is of our poor little country that we always hear and read of it as "one of the oldest kingdoms in the world." That is just the pity of it. If we were only a young country! There is only one way by which we can rejuvenate ourselves. First, to merge ourselves into a Scandinavia; then, when this is well done and well secured, to approach the Anglo-Saxon race to which we are akin. Moral: Become an Anglo-Saxon and study John Stuart Mill!

And I studied Mill with persevering attention, where he was difficult, but instructive, to follow, as in the *Examination of Hamilton's Philosophy,* which renews Berkeley's teachings, and I read him with delight where, accessible and comprehensible, he proclaims with freshness and vigour the gospel of a new age, as in the book *On Liberty* and the one akin to it, *Representative Government.*

II

During the months of February and March, my conversations with Giuseppe Saredo had been all I lived for. We discussed all the questions which one or both of us had at heart, from the causes of the expansion of Christianity, to the method of proportionate representation which Sar-

edo knew, and correctly traced back to Andræ. When I
complained that, by reason of our different nationality, we
could hardly have any recollections in common, and by reason of our different languages, could never cite a familiar
adage from childhood, or quote a common saying from a
play, that the one could not thoroughly enjoy the harmony
of verses in the language of the other, Saredo replied:
"You are no more a Dane than I am an Italian; we are compatriots in the great fatherland of the mind, that of Shakespeare and Goethe, John Stuart Mill, Andræ, and Cavour.
This land is the land of humanity. Nationality is milk, humanity is cream. What is there in all the world that we
have not in common? It is true that we cannot enjoy together the harmony of some Northern verses, but we can
assimilate together all the great ideas, and we have for each
other the attraction of the relatively unknown, which fellow-
countrymen have not."

He very acutely characterised his Italian compatriots:
"Our intelligence amounts to prudence and common sense.
At a distance we may appear self-luminous; in reality
we are only passivity and reflected light. Solferino gave
us Lombardy, Sadowa gave us Venice, Sedan gave us Rome.
We were just active enough to take advantage of fortunate
circumstances, and passively clever enough not to wreck our
advantage by stupidity. In foreign novels we are scoundrels
of the deepest dye, concocters of poisons and wholesale
swindlers. In reality we are indifferent and indolent.
Dolce far niente, these words, which, to our shame, are repeated in every country in Italian, are our watchword. But
things shall be different, if it means that the few amongst
us who have a little share of head and heart have to work
themselves to death—things shall be different. Massimo
d'Azeglio said: "Now we have created an Italy; there
remains to create Italians." That was a true saying. Now
we are creating the new people, and what a future there is
before us! Now it is we who are taking the leadership of
the Latin race, and who are giving back to our history its
brilliance of the sixteenth century. At present our Art is
poor because we have no popular type; but wait! In a few

years Italy will show a profile no less full of character than in the days of Michael Angelo, and Benvenuto Cellini."

III

Then the moment arrived when all abstract reflections were thrust aside once more by convalescence. I was well again, after having been shut up for over four months. I still felt the traces of the mercury poisoning, but I was no longer tied to my bed, and weak though I was, I could walk.

And on the very first day,—it was March 25th—armed with a borrowed stick (I possessed none, having never used a stick before), and equipped with a little camp-stool, I took the train to Frascati, where there was a Madonna Fête.

It was life opening out before me again. All that I saw, witnessed to its splendour. First, the scenery on the way, the Campagna with its proud ruins, and the snow-covered Sabine Mountains, the whole illuminated by a powerful Summer sun; the villas of old Romans, with fortress-like thick walls, and small windows; then the fertile lava soil, every inch of which was under vineyard cultivation. At last the mountains in the neighborhood of Frascati. A convent crowned the highest point; there, in olden days, the first Italian temple to Jupiter had stood, and there Hannibal had camped. Underneath, in a hollow, like an eagle's nest, lay Rocca di Papa. By the roadside, fruit-trees with violet clusters of blossoms against a background of stone-pines, cypresses, and olive-groves.

I reached Frascati station. There was no carriage to be had up to the town, so I was obliged to ascend the hill slowly on foot, a test which my leg stood most creditably. In the pretty market-place of Frascati, with its large fountain which, like Acqua Paola, was divided into three and flung out a tremendous quantity of water, I went into an *osteria* and asked for roast goat with salad and Frascati wine, then sat down outside, as it was too close within. Hundreds of people in gay costumes, with artificial flowers and silver feathers in their headgear, filled the square in front of me, crowded the space behind me, laughed and shouted.

The people seemed to be of a grander type, more lively, animated and exuberant, than at the fair at Fiesole. The women were like Junos or Venuses, the men, even when clad in abominable rags, looked like Vulcans, blackened in their forges; they were all of larger proportions than Northern men and women. A Roman beau, with a riding-whip under his arm, was making sheep's eyes at a young local beauty, his courtship accompanied by the whines of the surrounding beggars. A *signora* from Albano was lecturing the waiter with the dignity of a queen for having brought her meat that was beneath all criticism, yes, she even let the word *porcheria* escape her. A brown-bearded fellow came out of the inn with a large bottle of the heavenly Frascati wine, which the landlords here, even on festival occasions, never mix with water, and gave a whole family, sitting on donkeys, to drink out of one glass; then he went to two little ones, who were holding each other round the waist, sitting on the same donkey; to two youths who were riding another; to a man and wife, who sat on a third, and all drank, like the horsemen in Wouwerman's pictures, without dismounting.

I got into an old, local omnibus, pulled by three horses, to drive the two miles to Grotta Ferrata, where the fair was. But the vehicle was hardly about to start up-hill when, with rare unanimity, the horses reared, behaved like mad, and whirled it round four or five times. The driver, a fellow with one eye and a grey cap with a double red camelia in it, being drunk, thrashed the horses and shouted, while an old American lady with ringlets shrieked inside the omnibus, and bawled out that she had paid a franc beforehand, and now wanted to get out. The road was thronged with people walking, and there was just as many riding donkeys, all of them, even the children, already heated with wine, singing, laughing, and accosting everybody. Many a worthy woman supported her half-drunk husband with her powerful arm. Many a substantial *signora* from Rocca di Papa sat astride her mule, showing without the least bashfulness her majestic calves.

At Grotta Ferrata, the long, long street presented a human throng of absolute density without the slightest crush, for no one stuck his elbows into his neighbour's sides. The eye could only distinguish a mass of red, yellow and white patches in the sunlight, and in between them a few donkeys' heads and mules' necks. The patches were the kerchiefs on the women's heads. Folk stood with whole roast pigs in front of them on a board, cutting off a piece with a knife for anyone who was hungry; there were sold, besides, fruits, knives, ornaments, provisions, and general market wares. One *osteria,* the entrance to which was hung all over with sausages, onions and vegetables, in garlands, had five huge archways open to the street. Inside were long tables, at which people sat, not on benches, but on trestles, round bars supported by two legs, and ate and drank in the best of good spirits, and the blackest filth, for the floor was the black, sodden, trampled earth. Just over the way, arbours had been made from trees, by intertwining their branches and allowing them to grow into one another; these were quite full of gay, beautiful girls, amongst them one with fair hair and brown eyes, who looked like a Tuscan, and from whom it was difficult to tear one's eyes away.

After having inspected the courtyard of an old monastery, the lovely pillars of which rejoiced my heart, I sat down a little on one side in the street where the fair was, on my little camp-stool, which roused the legitimate curiosity of the peasant girls. They walked round me, looked at me from behind and before, and examined with grave interest the construction of my seat. In front of me sat an olive and lemon seller. Girls bargained with him as best they could in the press, others stood and looked on. I had an opportunity here of watching their innate statuesque grace. When they spoke, the right arm kept time with their speech. When silent, they generally placed one hand on the hip, bent, but not clenched. There were various types. The little blonde, blue-eyed girl with the mild Madonna smile, and absolutely straight nose, and the large-made, pronounced brunette. But the appearance of them all was such that an artist or a poet could, by a slight transformation, have portrayed from them whatever type of figure or special characteristic he required. In my opinion, the form Italian beauty took, and the reason of the feeling one had in Italy of wading in beauty, whereas one hardly ever saw anything in the strict sense of the word beautiful in Copenhagen, and rarely in Paris, was, that this beauty was the beauty of the significant. All these women looked to be unoppressed, full-blown, freely developed. All that makes woman ugly in the North: the cold, the thick, ugly clothes that the peasant women wear, the doublet of embarrassment and vapidity which they drag about with them, the strait-waistcoat of Christiansfeldt morality in which they are confined by the priests, by protestantism, by fashion, by custom and convention—none of this oppressed, confined or contracted women here. These young peasant girls looked as if they had never heard such words as " You must not," or " You shall not," and as here in Italy there is none of the would-be witty talk, the grinning behind people's backs, which takes the life out of all intrepidity in the North, no one thought: " What will people say? " Everyone dressed and deported himself with complete originality, as he, or rather as she, liked. Hence eyes were doubly brilliant, blood coursed twice as red, the women's busts were twice as rounded and full.

IV

From this time forth I had a strange experience. I saw beauty everywhere. If I sat at the window of a café on the Corso on a Sunday morning, as the ladies were going to Mass, it seemed to me that all the beauty on earth was going past. A mother and her three daughters went by, a mere grocer's wife from the Corso, but the mother carried herself like a duchess, had a foot so small that it could have lain in the hollow of my hand, and the youngest of the three daughters was so absolutely lovely that people turned to look after her; she might perhaps have been fifteen years of age, but there was a nobility about her austere profile, and she had a way of twisting her perfect lips into a smile, that showed her to be susceptible to the sweetest mysteries of poetry and music. My long illness had so quickened the susceptibility of my senses to impressions of beauty that I lived in a sort of intoxication.

In the Scandinavian Club I was received with endless expressions of sympathy, courteous remarks, and more or less sincerely meant flatteries, as if in compensation for the suffering I had been through. All spoke as though they had themselves been deeply distressed, and especially as though Copenhagen had been sitting weeping during my illness. I certainly did not believe this for a moment, but all the same it weighed down a little the balance of my happiness, and the first meetings with the Northern artists in these glorious surroundings were in many respects very enjoyable. The Scandinavian Club was in the building from which you enter the Mausoleum of Augustus, a colossal building in the form of a cross, several storeys in height. A festival had been got up on the flat roof for a benevolent object one of the first evenings in April. You mounted the many flights of stairs and suddenly found yourself, apparently, in an immense hall, but with no roof save the stars, and brilliantly illuminated, but with lights that paled in the rays of the Italian moon. We took part in the peculiarly Italian enjoyment of watching balloons go up; they rose by fire, which exhausted the air inside them and made them light. Round about the moon we could see red and blue lights, like big stars; one balloon ignited up in the sky, burst into bright flames, and looked very impressive.

Troops of young women, too, were sitting there, and dazzled anew a young man who for a second time had given the slip to the old gentleman with the scythe. There was one young servant girl from the country, in particular, a child of thirteen or fourteen, to whom I called the attention of the painters, and they went into ecstasies over her. The type was the same as that which Raphael has reproduced in his Sistine Madonna. Her clear, dark blue eyes had a look of maidenly shyness, and of the most exquisite bashfulness, and yet a look of pride. She wore a string of glass beads round her lovely neck. We ordered two bottles of wine to drink her health, and, while we were drinking it, the rotunda was lighted up from a dozen directions with changing Bengal fire. The ladies looked even handsomer, the glass lamps dark green in the gleam, the fire-borne balloons rose, the orchestra played, the women smiled at the homage of their friends and lovers—all on the venerable Mausoleum of Augustus.

V

I made the acquaintance that evening of a young and exceedingly engaging Frenchman, who was to become my intimate friend and my travelling companion. He attracted me from the first by his refined, reserved, and yet cordial manner.

Although only thirty-five years of age, Georges Nouf-flard had travelled and seen surprisingly much. He was now in Italy for the second time, knew France and Germany, had travelled through Mexico and the United States, had visited Syria, Egypt, Tunis, and Algiers to the last oasis. When the conversation touched upon Art and Music, he expressed himself in a manner that revealed keen perception, unusual knowledge, and a very individual taste.

The following morning, when we met on the Corso, he placed himself at my disposal, if he could be of use to me; there was nothing he had arranged to do. He asked where I was thinking of going; as he knew Rome and its neighbourhood as well as I knew my mother's drawing-room, I placed myself in his hands. We took a carriage and drove together, first to the baths of Caracalla, then to the Catacombs, where we very nearly lost our way, and thought with a thrill of what in olden times must have been the feelings of the poor wretches who fled there, standing in the dark and hearing footsteps in the distance, knowing that it was their pursuers coming, and that they were inevitably going to be murdered, where there was not even room to raise a weapon in their own defence. Next we drove to *San Paolo fuori le mure,* of the burning of which Thorwaldsen's Museum possesses a painting by Leopold Robert, but which at that time had been entirely re-built in the antique style. It was the most beautiful basilica I had ever seen. We en-

joyed the sight of the courtyard of the monastery nearly
1,700 years old, with its fine pillars, all different, and so well
preserved that we compared, in thought, the impressions produced by the two mighty churches, San Paolo and San Pietro. Then we dined together and plunged into interminable
discussions until darkness fell. From that day forth we
were inseparable. Our companionship lasted several months,
until I was obliged to journey North. But the same cordial
relations continued to subsist between us for more than a
quarter of a century, when Death robbed me of my friend.

Georges Noufflard was the son of a rich cloth manufacturer at Roubaix, and at an early age had come into possession of a considerable fortune. This, however, was somewhat diminished through the dishonesty of those who, after
the death of his father, conducted the works in his name.
He had wanted to become a painter, but the weakness of his
eyes had obliged him to give up Art; now he was an Art
lover, and was anxious to write a book on the memorials
and works of art in Rome, too great an undertaking, and
for that reason never completed; but at the same time, he
pursued with passion the study of music, played Beethoven,
Gluck and Berlioz for me daily, and later on published books
on Berlioz and Richard Wagner.

As a youth he had been an enthusiast such as, in the
Germanic countries, they fancy is impossible elsewhere, to
such an extent indeed as would be regarded even there as
extraordinary. At seventeen years of age he fell in love
with a young girl who lived in the same building as himself.
He was only on terms of sign language with her, had not
even secured so much as a conversation with her. None the
less, his infatuation was so great that he declared to his father that he wished to marry her. The father would not
give his consent, and her family would not receive him unless he was presented by his father. The latter sent him to
America with the words: " Forget your love and learn what
a fine thing industrialism is." He travelled all over the
United States, found all machinery loathsome, since he had not
the most elementary knowledge of the principles of mechan-
ics, and no inclination for them, and thought all the time of

the little girl from whom they wished to separate him. It did not help matters that the travelling companion that had been given him lived and breathed in an atmosphere of the lowest debauchery, and did his best to initiate the young man into the same habits. On his return home he declared to his father that he persisted in his choice. "Good," said his father, "Asia Minor is a delightful country, and so is Northern Africa; it will also do you good to become acquainted with Italy." So he set off on his travels again, and this time was charmed with everything he saw. Then his father died, and he became pretty much his own master and free to do as he liked. Then he learned that the father of the girl had been guilty of a bank fraud. His family would not receive hers, if, indeed, herself. So he gave up his intention; he did not wish to expose her to humiliation and did not wish himself to have a man of ill-fame for his father-in-law; he set off again on his travels, and remained a long time away. "The proof that I acted wisely by so doing," he said in conclusion, "is that I have completely forgotten the girl; my infatuation was all fancy."

When he commenced by telling me that for three years he had loved, and despite all opposition, wished to marry a girl to whom he had never spoken, I exclaimed: "Why, you are no Frenchman!" When he concluded by telling me that after remaining constant for three years he had abandoned her for a fault that not she, but her father, had committed, I exclaimed: "How French you are, after all!"

While mutual political, social, and philosophical interests drew me to Giuseppe Saredo, all the artistic side of my nature bound me to Georges Noufflard. Saredo was an Italian from a half-French part,—he was born at Savona, near Chambéry,—and his culture was as much French as Italian; Noufflard was a Frenchman possessed by such a love for Italy that he spoke the purest Florentine, felt himself altogether a Southerner, and had made up his mind to take up his permanent abode in Italy. He married, too, a few years afterwards, a lovely Florentine woman, and settled down in Florence.

What entirely won my heart about him was the fem-

ininely delicate consideration and unselfish devotion of
his nature, the charm there was about his manner and conversation, which revealed itself in everything he did, from
the way in which he placed his hat upon his head, to
the way in which he admired a work of art. But I could not
have associated with him day after day, had I not been able
to learn something from him. When we met again ten years
later, it turned out that we had nothing especially new to tell
each other. I had met him just at the right moment.

It was not only that Noufflard was very well and widely
informed about the artistic treasures of Italy and the places
where they were to be found, but his opinions enriched my
mind, inasmuch as they spurred me on to contradiction or
surprised me and won my adherence. Fresh as Julius
Lange's artistic sense had been, there was nevertheless something doctrinaire and academic about it. An artist like Bernini was horrible, and nothing else to him; he had no sympathy for the sweet, half-sensual ecstasy of some of Bernini's
best figures. He was an enemy of eighteenth-century art in
France, saw it through the moral spectacles which in the
Germanic countries had come into use with the year 1800.
It was easy for Noufflard to remain unbiased by Northern
doctrines, for he did not know them; he had the free eye
of the beauty lover for every revelation of beauty, no
matter under what form, and had the intellectual kinship
of the Italianised Frenchman for many an artist unap-
preciated in the North. On the other hand, he naturally
considered that we Northmen very much over-estimated our
own. It was impossible to rouse any interest in him for
Thorwaldsen, whom he considered absolutely academic.
" You cannot call him a master in any sense," he exclaimed
one day, when we had been looking at Thorwaldsen bas-
reliefs side by side with antiques. I learnt from my intimacy with Noufflard how little impression Thorwaldsen's
spirit makes on the Romance peoples. That indifference to
him would soon become so widespread in Germany, I did not
yet foresee.

Noufflard had a very alert appreciation of the early
Renaissance, especially in sculpture; he was passionately in

love with the natural beauties of Italy, from North to South, and he had a kind of national-psychological gift of singling out peculiarly French, Italian or German traits.   He did not know the German language, but he was at home in German music, and had studied a great deal of German literature in translation; just then he was reading Hegel's " Æsthetics," the abstractions in which veritably alarmed him, and to which he very much preferred modern French Art Philosophy.   In English Science, he had studied Darwin, and he was the first to give me a real insight into the Darwinian theory and a general summary of it, for in my younger days I had only heard it attacked, as erroneous, in lectures by Rasmus Nielsen on teleology.

Georges Noufflard was the first Frenchman of my own age with whom I had been intimate and whose character I partly understood and entered into, partly absorbed into my own.   If many of the various opinions evident in my first lectures were strikingly emancipated from Danish national prejudices which no one hitherto had attempted to disturb, I owed this in a great measure to him.   Our happy, harmonious intimacy in the Sabine Hills and in Naples was responsible, before a year was past, for whole deluges of abuse in Danish newspapers.

VI

One morning, the Consul's man-servant brought me a *permesso* for the Collection of Sculpture in the Vatican for the same day, and a future *permesso* for the Loggias, Stanzas, and the Sistine Chapel.   I laid the last in my pocket-book. It was the key of Paradise.   I had waited for it so long that I said to myself almost superstitiously: " I wonder whether anything will prevent again? "   The anniversary of the day I had left Copenhagen the year before, I drove to the Vatican, went at one o'clock mid-day up the handsome staircase, and through immense, in part magnificently decorated rooms to the Sistine Chapel.   I had heard so much about the disappointment it would be that not the very slightest suggestion of disappointment crossed my mind.   Only a feeling of supreme happiness shot through me: at last I am here. I stood on the spot which was the real goal of my pilgrimage. I had so often examined reproductions of every figure and I had read so much about the whole, that I knew every note of the music beforehand. Now I heard it.

A voice within me whispered: So here I stand at last, shut in with the mind that of all human minds has spoken most deeply home to my soul. I am outside and above the earth and far from human kind. This is his earth and these are his men, created in his image to people his world. For this one man's work is a world, which, though that of one man only, can be placed against the productions of a whole nation, even of the most splendid nation that has ever lived, the Greeks. Michael Angelo felt more largely, more lonely, more mightily than any other. He created out of the wealth of a nature that in its essence was more than earthly. Raphael is more human, people say, and that is true; but Michael Angelo is more divine.

After the lapse of about an hour, the figures detached themselves from the throng, to my mental vision, and the whole composition fixed itself in my brain. I saw the ceiling, not merely as it is to-day, but as it was when the colours were fresh, for in places there were patches, the bright yellow, for instance, which showed the depth of colouring in which the whole had been carried out. It was Michael Angelo's intention to show us the ceiling pierced and the heavens open above it. Up to the central figures, we are to suppose that the walls continue straight up to the ceiling, as though the figures sat upright. Then all confusion disappears, and all becomes one perfect whole.

The principal pictures, such as the creation of Adam, Michael Angelo's most philosophical and most exquisite painting, I had had before my eyes upon my wall every day for ten years. The expression in Adam's face was not one of languishing appeal, as I had thought; he smiled faintly, as if calmly confident of the dignity of the life the finger of God is about to bestow upon him. The small, bronze-painted figures, expressed the suspension and repose of the ceiling; they were architectonic symbols. The troops of

young heroes round about the central pillars were Michael
Angelo's ideals of Youth, Beauty and Humanity.   The one
resting silently and thoughtfully on one knee is perhaps the
most splendid.   There is hardly any difference between his
build and that of Adam.   Adam is the more spiritual brother
of these young and suffering heroes.

I felt the injustice of all the talk about the beginnings
of grotesqueness in Michael Angelo's style.   There are a
few somewhat distorted figures, Haman, the knot of men
and women adoring the snake, Jonas, as he flings himself
backwards, but except these, what calm, what grandiose perfection!   And which was still more remarkable, what imposing charm!   Eve, in the picture of " The Fall," is perhaps the most adorable figure that Art has ever produced;
her beauty, in the picture on the left, was like a revelation
of what humanity really ought to have been.

It sounded almost like a lie that one man had created
this in twenty-two months.   Would the earth ever again
produce frescoes of the same order?   The 360 years that
had passed over it had damaged this, the greatest pictorial
work on earth, far less than I had feared.

A large aristocratic English family came in: man, wife,
son, daughter, another daughter, the governess, all expen-
sively and fashionably dressed.   They stood silent for a moment at the entrance to the hall.   Then they came forward
as far as about the middle of the hall, looked up and about
a little, said to the custodian: " Will you open the door
for us? " and went out again very gracefully.

VII

I knew Raphael's Loggias from copies in *l'Ecole des
Beaux Arts* in Paris.   But I was curious to see how they
would appear after this, and so, although there was only
three-quarters of an hour left of the time allotted to me on
my *permesso,* I went up to look at them.   My first impression, as I glanced down the corridor and perceived these
small ceiling pictures, barely two feet across, was: "Good
gracious!   This will be a sorry enjoyment after Michael

Angelo!" I looked at the first painting, God creating the animals, and was quite affected: "There goes the good old man, saying paternally: "Come up from the earth, all of you, you have no idea how nice it is up here." My next impression was: "How childish!" But my last was: "What genius!" How charming the picture of the Fall, and how lovely Eve! And what grandeur of style despite the smallness of the space. A God a few inches high separates light from darkness, but there is omnipotence in the movement of His arm. Jacob sees the ladder to Heaven in his dream; and this ladder, which altogether has six angels upon it, seems to reach from Earth to Heaven, infinitely long and infinitely peopled; above, we see God the Father, at an immense distance, spread His gigantic embrace (which covers a space the length of two fingers). There was the favourite picture of my childhood, Abraham prostrated before the Angels, even more marvellous in the original than I had fancied it to myself, although it is true that the effect of the picture is chiefly produced by its beauty of line. And there was Lot, departing from Sodom with his daughters, a picture great because of the perfect illusion of movement. They go on and on, against the wind and storm, with Horror behind them and Hope in front, at the back, to the right, the burning city, to the left, a smiling landscape. How unique the landscapes on all these pictures are, how marvellous, for instance, that in which Moses is found on the Nile! This river, within the narrow limits of the picture, looked like a huge stream, losing itself in the distance.

It was half-past five. My back was beginning to ache in the place which had grown tender from lying so long; without a trace of fatigue I had been looking uninterruptedly at pictures for four hours and a half.

VIII

Noufflard's best friend in Rome was a young lieutenant of the Bersaglieri named Ottavio Cerrotti, with whom we were much together. Although a Roman, he had entered the Italian army very young, and had consequently been, as

it were, banished. Now, through the breach at Porta Pia,
he had come back. He was twenty-four years of age, and
the naïvest Don Juan one could possibly meet. He was beloved by the beautiful wife of his captain, and Noufflard,
who frequented their house, one day surprised the two lovers
in tears. Cerrotti was crying with his lady-love because he
had been faithless to her. He had confessed to her his intimacy with four other young ladies; so she was crying, and
the end of it was that he cried to keep her company.

At meals, he gave us a full account of his principal romance. He had one day met her by chance in the gardens
of the Palazzo Corsini, and since that day, they had had
secret meetings. But the captain had now been transferred
to Terni, and tragedy had begun. Letters were constantly
within an ace of being intercepted, they committed imprudences without count. He read aloud to us, without the
least embarrassment, the letters of the lady. The curious
thing about them was the moderation she exercised in the
expression of her love, while at the same time her plans for
meetings were of the most foolhardy, breakneck description.

Another fresh acquaintance that I made in those days
was with three French painters, Hammon, Sain and Benner,
who had studios adjoining one another. Hammon and Sain
both died long since, but Benner, whom I met again in Paris
in 1904, died, honoured and respected, in 1905. I was
later on at Capri in company with Sain and Benner, but Hammon I saw only during this visit to Rome. His pretty, somewhat sentimental painting, *Ma sœur n'y est pas,* hung, reproduced in engraving, in every shop-window, even in Copenhagen. He was painting just then at his clever picture,
Triste Rivage.

Hammon was born in Brittany, of humble, orthodox
parents, who sent him to a monastery. The Prior, when
he surprised him drawing men and women out of his head,
told him that painting was a sin. The young man himself
then strongly repented his inclination, but, as he felt he could
not live without following it, he left the monastery, though
with many strong twinges of conscience.

Now that he was older, he was ruining himself by

drink, but had manifested true talent and still retained a humorous wit. One day that I was with him, a young man came to the studio and asked for his opinion of a painting; the man talked the whole time of nothing but his mother, of how much he loved her and all that he did for her. Hammon's patience gave out at last. He broke out: "And do you think, sir, that *I* have murdered my mother? I love her very much, I assure you, *not enough to marry her*, I grant, but pretty well, all the same." After that he always spoke of him as "the young man who loves his mother."

IX

I felt as though this April, this radiant Spring, were the most glorious time in my life. I was assimilating fresh impressions of Art and Nature every hour; the conversations I was enjoying with my Italian and French friends set me day by day pondering over new thoughts; I saw myself restored to life, and a better life. At the beginning of April, moreover, some girls from the North made their triumphal entry into the Scandinavian Club. Without being specially beautiful or remarkable, they absolutely charmed me. It was a full year since the language of home had sounded in my ears from the lips of a girl, since I had seen the smile in the blue eyes and encountered the heart-ensnaring charm, in jest, or earnest, of the young women of the North. I had recently heard the entrancing castrato singing at St. Peter's, and, on conquering my aversion, could not but admire it. Now I heard once more simple, but natural, Danish and Swedish songs. Merely to speak Danish again with a young woman, was a delight. And there was one who, delicately and unmistakably and defencelessly, showed me that I was not indifferent to her. That melted me, and from that time forth the beauties of Italy were enhanced tenfold in my eyes.

All that I was acquainted with in Rome, all that I saw every day with Georges Noufflard, I could show her and her party, from the most accessible things, which were nevertheless fresh to the newcomers, such as the Pantheon, Acqua Paola, San Pietro in Montorio, the grave of Cecilia Metella, and the grottoes of Egeria, to the great collections of Art in the Vatican, or the Capitol, or in the wonderful Galleria Borghese. All this, that I was accustomed to see alone with Noufflard, acquired new splendour when a blonde girl walked by my side, asking sensible questions, and showing me the gratitude of youth for good instruction. With her nineteen years I suppose she thought me marvellously clever. But the works of Art that lay a little outside the beaten track, I likewise showed to my compatriots. I had never been able to tolerate Guido Reni; but his playing angels in the chapel of San Gregorio excited my profound admiration, and it was a satisfaction to me to pour this into the receptive ear of a girl compatriot. These angels delighted me so that I could hardly tear myself away from them. The fine malice, the mild coquetry, even in the expression of the noblest purity and the loftiest dignity, enchanted us.

I had been in the habit of going out to the environs of Rome with Georges Noufflard, for instance, to the large, handsome gardens of the Villa Doria Pamfili, or the Villa Madama, with its beautiful frescoes and stucco-work, executed by Raphael's pupils, Giulio Romano and others, from drawings by that master. But it was a new delight to drive over the Campagna with a girl who spoke Danish by my side, and to see her Northern complexion in the sun of the South. With my French friend, I gladly joined the excursions of her party to Nemi, Albano, Tivoli.

Never in my life had I felt so happy as I did then. I was quite recovered. Only a fortnight after I had risen from a sick-bed that had claimed me four months and a half, I was going about, thanks to my youth, as I did before I was ill. For my excursions, I had a comrade after my own heart, well-bred, educated, and noble-minded; I fell in love a little a few times a week; I saw lakes, fields, olive groves, mountains, scenery, exactly to my taste. I had always a *permesso* for the Vatican collections in my pocket. I felt intoxicated with delight, dizzy with enjoyment.

It seemed to me that of all I had seen in the world, Tivoli was the most lovely. The old " temple of the Sibyl " on the hill stood on consecrated ground, and consecrated the whole neighbourhood. I loved those waterfalls, which impressed me much more than Trollhättan[1] had done in my childhood. In one place the water falls down, black and boiling, into a hollow of the rock, and reminded me of the descent into Tartarus; in another the cataract runs, smiling and twinkling with millions of shining pearls, in the strong sunlight. In a third place, the great cascade rushes down over the rocks. There, where it touches the nether rocks, rests the end of the enormous rainbow which, when the sun shines, is always suspended across it. Noufflard told me that Niagara itself impressed one less. We scrambled along the cliff until we stood above the great waterfall, and could see nothing but the roaring, foaming white water, leaping and dashing down; it looked as though the seething and spraying masses of water were springing over each other's heads in a mad race, and there was such power, such natural persuasion in it, that one seemed drawn with it, and gliding, as it were, dragged into the abyss. It was as though all Nature were disembodied, and flinging herself down.

Like a Latin, Noufflard personified it all; he saw the dance of nymphs in the waves, and their veils in the clouds of spray. My way of regarding Nature was diametrically opposite, and pantheistic. I lost consciousness of my own personality, felt myself one with the falling water and merged myself into Nature, instead of gathering it up into figures. I felt myself an individuality of the North, conscious of my being.

X

One afternoon a large party of us had taken our meal at an inn on the lake of Nemi. The evening was more than earthly. The calm, still, mountain lake, the old, filled-up crater, on the top of the mountain, had a fairy-like effect. I dropped down behind a boulder and lay for a long time alone, lost in ecstasy, out of sight of the others. All at once I saw a blue veil fluttering in the breeze quite near me. It

---

[1] Trollhättan, a celebrated waterfall near Göteborg in Sweden.

was the young Danish girl, who had sat down with me. The red light of the evening, Nemi and she, merged in one. Not far away some people were setting fire to a blaze of twigs and leaves; one solitary bird warbled across the lake; the cypresses wept; the pines glowered; the olive trees bathed their foliage in the mild warmth; one cloud sailed across the sky, and its reflection glided over the lake. One could not bear to raise the voice.

It was like a muffled, muffled concert. Here were life, reality and dreams. Here were sun, warmth and light. Here were colour, form and line, and in this line, outlined by the mountains against the sky, the artistic background of all the beauty.

Noufflard and I accompanied our Northern friends from Albano to the station; they were going on as far as Naples, and thence returning home. We said good-bye and walked back to Albano in the mild Summer evening. The stars sparkled and shone bright, Cassiopæia showed itself in its most favourable position, and Charles's Wain stood, as if in sheer high spirits, on its head, which seemed to be its recreation just about this time.

It, too, was evidently a little dazed this unique, inimitable Spring.

INDEX